A Religious
Guide to Europe

A Religious Guide to Europe

DANIEL M. MADDEN

COLLIER BOOKS
A Division of Macmillan Publishing Co., Inc.

NEW YORK

COLLIER MACMILLAN PUBLISHERS

LONDON

Macmillan Publishing Co., Inc.
866 Third Avenue, New York, N.Y. 10022
Collier-Macmillan Canada Ltd.

A *Religious Guide to Europe* is also published in
a hardcover edition by Macmillan Publishing
Co., Inc.

Library of Congress Cataloging in Publication
Data

Madden, Daniel M.
    A religious guide to Europe.

    Includes index.
1. Christian pilgrims and pilgrimages—
Europe. 2. Christian shrines—Europe. 3. Europe
—Description and travel—1971-   —Guide-
books. I. Title.
[BR735.M23 1975b]   914'.04'55   75-6248
ISBN 0-02-097950-9 pbk.

FIRST COLLIER BOOKS EDITION 1975

Printed in the United States of America

For H U A N

*Remove not the ancient landmark
which your fathers have set.*

PROVERBS XXII:28

Contents

	ACKNOWLEDGMENTS	xi
1	THE PILGRIM'S PATH	1
2	AUSTRIA	7
3	BELGIUM	41
4	FRANCE	74
5	GERMANY	128
6	GREAT BRITAIN	167
7	GREECE	216
8	IRELAND	250
9	ITALY	283
10	LUXEMBOURG	329
11	THE NETHERLANDS	336
12	PORTUGAL	373
13	SCANDINAVIA	390
14	SPAIN	418
15	SWITZERLAND	458
16	TURKEY	494
17	EASTERN EUROPE	509
	INDEX	515

Acknowledgments

THE GATHERING OF MATERIAL used in *A Religious Guide to Europe* has taken me from Oslo to Istanbul, from Warsaw to Sofia. The routes I followed led to people and places I shall always guard in a warm corner of my memory.

Mine was not a unique experience. It can be any traveler's. There are memorable people and places galore, whether one lingers at the edge of Galway Bay or island-hops in the blue water off the Peloponnesus.

A Religious Guide to Europe is meant to help others have the same kind of experience I have had. I myself received much help, in a general as well as a specific way. For instance, over the years magazine editors for whom I was writing made suggestions and provided counsel that deepened and broadened my knowledge and understanding of Europe. I am thinking especially of editors such as Father Kenneth Ryan, Henry Lexau, Kay Sullivan, and John McCarthy of *Catholic Digest* magazine; Paul J. C. Friedlander of *The New York Times;* and Elmer Von Feldt of *Columbia* magazine.

In a special category also is Myra Waldo, a travel

authority whom I have found to be *sans pareil*. Her advice and encouragement were elements of basic help.

Longtime friends such as Karel Versluys, the Flemish writer, and Vincent McAloon, an old Roman hand, were invariably quick—and knowledgeable enough—to locate an elusive bit of information.

Fred Birmann, the Swiss government tourism official, is exceptional, too. For many years he has been a first-rate friend and first-rate provider of information about the land of the extraordinary Swiss.

Government tourism officials everywhere have been helpful. I salute, in particular, Nicole Garnier of Paris; Bruno Baroni of Switzerland; Count Sigmund Fago Golfarelli of Rome; Captain Gus Madden and Bill Maxwell of Ireland; Margareta Hjalmarsson of Sweden; Gregory P. Leventis and Philip Katsikas of Greece; Mrs. Dora Renz of West Germany; Nanna Lynneberg of Oslo; Michael Reece of Great Britain; Elizabeth Zeller of Austria; and Mette Franchetti of Denmark.

I thank Gunnar Rosvall of Sweden for the way he surprised me. It was no surprise that a high government official, such as he is, knew in detail the story of the Lucia feast of light, a warm tradition in Swedish families when winter is the darkest and dreariest. But with equal authority Mr. Rosvall sang "Santa Lucia" in the Italian. That was a nice surprise on a day of cold and snow in Stockholm.

DANIEL M. MADDEN

Rome, spring 1975

*A Religious
Guide to Europe*

1

The Pilgrim's Path

ONCE A MONTH a Franciscan friar guides a Land-Rover up a pitted mountain road at the edge of the Jordan valley. The friar's mission is to make certain that the small chapel on Mount Nebo is in good condition, that desert winds have not ripped away doors or pushed in windows. The friar is the caretaker of the chapel. Since the pilgrimage of St. Francis to Jerusalem in 1219, the followers of the *Poverello* of Assisi have been the Catholic Church's official guardians of the holy places of the Middle East. The chapel on Mount Nebo, although so remotely situated that few pilgrims ever can reach it, is a holy place. In the ground near the chapel a Byzantine mosaic, hidden usually by layers of warm dust, marks the spot from which the prophet Moses looked across the Jordan valley for the first time and saw the Promised Land.

The entire area first viewed by Moses from Mount Nebo became a holy land. Almost any path today's pilgrim takes in this area will cross or pass a place sanctified by a prophet, a saint, or an event. Jerusalem, Bethlehem, Nazareth, Galilee come at once to mind

1

when the Holy Land is mentioned. But there are scores of holy places—hundreds, even.

To a certain degree the situation is much the same along the roads which the early-day bearers of spiritual tidings followed westward across the Mediterranean and Europe to the British Isles. There are places everywhere which have become points of pilgrimage because of association with a recent or ancient, a real or traditional spiritual event or personage.

The great number of holy places in Europe became evident in 1954 when the Catholic Church was celebrating the centenary of the dogma of the Immaculate Conception. Pius XII proclaimed a Marian Year, and the pontifical commission in Rome dispatched a circular to the bishops of the world asking them to make known the names of the "sanctuaries consecrated to the Madonna, especially the most celebrated ones."

In response to the call from Rome, Father Jean Raymond, A.A., director for the Association de Notre Dame de Salut in Paris, produced a Marian map of France which pinpointed the location of more than 300 sites in the country dedicated to the Madonna—sanctuaries, cathedrals and places of Apparitions. This map, by definition, did not include the many other Catholic shrines of France—sites linked to Joan of Arc, to the Curé of Ars, to Martin of Tours and to other saints. Equally, the numerous non-Catholic holy places in France were not put on the Marian map, places such as the birthplace of John Calvin, the grottoes where the Huguenots carried on their religious services clandestinely, the lonely sites where people branded as heretics died for their religious beliefs, the ancient synagogue of Provence where refugees from the Iberian peninsula prayed.

The list of all pilgrimage places in France alone would be long. Similarly long lists would result for Spain, Italy, Germany, Britain, the Low Countries—in fact, most parts of Europe.

This is at once a source of joy and of distress for the pilgrim. It is no more practical for the pilgrim to visit all pilgrimage places than it is for the writer to write about them.

PLANNING THE PILGRIMAGE

Cicero made an observation that can serve as a guideline in outlining one's pilgrimage route: "We are only stirred by the very places that bear the footprints of those we love or admire."

For the ancient Greeks these "very places" were the temples of their gods at Ephesus, Olympus, Epidaurus. The Holy Sepulchre in Jerusalem is to the Christian what the Temple of Solomon was for the people of Israel. The custom of pilgrimage is an old one.

Passports

The basic travel document you will need is a passport. It is issued by the Department of State through branches of the U.S. Passport Office in Washington, D.C. and 10 main cities. Clerks of federal and state courts, and some post offices, also issue passports. When applying you will need two recent photos—not smaller than 2½ by 2½ inches, not larger than 3 by 3. If it is a first-time application, you will need proof of citizenship. Otherwise, your old passport, even if it has expired, will be enough. Western European countries have waived visas for United States citizens. Countries of Eastern Europe require them.

Travel Counsel

There are many sources of free, and helpful, advice during the planning stage. Your hometown travel agent is experienced, and is particularly excellent in making reservations for hotels and for transportation. Every government of Europe maintains an official tourist information office in New York and, in some cases, in other cities as well, such as Chicago, Los Angeles and San Francisco. These offices are staffed by citizens of the particular country. They have free pamphlets and maps, and are a prime source of detailed information.

Air or Sea?

If you have the time, a sea voyage is the most restful, enjoyable way of travel. Unfortunately, a number of the great passenger liners have been withdrawn from transatlantic service. The good news is that the Italian Line's sleek *Michelangelo* and *Raffaello* still sail regularly between New York and the Mediterranean's sunny ports. The cost is higher than excursion air fares, but worth every penny and more. Superb international cuisine is one of the many unique, memorable features. It is luxury traveling all the way.

With airplane travel, keep in mind that there are various tariffs to and from Europe even though all airlines which are I.A.T.A. members use the same rate structures. The first big price differential is between First Class and Economy. Within Economy there are numerous variations of the fare schedule which are determined by when you are going and how long you plan to stay. If you make a quick round trip in summer, the fare will be much higher than if you travel in the middle of winter and spend several weeks or more abroad.

The Eurail Pass

A guaranteed way of saving money on transportation in Europe is the purchase of a Eurail Pass which makes possible unlimited First Class travel on all trains in 13 countries for a flat sum. The Eurail Pass can be purchased for three weeks, a month, or two months. Its flexibility is one big attraction for the pilgrim. One can establish a travel base in Paris or Zurich, for instance, and make day excursions to pilgrimage points on fast express trains. If one reaches Cologne, for instance, and is told that he should have stopped on the way at Aachen, doubling-back on one's steps for the holder of a Eurail Pass does not mean spending any transportation money. It can be used day and night, for long or short journeys. The Eurail Pass is good also for reductions on many bus and steamer services. The point to remember is that the Eurail Pass cannot be bought in Europe. It has to be purchased in the United States or Canada. Your travel agent can obtain it for you.

Personal Finances

Principal credit cards can be used at airlines, at many hotels, restaurants and shops, and at international car rental agencies. This can be helpful in an emergency if cash runs low. In traveling from country to country it is a good idea to have $10 or so in each of a few major currencies—Swiss francs, French francs, German marks, for instance—along with dollars. This limits problems if banks are closed when you arrive at a town, and you have no local currency. If you have an assortment of foreign currencies, a hotel or restaurant will usually be willing to make change in one of them for you.

Driving in Europe

It takes only a few minutes to get the hang of the European driving style. The basic rule to remember is that, in general, drivers approaching from the right have the priority. There are lots of other rules, but they are mostly common-sensical ones. Gasoline is tremendously expensive. Italy for years has had a special coupon system for foreign motorists, making possible a big saving on gasoline purchases. Since the fuel crisis, the coupon system has been on again, off again. When reaching the Italian border, inquire whether the "gas" coupons are currently available. Your home-state driver's license is all that is needed in most countries, although it would be best to have an international driver's license because it is written in a number of languages. The international driver's license can be obtained through your hometown automobile club, or at any AAA office in the United States or Europe.

Information

Europe is superb on providing free information to travelers. Even the smallest town has an official tourist office. It is invariably in the heart of the town or city. A local map, a hotel list and a general-information pamphlet are the stock-in-trade of such official tourist offices.

Local Transportation

There is good public transportation throughout Europe. Many cities—German, Swiss, Italian, Austrian—have adopted some form of automatic system for fare-paying. It can be a pre-boarding ticket-purchase system from machines at tram stops, as in Zurich, or a coin machine aboard the bus, as on *some* buses in Rome. If there is no ticket-selling conductor on the bus or street-car, don't wait for one to appear. Ask a fellow passenger about the procedure for paying. There are stiff on-the-spot fines for passengers without tickets. Ticket-less tourists are usually let off scot-free—still, it can be embarrassing.

2
Austria

TWENTY CENTURIES of the Austrian story are projected in the trinity of titles traditionally used to salute the Madonna venerated at the Marian shrine of Mariazell. She is called *Magna Mater Austriae* (Great Mother of Austria), *Mater Gentium Slavorum* (Mother of the Slavic Peoples), and *Magna Hungagorum Domina* (Great Lady of the Hungarians). The use of the Latin language in the three titles is a reminder that Austria was a major settlement of the Romans. The designation of the Madonna as the Great Mother of Austria makes clear that this is basically, and historically, a Catholic land. Reference to the Slavs and the Hungarians recalls Austria's days of empire and the extension of its political and religious influence to tens of millions of people, much beyond its present borders.

The Celts were ancient inhabitants of Austria. About a dozen years before the birth of Christ the Romans conquered the territory that is now Austria, moving as far east as Vienna, given the name of Vindobona because its wine-growing capabilities impressed them. Not many centuries later Christianity also took root in the Roman settlement but, after flowering, was practically obliterated in the storm of Barbarian invasions that coincided with the decline of the empire of Rome. In the 8th century the rulers of Bavaria moved eastward, and Christianity traveled with them, pumping new life into the dormant Christian religion. The assignment of the dominion of the "eastern realm" (in German, *österreich*) to the Babenbergs in the latter part of the 10th century gave Christianity impetus and the land a name (Österreich).

Early in the 16th century, after the death of Maximilian, his grandson Charles V became emperor. In 1521 at Worms (see Index) Charles V divided the empire with his brother, Ferdinand I, taking Spain and the Low Countries (where he was born), and turning over the eastern territories. The accord produced a separation of the Hapsburg dynasty into Spanish and Austrian houses. Although "Defenders of the Faith," Charles V and Ferdinand I recognized that the support of the Protestant princes in Germany was of help in protecting their respective hegemonies from hostile encroachment.

Ferdinand did try to slow the coming of Lutheranism to Austria. For several years he banned all writings of the Reformation. But the founding of Protestant churches grew apace. The vigorous Counter-Reformation put Austria back in the ranks of Catholicism. The return was encouraged in some parts of the country by urgings to accept Catholicism or get out. The Austrian Hapsburgs carried the Catholic banner in the Thirty Years' War (1618–48). The Treaty of Westphalia called for the recognition of Lutheranism, Calvinism and Catholicism throughout the empire, but in Austria it did not work out that way. The Hapsburgs repeated in Austria the kind of anti-Protestant measures that had been taken in Bohemia—banishment of non-Catholic clergymen and the prohibition of non-Catholic religious services, for example.

One of Empress Maria Theresa's many children, Joseph II, when he became sole ruler of the Austro-

Hungarian empire in 1780, sought in his own fashion to establish religious equality. Lutherans, Calvinists and Orthodox were assured the right to public practice of their religion. But they were restricted on the adornment of their churches—no bell, no tower, no entrance from a main street. The Catholics were restricted, too—when and where Mass could be said, the number of churches, the quantity of candles for Mass. Alarmed that Joseph II might set up a national church independent of Rome, Pius VI took the unusual step of traveling to Vienna for a month of consultations. Joseph II did not cancel anything already done, but he agreed to respect the primacy of the Pope in matters of faith and morals. In 1824 the Jesuits, banished by Joseph II, were allowed to return to Austria. The First World War broke up an empire that had included 50 million people. Nonimperial Austria's postwar population dwindled to 7 million. In 1938, after years of political turmoil, Austria was annexed to Germany by Adolf Hitler. (Hitler was born in Austria at Braunau.)

Hitler replaced government subsidies to the church in Austria with a system of compulsory church taxes. His thought, seemingly, was that the taxes would drive the Austrians out of the church. This did not happen. Austrians remained Catholic, and paid the taxes. They still pay church taxes and some do not like it at all. When a 10-schilling payroll tax was imposed in Vienna a few years ago to finance an extension of the city's subway (U-bahn) system, a Viennese coffeehouse waiter remarked to a customer: "At least I'll use the subway. I never go to church, but I still have to pay taxes."

MARIAZELL

On the first of May in 1954—the Marian Year—7,000 members of Austria's Catholic Young Workers organization came on pilgrimage to the alpine shrine of

Our Lady of Mariazell to pray for young people behind the Iron and Bamboo Curtains. The youths brought with them 9 candles—one for each province of Austria—and placed them in a side chapel dedicated to St. Ladislas, a king of Hungary in the 11th century. The candles burned while Mass was celebrated. After Mass the candles were extinguished. The Catholic Young Workers of Austria plan to leave them unlighted until religious freedom returns to Eastern Europe.

Each candle is marked with the name of the Austrian province which donated it, and the nation for which it is to be lighted some day. The candle from the province of Carinthia has been removed. It had been marked for Yugoslavia.

"Many Yugoslavs go to Mariazell," a woman with an armband says in the Westbahnhof in Vienna. "But no one from the other Eastern countries. In Dubček's 'Czechoslovakia spring' there were many Czechs from Bohemia and Moravia—many hundreds of them. But after that, almost no one."

Bahnhof Mission is stamped on the woman's armband. The "railroad station mission" was organized by Vienna's *Caritas* (Catholic Charities) in the postwar years when Austria was occupied by the Big Four (U.S.A., Britain, France, Russia). Lower Austria, the province surrounding Vienna, was in the Russian zone of occupation and Vienna itself was divided into four sectors. Bahnhof Mission volunteers were the first Westerners many refugees talked to on their arrival from Eastern Europe.

Mariazell is in the foothills of the Alps. An estimated 1 million people visit Mariazell each year. It is 90 miles from Vienna. The express train ride from Vienna to St. Pölten takes only 45 minutes. From St. Pölten to Mariazell, it is a journey of 3½ hours on a narrow-gauge railway which travels to an altitude of 2,895 feet.

The train conductor is not sure of the origin of the name "St. Pölten." He thinks the name might have come from an old monastery in the area that had been dedicated to St. Hippolytus, an early Roman martyr.

The conductor—chunky, genial, and fortyish—says: "Eight centuries ago there were some people at Maria-zell making a living by digging salt and iron from the mountains. Nothing was there then, of course, and the people were refugees or nomads of some sort. Word about them eventually got to the Benedictines at St. Lambert's Monastery—that's a bit over one hundred miles southwest of Mariazell, on the other side of the Alps. The abbot nominated a monk named Magnus to go to the miners' camp, and do what he could for the people. Magnus took with him a wooden statue of the Madonna he had carved himself. When he was just about at the camp, an enormous boulder blocked the way into the valley. He put the statue up against the boulder, as you would in a chapel, and prayed to the Madonna for guidance. Instantly, the rock split in two, making a path for him into the valley. When he got to the camp he placed the statue on a tree stump and in the following days built a little house around it, like a hermit's cell. They began calling it Mariazell—*zelle* being 'cell.' The name has been Mary's Cell ever since."

At the side of the track "milestones" were posted every 100 meters in each kilometer section—ten 100-meter markings a kilometer. The markings make it easy to instruct repair crews where work has to be done.

The conductor thoughtfully repeated the question that had been asked: "What made Mariazell the shrine of the Slavs? That's easy. When you get to the basilica you'll see two stone reliefs above the entrance. One portrays the crucified Christ. In the other the Madonna is on a throne, and at her feet are a number of men and women. Records show that two of these figures are Margrave Henry of Moravia and his wife. Both of them had been sick—something like arthritis. One night St. Wenceslaus appeared to the margrave in a dream and said if he wanted to get well he and his wife should make a pilgrimage to Mariazell. That was a very long journey in those days—it was about the year 1200—but the margrave and his wife made it. They prayed at the shrine, and went home recovered. The fame of Mariazell spread among the Slavs very quickly."

The train conductor anticipated the next question.

"As for the devotion by the Hungarians, that started almost two centuries later—in 1377, to be precise. The Christian king of Hungary, Ludwig, was threatened by an overpowering army of Bulgarians who had invaded his land. The Madonna appeared to him in his sleep and encouraged him to put up a fight, saying she would be at his side. He went into battle with the Bulgarians, and really beat them. They fled. Ludwig made a pilgrimage with his wife to Mariazell and had a large Gothic church built around Magnus's cell, replacing a smaller stone church of the margrave Henry."

At some stops the train station is the only building in sight. The stationmaster and his family live in an apartment on the second floor. When the train arrives, the stationmaster puts on his red cap—his badge of authority—and walks over to talk to the driver. The stationmaster's wife leans out the window to watch the goings-on. When it is time for the train to leave, the stationmaster raises a short metal rod with a disk at the end. Red and green lights are inserted in the disk. When the woman sees her husband flashing the green light, she closes the window slowly, knowing that there will be nothing new until the next train.

"The basilica you'll see," the conductor says when he returns, "is not the church of King Ludwig. His church was enlarged in the seventeenth century. I doubt whether you have ever seen one like it, though, because of its towers. There are three of them. Two Baroque towers at the sides and the Gothic one of King Ludwig in the center. They think it might have hurt the feelings of the Hungarians if they had done away with King Ludwig's church completely."

He says the Gothic tower figures in the biggest celebration of the year at the shrine.

"The official feastday for the arrival of the monk Magnus is the twenty-first of December. The celebration continues right through Christmas. On Christmas Eve, an hour before the Midnight Mass begins, Mariazell youths climb to the top of the Gothic tower with their brass trumpets and play 'Silent Night.' It's like a family celebration. There's sometimes as much as three or four feet of snow right in Mariazell itself, so except for the tourists in the ski resorts there are not too many foreigners around. Then, too, 'Silent Night' is our own religious song. It was written not far from here at a little place called Oberndorf.

"After the trumpets play 'Silent Night,' the five big bells of the basilica ring, and you can hear them across the valley. Speaking of bells, you'll hear them peal for the Angelus at *eleven* A.M., so don't think your watch is an hour slow. The custom began with the Turks, our old adversaries. During their invasion of Austria in 1683—their last one, as it turned out—they came along this valley through which we are riding. Their leader declared that he would reach Mariazell before noon so that its bells could never sound again. Somehow or other, the bells rang an hour earlier than they were supposed to. No one knows how this happened, but it completely rattled the Turks. They scattered as fast as they could, and left the shrine alone."

Mariazell is the last stop on the mountain railway. Many of the passengers getting off are wearing local dress—the women in pretty dirndls, white blouses and black vests with silver buttons. A middle-aged woman helps her husband fit his rucksack comfortably, tugging at the bottom of his lodencloth jacket till it is just right. He is wearing leather breeches, woolen socks and heavy shoes, and clings to a walking stick.

"We Austrians are great walkers," the conductor says. "Some pilgrims still walk to the shrine from their own villages. In the old days everyone walked. Where the shrine came into view for the first time, a cross was erected. People would stop at the cross when they reached it to say a prayer for their safe journey, and on the way home would stop to say a prayer of thanksgiving."

The town lies along the slopes of a valley. This is a favorite place for walks through the mountains, and walking itineraries of up to 4 and 5 hours are charted on maps which are displayed at various points in the town. Wienerstrasse, the main street, is paved but narrow, and almost solidly lined with hotels, pensions and eating-places, ranging from a cosy *Gasthaus* with plain wooden tabletops and a menu featuring sausages and wine to a restaurant with white tablecloths and an elaborate bill of fare. Austrians like to eat. In Lent they produce a typically Austrian compromise to abstinence demands and their perennial yearning for food. A favorite Austrian dish, for instance, is a *Bauernschmaus,* a "peasant's feed" of sauerkraut, sausages and various cuts of pork. During Lent, restaurants in Mariazell substitute as the big dish a *Heringschmaus*—shrimp, eel, *Fischfilet* and other fruits of the sea.

The soft red of the basilica's fabric blends smoothly with the vividly crimson geraniums fringing the stone railing at the main entrance. Pilgrims from Austria and the eastern countries traditionally use one of the three side entrances. The portal just to the left of the main entrance is for pilgrims from Yugoslavia and southern Austria; the one on the north, identified by statues of St. Leopold and St. Wenceslaus, is for Viennese and Czechoslovaks; and the one on the east for Hungarians.

The Chapel of Grace containing monk Magnus's

statue of Our Lady of Mariazell is halfway down the center of the basilica. It is shaped like a diamond. Italian marble in shades from red to gray coat the outer walls. It is a sumptuous piece of work done in flamboyant Austrian Baroque style.

A baldachin formed by a dozen thin columns of silver rests on an altar of solid silver and is the framework for the wooden statue that Magnus brought over the Alps 8 centuries ago. The statue is not much more than 18 inches high, but seems bigger because the figures of the Madonna and of the Child she holds in her lap with her right arm are clothed in robes of silk and brocade.

"There are some sixty changes of costume," an Austrian guide, speaking good English, tells a tour group of Americans in a lowered voice. "We'll see them later when we visit the basilica's treasury room. The only time the statue is not robed is on the feastday of Our Lady of Mariazell."

The guide directs the attention of the tour group to the Madonna's face.

"You notice that she seems to be smiling, but there have been times when pilgrims have reported her looking crestfallen and troubled. Some have even seen her eyes move."

A woman in the group asks about the crowns, and the guide seems to be annoyed with himself for not having said anything about them.

"The crown on the Virgin is made of diamonds and pearls, and solid gold crosses. Princess Regina of Saxe-Meiningen wore it at her marriage to Archduke Otto von Hapsburg. They were married in Nancy, France, in May 1951, and the crown was created for her. She made a gift of it to Our Lady of Mariazell. The archduke arranged to have the Child's crown made."

Several women in the group were gazing at the chapel's silver gate, and seemed to be puzzled by the golden initials on its doors. The guide noticed this.

"The F.I. is for Emperor Francis I and the M.T. on

the other side stands for the name of his wife, Maria Theresa, the empress. They presented the gate in 1757 when the six-hundredth anniversary of the shrine was observed. There had been another silver gate before that, one given by Emperor Leopold I who was Maria Theresa's grandfather. So many pilgrims were here one day that the gate was literally crushed. Both times the gates were thanksgiving gifts for the birth of children. Maria Theresa and her husband, you know, had quite a large family—sixteen children, one of whom was Marie Antoinette.

From the choir loft the voices of choristers rehearsing for their next appearance in the basilica interrupted the guide. He closed his eyes momentarily as he listened to the choir.

"That's the Mariazell Mass," he continues. "It was written by Franz Josef Haydn. He sang in the choir here when he was a young boy. He was born not far from here, at Eisenstadt."

Some pilgrims in local dress enter the basilica. The guide says that the costumes are not Austrian.

"These are people from Yugoslavia, and Hungary and Czechoslovakia—people who are now living in Austria."

The group of Eastern Europeans kneels silently in front of the Chapel of Grace for several minutes and then walks down the left side of the basilica toward the immense main altar, the work of Fischer von Erlach, who did so much to beautify Austria. The Eastern Europeans in the folk costumes proceed to the St. Ladislas Chapel at the end on the left side. For quite a while they merely stand in front of the chapel, as motionless as the tall unlighted candles. Then, without any signal, they begin softly singing. A young monk in a black cassock is passing through the basilica at the time, and he stops to listen. He says they are singing the Mariazell pilgrims' hymn: "To love Mary is always my aim; in joy and sorrow am I ever her servant."

In answer to a question about the office of the pilgrimage director, the young Benedictine offers to show the way. The monastery is at the right of the basilica, separated from it by a narrow open area. The parish office is at the beginning of the long ground-floor vaulted corridor. Some letters, numerals and crosses are written in chalk, against a black painted background, above the door of the parish office: 19 + K + M + B + 74.

"That's an Austrian tradition," the monk explains. "It's a house sign. The letters stand for the Three Kings—Kaspar, Melchior and Balthasar. It shows the house is under the protection of God. The house sign was written there in the Christmas period, and will remain there all year. At Christmas time the priest goes around blessing the houses in his parish or village."

The office of the pilgrimage director is next to the parish office. A tablelike desk stands in a corner near the window where the light is good. A smaller table, with drawers at each side, holds a semiportable electric typewriter. Along the wall near the desk is a Baroque cabinet. Its inlaid wooden doors are of several honey shades. A splendid, huge ceramic stove, *Kachelofen,* literally fills the corner diagonally opposite the desk. There is no sign of any *Briketts,* the bricks of compressed coal dust used for fuel.

"It works," Father Veremund Hochreiter says, gesturing toward the gleaming ceramic stove. "But it's not used now because we have central heating."

The pilgrimage director, a pleasant, dark-haired monk with rimless glasses, is fiftyish. Instead of the usual Benedictine cassock that is fastened from the inside, his cassock has six buttons at the top.

He is amused by the question.

"Buttons are an Austrian custom from the Middle Ages. It's easier to put on and take off with buttons. Some monasteries have five, or four, or even three. We have six."

Father Hochreiter is one of 6 monks now at Maria-

zell, but he actually belongs to the Monastery of
Kremsmünster, in Upper Austria, which was founded
in A.D. 777. (See Index.) The status of the Mariazell
monastery has changed several times through the centuries, and it is now administered by the abbot of
Kremsmünster.

"For a long while the monks at Kremsmünster have
been raising carp and trout in a big pond there. They
started that because there was not enough meat in the
area in the past. This is probably unique among monasteries. There are ninety monks there. We have oil, too,
but it's expensive to drill and to produce."

TRANSPORTATION: On weekends buses travel to Maria-
    zell from Vienna.
HOTELS: Facing the basilica are *Schwarzer Adler* and
    Goldener Löwe. Lower-priced are *Drei Hasen* and
    Scherfler.

STYRIA

Mariazell, being the national shrine of Austria, is ipso
facto the outstanding point of pilgrimage in the province of Styria where it is situated. But there are other
holy places of historic and religious renown in the
province. Among them are:

The Graz Cathedral: The cathedral at Graz, the capital of Styria, is dedicated to St. Giles, the Benedictine
monk who is associated primarily with southern France
but probably was born in Athens. It was assigned to the
Jesuits in the Counter-Reformation and they used it as a
parish church until their expulsion from Austria by
Joseph II. There are many features and fixtures associated with the Jesuits, such as two reliquaries which
once were chests holding the dowry of a member of the
Gonzaga family.

The Rein Monastery: This is the oldest Cistercian
monastery in Austria. Not far away is the 14th-century
Maria Strassengel Church, a site of pilgrimage.

Seckau Abbey: A 12th-century painting of Our Lady of Seckau has been honored here since shortly after the monastery was founded in the middle of the 12th century.

Admont Monastery: A Benedictine monastery founded in 1074, Admont has what is considered to be the largest and most important monastic library in the world.

LOWER AUSTRIA

In other countries, districts and provinces with variations of the word "low" in their names have demanded, and obtained, new designations from the competent authorities. Thus, the name of Basses-Alpes (Low Alps) *département* of France's Riviera has been changed to Alpes-Maritimes. The use of "low" in such names was intended only to indicate the particular region's geographic situation, but some residents began reading derogatory implications and insisted on changes. Such a thought would never occur to the people of the province of Lower Austria. They know the word "lower" tells the province's location along the Danube compared to the neighboring province, Upper Austria, which is upriver. They also know that anyone looking for Austria's historic milestones will find most of them within its borders. The Babenbergs were given rule over Austria, the eastern march (*Ostmark*), by Emperor Otto II in A.D., 976, two decades after the Magyars had been repulsed in the Battle of Lechfeld and driven down the Danube valley. At Melk, the Babenbergs established their government. When they later moved eastward to the Vienna Woods the Melk palace became a monastery, one of Europe's most splendid Benedictine abbeys. Many of the monasteries in Lower Austria were built on the sites of temples to Greek gods or of places where the Celts made sacrifices to the pagan idols they had deified.

MARIA TAFERL

Maria Taferl dominates the Danube between Linz and Vienna. The pilgrimage church, bright white with dark bulbous towers, rests in a wood-circled clearing 780 feet above the river station for the Danube passenger ships at Marbach.

A huge stone in front of the church is compared by archaeologists with the kind of Celtic altar used in pagan rituals and sacrifices. The stone is thought to be the possible source of pilgrimages to the hilltop before the church itself, just three centuries old, was built. Motivated possibly by an urge to drive away lingering memories of the heathen spirits of old, someone in the area had attached a painting of a crucifix to an oak tree near the weather-riven stone. Shepherds, farmers and riverains made a point of stopping at the "tablet" (*Taferl* in the local dialect) on which the crucifix was painted whenever they were on the hill.

On a winter's day early in 1633 a farmer named Pachman tried to cut down the oak tree. He struck at the tree a couple of times, but nothing happened. The third blow landed across his own legs. At this point he saw the crucifix image on the wooden tablet. He was horrified at how close he had come to destroying the simple shrine, and unmindful of his bleeding wounds began to beseech forgiveness in prayer. The story told in the area is that the man's bleeding halted, and he was able to walk away without anyone's help. A few years later a local official replaced the crucifix image with one of the Madonna, known as Our Lady of Sorrows.

The first Masses on the hill were said on the feast of St. Joseph (Mar. 19) in 1660 and a month later the building of the present church, known as Maria Taferl, was started. In the months before and after the laying of the foundation stone more than two dozen Apparitions were reported. In a few cases an unusual light was seen. The other Apparitions were of figures in white. An ecclesiastical commission heard a number of witnesses but never announced any conclusions.

Five years before the 100th anniversary of the shrine, the oak tree caught fire and the Madonna image which had remained fixed to it all this time was destroyed. This misfortune did not stop pilgrims from coming. In the centenary year of 1760, more than 325,000 Communions were distributed. During the reign of Joseph II pilgrimages were prohibited, but they were resumed early in the 19th century.

Like other Danube ferries, the one serving the Maria Taferl shrine is a flat-bottomed, raft-type craft which can carry about 100 persons and a few cars. It has no motors. It is driven from one bank to the other by overhead cables and the rushing power of the river.

The steep road that curls upward from the Danube to Maria Taferl is 2½ miles long. Just before reaching the summit of the hill the pilgrim passes along the *Bussweg*, "The Way of Atonement," marked by chapels and other memorials put there to recall the Seven Sorrows of Mary. The major pilgrimage at Maria Taferl takes place on the afternoon of the Sunday after the feast of the Seven Sorrows of Mary, Sept. 15. A procession of pilgrims follows each of the seven stations along the hill.

"In the past," Father Anton Hommer says, "pilgrims would make a special offering, like fasting beforehand or promising to say certain prayers, or they would go on their knees from station to station. That's why it has the penitential name, Bussweg or Busse. From May till the Rosary feast in October there are always pilgrimages. Sometimes a whole townful of people will come, with the mayor leading them."

Father Hommer, the Maria Taferl pastor, is dark-haired, not too tall. At the long table in the refectory, he tells about himself. He was born in southern Czechoslovakia of a Sudeten Deutsch family. He did his military service in the German army and then after the war, when his family was expelled from Czechoslovakia, he entered the priesthood.

A Holy Cross Sister tidying up the table replies that she is from Chile. Her German seems to be too natural for a foreigner, and she has no Latin American accent.

"I was really born in Germany but I have spent thirty-six years in the missions in Chile. Now I am on home leave. I spent a month at my family's home in Bavaria, a month or so at my congregation's house in Altötting, and now another month at Maria Taferl."

She seems to be counting the days till her departure for Chile, and agrees that missionaries usually long to go back to the mission lands. She smiles.

"That's natural. It's their vocation."

TRANSPORTATION: Marbach is a port for the passenger ships on the river.

HOTELS: At Maria Taferl: *Krone,* the leading one; *Kaiserhof,* medium-priced; and *Rose,* comfortable.

Maria Taferl is not far from a number of other holy places in Lower Austria. Among them are:

Melk Monastery: Duke Leopold, after being given dominion over the territory of Austria in A.D. 976, subsequently built his palace on the cliffs at Melk overlooking the Danube. The palace, a fortified castle, included a chapel where religious services were held regularly. The government of the new territory was subsequently moved eastward along the Danube, but Melk remained a religious center, and in the 11th century Leopold II invited Benedictine monks to take the place of the secular priests who had been there. The monastery library has an illuminated manuscript of the Venerable Bede.

Göttweig Monastery: Forty-eight river towns are said to be within view from the gardens of Göttweig monastery which is 800 feet above the right bank of the Danube, opposite the medieval town of Krems. It was established by St. Altmann, bishop of Passau, in 1074, and before becoming a monastery of the Benedictines had been assigned to the Augustinians. In restoring the monastery early in the 18th century, after a devastating fire, the Baroque architect Johann Lukas von Hildebrandt hoped to make it a "fortress of faith." One of the artistic master strokes is "The Emperor's Staircase," with a frescoed ceiling. A museum displays a collection of ancient copperware. The monastery has a *Kellerstüberl* which serves moderately priced characteristic Austrian food. The open-air wine garden has a 180-degree view of the Danube valley.

Klosterneuburg Monastery: In the 12th century Klosterneuburg, in the Vienna Woods, became for Margrave Leopold III of the Babenbergs what Melk had been over a century earlier for Leopold I. When transferring the court here, he had the construction of a monastery and a church started in 1113. Particularly attractive are 14th-century altar panels, shimmering works of gold and enamel. Leopold III was honored as a saint, and his relics are in the chapel named after him in the monastery. Viennese men traditionally make a pilgrimage to Klosterneuburg on Nov. 15, the feast of St. Leopold, patron of Lower Austria. The monastery has an immense wine cellar, Babenberger Keller, which sells food and local wine. A center of attention on the feast of St. Leopold is a tremendous wine barrel. It is rolled out, and many of the celebrants slide down its sides.

Heiligenkreuz: Another foundation of the Babenbergs, Heiligenkreuz was established in 1135 for the Cistercian monks in the Vienna Woods. Many of the monastery's early-day facilities, such as the sleeping quarters (*Dormitorium*) and washroom (*Lavatorium*) are still visible.

Altenburg: A Benedictine monastery, founded in 1144, is near Horn. An unusual feature is the monastery

crypt which is vividly decorated with fantastic and
bizarre paintings, including a Dance of Death. What
makes the crypt totally unusual is that no one has ever
been buried in it.

Liebfrauenkirche Wiener-Neustadt: Our Lady's
Church has been a Marian shrine since its consecration
in 1269.

THE TYROL

Austria's western province of the Tyrol is a land of
modern ski resorts and ancient shrines, of tall peaks and
slender valleys. All year round it is a place of enchant-
ment, particularly its capital city of Innsbruck.

INNSBRUCK

The Berg Isel, on the south side of Innsbruck, has
been a landmark in the history of the Tyrol for centuries. In 1964 its slopes wers so satisfactory as a ski
jump for the Winter Olympics that they were designated for a similar use in 1976. A museum on the
mountain preserves the uniforms worn by the Tyrolean
patriot Andreas Hofer and his men when they resisted
the troops of Napleon in 1809. At the foot of Berg Isel
is the Praemonstratentian Monastery and the Wilten
Basilica. The church is built on the site of the ruins of
the fort, Veldidena, that had been used as a bastion by
Roman legionaries. Above the main altar in the church
is the sandstone statue known as "Our Lady under the
Four Pillars." It is a Madonna holding on her knee a
standing Child. The statue has been an object of pilgrimage since at least the early part of the 14th century. It gets its name from the columns supporting the
resplendent baldachin which is raised above the altar
like a canopy.

Like the church itself, which has been renewed
several times, the statue has been embellished over the

years. In the 18th century, for example, it was clothed in rich garments. In 1893 high-domed gilded crowns were placed on the heads of the Madonna and Child, and a circle of stars added as a backpiece, like an oversized halo. In 1953 the statue was set in a gilded frame from which issue bright rays in all directions like a nimbus, the shining cloud of light that in ancient times would surround gods or goddesses when they appeared on earth.

The church is in the Wilten district of Innsbruck, less than two miles from the center of the city and along the main road leading to the Brenner Pass. Till the 19th century Wilten had been an independent community. The borderline was the Arch of Triumph which Empress Maria Theresa erected. The jubilation side of the Arch celebrates the marriage of a son; the other side commemorates the death of her husband, Franz Stefan.

Across the Brenner highway from the basilica is the monastery of the Praemonstratentian canons, a massive rose-colored complex. The monastery church sustained a direct hit from an Allied bomb on June 13, 1944 and, as one of the canons wrote at the time, its roof was "robbed of the 120,000 shingles." Our Lady under the Four Pillars Basilica across the way was not touched.

Robert Hodges, of Columbus, Ohio, says the monastery church was probably hit because it lies along the main railroad line to the Brenner Pass, and is just a mile south of the railroad marshaling yards and the station. Hodges, 26 years old, is studying theology at the University of Innsbruck as a seminarian in the Order of the Praemonstratentians. The Order gets its name from the valley of Premontré, near Laon in northern France, where it was founded by St. Norbert early in the 12th century to join together the active apostolate of country priests and the spiritual discipline of monastic life.

The young American seminarian is tall and wears steel-framed glasses. He speaks with such deliberation that it takes a few moments of listening to his speech before it is evident that he is an American. He has been studying at Innsbruck for 6 years, and expects to be ordained soon. He tells how he happened to join the Order.

"I met a priest from the St. Norbert community of El Toro [California] when I was at a Cardinal Mindszenty Conference in St. Louis. We talked about the Order—its work, its history—and I eventually accepted an invitation to come to California and visit them."

Innsbruck is a state university but like all state universities of Austria it has a Catholic college of theology.

"In the theology school," the seminarian says, "there are diocesan candidates (for the priesthood) from Vietnam, Africa, the U.S.A.—lots of different places. There used to be many from the U.S.A. but now only ten to fifteen or so. It costs much less to educate abroad than in the States—perhaps seventy-five dollars a semester, here, for foreign students. The local people pay nothing. Up until the Council many American bishops sent someone to Innsbruck from their diocese. There were perhaps forty or fifty here at one time. The bishops did this for various reasons, including the sentimental one that they had studied here themselves."

When he returns to California, he expects to teach.

THE HOFKIRCHE

The Hofkirche (Court Church) of Innsbruck was built in the middle of the 16th century to provide a suitable setting for the mammoth black marble memorial monument to Emperor Maximilian I, called "the last of the knights." Twenty-eight bigger-than-life bronze figures are posted as a guard around the monument. Among the figures represented are the legendary King Arthur of England and the real Ostrogoth King Theoderic. The church also contains the tomb of the Tyrolean national hero Andreas Hofer.

TRANSPORTATION: Innsbruck is on the main east-west (Vienna-Zurich) and north-south (Munich-Italy) rail lines.

HOTELS: *Maria Theresa, Holiday Inn, Europa* and *Tyrol* (closed in winter) are the leading ones. *Central* and *Mozart* are in the moderate price range.

POINTS OF INTEREST: The Europa Bridge, the 897-yard-long span across the Wipp valley. At 624 feet above the valley floor, it is the highest bridge on the Continent.

CARINTHIA

Italian influences in architectural style and interior design are discernible in a number of the religious centers of Carinthia, the southernmost of Austria's provinces. In the diocesan museum at Klagenfurt, the provincial capital, is a representation of Mary Magdalene, the oldest Austrian painting on glass (about 1170). Among Carinthia's principal points of religious interest:

Gurk Cathedral: Each Easter the altar of this 12th-century church is dressed in what is known as the Lenten Cloth, a fabric of 100 sections that was woven in 1458. Biblical scenes are portrayed in the various sections. The cathedral was built by a local noblewoman, Countess Hemma, who subsequently was venerated as a saint. She is buried in the crypt, a magnificent work of art. Its vaulted ceiling rests on 100 pillars. From medieval times the tomb of St. Hemma has been the goal of pilgrims—originally, pregnant women; more recently, those with eye diseases.

Maria Saal: St. Modestus, the latter part of the 8th century, established a church on the Saal Hill, 5 miles outside of Klagenfurt, and dedicated it to the Madonna. Ever since, Maria Saal has been the focus of religious devotion in Carinthia. St. Modestus is buried in the church. On a nearby mountain, Kronburg, is a church from Carolingian times.

UPPER AUSTRIA

What the province of Upper Austria lacks in mountain peaks is compensated for by some of the country's finest lakes. The provincial capital, Linz, is at once an industrial hub and a point of cultural greatness.

LINZ

A man tending grapes in the vineyards of the Capuchins at Linz early in the 18th century was advised by a friar one day to include a book about the sufferings of Christ in his spiritual reading. The man, named Franz Obermayr, followed the friar's advice and was so taken by what he read that from then on, day and night, according to chronicles of the parish, he thought of nothing else but the Crucifixion of Christ. He decided to give a practical turn to his thoughts and had a wooden statue made, showing the sorrowful Madonna holding the body of the crucified Christ across her lap.

In the fields and hills bordering the Danube he sought a suitable place to install the statue. Finally he decided on the mountain known as Pöstlingberg which overlooks Linz, the capital city of Upper Austria, from the left (north) bank of the Danube. The site was on property belonging to Count Josef Starhemberg, and the nobleman gave his permission for the tiny shrine. The pious Obermayr installed the statue on the Pöstlingberg, at 7 o'clock in the morning of the first Sunday after Advent in 1716, and from then on would climb to the top of the 1,745-foot mountain each Sunday and holy day to pray. The special devotion of the Capuchins' winegrower became known to the people of Linz. Friends of a badly crippled woman by the name of Mayrin were among those who heard about it. They suggested to Mayrin that she should make her way to the little shrine and in prayer tell the Madonna of the

Seven Sorrows about her own particular grief. Mayrin took the advice. It is said that she had arrived with the help of two crutches, but was able to walk home without them. The experience of Mayrin, when it was recounted, induced others to visit the shrine. In 1738 Count Starhemberg had a church built.

Some pilgrims seek out the old paths from the river to the mountaintop. Others make the journey to the sanctuary by the mountain railway which was inaugurated on May 29, 1898. The *bergbahn*, as it is called, follows a mountain route that is exactly 2.9 kilometers long—1.8 miles. It takes the train 20 minutes to make this relatively short, but uphill, journey. It is a wonderful ride. A school is halfway up the mountain, and often children are aboard the train, making a lighthearted contrast to solemn, contemplative pilgrims.

TRANSPORTATION: Linz is a main station on the Vienna-Salzburg-Innsbruck railroad line. Danube steamers call at Linz.

HOTELS: The large *Hotel Pöstlingberg* is a few dozen yards from the shrine, and a number of guest-houses are also nearby. In Linz, the newest hotel is *Tourotel*.

POINTS OF INTEREST: St. Martin's (8th century) is the oldest church in Austria which has retained its original form.

Among the other places of religious interest in the province of Upper Austria are:

Enns: St. Florian, an early-day Christian missionary, was martyred at Enns in A.D. 304 during the reign of the Roman emperor Diocletian, and according to legend was buried on the estate of a noblewoman here. In the 6th century St. Severin, as bishop, founded a church at Enns. Not far away, at the community named after St. Florian, a monastery was established about the start of the 9th century. Anton Brückner played the organ here, and is buried in the church crypt.

Kremsmünster: When Gunther, the son of a Bavarian duke, was killed by a ferocious bear, his father, Tassilo III, established a Benedictine monastery at Kremsmünster on the spot where the fatal attack reportedly took place. He also presented the new monastery with a memorial chalice. The Tassilo Chalice is still in the monastery collection. Kremsmünster is a captivating monastic complex of moats, drawbridges and towers. Just inside the Eichtor entranceway is the fishpond built three centuries ago for breeding carp and trout to support the monks.

Lambach: The monastery's art collection includes the sketchbooks of Johann Martin Schmidt, known as Kremser-Schmidt. On the other side of Traum Lake—a walk of a few hundred yards—is the votive Trinity Church at Stadl-Paura built by the monastery early in the 18th century as a thanksgiving offering for being spared in the plague of 1713. Trinity Church is theologically and artistically noted for the deliberately repeated use of 3's in the design—3 altars, 3 organs, 3 towers, 3 doors, a 3-sided lantern atop the cupola. The basic plan of the church is an equilateral triangle.

Wilherinn: The 12th-century Cistercian monastery was destroyed in a fire of 1733 but rebuilt on an impressive scale. Frescoes in the chapels and on the church ceiling are a visual recital of the Litany of Loreto, hailing Mary as queen of the angels, of the prophets, of the martyrs, of women, of virgins, and so on.

VORALBERG

The Lake of Constance, on which the city of Bregenz is situated, was a missionary area of St. Gall, the 6th-century Irish monk. Bregenz, an early Roman settlement, has a Benedictine monastery dedicated to the Irish monk. Voralberg is the most western of the Austrian provinces. Among the other points of religio-historic interest are:

Bildstein: The sanctuary itself was built between 1663 and 1676, but the wooden statue of the Madonna and Child is from the 14th century.

Rankweil: The Visitation of Mary Sanctuary, which is attached to the local church, contains a 15th-century wooden statue of the Madonna and Child.

SALZBURG

MARIA PLAIN

A composer who was born a few miles from the Madonna shrine on the Plain hill outside the city of Salzburg wrote the special Mass which highlights the annual celebration of the crowning of the image of the Mother and Child. Wolfgang Amadeus Mozart's "Coronation Mass" was performed for the first time, it is believed, during the celebration at the shrine in 1779. The original crowning took place in 1751. The two golden crowns had earlier been carried to Rome for the apostolic blessing of the Pope, Benedict XIV.

The image is not a native of Salzburg. It belonged originally to a master baker who lived near Regensburg in Bavaria. In December 1633, during the Thirty Years' War, his house was set afire by Swedish soldiers. The only possession that survived was a painting which showed the Madonna in the process of covering the naked infant on her lap with a large white cloth. The survival of the image seemed to be a miracle, and a woman neighbor named von Grimming eventually persuaded the baker's wife to part with it. The new owners of the image eventually moved to Salzburg where they owned property that included land on the Plain hill. When they died, their son carried the Madonna image to the hill and installed it in an oakwood shelter. This was at about the time of the feast of the Immaculate Conception in 1652. Ecclesiastical authorities inter-

vened, suggesting that the image should be placed in a
church. Its owner did not care for this proposal, and
removed the image, taking it to his home.

Financial difficulties developed for the owner in
1658. His possessions—all except the image—were auc-
tioned off and he returned to Bavaria. Near Augsburg
he built a small chapel and installed the image. Once
again people found their way to the private shrine, and
the Augsburg bishop stepped in this time, insisting that
the image be brought to the episcopal office for safekeeping. The bishop, like the one in Salzburg, had been
preoccupied about the possibility of a private cult
springing up outside the theological framework of the
church.

Meanwhile, in Salzburg the devotion to Maria Plain
had not been halted by the removal of the image to
Augsburg. A copy was made and set in the original
oakwood shelter. Soon the Salzburg bishop built a
chapel. When pilgrimages grew to the point that an
average of 2,000 Masses were being celebrated a year,
it was decided to build a church, and the copy of
the original image was placed above the main altar.
The use of the copy was only temporary. Now that a
church was available to receive the image, arrangements were made for its return from Augsburg in May
1676.

In November 1681 the bishop of Salzburg publicly
consecrated the diocese to the Madonna and besought
her protection. The act of consecration was recorded on
parchment by the bishop. He signed it in his blood, and
fastened it to the back of the painting.

The sanctuary is in one of those marvelous alpine
settings for which the province of Salzburg in particular,
and Austria in general, is known and loved—snow-
tipped peaks, vividly green meadows, vistas spreading
everywhere for miles. It looks across a small valley to
the Salzburg landmark, the *Festung* (fortress). The

road to the sanctuary swerves across a series of hills past farmhouses, men in shirtsleeves chopping wood, and barnyards of chickens and cows. The lower part of houses along the way is of brick or stone, and surfaced in stucco. The upper part is made from dark wood. Religious scenes are painted on the sides of many.

TRANSPORTATION: Salzburg is on the east-west and north-south rail lines.

HOTELS: *Bristol, Goldener Hirsch* and *Kobenzl* are great. *Stein* (superbly situated on the Salzach's banks), *Winkler* (great view) and *Pitter* are moderately priced.

POINTS OF INTEREST: Mozart's birthplace; the salt mines outside the city; the tomb of Paracelsus, the 15th-century Swiss physician and alchemist, in St. Sebastian's Church.

The city of Salzburg is filled with churches designed by Fischer von Erlach. As a matter of fact it is filled with as much beauty as man and nature can cram into a small city along a river. Among the churches of Salzburg that stand out from outstanding ones are:

Saints Rupert and Virgilius Cathedral: St. Virgilius, the bishop of the diocese, built the first cathedral on the site of the forum of the town which the Romans called Juvavum. It was consecrated on Sept. 24, 774 A.D. The present cathedral was completed in 1628. One of its three new doors—they represent Faith, Hope and Charity—was made by Giacomo Manzú. The façade of the cathedral serves as a backdrop each summer for the presentation of *Everyman* during the Salzburg festival.

St. Peter's: Rupert, a native of Franconia, established a Benedictine monastery amid the ruins of the Roman settlement somewhere around A.D. 700. Since then God has been worshiped on this site continuously—one of the handful of places north of the Alps which can claim such a long record of religious continuity. The graveyard is the oldest known cemetery in the province, and there are catacombs which might have been used by Christians in Roman times.

"Silent Night, Holy Night"

Folk Masses—those at which a guitar accompanies the singing—are not new in Salzburg. In 1818 the organist in the Oberndorf village church, a dozen miles north of Salzburg, used a guitar for the Christmas Midnight Mass when the organ broke down at the last minute. The organist also had with him the music he had composed for the Christmas poem written by the assistant pastor. That Christmas Eve the townspeople of Oberndorf assisted at the première of "Silent Night, Holy Night."

Literally by word of mouth the song traveled along the Salzach River into the Tyrol and then north into Germany. Thirty-six years later it reached Berlin, and a member of the Imperial Orchestra decided to trace its lineage. Father Josef Mohr, 26 at the time he wrote the words, was dead. Organist Franz Gruber, five years older than the priest, had retired as a village schoolteacher but was still alive. Gruber wrote to the Berlin orchestra member, giving him the background of the Christmas song's birth.

Oberndorf looks like a place where "Silent Night" would be written and sung. The surrounding mountains are always brimming with snow in the late fall and winter. The townspeople, as in the old days, are mostly farmers. At Midnight Mass women wear dark velour hats, and the men self-consciously cling to black fedoras which have high green bands that make clear they are alpine people. Rhinestone pins adorn women's hats or brighten their blouses. There is still a *Schifferschützenkorps*—as there has been for 696 years in Oberndorf. But it is not as important as it used to be and now is retained for ceremonial and nostalgic reasons. It had been founded to protect salt-carrying river boats from pirates. But the members of the oldtime protection group still appear at Midnight Mass in red coats and white trousers as a guard of honor.

An 1899 flood damaged the foundations of St. Nicholas's Church in which "Silent Night" was first sung. The new village church is built farther back from the river, but a memorial chapel dedicated to the two authors of "Silent Night" is on the site of the old church. Masses are said in the chapel on the anniversaries of the authors: Father Mohr's, Dec. 11; Organist Gruber's, Nov. 25. There is a Mass at the Silent Night Chapel at 5 P.M. on Christmas Eve. The mayor leads the procession of townspeople to the chapel.

Franz Gruber used to teach school in Arnsdorf, a hamlet 2 miles away. He lived with his wife and children on the second floor of the schoolhouse. His home is now kept as a memorial, and the present teacher lives nearby.

Gruber moved away from Oberndorf, possibly because he was disappointed at failing to land a teaching job in the town itself. It is not clear why he did not get the job. There were 5 candidates, and the district school superintendent gave him a high rating: "He knows very much, can paint, and is a musician. He is industrious. He handles children very well. People like him. He is very specially trained in every sense."

He obtained a job as choirmaster and teacher at Hallein, outside Salzburg, and died there. The house where he died is across the street from the parish church. In 1934 Los Angeles teachers made a pilgrimage to the site and erected a plaque on the outside wall of the house. It says: 'In honor of a teacher for his universal message of peace and goodwill."

Father Mohr is buried in the churchyard of the alpine town of Wagrain, 50 miles south of Salzburg, where he had been made pastor.

The guitar which accompanied the première of "Silent Night" is in the museum at Hallein.

BURGENLAND

Burgenland, south of Vienna and bordering Hungary, is the smallest province in Austria but it has a Baroque representation of the Mount of Calvary and Via Crucis that is one of a kind. The Calvary is at the Bergkirche (Mountain Church) in Eisenstadt, the same church which contains the mausoleum of Franz Josef Haydn. Prince Paul Esterházy had a Franciscan friar named Felix Nierinck create the Calvary. It was started in 1701 and completed 6 years later. The cross itself is on a man-made hill. The Via Crucis stretches to the hill along a route of chapels and grottoes. A later Prince Esterházy, Nikolaus, arranged for the transfer of Haydn's remains from Vienna to the Bergkirche. Eisenstadt was the composer's birthplace.

VIENNA

The 8-century-old St. Stephen's Cathedral is the centerpiece of the capital of Austria in every sense. It is dedicated to the son of Duke Geysa of Hungary who saw the martyr St. Stephen in a vision. St. Stephen told the duke that the son who was to be born to him in A.D. 977 would complete the task of bringing Christianity to his realm. The duke's son was given the name Stephen and became saint and king, founding churches and monasteries throughout the land of the Hungarians. St. Stephen is the patron of the diocese of Vienna, a city once called the eastern frontier of the Holy Roman empire. In the central nave of the cathedral is a statue of the Madonna of the Servant Girls, made about 1320. The sculptor of the cathedral's Gothic stone pulpit immortalized himself by including his sculpted head peering from a half-opened door at the base of the stairway. St. Stephen's gigantic bell, the Pummerin, is the largest in Austria.

Vienna was the birthplace of many Jewish physicians, painters, musicians, writers, scientists, actors, educators and other men and women of culture and learning who enriched the city and the world. The homes and places associated with some of them—such as Sigmund Freud—are identifiable and can be viewed. In the Nazi occupation of Austria which followed Hitler's annexation of the country in 1938 the Jewish population of Vienna literally disappeared, either by forced migration for safety's sake or by transportation to concentration camps in western Austria and Germany. Many of the places sacred to the Jews were destroyed, particularly in the second bezirk. A synagogue built in 1824 is in the first bezirk at 4 Seitenstettengasse.

St. Peter's (Peterskirche) is easily the oldest church in Vienna but there is some argument about its beginnings. One story is that it was founded by Charlemagne. Some believe the original church was a chapel used by the first Christians among the Roman legions. In the 17th century it was assigned by Emperor Leopold I to the Fraternity of the Trinity, a lay community to which he and Viennese aristocrats belonged. When the city was threatened with a plague in 1679, the emperor prayed in the church and promised to erect a memorial to the Holy Trinity if the pestilence (*pest*) ended. The "pest statue," as it is called, is in the Graben, not far from the church.

Disciples of Francis of Assisi settled in Austria during the saint's lifetime. Four of the friars on reaching Vienna were welcomed by Duke Leopold VI of the Babenbergs and given a piece of land for a church in the area where the imperial palace (Hofburg) was later built. The church, Minoritenkirche, took the name of the Friars Minor, or Minorites. For a brief time at the start of the Reformation Protestants used the church. Emperor Joseph II in the 18th century ordered the transfer of the Franciscan friars to a church in the suburbs, and assigned the Minoritenkirche to the "Italian nation" for use of Italians in Vienna.

The Hapsburg emperors used to attend Sunday Mass in the Hofburg chapel where the Vienna Boys' Choir still sings. But the parish church for the employees and middle-level members of the imperial court was the nearby Augustinerkirche of the Augustinian canons.

VIENNA BOYS' CHOIR

Nowadays hundreds of thousands of people around the world hear the Vienna Boys' Choir in concerts each year, but when the Holy Roman emperor Maximilian I established it in 1498 the youngsters were to sing only at Mass in the chapel of the imperial palace, the Hofburg. The end of the Hapsburgs' Austro-Hungarian empire in 1918 almost meant the end of the Vienna Boys' Choir, too. But a Viennese priest named Joseph Schnitt thought it was something too good to lose and, along with begging funds, sold some property he had inherited to get the choir started again. By 1924 the Vienna Boys' Choir was once again singing at Sunday Mass in the Hofburg Chapel, and two years later it began the concert tours that have made its voices known to people everywhere. The first tour to the United States was in 1932. There was a rough period during the Second World War when the Nazis occupied Austria, and Father Schnitt was imprisoned. By the time of Father Schnitt's death in 1955, at the age of 70, the Vienna Boys' Choir was able to carry on without him. He had set up a nonprofit organization of former choristers to direct the administration of the choir, and the education and training of the singers.

There are really four choirs, each composed of about a score of 10- to 14-year-old boys. The four groups are so perfectly trained that it is said even their director cannot tell them apart if he hears them separately. One choir is always on hand for the Mass in the Hofburg Chapel at 9:30 A.M. on Sunday. The other choirs are at various stages of resting, touring or preparing for a tour.

The boys' home while they are choir members is the Augarten Palace on the banks of the Danube. In the summer they vacation in the Tyrolean Alps at Hinterbichl. The choir boys have their own private tutors at the Augarten Palace. If they do not keep up their studies, they are dropped from the choir. That happened to Franz Schubert in the early part of the last century. The choirmaster liked his voice, but the tutors were disappointed in his Latin and mathematics.

One disappointment faces every choir member: his voice eventually "breaks." This can come with a warning, such as a hoarseness that lingers on longer than a typical sore throat should. Or it can happen in the middle of an aria on the concert stage in a far-off city. In the lean, ration-coupon days of the Second World War the voice change usually did not take place till the singer was 15 or 16 years old. When good food became plentiful once again, voices began breaking at the age of 13½ on the average. Some youngsters try to postpone the inevitable change in their voice by passing up meat and milk, and sticking to chicken and potatoes. The voice-change, of course, means that they no longer can sing in the choir. But they continue to live in the Augarten Palace, and finish high school. They usually are about 18 at the end of high school, and most return to their homes at that time. If they wish they can continue living at the Augarten Palace while they attend the University of Vienna or the Academy of Music.

TRANSPORTATION: The city's international airport is in a lovely part of the Vienna Woods. The Westbahnof is the rail station for trains from the West.

HOTELS: Among the leading hotels are the *Sacher,*

Bristol, Imperial and *Inter-Continental.* The *Europa, de France, Astoria* and *Stephansplatz* are not quite as expensive.

POINTS OF INTEREST: The Schottenkirche, founded in the 12th century by Hibernian monks identified as "Scots"; Roman ruins under the Hoher Markt and at Am Hof; Schönbrunn, summer residence of the emperors; and the Votive Church, built to commemorate Emperor Franz Josef's escape in 1853 from an assassination attempt.

3

Belgium

WHEN JULIUS CAESAR encountered the people of Gaul he remarked: "Of all these the bravest are the Belgians." Missionaries who followed the legions of Rome northward brought Christianity. Through the centuries churchmen in assessing the Belgian people have given them as high marks for their spirituality as Caesar once did for their physical courage.

At the time the Reformation reached the Low Countries, the Northern Provinces (now the Netherlands) accepted the teachings of Luther, while the people of the Southern Provinces (now Belgium) stood fast on their Catholicism. A massive practical reason for this, to be sure, was that Emperor Charles V—who also was King Charles I of Spain—maintained his court in Flanders where he was born. The direct rule of the Catholic monarch encouraged the Belgians to keep to the faith.

Popes established universities in various parts of Europe and some of these are older than the University of Louvain which came into being by a Papal Bull of Martin V in 1425. Unlike its seniors, the Belgian university has remained Catholic through 5½ centuries of change—political, military, economic and cultural. Bel-

gium's University of Louvain is the oldest Catholic
university in the world.

France was the last of Belgium's foreign occupiers,
moving into a vacuum created by the withdrawal of
Spanish and Austrian influences. France's tenure ended
with Napoleon's defeat at Waterloo, now a glum monument in the suburbs of Brussels. When the major
powers met at the Congress of Vienna in 1814 to fashion a permanent pattern of peace for Europe, Great
Britain proposed the unification of all the provinces of
the Low Countries (including Belgium) into a single
kingdom of the Netherlands. Britain's strategy was that
the new kingdom could provide a substantial buffer
against any future expansion moves of France. The
Belgians endured their enforced political condition for
16 years, breaking away in 1830 to form their own
independent kingdom.

It was a rebellion directed both at the religion—predominantly Protestant—of their northern neighbors of
the Low Countries and at the Dutch language spoken
in the north. To emphasize their difference from the
northerners, the Belgian rebels used French as their
main language although well over half of the 9.5 million
residents of the new kingdom of Belgium were Dutch-
speaking Flemings.

From the start of Belgium's independence the French
language had a louder voice in public affairs than
Flemish, a language the same as written Dutch. The
economic lay of the land also worked against the Flemish people. While the power sources for the industrial
revolution of the 19th century were in the backyard of
the French-speaking Walloons, the Dutch-speaking
Flemings of the north were surrounded by farm lands.

The French language dominated Belgium's life until
early in this century. Flemish men not understanding a
word of French were tried in French-speaking courts.
Belgian diplomats were chosen mainly from Walloon
ranks. Flemish soldiers fought in the First World War

under officers who spoke only French, and the Germans added psychological warfare with leaflets saying only fools obey people who do not speak their language.

At the Catholic University of Louvain, which is under the administration of the country's bishops, the first course in the Dutch language was not given until 1911.

From 1930, when the first Flemish high school in the country was established, language has been not a means of dialogue but a separator among the Belgians. Impetus for linguistic equality came after the Second World War when international businessmen seeking sites for new plants and investments found much of what they were looking for in Flanders. The economic fortunes of the Flemish noticeably improved, and so did their political standing. In 1960 the Flemings were the majority voice in Parliament for the first time.

In 1963 a linguistic boundary line was drawn across the center of the country. North of the line was the Flemish-speaking zone; south, the French. Brussels, just above the line, was made an exception because it is the capital. It was agreed that Brussels would be bilingual. The Flemish city of Louvain was also above the line— by 7 miles.

The bishops at first refused to recognize that the matter affected the Catholic University of Louvain itself. They insisted on the unity of the University of Louvain *at* Louvain, thereby ignoring suggestions that the French branch be split off and moved into the French-speaking zone of the country. Early in February 1968 Flemish Bishop Émile-Joseph De Smedt of Bruges, who was lauded by the world press for his progressivism at the Second Vatican Council a few years earlier, broke the solid episcopal front. He told some country people at Kortrijk that he had been "grossly mistaken" in agreeing with the unity-of-the-university declaration of Belgium's bishops, and that he would "remain faithful to the Flemish people."

After that, it would have been difficult for another Flemish bishop to take any other view.

The linguistic confrontation at Louvain was also splitting the government. New linguistic laws already required primary and secondary schools to use the language of the area. A few days after Bishop De Smedt's statement, a Flemish deputy asked Parliament to extend the same law to higher education—meaning the University of Louvain. The government fell over the issue. In the summer of 1968 the new government gave the French branch of the university its official moving notice. A few weeks later the bishops tacitly agreed to splitting the Catholic University into two by asking the French branch to submit its building plans for new locations in Brussels and in the French zone.

The Catholic University of Louvain will be 450 years old in 1975.

LOUVAIN

The Catholic University of Louvain is dedicated to the protection of Our Lady, Seat of Wisdom, and a great statue of the patroness is in the main building.

The only Pope from the Low Countries, Hadrian VI, studied and taught at Louvain. Erasmus of Rotterdam organized its "school of three languages" for comparative study of the New Testament in Latin, Greek and Hebrew. Gerard Mercator, the 16th-century cartographer, was educated at Louvain.

Louvain has close ties with the United States. Contributions from Americans helped rebuild, and re-equip, the library that had been destroyed in the First World War. The gifts poured in from Americans everywhere: universities (M.I.T. to the Ivy League), the Jewish Theological Seminary of America, a South Carolina Y.M.C.A. branch, the New York Police Department, service academies (West Point and Annapolis). A statue of Herbert Hoover stands in a square near the

library in remembrance of the way he directed relief to
Belgium after the First World War.

The oldest link is the 117-year-old American College,
which was founded for the training of Belgian priests
who would go to the United States as missionaries.
When America ceased being a "mission land," many
dioceses began the tradition of sending one or two
theology students to Louvain to complete their training
for the priesthood. The Irish College of the Franciscans
is even older, going back centuries. At times of persecution when Catholic printing presses in Ireland were
outlawed, catechisms were printed by the friars at
Louvain and shipped home.

During "the troubles" of the 17th century in Ireland,
when monasteries were threatened, four friars from the
Irish College at Louvain returned home and laboriously
copied entries from old manuscripts before they could
fall into hands that might destroy them. The Irish friars
returned to Louvain with their copies, known as *The
Annals of the Four Masters*. In Napoleon's invasion of
Belgium a century later, the friars worried about the
safety of their manuscript copies and had them taken to
Rome for safekeeping, to the Irish Franciscans at St.
Isidore's Church. Almost a century later they were
again endangered during the fighting in Rome over
independence from temporal rule of the Popes. At this
critical point the British government stepped in and
offered its "good offices" to make certain that the
precious manuscripts were safely returned to Ireland.

Father Damien

A little over a hundred years ago a Belgian priest,
born at Tremelo, 12 miles from Louvain, on Jan. 3,
1840 as Joseph De Veuster, volunteered to take on the
mission of aiding the lepers on the island of Molokai.
He remained 16 years at the Hawaiian leper colony,
revolutionizing the despairing conditions of the 200

inmates to bring about a community of hope based on Christian principles. Four years before his death at the age of 49 he had contracted leprosy himself. He is known by the religious name he took when he joined the Congregation of the Sacred Hearts (the Picpus Fathers), calling himself Damien after an early Roman martyr. He was 23 when he sailed for Honolulu on Nov. 2, 1863, and was ordained there the following spring.

"People are always putting flowers on his tomb—including leis," says Father Bosquet Telesphore, the archivist of the Picpus Fathers in Belgium.

Father Damien's body was exhumed in Hawaii on Jan. 1, 1936. It was brought to Louvain and placed in the crypt of the church known as the Sanctuary of St. Joseph.

Mass is said each morning in the crypt, but that, the priest archivist explains, is only because it is too difficult to warm the upstairs church. Sunday Masses are upstairs, however.

"Church law," he says, "is very strict about a devotion developing around someone who is not canonized. But all the preliminary steps to canonization have been taken. The archbishop of Malines established a commission in 1938 to investigate Father Damien's life. His reputation for sanctity has been carefully looked into here in Belgium and in Hawaii—and in Rome they read all his letters and papers to be sure he had never strayed from the teachings of the church. Everything so far has been favorable."

A painting near the tomb shows Damien as a youngish, black-haired priest in a white cassock, supporting an obviously weak brown-skinned man.

Damien went to school at Werchter till he was 13, and then worked on the farm at home.

"We have restored the family house in which he was born, putting it in the old manner as it was," the archivist says. "The zone is still farming, but it is gradually changing. The house is in a new parish between

Tremelo and Keerbergen which is called Ninde. A museum has been added to the house. It contains his books and clothes, and also the wooden altar of the Philomena Church of Kalawao, the Molakai leper settlement. Damien built the wooden church there."

St. Joseph's Chapel is in the upstairs part of the sanctuary, above the crypt containing Damien's tomb. The walls are lined with small marble ex-voto tablets engraved in gilt letters with words of thanks—*Merci, St. Joseph,* usually—and a date. The dates of the ex-votos are old. There are many banks of lighted candles.

"Mothers, and girls seeking a husband, especially like to make the pilgrimage to St. Joseph," the archivist says. "A few years ago we stopped having processions in the streets on St. Joseph's feast day. There are twenty thousand students in Louvain, and they don't seem to care for processions."

TRANSPORTATION: Louvain (in Flemish, Leuven) is a 20-minute train ride from Brussels.

DIEST

The Flemish village of Diest, 18 miles northeast of Louvain, is one of the few places in Belgium where beguines still live. They are also at Termonde, between Aalost and Ghent, and at Kortrijk in West Flanders. The beguines—holy women who do not take formal religious vows—first settled in Diest early in the 13th century. Their houses are along the four streets of the beguinage at the Porte de Schaffen in the western end of the city. Each house is dedicated to a saint, and the medieval practice of ensconcing an image of the patron in a niche near the door was followed.

St. John Berchmans

The patron of Belgian youth, the Jesuit saint, John Berchmans, was born in Diest on Mar. 13, 1599, and baptized the following day in the Church of St. Sulpice. The street on which he was born—now named for him—starts at the church. It is a narrow busy street crammed with pastry shops, clothing boutiques and various small stores. The Town Hall is at the head of the street, too, across from St. Sulpice. A worn brass-plated wooden stairway, at the middle of the ground-floor entrance to the Berchmans house, leads to the open floor above where there is an altar. Mass is said each morning in the chapel, and on Tuesday evening also. There are several Masses on Berchman's feastday which, in Belgium, is celebrated on Nov. 27. He was 22 when he died on Aug. 13, 1621.

"His heart is with the Jesuits in Malines," says the dean of St. Sulpice, Father Verbiest. "I've asked them for it so that it could be displayed here, but they say No. It is a very beautiful relic."

The dean is an agreeable white-haired man of medium size. His hair seems to have whitened prematurely. The cigars he smokes give off lots of black smoke.

Is the Berchmans house a Jesuit chapel?

"Not at all," the dean says, laughing. "It is curious but the Jesuits do nothing for the chapel here. It is maintained by the parish. I am going to restore it now, and that is why I asked for his heart so it could be exposed."

TRANSPORTATION: Diest is 35 miles from Brussels. Express trains serve Louvain and Hasselt, and there are bus connections to Diest. Local trains also stop at Diest.

POINTS OF INTEREST: The village church of Kortembois, between Hasselt and St. Truiden, has five steeples. A shrine to St. Appolonia, the patroness of people with tooth problems, is at Niel-As, a village about 2 miles from As.

SCHERPENHEUVEL/MONT AIGU

"I think after Lourdes, Notre Dame of Mont Aigu is the biggest shrine in Europe," the woman owner of one of the cafés on the main square of Scherpenheuvel (in French, Mont Aigu) remarks.

The woman serves coffee in the old-fashioned Belgian way—in a glass with hot water filtering through a silvered metal holder. She is Flemish, with dark red hair, aged about 40. The shrine is at the center of the main square, at the door of her café. Many of the square's cafés have religious names, like "St. Joseph" and "Our Dear Lady." They are small buildings of two or three floors, with the café on the ground floor and rooms for pilgrims upstairs.

"May is the month for the real pilgrims," the woman continues. "I've seen as many as thirty thousand people here on the first of May. Some of the young come on foot, and spend the night here. There are about two thousand beds in the village—but a dozen beds in a room, I mean. It is pretty crowded. Some of the pilgrims also use the old stables of farmers near the basilica. Farmers give hay to the pilgrims who as a form of penitence spread it on the floor of the stables, and sleep on it."

The basilica is at the end of the highway on a gently rising hill. Eight centuries ago when pilgrims first began visiting the "pointed hill" (*scherpenheuvel,* in Flemish), the area was wild and uninhabited, and the closest village was Zichem. The pilgrimages began sometime in the 12th century after an unknown person had installed a statue of Mary in the bough of an oak tree. The local people associated the statue with health cures and graces they had received. About 1415 a passing shepherd noticed the statue on the ground, and picked it up. All at once he found that he could not move, that the statue seemed to be too heavy. He remained immobile until, hours later, his employer came looking for him and, seeing the statue, replaced it in the tree. The shepherd was then able to walk. News of this happening increased the number of pilgrims.

In 1603 Archduke Albert and the Archduchess Isabella of Austria visited the shrine. The royal visitors came with an entourage of some two dozen people, all of whom ceremoniously signed the shrine's first golden guest book, *album amicorum,* which was a collation of sheets of parchment. The archduke and archduchess also arranged to have a stone church built. Archduke Albert died before the church was completed in 1627, but his wife continued to help expand the shrine. She invited the Oratorian Fathers to come to Mont Aigu to assist the pilgrims—their first foundation in Belgium. She also proposed that the village be laid out in the form of a star, as a tribute to the Madonna.

The church, of white stone, looks like a miniature St. Peter's. The interior is paneled in marble, and lavishly ornamented with silver. The miraculous statue is above the tabernacle. A sculptured replica of the old oak tree, realistic with leaves and branches, has been set symbolically high over the main altar. There are seven chapels for seven prophets, starting with Daniel.

Because of the numerous objects of art, a caretaker is on duty. He is middle-aged and tall. His name is Antoine.

At the right of the main entrance is a small chapel with many ex-voto offerings. Most seem to be children's things. There are tiny nightshirts and many pairs of baby shoes. Antoine points out that the baptismal font is in the chapel, and therefore it is a favorite with mothers.

"Just recently," Antoine says, "a mother brought a knitted blue sweater and a picture of her little girl of three or four who had been cured."

At the left side of the main entrance is the Chapel of

the Candles, sharply illuminated with hundreds of imploring fingers of light. Small sheets of paper and pencils lie on the chapel altar. Pilgrims write out the things they are praying for on a piece of paper, and slip it into a chute marked INTENTIES (Intentions). The pieces of paper, Antoine says, are collected and placed behind a glass on the wall of the chapel.

The vicar of the shrine—it is also the parish church—is a robust priest in his 50s with glasses who seems to have time for everyone. His name is Janssens. He estimates that 1.4 million people hear Mass during the 4 summer months alone, starting the first of May.

Like a Roman ruin in southern France an ancient brick corridor stands mutely, unused and unusable, behind the basilica. It once led to the monastery built by Archduchess Isabella for the Oratorian Fathers. (See Index.)

"There are no Oratorians left in Europe, except in England and Spain," the vicar says. "They were banished from here in the French Revolution, and taken to Caienne, a colony off the African coast. None ever left that island alive. They were considered too dangerous. Their monastery here was burned out, but the flames did not harm the basilica. They didn't quite reach it."

TRANSPORTATION: There is bus service to and from the nearby town of Diest, which is on the main railroad line between Brussels and Hasselt. By highway, take the Brussels-Hasselt auto-route.

LIÈGE

Liège was founded in A.D. 558 at one of the prettiest points on the Meuse River by Bishop Monulphe, of Tongrès, 15 miles to the north. Tongrès still exists. Liège not only has survived, but has become the capital of the French-speaking Wallonia zone of Belgium, and one of the most important cities, industrially, of the Common

Market. From earliest days, Liège has been a religious center. The martyrdom of Bishop Lambert in A.D. 705 set off a chain of pilgrimages that remained unbroken for centuries. Clovis, a native of Tournai in western Belgium, encouraged the development of the Liège area as a sanctuary subject only to the bishop's jurisdiction. Charlemagne was born not far away, at Jupille, and maintained his court at either Aachen (usually) or Herstal. The feast of Corpus Christi was instituted in 1246 at the *Church of St. Martin.* In the 10th-century *Ste. Croix* (Holy Cross) *Church* is a reliquary containing what is believed to be a relic of the True Cross. The church also possesses a symbolic "Key of St. Peter," which early Popes used to present to outstanding personages. Such keys contained what were said to be iron filings from the chains of St. Peter. Pope Gregory gave the Liège key to Bishop Hubert in A.D. 722. The only other known Key of St. Peter is the one presented to St. Servais in Maastricht. (See Index.) The *Sacre Coeur Basilica* overlooks the city from a height of more than 350 feet above the Meuse. It was built as a companion to the memorial honoring the Allied dead of the First World War.

TRANSPORTATION: Liège is about 60 miles east of Brussels and 30 miles west of Aachen (Germany). It is on the main railroad line between Brussels and Germany.

HOTELS: *Holiday Inn, Couronne* and *Ramada Inn* are the leading places. *Boulevard, Cygne d'Argent* and *Métropole* are somewhat less expensive.

BANNEUX

In 1934, the year after 12-year-old Mariette Beco reported seeing the Madonna 8 times, the late Father Louis Jamin sent an urgent message to her home in the pine forest a mile from the center of the town of Banneux.

"An important man from Paris, the vicar general, is here and wants to talk with you," Father Jamin, the village pastor, said.

Mariette declined the summons to see the visiting priest.

"Tell him he came for the Blessed Virgin—not for me."

That has been Mariette's standard reply ever since to unofficial questioners, says Father Arthur Merlot, who came to Banneux from Liège in 1935 to assist Father Jamin because he was sick. Father Merlot was put in charge of pilgrimages to the shrine of Our Lady of Banneux in 1952.

"Sometimes pilgrims recognize Mariette in town and ask her to talk about the Apparitions," Father Merlot says. "Mariette points out to them that she related every detail to an ecclesiastical commission, and that it has all been written down. She has not one word to add."

What has been written down in the official archives of the bishop of Liège is that Mariette was looking out of the window of her home on a winter evening when she saw the Madonna. At the time she was the oldest of 7 children. Four other children were later born. The family's home was a two-story brick building, shaped almost like a perfect square. Mariette's father was a laborer and the home, practically isolated in the pine woods, was typical of families who were not too well off. Banneux is in the Ardennes which sweep across southeastern Belgium. In summer they are a welcome, cool forestland. In winter, they are shrouded in fog, rain or snow.

At 7 o'clock on Sunday evening, Jan. 15, in 1933, snow and ice were packed around the Beco house when Mariette, while watching for her 10-year-old brother Julian who had been gone all day, saw the first Apparition. . . .

"Oh, mama!" she exclaims. "There is a beautiful Lady in the garden. . . . I tell you it is the Blessed

Virgin. She is smiling at me. She is wonderfully beautiful!"

Mariette heads for the door but is stopped by her mother who, confused by the child's report, believes it is the work of witches. When Mariette returns to the window the Lady is gone.

Again, about 7 o'clock three evenings later—Wednesday, Jan. 18—there is an Apparition. Mariette, ignoring the darkness and cold, had gone into the garden. The figure approaches slowly, growing larger all the time, and comes to a halt, above the ground, a few feet from where Mariette is kneeling. The figure seems to be standing on a small cloud of gray. Mariette continues to recite the Rosary, and the Lady, smiling, also appears to be saying a prayer because her lips move softly. Mariette later estimates that the interval of mutual prayer lasts 20 minutes. The Lady then motions Mariette to follow her. Mariette does, but after a few yards falls to her knees to say some *Aves*. A little farther along, she again kneels in prayer, and once more the Lady indicates she should follow her. Mariette does and then, looking to the right, sees water gushing from a spring. "Plunge your hands into the water," Mariette is told. Mariette washes her hands carefully in the spring, and the Lady says: "This spring is reserved for me." The Lady then says goodnight to Mariette and, still facing the child, moves backward, growing progressively smaller until she no longer is visible.

The following evening, toward 7 o'clock, Mariette covers her head with an old coat and, a few steps from the door of the Beco home, kneels on the snow-covered ground. Soon she stretches out her arms and cries: "Ah, there she is!" Mariette remains silent a moment, and then asks: "Who are you, my lovely Lady?" She is told: "I am the Virgin of the Poor." Nearby are her father and neighbors, but the child seems to be unaware of their presence.

Mariette remains in bed the following day, Friday,

Jan. 20, because she is not feeling well. About 6:30 P.M., however, she gets up and, dressing, persuades her parents to let her go outside. There are dozens of people waiting. After reciting the Rosary for 2 minutes, Mariette cries out: "There she is!" Mariette asks: "What do you want, my lovely Lady?" She is told: "I would like a small chapel." The Lady makes the sign of the cross. The witnesses notice Mariette bend, lean forward, and then collapse on the cold ground, as if she has fainted. Her father takes her home and she regains consciousness quickly.

The next morning, for the first time, Mariette goes alone to the parish office of Father Jamin to tell him about the four Apparitions. The priest is certain that the series of Apparitions has ended, and asks Mariette to remain at home in the evening, and not go outdoors. She thinks the priest does not believe her and, bursting into tears, declares: "I have seen her. I have heard her."

Each evening for the next three weeks Mariette takes her rosary and, kneeling outside her home in the snow, waits for another appearance of the Lady. She does not appear. During this long period Mariette is taunted by young and old alike in the village, some saying, "Bonjour, Bernadette."

On Saturday, Feb. 11, at 7 P.M. Mariette is kneeling in the yard of her home with some villagers. Together they are reciting the Rosary, taking turns with each decade. They have just reached the fifth decade when suddenly Mariette gets to her feet and walks toward the spring, stopping at the now familiar two spots along the way to recite *Aves*, half-aloud. "I come to ease suffering," Mariette hears the Lady say. A thankful Mariette says: "Merci, Merci." The Lady says: "Au revoir." The words thrill Mariette. They mean she will see the Lady again.

That same evening Mariette rushes to tell Father Jamin, and to ask him if she can make her First Communion the next morning. Her parents had been in-different about religion, and she had never made her First Communion when her 7-year-old friends had. Father Jamin agrees to give her Communion in the morning after hearing her Confession.

The Lady does not appear that Sunday evening, or any other evening until the following Wednesday—Feb. 15. "Blessed Virgin," Mariette says to the Lady, "the priest has told me to ask you for a sign." Mariette is told: "Believe in me; I will believe in you."

For the next five evenings Mariette recites the Rosary punctiliously at 7 o'clock. Nothing out of the ordinary happens on the first four evenings. On the fifth evening, Monday, Feb. 20, the Lady appears and leads her to the spring. "My dear child, pray a great deal," the Lady tells Mariette.

Each of the following mornings Mariette goes to the parish church, a half mile from her home, to receive Communion. In the evening, with some friends, she prays in the front yard. The Lady does not reappear until 7 P.M. on Thursday, Mar. 2. It is raining fiercely. When Mariette and her friends reach the third decade of the Rosary, the rain abruptly stops, the sky clears, and the stars shine brightly. The Lady is making her eighth and last appearance. She tells Mariette: "I am the Mother of the Redeemer. The Mother of God."

She announces the end of the series of Apparitions by saying "Adieu" instead of "Au revoir."

"Father Jamin," his successor Father Merlot says, "went to Bishop Kerkhofs in Liège and told him of the Apparitions. The bishop counseled Father Jamin that he must be prudent. And he was prudent—that I know."

Father Merlot was ordained in 1935, the year he came to Banneux to help Father Jamin. He is big and tall. His face is florid. He gives the impression of hiding nothing. He obviously wants to share, with anyone who asks, every bit of information in his possession.

Affirmative reaction of laymen to the Apparitions was faster than the church's.

"At the time," Father Merlot says, "laymen active in the St. Vincent de Paul Society in Liège came to Banneux, and asked Father Jamin if they could help him. They formed a nonprofit corporation called Notre Dame of Banneux Caritas, and in 1934, the year after the Apparitions, bought the Beco family house. When I came here in 1935 the Becos had built a larger house about twenty-five yards away. I came for two months. The only thing here then was the Beco house where Mariette had lived at the time of the Apparitions and a little chapel that had been built in 1933 in the garden.

"I came back in 1943, on the feast of the Assumption, as the village *curé* and assistant to Father Jamin. The year before Bishop Kerkhofs had recognized the *devotion* to Our Lady of Banneux—not the *facts* of the Apparitions, mind you; only the devotion. But that made it possible for priests to join the laymen in the nonprofit Caritas corporation that was developing the shrine. By the time of my return in 1943, too, the second Beco home had been bought by the society and was being used as a priests' house. About 1940 Mariette's parents built their third home—this time a couple hundred yards away, on what is now the main square at the entrance to the shrine."

On Aug. 22, 1949 Bishop Louis Kerkhofs announced in a pastoral letter his recognition of the facts of the Apparitions that had been reported by Mariette 16 years earlier.

The announcement increased the number of pilgrims. When Father Merlot was put in charge of pilgrimages in 1952, there were 300,000 pilgrims that year. Now, he estimates, 700,000 persons visit the shrine annually. Among the pilgrims is the bishop of Liège.

"As I said, Bishop Kerkhofs at first was cautious. But later when he recognized the facts, he came often. Bishop Kerkhofs died around 1961 or 1962, and I remember that his successor, the present bishop, Monsignor Guillaume Marie van Zuylen, was sick in Switzerland, and right after his recovery he came here twice. He might have been here more than that but we saw him twice. He comes each year on the feast of the Apparitions, although this year he couldn't because he was ill."

From the end of April till October about 4,000 sick and invalid pilgrims arrive on special trains and remain for four days at the 300-bed Hospitality Center. Most pay their way, but those who cannot are financed by the nonprofit Caritas Society.

Mariette's mother and father have died, but her brothers and sisters are still alive. Most of them live in the Banneux area. Her brother Julian's wife died three years ago.

The house in which Mariette lived at the time of the Apparitions is now the residence of the sacristan of the shrine. The second family home is still the priests' house. The third house has been turned into a family-run commercial establishment. Mariette's sister Simone operates the hotel part; her brother Guy, the restaurant; and another brother, André, the religious-articles shop.

Mariette married relatively young. She has two children, a son and a daughter: Jean-Marie, born in 1943, and Miriam, who is in her late 20s. The son is married and lives near his mother, about 2 miles from the shrine. The daughter lives in Banneux. A third child died at birth. With her son, Mariette operates a restaurant near the shrine, called Friterie Saint-Michel, and a souvenir shop.

"Most people," Father Merlot says, "do not know the Beco family history or details of Mariette's present life. Some talk with her in her shop, and think she is a clerk. She comes to the shrine quite often, but without any ceremony—and never when it is likely she might be recognized by pilgrims."

Father Merlot says he has known Mariette's husband, Mathieu, for years.

"One night he stayed in the rectory with me talking till one in the morning. The man was very upset. I was afraid he was going to do something—I don't know what.

"I don't believe Mathieu understands the psychology of Mariette. He is Dutch. He told me one time he does not believe Mariette saw the Virgin. I said to him: 'You know Bishop Kerkhofs. He is a very serious, intelligent man, isn't he? Well, he believes what Mariette has said. Isn't that enough for you?' He said, 'Yes.' "

Mariette and Mathieu are separated. He still lives in Banneux, a mile or two away from Mariette.

"The separation has been a difficulty for the shrine," Father Merlot remarks spontaneously, adding: "We are the shrine of the Virgin of the Poor." He makes the same remark each time something negative is mentioned. Thus, when Canon Maurice Van Lon, the general director of the shrine, observes that the supply of a particular leaflet is low, Father Merlot smiles, and says: "We are of the poor." But he makes a note to have more copies printed.

Banneux's spring still flows but it has been covered over, and the water is funneled into a stone basin with a brass spigot. Pilgrims drink the water from picnic cups they have brought with them, and dampen their faces and hands with it. Villagers come with plastic bottles and containers to fetch water for their homes. One youngish village woman in a sweater and wool skirt remarks as she fills a 2-liter plastic bottle:

"Sometimes the water at home is yellow, and not good for cooking. This is always good."

TRANSPORTATION: All trains on the main Liège-Aachen rail line stop at Pépinster (the town of Pépin, father of Charlemagne), 6 miles from Banneux. Buses connect with the shrine. There is also bus service from Liège, 20 miles from Banneux.

HOTELS: There are rooms for 500 persons in medium-comfort hotels at Banneux. At Verviers, the *Amigo* is excellent; the *Grand*, less expensive.

BRUGES

In Flemish the word *brug* means "bridge" and the city of Bruges, once the main center of Flanders, has been a bridge through more than a dozen centuries of the history of the Belgians. The Procession of the Holy Blood, on the Monday following May 2, is a religious event with a long tradition in Flanders. In 1149 Thierry, Count of Flanders, received from the Patriarch of Jerusalem a few drops of the blood of Christ. This sacred relic has been conserved in a gold and silver reliquary, adorned with precious stones and enamel work, and is carried in the annual procession. During the rest of the year the reliquary is in the Chapel of the Holy Blood, next to the Town Hall.

St. Saviour's Cathedral is the oldest brick church in Belgium. Its foundations were laid in the 7th century. The stalls of its choir already existed when the Knights of the Golden Fleece met in Bruges in 1468.

Michelangelo's statue "The Virgin and Child" is in the Church of Notre Dame.

Bruges is noted, also, for its artistic lacemakers, and this ancient art is continued today by the Apostoline Sisters whose convent is near St. Anne's Church. The Sisters have a lacemaking school. On warm sunny days lacemakers work on the doorsteps of the small houses along rue du Poivre. Nearby is the Jerusalem church of the 15th century. It was built according to designs brought back from the Holy Land of the church built around the Holy Sepulchre.

TRANSPORTATION: Bruges is linked to Britain by car
   ferries at Ostend and Zeebrugge. Direct trains from
   Brussels.
HOTELS: The *Duc de Bourgogne, Portinari* and *Bour-*
   goensch Hof are the leaders; *Bryghia* and *Sneeuw-*
   berg are less expensive.

GHENT

Every five years—1975, 1980 and so on—the extraordinary flower show known as the Floralies takes
place in Ghent. It has earned Ghent the title of City of
Flowers. In 1500 the future Charles V, Holy Roman
emperor and king of Spain (as Charles I), was born in
Ghent. Through the centuries Ghent has been known
for its cloth and for its art. Its Cathedral of St. Bavon is
Belgium's greatest repository of religious art.

THE MYSTERY OF THE "MYSTIC LAMB"

The most precious art treasure in the Ghent cathedral
is the 15th-century group of paintings by the Van Eyck
brothers known as "The Adoration of the Mystic
Lamb." It is an immense altarpiece, technically called a
polyptych, a central group of paintings associated with
paintings on lateral panels that fold shut like doors. It
was unveiled in 1432, and probably has had the most
bizarre history of any painting.

Emperor Joseph II ordered the panels of Adam and
Eve removed because to him they seemed indecent. In
the French Revolution the central piece was carried off
to Paris as a trophy and mounted in the Louvre. A half
dozen of the side panels, after moving through various
hands, reached the king of Prussia who ceremoniously
presented them to the Berlin Museum. Belgium got the
panels back as war reparations, thanks to the Treaty of

Versailles. But in the Second World War, during the
Nazi invasion of the Low Countries, the entire polyptych was taken out of the country for safekeeping in
southern France. The Nazis found it and transferred it
to Germany. Americans in liberating Austria discovered
it hidden in the salt mines near Salzburg, and in 1945
returned it to Belgium.

That was not the worst of the strange experiences of
this masterpiece of religious art. One of its panels was
stolen in 1934 and has never been found, even though
police identified the thief.

The theft was discovered on the morning of Apr. 11,
1934 by the sacristan after he noticed an early Mass-
goer entering by the side door. He was startled because
he had not as yet opened that door. In his inspection
the sacristan discovered that two panels, "The Upright
Judges" and "St. John the Baptist," were missing from
the Van Eyck altarpiece. Each oakwood panel was
nearly 5 feet high and 2 feet wide.

It was a month before the thief showed any signs of
life. He sent a letter to the bishop of Ghent, saying he
possessed the two panels, having in some unexplained
way outsmarted the actual thieves. For his efforts he
wished 1 million francs—close to a half million dollars.
There followed an exchange of coded messages in a
Brussels newspaper, and a demand that the letter-
writer show proof he really had the painting. He did
this by mailing a Brussels railroad station baggage
check. The baggage check, it turned out, was for a
package that contained one of the two missing panels,
St. John the Baptist. Having given spectacular proof
that he was not a prankster, the letter-writer demanded
the 1 million francs for the safe return of the other
panel. Antwerp was arranged as the delivery point for
the money and the painting. The thief picked a parish
priest as the intermediary. He was to be given a sealed
envelope containing the money and, with it, half of a
page from a newspaper. When someone appeared with

the matching half-page, the priest was to hand over the envelope.

One summer afternoon the priest was told that a caller was at the door. The visitor said he was there to "pick up something," and presented the matching piece of newspaper. The priest turned over the envelope.

It is not clear why the police did not move in at this point. They did not. But the caller's license number had been taken. It was found to be the number of a taxi. The driver's story was a simple one. He had been engaged at the railroad station and given an address. On reaching it, the passenger asked the driver to pick up a small package while he waited in the taxi, and gave him the torn newspaper to identify himself. Later he drove the passenger back to the railroad station.

A few days later, the bishop received a complaining letter. Only 25,000 francs—not 1 million—had been in the envelope! The thief broke off the contact, and never resumed it.

The following autumn a speaker at an election rally in Dendermone, 20 miles from Ghent, collapsed in the street. He was a 58-year-old money-exchange agent who was active in civic works. The man sensed he was about to die, and asked to speak to a lawyer friend. He told the lawyer that everything that had to do with the missing painting was in a desk drawer in his home. He said he was the only person who knew where it was hidden. At that point, as in a TV drama, the man died.

Police found copies of the ransom letters to the bishop in the man's home in Wetteren, a town near Ghent. The typewriter on which they had been written was located. There was also a letter, which the man had apparently written to himself, asking him to please do a favor for the "writer," and pick up a package in Antwerp. Police theorized that the man had acted alone and had stolen the painting to make good some business losses.

The only clue police have as to its whereabouts is a statement in one of the letters from the thief. "I cannot remove it without attracting attention," he had written, "for it is in a public place." Police believe the "public place" might be the cathedral itself, but they have searched it from bell tower to sacristy without success.

Meanwhile, a copy has replaced the missing panel. But the effect is not the same as the original. In the modern copy, for instance, the blue sky over the heads of "The Upright Judges" is fading. In the rest of the polyptych the sky is vividly bright and fresh after more than 5 centuries.

TRANSPORTATION: Ghent is at the nucleus of auto-routes fanning out to Brussels, Antwerp, Bruges and Kortrijk. It is 35 miles from Brussels, and is on the main rail line between Brussels and Ostend.

HOTELS: The *Cour St. Georges* is full of history and comfort.

PLACES OF INTEREST: St. Elizabeth's Beguinage; the museum of the Treaty of Ghent (Dec. 24, 1814), which brought an end to the war between the United States and Britain.

BEAURAING

Until Tuesday evening, Nov. 29, 1932 the town of Beauraing in southern Belgium was a dot on the map for most Belgians. But at 6:30 that evening 12-year-old Albert Voisin, walking toward the girls' boarding school of the Sisters of the Christian Doctrine with some companions, suddenly pointed to the railroad viaduct that runs close to the building, and exclaimed excitedly: "Look! the Virgin! She's walking all in white above the bridge!" . . .

At first Albert's companions think the brightness is from a car's headlight. But as they stare toward the corner of the school garden, in the vicinity of the grotto of Notre Dame of Lourdes, they perceive someone in white also. By the evening of Jan. 3, 1933 Albert and his companions are known throughout Belgium as "the five children of Beauraing" and 30,000 persons, including priests and doctors, are present in the Ardennes town for what is to be the last of 33 Apparitions by the Lady in white.

The Five Children of Beauraing were Albert; his two sisters, Gilberte, 14, and Fernande, 16; and the two girls of the Degeimbre family, Andrée, 15, and Gilberte, 9½, who was called "Little Gilberte" to distinguish her from her older friend with the same name.

"Today, more than forty years later," an Assumptionist priest, Father Leopold, says, "the Apparitions are *très vivantes*—very much alive—for the five principals." The priest, a youngish, slender man with glasses, nods his head as he contemplates what he has just said.

"After each Apparition," Father Leopold continues, "the children, one by one, were interrogated by a doctor of the village who had an office near here. On December 8, 1932, during the evening Rosary, the five were here and went into an ecstasy. There were doctors present, and they examined the children, putting matches to their hands and pinching them. But there was no reaction. One doctor even tried a lighted match on himself and shouted, 'Ouch!' That is why so many doctors were present on the night of the last Apparition. There were eighty doctors here."

Sometimes one of the children heard a message which others did not hear. On the day of the last Apparition, Jan. 3, 1933, for instance, Fernande was in tears because the others saw the Lady in white, and she had not. Fernande lingered at the site, continuing to say the Rosary, and was rewarded with an Apparition. Furthermore, it was to Fernande on this occasion that the Lady identified herself as "The Immaculate Conception, the Mother of God, and the Queen of Heaven."

To the children who saw the Apparitions, she seemed

to come and go swiftly, like a bright light being turned on and off. The whiteness of the figure was indescribable—"whiter than snow." She had rosy cheeks, blue eyes, and her face was shaped like a white egg. She held her hands joined together in prayer, and her eyes were turned toward heaven. She smiled a great deal. Golden rays burst from her head. Her voice was gentle—"like a woman's." Her robe was long, reaching to her feet, and there were many folds in it. In the last of the Apparitions, from Dec. 29 until the final one on Jan. 3, a golden heart with a sunburst of rays appeared also on her breast. Her general message was to pray and make sacrifices.

When she first appeared on the evening of Nov. 29 only four of the children saw her. They were on the way to the boarding school of the nuns to meet Gilberte Voisin, Albert's 14-year-old sister who was a student there, and accompany her home. Greatly agitated by what they had seen, they related their experience to Sister Valeria, the nun doorkeeper. Peering in the darkness toward the Notre Dame of Lourdes grotto, the nun asserted that it was impossible for a statue to move from its shrine and walk back and forth along the railroad bridge. When Gilberte Voisin joined her companions she, too, saw the figure in white. Their parents scoffed at them when they arrived home and told what they had seen.

"In the beginning the bishop was *très reservé*, very circumspect," Father Leopold says. "Every night at six-thirty, the hour of the Apparitions, the children came for ten years, and recited the Rosary together. In 1942 the bishop asked them to withdraw, saying they had performed their role. They still come today, particularly those who are at Beauraing."

Despite the official silence of the church, laymen began making pilgrimages at once. Finally, 10 years after the events, Monsignor André-Marie Charue, bishop of Namur, gave official approval for the devotion

to Notre Dame of Beauraing. This was Feb. 2, 1943.
Six years later, on July 2, 1949, he recognized that two
reported cures could only be explained as due to supernatural causes—that is, miracles. In a letter to the
clergy of the diocese that day he said: "These two
miraculous cures constitute the final element that wins
our conviction on the supernatural nature of the facts.
. . . We can in all serenity and prudence affirm that
the Queen of Heaven appeared to the children of
Beauraing in the course of the winter of 1932–33."

To accommodate the throngs of pilgrims, the shrine's
nonprofit Pro Maria Society in January 1946 bought a
château and 45 acres of land on a hill behind the convent of the nuns. A Way of the Cross was installed, and
the château made into a house for retreats. Later that
year, on Aug. 22, Bishop Charue led a solemn procession from the château to the corner of the nuns' garden,
where the Virgin had appeared, and a statue made
according to the description by the children was installed there. During the ceremonies Bishop Charue
declared Aug. 22 to be the summertime feast of Notre
Dame of Beauraing, and on that date each year since
there is a candlelight procession. (The wintertime feast
is Nov. 29, the date of the first Apparition.)

About 40,000 pilgrims were at Beauraing on May 31,
1951 for the celebration of the dogma of the Assumption of the Virgin Mary which Pius XII had proclaimed
the previous Nov. 1, during the Holy Year of 1950. The
bishop of Lourdes, Monsignor Theas, was invited to
Beauraing to speak at the celebration.

The bishop of Lourdes again spoke at Beauraing
when the 25th anniversary of the first Apparition was
observed on Nov. 29, 1957. For the pilgrims a highlight
of the day was seeing "The Five Children of Beauraing"
once again kneeling in prayer together as they had done
a quarter of a century earlier. On the following Aug. 22,
the summertime feast of the shrine, the Apostolic Nun-
tius in Belgium, Monsignor Forni, celebrated the Mass

in the presence of all the bishops of Belgium and many from other countries.

"All the children are alive," says Sister Anne, a nun at the convent. Sister Anne deals with the pilgrims, and gives a lecture with diapositive colored slides, which she briskly calls "dias." She is tall and handsome, and her face is particularly white and serene. She is probably in her 30s. She wears a nondescript nun's garb with a small coif.

"They all married and have children of their own. Three are right here at Beauraing yet—Andrée, who comes to the chapel every day; Gilberte Voisin; and Albert Voisin. The three children of Andrée are already married themselves. Gilberte is a widow. She was married to a gendarme but he was killed in line of duty. She has two married children. Albert is a teacher here in the village school of the Christian Brothers, and has three children. The other two who are not at Beauraing are Fernande and Little Gilberte. Fernande is the mother of five children, and is at Namur. Little Gilberte lives in northern Italy, and has two children.

"Little Gilberte says that in the beginning no one in the village where she lives in Italy knew that she was one of the Five Children of Beauraing, and therefore she was able to lead a normal life. When people there found out her background, life for her became a Calvary—people always posing questions about their future, their lives, and so on.

"Albert, when he was younger, was away from Beauraing for quite a while, too. He was in the Congo for many years. His son Claude remembers as a child in the Congo that the family always assembled each evening at six-thirty to say the Rosary. But his father never once mentioned the Apparitions. It was only when the family returned to Belgium, Claude says, that he heard about his father's part in them."

Sister Anne says that there are 700 different statues of the Madonna in the Marian Museum that was established at Beauraing on the first of May in 1951. The statues are from all over the world. The museum displays various articles associated with the shrine, such as the clothes worn by the children at the time of the Apparitions. Princess Josephine, sister of the late Albert I, king of the Belgians, presented her wedding veil to the shrine.

The Sisters still own the garden and the school building where Little Gilberte was a student, but they reestablished the school at a new location in town. The former school is used to house up to 100 sick and invalid pilgrims who make 3-day visits to the shrine, accompanied by priests, nurses and stretcher-bearers.

"Sometimes the sick ask to speak to the children," Sister Anne says. "The children are very discreet. Andrée was talking to one who posed some questions. 'It is not I who am important,' Andrée said. 'It is the Virgin.'"

The shrine is in a crowded corner of the town, and the buses bringing pilgrims have a hard time finding a place to park. Trains rattling along the viaduct nearby seem to make the hundreds of candles shudder in the chapel at the corner of the garden, but the flickering is probably caused by a wind from the Ardennes. Noting the railroad tracks and the crowded street outside, Sister Anne says: "Our Lady does not always choose the beautiful places for her appearances."

TRANSPORTATION: Beauraing is 12 miles south of Dinant. There is rail service from Brussels.

HOTELS: The *Aubépine, Salve Regina* and *Métropole* are very comfortable. The *Touristes* is a bit less expensive.

PLACES OF INTEREST: The Benedictine Monastery of Chevetogne, in the Ardennes, where half the community of monks celebrate the daily liturgy in the Latin rite; the other half in the Byzantine, or Oriental, rite.

GHEEL

Long before psychology had evolved as a word and as part of medicine it was practiced in the Flemish town of Gheel, 30 miles east of Antwerp. Many centuries ago mentally disturbed people began making pilgrimages to Gheel, seeking cures. The people who helped them—religious and laymen, alike—did not realize they were practicing psychology. All they thought they were doing was following the principles of Christ by showing the mentally sick kindness and making a place for them as boarders in the homes of the townspeople. The idea was to make the sick pilgrims feel at home and free to move around the town like any other resident.

Gheel is still that kind of place, although it has added modern psychiatric facilities.

About a tenth of Gheel's population are mental patients. The 200-bed infirmary is primarily a check-in point. After being diagnosed in the 5 days following their arrival, each patient is assigned to a family. There is an attempt to match interests—a baker or tradesman, for instance, moving in with a shopkeeper's family. Sometimes it takes as many as a dozen "tries" before the patient is matched up with a family that is right for him or her. Many of Gheel's patients are technically "incurables"—psychotics (schizophrenics, mostly), feebleminded, and some manic depressives who have not responded to treatment in "closed" institutions. It is felt at Gheel that if an "incurable" has any chance of being cured it will be by its family-care method. About 100 are able to return home each year. "Escape" is not a problem at Gheel. "Why should they?" a doctor asks. "Gheel is a typical town, and they lead more or less typical lives."

Gheel became a pilgrimage point because of a young Irish princess named Dympna. She was the daughter of a pagan Irish king of the 7th century and a Christian mother. When the mother died, Dympna was chosen to be her father's next wife. Dympna fled to the Low Countries. The mad king pursued her, and at Gheel slew her with his sword, according to legend. Soon "miracles" were reported on the site where Dympna had been slain. It was noted that most of the extraordinary cures were of people who had been mentally deranged. Dympna was made the patron saint of the mentally ill, and relics from the body of the young Irish princess were placed in the town church. Pilgrimages began, and a religious congregation took on the responsibility of caring for the mentally ill pilgrims. Somewhere around the 14th century—perhaps earlier—residents observed that the mentally sick did not behave badly if they were treated kindly, and began accepting them in their homes. At times half the families in Gheel have had patients as boarders. In 1852 the Belgian government began making payments to families who accepted patients. The patients are treated like members of the family. When some families fled Gheel during the Nazi occupation of Belgium in the Second World War they took their patients with them.

TRANSPORTATION: There is bus service to Gheel from the train stations at Antwerp and Turnhout. Gheel is just north of, and midway along, the Antwerp-Hasselt auto route.

HOTELS: In Antwerp, the *Plaza, Waldorf* and *Century* are the main hotels. The *Empire, Theater* and *City Park* are less expensive.

BRUSSELS

The headquarters of Europe's Common Market community today, Brussels began life in A.D. 580 as a small chapel built by St. Géry, bishop of Cambrai (France). As the town developed, St. Michael was made the patron saint, and a church in his honor was built atop a hill. In the middle of the 11th century Duke Lambert II of Brabant decided to move to St. Michael's Church the ashes of St. Gudule which were in his castle in Brussels. By the 13th century the Church of St. Michael and St. Gudule (now the cathedral of Brussels) had become a major place of pilgrimage. Among its striking features are the huge statues of the twelve apostles which decorate the main pillars. The painter Peter Breughel is buried in the *Church of Notre Dame de la Chapelle*. In the 14th century *Church of Notre Dame of the Victories*, the Mass of St. Hubert (patron of hunters) is celebrated to the sound of hunting horns. The most visited church in downtown Brussels is *Finistère* on the main shopping street, rue Neuve. The church is said to have been designed by Rubens, but it is visited because of a Madonna image known as "The Virgin of Good Fortune."

In the communes that comprise Greater Brussels are many points of religious significance. Erasmus lived at Anderlecht, and the house where he wrote many of his letters is now a museum. The church at Laeken is a royal parish because it is near the summer palace. In its crypt are buried all the Belgian rulers. A Russian-Orthodox church, with bulbous spires and golden crosses, is in Uccle. On the plateau Koekelberg is the national Basilica of the Sacred Heart, built in thanksgiving on the 75th anniversary of Belgium's independence in 1905.

Many villages around Brussels, and in Belgium generally, have local fairs which are held on the same day as the annual feast of the patron saint of the town church. This is not a coincidence. The celebration has been a joint one from the start. The word for "fair" in Flemish is *kermis*. It is derived from the Flemish for "church," *kerk*, and "Mass," *mis*. The French-speaking Belgians frenchified the Dutch word *kermis* and made it *kermesse*.

TRANSPORTATION: Brussels is on main rail and air routes to London and other European capitals.

HOTELS: *Sheraton* and *Lendi* are brand-new, luxurious; *Palace* and *Plaza* are old-timers but very comfortable. *Ramada Inn*, *Scot*, *Europa* and *Arenberg* are a bit less expensive.

4
France

A BRASS PLAQUE in the paving in front of the Cathedral of Notre Dame in Paris is used to measure the distance between the French capital and other cities of France. With the same precision as the spacing of military stones, more than two dozen centuries of French history can be measured along the highways fanning out from the streets of Paris.

The first known date in France's history was the founding of Marseilles 25 centuries ago. Wandering Phoenician traders sailed into the port city while the king of the Ligurian tribe, which inhabited the Mediterranean coast, was host at a banquet for his daughter, Gyptis. The climax of the festivities was to be the selection by Gyptis of a husband from among the warriors of the tribe. She would hold a bowl of wine in her hands and, when she had made up her mind, present it to her choice. She and the warrior would then share the bowl of wine, a prelude to a lifetime of sharing. The only surprise in the ritualistic ceremony was that the Ligurian princess handed over the bowl of wine to the chief of the Phoenician traders who had joined the crowd to watch the goings-on. The princess and the Greek visitor were married, and as a dowry she offered the towering hill from which, today, the Notre Dame de-la-Garde Basilica overlooks the city.

Shortly after the foundation of Marseilles by the Phoenicians in 600 B.C., tribes of Celts, or Gauls, began streaming into southern France. They joined with remnants of the oldtime Ligurians, and established a capital just north of Aix-en-Provence. When the Celts gave signs of seizing Marseilles, the Phoenicians appealed to Rome. Roman legions in 122 B.C. wiped out the Celt-Ligurian capital and founded an empire beyond the Alps, known as Gaul, with capitals at Aix-en-Provence and Narbonne. About 20 years later, Germanic tribes from northern Europe invaded southern France. The Roman general Marius halted them in a massive annihilation. Still today, many people of Provence baptize their first son Marius in honor of the first conqueror of the Germanic invaders.

Caesar and his successors solidified the Roman hold on France, but by the 5th century A.D. the Roman empire was withering away, and Barbarian tribes had settled in three main parts of the country: the Visigoths, from the Loire to the Pyrenees (and beyond to Andalusia); the Burgundians, in the valleys of the Rhône and the Saône; and the Franks in northern Gaul.

The Franks subsequently gave Gaul its new, permanent name: France. But at the start they were outshone by the Visigoths and Burgundians who were more cultured, and also were Christians even if, in some cases, considered heretics. The fortunes of the Franks suddenly improved, however, when Clovis (A.D. 466–511), a king of one of the tribes, was converted to Christianity by his wife Clotilda, a Burgundian princess. He was crowned in the cathedral at Rheims, the first Christian king of the Franks, and Christianity became the active means for uniting the nation. His Merovingian dynasty, split among four sons, collapsed after 2½ centuries.

Charles Martel (A.D. 689–741), the grandfather of Charlemagne, and the Carolingians, reunified France. He stopped the Arab invaders of Europe at Poitiers, winning the name Martel (hammer) for himself and becoming king of the Franks, but not in name. His son and successor, Pepin the Short, discussed the anomalous situation with Pope St. Zachary. "The person who exercises the king's power should enjoy the king's title," the Pope said, and Pepin had himself crowned king at Soissons. Pepin's kingdom was divided, in the old Frankish custom, between his two sons, Carloman and Charles. Carloman died in a few years and Charles broadened the Frankish territory into an empire. He was called Charles the Great, Charlemagne, and was crowned emperor of the West by Pope St. Leo III on Christmas Day, A.D. 800, in Rome. During the reign of the 14 Capetian kings (A.D. 987–1328) the local princes and dukes grew in power, and religion became increasingly involved in the life of France.

In A.D. 1095 Pope Urban II preached the First Crusade at Clermont-Ferrand to a throng of thousands, including several hundred bishops. In A.D. 1146 St. Bernard of Clairvaux preached the Second Crusade at Vézélay, 140 miles south of Paris. In the crowd was King Louis VII. In the same hillside town King Philip-Augustus of France and England's King Richard the Lion-hearted met for the Third Crusade.

Once a unifying element, religion soon was transformed into a divisive one in the kingdom.

In the early part of the 13th-century Toulouse, France's fourth-largest city and gateway to the Pyrenees, was the center of a violent religious struggle. The conflict involved the Albigensians, given the name from the nearby town of Albi (where Toulouse-Lautrec was born). The Albigensians were an extremely ascetic sect, which had an organized church. Albi was a center. To them the material world was evil, and in their dualistic view they attributed its creation to the "bad" god rather than the "good" god. Less radical members of the group believed that Satan, rather than being a separate deity, was a fallen angel. All felt that man's spirit was imprisoned in a material (and therefore evil) body. Because procreation meant for them that more spirits would be imprisoned in the world of flesh, the Albigensians by implication looked affirmatively upon abortion, suicide, and starvation. Pope Innocent III tried persuasion, and the dispatching of Cistercian monk-preachers. When these efforts produced few results, the Pope unloosed a crusade which continued more than 20 years. The last of the Albigensians were killed in the Château Montségur in the Pyrenees, southeast of Foix, where they had fled.

The Spanish canon St. Dominic arrived in France with his superior, the bishop of Osma (Soria), at the time the Albigensian heresy was peaking. Distressed at the headway it was making, he determined to combat it, establishing his threefold religious Order. At Prouille, 16 miles from Carcassonne (Route 119), he set up a convent for women, and initiated the Rosary devotion. Next, at Toulouse, the pious men who had gathered around him were joined together as friars in the Order of Preachers. The third Dominican branch formed by St. Dominic was the Tertiaries (from the Latin *tertius* for "third"), men and women who as civilians sought to promote Catholic life and action.

A war with England in the 15th century exacerbated the politico-economic situation created by the Hundred Years' War involving the future of Flanders. A young maid from Domrémy, in Lorraine, came to the support of the beleaguered Charles VII. "Voices" admonished Joan of Arc to help the young dauphin raise the siege of Orléans, and then lead him to Rheims for his coronation.

During the reign of Francis I (1515–47), the Reformation commenced to spread throughout France. The followers of French-born John Calvin eventually formed a political party. France became the scene of 8 civil wars between Protestants and Catholics, threatening its very existence. Neighboring nations chose sides, according to religion. By the latter part of the 16th century, the French kingdom consisted of Blois, Tours, Bordeaux, and little more. Even Paris was gone.

On Aug. 24, 1572, the feast of St. Bartholomew, thousands of French Protestants (Huguenots) were murdered in Paris in what has been known since as the St. Bartholomew's Day Massacre.

Henry IV (1553–1610), a Huguenot, had the task of reunifying the French kingdom. Not until five years after he had come to power did he succeed in entering Paris. The year before, 1593, he had renounced his Protestant religion and been crowned king at Chartres.

The days of Richelieu (1585–1642), Paris-born statesman and cardinal, followed. Armand Jean du Plessis, the duc de Richelieu, in taking office in 1624 as chief minister told Louis XIII: "I promise to devote all my energy, and all the authority·that it may please you to place in my hands, to the destruction of the Huguenots, to the lowering of the pride of the great nobles, to the restoration of all your subjects to their duty, and to raise the name of your majesty among foreign nations to its rightful place."

Jules Mazarin (1602–61), another cardinal but Italian-born, took up where Richelieu, his mentor, had left off. He and Anne of Austria, the widow of Louis XIII, ruled France until her son Louis XIV came of age. Louis XIV, builder of Versailles and of French glory, was called the Roi-Soleil, the Sun King. He identified himself, in a classic solipsism, with the state.

The secular-oriented Renaissance and France's homegrown Gallicanism, elevating the national church at the expense of Rome, and the blunting of religious authority by the Reformation weakened Catholicism. But the most effective allies against the church in the 17th and 18th centuries, perhaps, were Voltaire and his colleagues in the intellectual establishment. The Jesuits fought back, but they themselves were suppressed in 1764.

When Louis XVI summoned the States-General in May 1789, seeking advice, the clergy, the nobility and the bourgeoisie were the three main groups of citizens represented. This set of three orders, or estates, was changed by the Revolution which opened on July 14, 1789 with the seizure of the Bastille in Paris. Napoleon, seeking to unite France, negotiated a Concordat with Rome in 1801 and, soon after, *Les Articles Organiques* for the Protestants. In 1814 the Jesuits returned, but in 1880 were banished once more.

Prime Minister Émile Combes in 1905 effected adoption of a law separating church and state, and brought himself, a former seminarian, into a confrontation with the Pope. The law set up a government organization to serve as caretaker for schools, seminaries and other church properties. Pius X ordered France's Catholics to give up all right and revenues to their properties rather than have anything to do with the law.

The separation law still exists, but it has its anomalies.

In Alsace-Lorraine, which Germany seized in 1871 and once more in 1940, bishops are nominated with the approval of France's president.

And in Rome itself the president of France has the right to a seat in the chapter of canons at the Pope's cathedral as bishop of the city, St. John Lateran. The custom goes back to the days of the kings of France. In the atrium of the basilica is a statue of Henry IV, erected by his "fellow canons," in memory of his renunciation of the religion of the Huguenots on becoming king in 1593.

NÎMES

Nîmes, the Protestant capital of the southern region of France known as Languedoc, has been caught in religious struggles through the centuries. In the 5th century it was overrun by the Visigoths, the heretical practitioners of Arianism. In the 13th century the Albigensians took over. Later in the century the Jewish residents were driven from the town. In the 14th century Nîmes became a center for the Huguenots.

During the reign of Constantine, the first Christian emperor, Arles (*Hotel Jules César*) was second only to Rome in the Western branch of the empire. It is 20 miles southeast of Nîmes on Highway N-113. Its cathedral is dedicated to St. Trophinos who came from Greece to spread Christianity in Provence. Tradition is that the original church was built during the lifetime of the Virgin Mary. Frederick Barbarossa received the royal crown of Arles in the cathedral in the 12th century, and the jovial Provençal ruler, King René, was married there.

At Avignon (*Hotel d'Europe, Holiday Inn* and *Novotel*), 26 miles northeast of Nîmes on Highways N-86 and N-100, Catholicism had its capital for most of the 14th century. The Popes, alarmed at political events in Italy, took up residence there. Seven French Popes resided at Avignon. In 1377 Gregory XI decided to return to Rome. He died a year later, and disagreement over the policies of his successor led to the great schism in the Western church. A group of the cardinals chose another Pope who returned to Avignon as the anti-Pope. While the Popes were at Avignon a tremendous château palace was constructed and the city was encircled with ramparts as protection against bandits. The Papal Palace can be visited, and one of the delightful walking tours of Avignon is along the ramparts. Children have been dancing on, under and around the bridge of Avignon ever since a gifted friar named Béné-zet built it 8 centuries ago. At the Carthusian Monastery in Villeneuve-les-Avignon, on the west bank of the Rhône, Enguerran Charenton's painting, "The Crowning of the Virgin," is exhibited. In the rue Heldique at Cavaillon, 15 miles southeast of Avignon on Highway N-573, is France's oldest synagogue.

The Church of Saintes-Maries (the Holy Marys) overlooks the Mediterranean beach on which, tradition says, friends of the crucified Christ landed in A.D. 40. Saintes-Maries (*Hotel Brise de Mer*) is 44 miles south of Nîmes, via Arles and Highway N-570. The friends of Christ had been forced to leave the Holy Land on a raft, without provisions or sailing equipment. The group included Mary Jacob, wife of Cleophas and mother of James-the-Less; Mary Salome, mother of the apostles James-the-Greater and John; their black servant Sarah, and Lazarus and his two sisters. After their miraculous safe arrival in the Camargue coastal district, the group scattered on evangelical missions throughout Provence. The two Marys and Sarah remained in the little settlement by the sea. At their death, their relics were placed in a small oratory, beginning 19 centuries of pilgrimages. Sarah has been traditionally chosen by gypsies of the world as their patron saint. Each year (May 23 and 24, and Oct. 29 and 30) nomads from everywhere gather at Saintes-Maries-de-la-Mer, and there is a religious procession through the streets. During their springtime assembly, the gypsies elect a king and a queen.

At Vauvert, between Nîmes and Saintes-Maries-de-la-Mer, is the château birthplace of General Montcalm who commanded French troops in the conquest of Canada in the time of Louis XVI. He is buried in Quebec, but his natal home is a point of pilgrimage for French Canadians.

At Gran-du-Roy, 4 miles south of Aigues-Mortes, the king-saint Louis IX embarked for the Holy Land in

1248, beginning the Seventh Crusade. Gran-du-Roy is a beautiful beach area, and also a fishermen's village. St. Louis's son, Philip the Bold, constructed the ramparts at Aigues-Mortes, building them so well they have never needed restoring. Almost the entire town is within the walls, and there are three picturesque churches—the parish church and the chapels of the Penitents Blancs (White Penitents) and the Penitents Gris (Gray Penitents), medieval associations of lay people which still exist. Before leaving for the Seventh Crusade, Louis IX had the Tower of Constance built at Aigues-Mortes on the site of a Roman one. Louis XIV made it a prison for the Huguenots in 1686, and starting in 1705 it was used for imprisoning Protestant women.

Another point of pilgrimage in the area is St. Giles, 12 miles directly south of Nîmes on Highway D-42. An impressive crypt in the parish church holds the remains of St. Giles, a hermit from Greece, who was shipwrecked here in the 8th century.

Roman ruins exist throughout the area. Fourteen miles northeast of Nîmes is the opulent double tier of arches of the Pont du Gard, an aqueduct built by the Romans 20 centuries ago to funnel water into the city.

Nîmes calls itself, because of its association with the ancient Roman empire, the "French Rome." But religiously its link with French Protestantism is every bit as strong. At the time of the Reformation residents of the Cévennes, the mountainous area west of Nîmes, adopted Protestantism and, during later persecutions, the Huguenots took refuge in the high isolated places, living in a desert until once again free to practice their religion. Nîmes has a population of 130,000, with 10 percent of the residents Protestant—a high percentage for a French city. One block from the Roman temple (Maison Carrée) is a Welcome Center for Visitors maintained by French Protestantism. It is at 3 rue Claude Brousson.

THE HUGUENOTS

The origin of the term *Huguenot* is not clear. Some think it is a frenchified version of the German *Eidgenossen* (confederates) which was used in the 16th century by Swiss cantons in describing themselves. Others think it is derived from Hugues (Hugh) Capet, founder of the royal house of Capet, or Bezanson Hugues who led the *Eidgenossen* in Geneva. The Huguenots figured prominently in the religious wars of the 16th century, and their early leaders were religious exiles such as French-born John Calvin who took refuge in Geneva. Aristocrats with wealth and a political base joined the Protestant movement, and its political leadership was highlighted by the support of the Bourbons and the House of Navarre.

A powerful Huguenot leader was Gaspard de Coligny, a nobleman, and a friend and counselor of kings. He became admiral of France, and a convert to Calvinism. He suggested that the king unify France by supporting the Low Countries in their revolt against Spain. The king's mother, Catherine de Médicis, and the duc de Guise, did not want to get into another war with Catholic Spain, and they intrigued to do away with Coligny. But the plot fizzled, and the admiral was only wounded in the attempt that took place on Aug. 22, 1572. The queen was alarmed, fearing that the whole thing could be traced to her. The Huguenots were descending upon Paris at the very moment for the marriage of Henry of Navarre, a Huguenot, and the king's sister, Marguerite. Catherine persuaded Charles II that the Huguenots were out to kill her and him. Two days after the abortive attempt on the life of Admiral Coligny, Huguenots were massacred in Paris by the thousands on the feast of St. Bartholomew after Charles II had given his approval. The killings spread through France, continuing until Oct. 3 and claiming 25,000 to 50,000 victims. Admiral Coligny himself was killed and his body shredded by cohorts of the duc de Guise. Henry II of Navarre, a supporter of the Huguenots, came to the throne as Henry IV in 1589. Four years later he turned Catholic and concentrated on broadening the base of support in his kingdom, and on expanding the kingdom itself. He issued the Edict of Nantes, reaffirming Catholicism as the official religion of France but giving Huguenots a basic religious freedom. They would be allowed, for instance, to hold certain political offices and to maintain military forces for defense of specified cities, such as La Rochelle. In the 17th century, when the Edict of Nantes was revoked, the Huguenots were persecuted once more, and their preachers had to go underground.

The period of the Desert lasted from 1685 to 1787 when Louis XVI issued the Edict of Tolerance, declaring the end of persecution for the Protestants.

"After the revocation of the Edict of Nantes," says Protestant pastor Benjamin Muller, "the French Huguenots had the choice of becoming Catholic, of leaving, or of resisting."

Pastor Muller is a painter and sculptor, and has a huge library. "That library is my vice," he says. He is a pastor in the Reformed Church of France at Alès, a city of 44,000 which is 30 miles northwest of Nîmes and at the gateway to the Cévennes. He is in his late 30s and has a small beard. He smokes a pipe with a tiny bowl and a stem that is nearly a foot long. His parents come from Montpellier, 30 miles southwest of Nîmes. His first parish was in a little hamlet in the Cévennes, near Forlac.

"The real resistance took place in the Cévennes mountains," Pastor Muller says, "and went on for a century, there and in other areas, like Bergerac and the Charente. People pretended to have turned Catholic but in their homes at night they practiced their religion.

Then, after the revolution, these people came out of hiding, and said, 'Here we are.'

"In the Cévennes the war of resistance for freedom of conscience lasted for two years, from 1702 to 1704. At least these were the most dramatic moments. There were battles before and after, however, but this was the main time. In 1704 Marshal de Mont Revel crushed more than four hundred villages and hamlets in the Upper Cévennes—*Le Razement des Cévennes*, it is called. But the people, without homes, continued to have their services in the open air, keeping up their spiritual resistance.

"Men who were surprised at an assembly during the period of the Desert were put on military vessels in chains, and used as rowers, given the same treatment as criminals, assassins and scoundrels. The women were put in the tower at Aigues-Mortes. One woman, Marie Durand, resisted for thirty-eight years, and remained imprisoned in the tower. It is called the Tower of Constance because Marie Durand and her companions refused to become Catholics. Many died during this period."

Was Marie Durand from Nîmes?

"No. She and her husband came from the Vivarais, from a little town called Bouschet-de-Pranles, not far from Valence. A museum is at her birthplace, and each year there is an assembly on the Monday of Pentecost."

Were the Protestants wiped out?

"Not at all. From about 1710, Antoine Court, a pastor, began to reorganize the Protestant churches secretly, and there were assemblies of the people."

And today—how many Protestants?

"About five hundred thousand to six hundred thousand in all France—a real minority, mostly in the old areas of refuge in the south, but some are in the north, too, nowadays. Under Napoleon III pastors were in the north of France but there was a saying that the only Protestants in a district were the prefect and the pastor.

In the valley of Queyras, in the Alps near Briançon, which is the highest walled city in Europe, several villages have many Protestants. One village, St. Veran, has two parishes from the old refugee days. The valley of the Vaudois (Waldenses) is on the other side of the border which is now Italy. Pierre Waldo, the son of a Lyons merchant, preached all along the valley of the Rhône in the thirteenth century. His successors were persecuted by the princes of those days, and at Lourmarin, near St. Rémy and Baux, almost all the Waldenses were massacred in the time of Louis XIV. But this did not happen to the Waldenses who fled to the valleys of the Alps near Briançon, which were then part of the kingdom of the House of Savoy. The valleys were high and out of the way, and no one bothered them. The kings of Savoy were more tolerant than Louis XIV. In the time of Luther these Waldenses heard of the Reform, and made connections."

And the Protestant museums?

"They exist in zones where Protestants were found in the early nineteenth century, and which were rich in articles and souvenirs. Like the Museum of the Desert, in the Cévennes, which recalls how the Camisards fought the soldiers of Louis XIV in the early 1700s."

The Camisards?

"Yes, the Camisards. It comes from *camisa,* an old Provençal word for a kind of night shirt. The Protestant resistance fighters wore a *camisa* over their regular clothes at night so they could pick out their friends in the darkness."

The Museum of the Desert is at Mas-Soubeyran, 10 miles west of Alès. At Ganges, not far from the museum, is the Grotto of the Demoiselles, one of the caves in which the Protestants lived during the persecutions. It can be visited. Another nearby cave is the Grotto Trabuc, which served as an infirmary and a depot of supplies and provisions for the Camisards. The Museum of the Desert is inside the house of the chief Camisard,

Rolland Laporte. It contains furniture, costumes, household articles, paintings and historical documents. In winter visiting arrangements should be made through the Maison de Protestantisme, 5 rue Frédéric Mistral, at Alès.

"Since 1910, when the Museum of the Desert was founded, there has been an annual assembly there, too," Pastor Muller says. "The assemblies were started for historical reasons, to recall the past—and for spiritual reasons, also. But now with temples everywhere it is not really necessary to have assemblies.

"The Assembly at Mas-Soubeyran is on the first Sunday in September. There are fifteen thousand to twenty thousand people who come for a day's program. In the morning there is the service in the open air, and they take Holy Communion. The old vessels have been found—the plate and the bowl—which were used in the Desert, and which had been hidden by the people. Each person arrives with a picnic basket. This is before the *vindange*, the grape harvest, and the weather is usually still good. In the afternoon there are discourses on a theme—often by a famous Protestant, a man of the hour, or a historian. And always there is a pastor to close the assembly on a spiritual note."

Is the term *Huguenot* still used?

"Oh, yes. But in the Midi here, Protestants of southern France are also called *Parpaillots*. That word comes from the Languedoc patois for 'butterfly,' *papillon*. The people of Languedoc say *parpailloun* instead of *papillon*. Catholics used to say that Protestants fluttered from one flower to another in the garden of Christianity. The word usually was spoken in a pejorative sense, but now Protestants happily say, 'I am a Parpaillot.' "

TRANSPORTATION: There is relatively frequent train service from Nîmes to Alès. From Alès to Mas-Soubeyran, taxis are available. A secondary road, N-107, north of Nîmes, leads to Anduze and then Mas-

Soubeyran, but it is advisable to go by way of Alès on Highway N-106.

HOTELS: The *Imperator* is the leading hotel at Nîmes. The *Novotel* resembles an American motel in style and price. The *Mercur* is new and moderately priced.

NOYON

Noyon, 60 miles north of Paris, is in the heart of Picardy. It has been burned to the ground in wars a dozen times—by the Normans, Spaniards, Burgundians, and so on—says the woman in the Syndicat d'Initiative, the local tourist office, because it is a central crossroads. Compiègne is southwest; Soissons, southeast; Verdun and the valley of the Marne are not far away. Noyon is also a center of Christianity. John Calvin was born there on July 10, 1509.

The tourist office director is heavy-set and middle-aged, and is at work on a "little book" about the city.

"Calvin's birthplace had been established as a museum by the Society of the History of Protestantism in 1930," she says. "After the house was destroyed in the war, the city of Noyon assumed responsibility for it in 1954, and on July 17, 1955 they reopened it as a museum. They found the big heavy beams from the original house, all hewn by hand; the iron work; and even the *culs-de-bouteilles,* the bottoms of glass bottles which had been made part of the wall at the front of the house. You can see out from the inside, but not from the outside in. Engineers from a glass factory not far from here have visited the Calvin Museum and are captivated by this ancient type of one-way glass. Some people think one-way glass is a modern invention."

Calvin was the son of a clerk at the 12th-century Cathedral of Notre Dame of Noyon. The family name of his father, Gerard, was Cauvin, and in the Latinization became Calvin.

In 1523, at the age of 14, he goes to Paris to study,

eventually attending the Montaigu College where, not too many years later, Erasmus and Ignatius of Loyola, are students. His father objects to the theological studies, and in 1528 he transfers to Orléans, and then Bourges, to study law, obtaining a degree. In 1534 he openly takes sides with the Reformation, following what he himself calls a "sudden conversion," and soon leaves for Basel. There he does much writing, first collaborating in the translation of the Bible and then producing his masterpiece, *The Institutes of the Christian Religion.* In 1536 he accepts an invitation to remain in Geneva. (See Index.) Four years later he marries Idelette de Bure. Their only child, a boy, dies within a few days and Idelette herself dies in 1549. In 1559 the first national synod of the Reformed Churches of France is held in Paris, adopting a Confession of Faith and a Discipline inspired by Calvin. He dies on May 27, 1564, not quite two months before his 55th birthday.

The house where he was born is on the Place Aristide Briand, 100 yards from the Hôtel de Ville. In Calvin's time the square was called Place au Blé because wheat was sold there.

"Briand tried to bring a rapprochement between the French and German people," the tourist director says. "All cities and towns in France remember him with a square or a street."

In the streets between the Hôtel de Ville and the Place Aristide Briand an open-air market takes place on the first Tuesday of each month, with several hundred merchants setting up stands of clothes, cheeses and household wares of all sorts. Even banks from Compiègne arrive in mobile offices on market day.

John Calvin was born in a large room on the main floor of what is now the Calvin Museum. The floor is covered with flagstones, a wall is broken by a fireplace, and the ceiling is lined by big beams. An adjoining room, somewhat larger, serves for Sunday morning services at 9 o'clock. It is about 30 feet long, 10 feet wide. The floor is plain wood. Wooden benches are along the walls, and an organ stands in the corner. At the front a table holds an open Bible. Among the furnishings is a Chair of the Desert, a pulpit used by the Protestants when they had to hide from persecution. It was assembled from dozens of parts, each of which was held for safekeeping by one of the people until the chair was again needed. Only 6 or 7 attend Sunday services, the woman tourist director says. The pastor comes from Compiègne, 15 miles away.

"The pastor arranges youth programs—like a car *rallye* in which the contestants try to be first at a point one hundred kilometers away by discovering hidden clues along the route. This is the kind of game the whole family can play. The *rallye* starts after services on Sunday, and concludes with a dance in the *salle des fêtes* of Noyon around 6:30 P.M."

TRANSPORTATION: Noyon, 90 miles north of Paris, is on the main rail line between Brussels and Paris.

HOTELS: *Le Grillon* and *St. Eloi* are the leading hotels. *St. Jacques* and *Bon Pêcheur* are moderately priced.

POINTS OF INTEREST: The tower at Compiègne is where Joan of Arc was held prisoner after being wounded in 1430. The cathedral at Soissons is considered by some to be France's finest monument.

JOAN OF ARC

The full name of Domrémy is Domrémy-la-Pucelle, Domrémy-the-Maid. "The Maid" is Joan of Arc who was born in the startlingly unspoiled Lorraine village of Domrémy on Jan. 6, 1412, the daughter of Jacques and Isabelle d'Arc. From the window of her bedroom she could look across a small yard to the 14th-century village church where she was baptized. A mile and a half south of Domrémy is the Basilica of the Bois-Chênu

(Old Wood), built in the past century on the site of one of the places where Joan, as a 13-year-old, began hearing her "Voices." Angels and saints, she reported, urged her to be good and holy. Later, these Voices sent her on her mission of aiding the dauphin whose claim to the French kingdom was threatened by the king of England who was overrunning northern France.

Two miles north of Domrémy is the chapel in the woods at Bermont where Joan went to pray each Saturday in front of a 14th-century statue of the Madonna. Through the Porte de France at Vaucouleurs, 13 miles north of Domrémy, Joan of Arc departed with a handful of companions on her mission. She had persuaded the military commandant of the town that she, a 16-year-old shepherdess, was actually an ambassador of God. The castle where the governor received Joan is now in ruins. A new chapel has been built like the one which was there in Joan's time. In the chapel is the statue of Notre Dame before which she had prayed.

On May 17, 1429 Joan drove the English troops from Orléans after they had made a final stand among the fortified ruins of the Augustinian monastery. In the Cathedral of the Holy Cross is a chapel dedicated to the Maid of Orléans. Each May 7-8, Orléans remembers its deliverance from the English by Joan of Arc with a massive celebration.

From Orléans Joan of Arc went to Rheims for the coronation of the dauphin.

Just a matter of yards from where the railroad station is now situated in Compiègne, Joan of Arc was wounded and captured in May 1430 as she was surveying the battle-lines drawn up by the English and their Burgundian allies. The tower in which she was imprisoned is named after her. (Relics traditionally believed to be from the veil of Mary are in the Chapel of the Virgin in the Church of St. James.) A stone marking the place of the signing of the First World War armistice was ripped away by the Germans in 1940, but has been replaced. The Germans also burned the railroad coach in which Marshal Foch had directed the armistice talks (a replica has been substituted).

Joan was charged with witchcraft and heresy, subjected to a long trial at Rouen before an ecclesiastical court, condemned, and burned at the stake on May 30, 1431 at the age of 19. A revision of her trial was obtained, and her innocence declared in 1455.

A mosaic in the floor of the Vieux-Marché (old market-place) at Rouen, 90 miles northwest of Paris, identifies the spot where Joan of Arc was burned to death. The ashes of the Maid of Orléans were taken to the Seine, a few hundred yards away, and thrown into the river. A museum in the Vieux Marché presents the life of Joan of Arc in a series of waxwork groups. Her feast is celebrated at Rouen on the last Sunday in May to coincide with the anniversary of her execution. She was canonized on May 13, 1920.

DOMRÉMY

The fields near the Meuse are usually flooded in early spring for hundreds of yards inland, and the fence posts poke through the water like a line of tiny reefs. Farmhouses of stone, and barns with cattle and chickens, border the main street and an ambulant if motorized butcher-grocer moves from door to door to serve the townspeople. The house in which Joan was born is small, made of stone, and has what looks like a half roof. The roof slopes at a 45-degree angle. It is one of three 15th-century roofs still in Domrémy and is described by the term *cou levé* (neck raised). The roof was designed that way as a protection against rain and snow.

Joan was born in the main ground-floor room which in Lorraine is called *la puille*. The furnace was in the room; the kitchen and dining-room table, too. When

Joan was older, she shared a room with her sister Catherine.

The house, and a neighboring one-room stone structure which is a museum, are in a grassy enclosure which faces the bridge across the Meuse.

A helpful, cultured middle-aged man, the conservator of the museum, shakes his head when he thinks of how family members treated Joan's birthplace after her death.

"They used the house as a stable and as a place for making wine," he says. "In front they built other stone houses to live in. The foundation stones of these houses can still be seen in the ground, but the buildings themselves have been swept away.

"In 1817, a pilgrimage led by Ferdinand of Austria visited Domrémy and was appalled by the conditions of Joan's birthplace. They offered to buy it from the relatives for six thousand francs in gold—golden louis. The French government stepped in, and decided this historic site should not pass into foreign hands, and it was bought by the Vosges *département* which restored it."

The Basilica of the Bois-Chênu at the southern outskirts of Domrémy is on the site of a chapel which was built a quarter of a century after Joan's death, following her rehabilitation. The chapel was installed on the site of a tree which had figured in her sorcery trial as "the tree of the fairies."

A Carmelite cloister is on the Meuse side of the country road which skirts the basilica. A young extern nun in rubber boots and a working habit of blue denim is on her knees in the yard of the convent, resetting stones sent askew by the latest rainstorm. "Why, certainly, I am sure Mother would be happy to talk with you," she says.

The prioress of the Carmelite convent is Mother Teresa of Christ. She talks from behind a grilled window, made from strands of thread rather than metal.

Because of the grille, and because she smiles almost continuously, it is difficult to estimate her age. She talks in an open, friendly way as if the visitor is the first one there in a mighty long time. Actually, she explains, about four hundred thousand people come to Domrémy each year.

"Our convent," she says, "was started early in the century, and then with the wave of religious suppression it was closed before the First World War. Then in 1968 I came here from Valenciennes with ten young Sisters. There were beginning to be too many Sisters at Valenciennes. We put the convent back into working order."

How many Sisters are here now?

"We are eighteen—and eleven of the Sisters are under thirty-two years of age. Eleven young out of eighteen is not bad, is it?"

How do you support yourselves?

"We make bonbons out of honey, and we do enamel-work—and we sell what we make to pilgrims. A Trappist brother from the Sept Fons Monastery near Moulins came for fifteen days to teach the Sisters how to make the candies. Then a Benedictine monk came from the monastery at Croirault in the Somme *département* near the Channel. That is the monastery that was founded to help physically handicapped people. The Benedictine showed us how to work in enamel. There's a lot of charity in the world."

TRANSPORTATION: By railroad, to Chaumont; at Chaumont, connecting bus to Neufchâteau, 6 miles from Domrémy.

HOTELS: *Hotel de la Basilique,* is alongside the Basilica of the Bois-Chênu.

LYONS

There is a running argument between Marseilles and Lyons as to which is larger, and therefore the claimant to the title of being France's second city. Marseilles usually wins, possibly because of its age. But no one disputes that Lyons was the first city of Gaul in which Christianity took root. The first Christians were people from Asia Minor, the last survivors of the Age of the Apostles. They arrived at Lyons in the 2nd century from Smyrna (now Izmir, Turkey; see Index), and quoted works of the apostles. Marcus Aurelius in A.D. 177 ordered the persecution of these Lyons Christians. Some survived, and together wrote a letter back home. The letter, still preserved, is a magnificent declaration of faith.

Each year on Dec. 8 a pilgrimage is made to the Basilica of Notre Dame of Fourvière. Its Marian Museum tells the history of the pilgrimages to the hill on which the Romans had built a temple. One hundred statues of the Madonna are exhibited. Lyons is in the Rhône valley, 300 miles south of Paris. It is a main rail center.

HOTELS: *Terminus-P.L.M., Bordeaux-Parc, Bristol,* and *City.*

ARS

Jean-Baptiste Marie Vianney, a shepherd boy in the hills outside Lyons, did not seem to be a good prospect as a priest. But the bishop approved, commenting: "I don't know if he is well educated, but I do know he is enlightened." He was assigned as the village priest for Ars, and his sermons and simple way of life attracted increasing numbers of pilgrims. The rectory of the church has been preserved the way it was when he died there in 1859. The *Curé of Ars,* as he became known, was canonized in 1925, and the village is a major pilgrimage site. The saint's body is in a reliquary in the new basilica. Each Aug. 4, the anniversary of his death, the village is crowded with pilgrims. (Ars is reached from Lyons—or from the north—by leaving the Riviera

Auto-route A-6, at Villefranche, and proceeding east on
N-504. It is 21 miles north of Lyons. *Hotel Regina.*)

Paray-le-Monial

On the feast of St. John the Evangelist, Dec. 27, in
1673, the pious daughter of a royal notary received an
Apparition of Christ in which He revealed the "inex-
plicable secrets of His Sacred Heart." The young
woman, Margaret-Mary Alacoque, had become a nun
two years earlier in the Convent of the Visitation here.
From that first Apparition until her death on Oct. 17,
1690 she continued to report other revelations in which
Christ asked for a special devotion to His Sacred Heart.
The devotion was started. From this little Burgundian
town of 9,000 inhabitants the Sacred Heart devotion
spread across the world, and inspired the building of
the Sacre-Coeur Church on Montmartre in Paris. The
young woman was beatified in 1864, and canonized as
St. Margaret-Mary on May 13, 1920.

"Until she was canonized," a small, aged nun says in
the Visitation Convent Church, "the reliquary of St.
Margaret-Mary was at the Communion rail. The people
liked that because they could be very close to her, and
could touch the reliquary. But after the canonization a
special chapel was built, and the reliquary is now out of
reach of the people."

The nun describes herself as the archivist at the convent. She is one of 40 Sisters there.

"When her tomb was opened," the Sister-archivist
says, "the body was not intact. But there were bones,
and her brain was intact. This is extraordinary because
they said she was sick. This [the brain] is kept in a
glass container in our convent, behind the wall of the
church chapel which has her reliquary. Her body has
been simulated and dressed in the reliquary, and the
relic bones placed around it."

The image of the saint is vested in a black robe, and

the head reclines against a white satin pillow. A sign reads: "While awaiting the Resurrection the bones of St. Margaret-Mary rest in this reliquary."

On the face of the altar are the words: "If you believe, you will see the power of my Heart."

"Twice a year," the Sister-archivist says, "the Sisters leave their cloister and there is a procession in the garden—the Sunday after Corpus Christi and the Sunday following October 17, the day she died."

St. Margaret-Mary was born at Lhautecour, 20 miles east of Paray-le-Monial on July 25, 1647. Franciscan nuns have acquired the house where she was born, and it adjoins a school they operate for teaching girls domestic science.

The procession on Corpus Christi and on the saint's feastday, begins in a large area about 200 yards from the shrine, known as the Chaplains Park, and continues to the garden of the convent. At the Chaplains Park a diorama, a visual exhibit in charts, photos and designs, traces the life of St. Margaret-Mary. Next to the house of the chaplains is a room of souvenirs of the saint— clothes and other articles.

"About four hundred thousand to five hundred thousand persons come to Paray-le-Monial each year," Father Jean LaDame, one of the chaplains, says. "But they are not all pilgrims. There are many curious visitors."

TRANSPORTATION: Paray-le-Monial has train service from Lyons, 75 miles southeast.

HOTELS: The *Hotel Basilica* and the *Foyer Sacre Coeur*, a retreat-house which also accepts pilgrims, are near the shrine.

POINTS OF INTEREST: Not far from Paray-le-Monial is the Taizé monastery which was founded by Protestant monks in 1962. The Taizé monastery has become noted for its ecumenical work, and is particularly popular with young people. It is west of

Tournus and 10 miles north of Cluny. At Cluny are remains of the Benedictine monastic settlement which had enormous influence on medieval Europe.

LOIRE VALLEY

Night driving is not a good idea, except in the valley of the Loire where electricity has brought to its châteaux a muted brilliance never known by the kings and lords who inhabited this bright fairyland. At many, sound is added to the spectacle of nighttime light, and scores of costumed figures parade as if in an operatic finale. Most of the châteaux are between Gien and Angers.

CHARTRES

Sorbonne students, at Pentecost, walk the 40 miles from Paris to Chartres Cathedral where, in the Middle Ages, the Madonna made her appearance for the first time at the entrance to a church. Chartres is on the route from Paris to the Loire valley. It has been a major religious site since pagan times. Caesar wrote about the Druids and their form of worship at Chartres. With the coming of Christianity in the 4th century, a church was erected. A series of fires destroyed one new church after another until the present cathedral was built. The crypt is said to be the cave into which early Christian martyrs of Chartres were thrown. In the 9th century Charles the Bald gave to the cathedral a robe known as "The Tunic of the Virgin." In the cathedral is a 16th-century wooden statue of Notre Dame which is venerated by pilgrims.

The Cathedral of Notre Dame of Chartres is one of the world's most impressive churches. The precise sculpture of its façade and the passage of light through its windows are known wherever art is discussed. The particular shade of blue mirrored by the windows has been described as the cathedral's own *Chartres blue.* The main part of the present cathedral was built toward the end of the 12th century. Some people gave both money and labor, with nobles from the valley working side by side with farmers. (Forty miles southwest of Paris. *Hotel Grand Monarque.*)

CHÂTEAUDUN

The castle looks down the Loire valley from a rocky plateau, and in 10 centuries passed through a series of hands, starting with the Counts of Blois. In the middle of the 15th century it was given as a present to a young man of Orléans named Jean Dunois. The youth, noted for his bravery, had joined Joan of Arc in her encounters with the English. Dunois had a Gothic chapel built in the castle. (Twenty-seven miles south of Chartres. *Hotel St. Louis.*)

TOURS

Pilgrims started coming to Tours in the 4th century to honor St. Martin, the apostle of Gaul. Martin is the Roman legionnaire who, near Amiens in northern France, used his sword to cut his cloak in two so that he could share it with a freezing beggar. Near Poitiers (65 miles south of Tours) he founded the first monastery in France, and was made bishop of Tours in A.D. 372. When his body was brought to Tours on a cold November day at the end of the 4th century, legend says that the sun suddenly shone, flowers blossomed, and trees grew green. The "Summer of St. Martin," as it was called, inspired pilgrimages to his burial place in the basilica. (Sixty miles south of Châteaudun. Hotels: *France,* and *Métropole.*)

St. Bénoit-sur-Loire

St. Benedict, founder of monastic life in the West, is venerated in the town named for him on the Loire River. Monks from this abbey went to Monte Cassino in Italy in the 7th century in search of relics of St. Benedict when they heard that the Great Abbey of the Benedictines had been pillaged by Barbarians. (See Index.) The porched-in Bell Tower of the basilica is sculpted with episodes from the life of Christ and the Madonna, scenes from the Apocalypse, and figures of animals and flowers. (It is almost halfway between Orléans and Gien. *Hotel Grand Sully*, at nearby Sully-sur-Loire.)

THE ALPS

Grenoble is at the doorstep of the wintertime ski resorts and the summertime meadows and paths of the Alps. In March 1815 Grenoble was the goal of Napoleon Bonaparte. The rulers of Europe were at a summit meeting in Vienna when word reached them that Napoleon had left his place of exile on the island of Elba. A year before—April 1814—Napoleon had abdicated and made his *adieux* at Fontainebleau. But he did not remain at Elba. On Mar. 1, 1815 he landed on the Riviera coast with a handful of men, and headed north through the Alps for the Hundred Days That Shook the World. Napoleon landed at Golfe-Juan, 16 miles west of Nice.

Napoleon's journey through the Alps to Grenoble took seven days, with him averaging about 50 kilometers a day. Some stretches he made on muleback, and others with a horse.

In a meadow near Laffrey, 15 miles south of Grenoble, is a statue of Napoleon astride a horse. The statue is a few hundred yards from the highway, N-85.

It pinpoints the *Meadow of the Meeting* where Napoleon encountered the soldiers sent from Grenoble to arrest him. The soldiers more than outnumbered Napoleon and his handful of companions.

Napoleon adjusted his jaunty bicorne hat, opened his green *chasseur de la garde* coat, and advanced toward the soldiers.

"I am your emperor," he told them. "If any one of you wants to shoot your general, here I am."

No shots were fired. Instead of arresting Napoleon, the soldiers embraced him. As he left for Grenoble, they shouted, *"Vive l'empereur!"*

He himself later noted: "Before Grenoble, I was an adventurer. At Grenoble, they made me a prince."

Twenty days after landing at Golfe-Juan, Napoleon was at the Tuileries in Paris. Louis XVIII had fled to Ghent. Outside of Brussels a few months later, Napoleon's journey came to a final halt at Waterloo. He sought asylum in England, but was sent to St. Helena instead.

Corps

The Hotel du Palais, a pinkish two-story structure in the alpine village of Corps, carries a plaque on its façade saying that Napoleon on his return from Elba slept there on the night of Mar. 6, 1815. Corps, 40 miles south of Grenoble, is on the Route of Napoleon. It is also the doorway to the shrine of Notre Dame of La Salette. The monastery at the shrine is, at nearly 6,000 feet, the highest habitation in the Alps.

Higher than ski resorts?

"Well, yes," says Pascal. "There aren't many ski resorts at one thousand eight hundred meters."

On a winter morning Pascal is usually the only person scurrying through the snow-packed streets of Corps. Pascal, chunky, mustachioed and cheerful, used to drive a small bus up the winding mountain road which leads from Corps, at an altitude of 2,925 feet, to the shrine. The mountain road is 10 miles long and, since its widening, full-sized buses can travel it in the summer. Pascal has given up his minibus and now drives a taxi. In the winter he has to telephone to the shrine to find out if the road is open all the way, or whether it is still blocked by the latest snowstorm.

The village church is in a little square, a few dozen yards from the highway, and the parish house is across from it. The *governante* who answers the knock on the door of the parish house is a tall, middle-aged woman in a heavy sweater and fur hat. The bell does not ring, she explains, because the snow has snapped power lines and there is no electricity. The curé, she says, is busy but she will let him know he has a caller. Within a half minute, the curé comes to the door. He is in a white shirt and black sweater, and holds a book in his hand. He is short, stocky and balding, and wears glasses.

"This is Wednesday, a busy day," he says, pleasantly. "There is no school on Wednesday, so I have catechism classes straight through the day."

His classroom is the dining-room. The long table is covered with a plastic cloth. In the corner a cross reaches to the ceiling. On a wall is a reproduction of a Picasso painting of a child and a white dove. About a dozen boys and girls are in the dining-room for the catechism class. The children are about the same ages as the two youngsters who saw the beautiful Lady, La Belle Dame, on the mountaintop above Corps on the afternoon of Sept. 19, 1846. They were from poor families—Pierre-Maximin Giraud, 11; and Mélanie Calvat, nearly 15. Neither child had any education. The girl, Mélanie, had been rented out by her family as a shepherdess since she was 10. Maximin had gotten a job for a few days to guard some cows. . . .

About 3 o'clock in the afternoon they awake after a nap. Mélanie sees a roundish light with the figure of a Lady at the center, and points it out to Maximin. The figure is seated. "Come here, my children," the figure says. "Do not be afraid. I am here to announce to you a great news."

What the children call a *bonnet* covers the head, ears and neck of the Lady. It is vividly white, and gives off brilliant rays. There is a crown of roses of all colors. Her dress is white, and seems to be speckled with shining stones, like pearls.

"If my people are not willing to submit," she tells the children, "I shall be forced to let fall the arm of my Son. It is so heavy and so great that I am no longer able to hold it back." Her voice filled with sorrow, she tells the two youngsters that men work on Sundays, and use blasphemy.

Then she talks of the potato harvest, and says it is not the farmers but God who determines whether the crop is good or bad. For Christmas, she warns, there will be no more potatoes—a staple of the mountain people of the area. Whereupon she exhorts the children to pray, and to pass on her message. As the figure begins to glide away, Mélanie cries out that perhaps it was a "great saint." If that was the case, Maximin says, he and Mélanie should have asked her to take them along with her.

The village curé, a 63-year-old priest, on hearing the children's story, tells them they are fortunate, that they have seen the Holy Virgin. Ignoring the canonical rules of the church against discussing such happenings until they have been investigated thoroughly, the curé blurts out the news at Sunday Mass. During a long interrogation that lasts for hours townspeople write down an account of what the children saw and heard, describing it as a "letter dictated by the Holy Virgin to two children on the mountain of La Salette-Fallavaux."

Five years later, the bishop of Grenoble, Monsignor Philibert de Bruillard, issues a *mandement* (an ecclesiastical charge) which, in effect, is official recognition, and declares: "We judge that the Apparition of the

Holy Virgin to the two shepherds on Sept. 19, 1846 on a mountain of the chain of the Alps, situated in the parish of La Salette, of the archpriestry of Corps, carries in itself all the characteristics of the truth and that the faithful have grounds to believe it indubitable and certain."

On May 25, 1852 the first stone of a church was laid. A stairway is now stretched along the path which the Madonna took after talking to the children. Main pilgrimage days are Sept. 19, anniversary of the apparition; Aug. 15, the Assumption; and Sept. 8, feast of the Nativity of the Virgin.

Abbé Louis Moriceau, the present curé, shows an insert he has kept from an old edition of *Paris Match*. The photo-reportage deals with "The Kennedys—The Rise of a Family, 1848–1941."

Why does he save it?

"Because the Message of La Salette in 1846 talks about a potato famine. This article about the Kennedys points out that the 1846/47 winter was the second without potatoes in Ireland, and the Kennedy emigration began in 1848. Hunger and typhus killed one million people in Ireland."

Maximin, the boy who saw the Apparition, was born in a two-story building at the corner of rue du Four and rue la Voirie, a few doors from the parish church. The building's owner says Maximin's family has disappeared. The curé says no one knows where Mélanie, the little girl, was born.

"Mélanie lived for a while at Cannes and Le Cannet with her mother," the curé says. "When the mother died, she went to Marseilles, then Italy, then Allier *département*. Finally, Italy. Mélanie never entered the religious life with vows, but she led a life of prayer. On December 15, 1904 she died at Altamura, near Bari, and is buried there.

"Maximin was always faithful to the Apparition. He never married. He worked for a while near Grenoble, and Paris, but mostly at Corps. He did all kinds of work, including wine salesman. He is buried here in Corps."

The cemetery is ½ mile north of the village. It is a small rectangle fenced off from valley meadows. A large engraved stone heading Maximin's tomb says: "Here lies Maximin Giraud, witness of the Apparition of the Very Holy Virgin on the mountain of La Salette in 1846. He died at Corps on May 1, 1875 at the age of 40."

TRANSPORTATION: Corps is 40 miles south of Grenoble, and 25 miles north of Gap on Highway N-85. Grenoble is a main rail center, but there are no trains at Gap. Buses travel between Grenoble and Corps. Visitors should make reservations in advance for accommodations at the shrine's guest house. The address is Hôtellerie de La Salette, Corps; telephone 38–970.

HOTELS: In Corps, *Hotel Le Napoleon* is comfortable. *Hotel du Palais* and *Hotel de la Poste* are moderately priced.

THE RIVIERA

Southern France has been a particular favorite of artists. Renoir called it "the most beautiful country in the world," and many artists have followed him here. Some of their creations are great works of religious art—not only paintings, but chapels. At *Vence,* the lovely back-country town between Cannes and Nice, Matisse decorated the Rosary Chapel of the Dominican nuns, relying mostly on black and white—the colors of the Dominican habit. Mauve rose, the only suggestion of color, seeps through the stained glass windows. The Rosary Chapel can be visited on Tuesday and Thursday from 10 A.M. to 11:30 A.M., and 2:30 P.M. to 5:30 P.M. There is no admission fee. *Villefranche,* between Nice and Monte Carlo, is a classically beautiful fishermen's port. St. Peter's 14th-century chapel at the shore had been used for centuries to store nets of the fishermen. Jean Cocteau has guaranteed the chapel's longevity by painting its walls with light-colored frescoes depicting scenes from the life of Christ, and of the fishermen of the beautiful port. At the Matisse Museum in Nice are studies the artist made for the line drawings at the Rosary Chapel in Vence.

St. Patrick was a monk on the offshore island of St. Honorat, within sight of the Croisette at Cannes. He stayed there before going to evangelize Ireland. (See Index.) Cistercian monks, spiritual descendants of the 5th-century monastic settlers of the island, live in the monastery on St. Honorat, and grow their own vegetables, citrus fruits and grapes which they market in Cannes.

TRANSPORTATION: Nice, the capital of the Riviera, is a major rail, air and bus center.

HOTELS: *Negresco* is superbly located on the Promenade des Anglais at Nice. *Splendid* and *Royal* are comfortable.

ROC AMADOUR

On the southern edge of the Massif Central, an ancient shrine is tucked into the 500-foot-high wall of a canyon. "Roc" in the name of the shrine refers to the sheer cliff. "Amadour" is the name of the hermit who built an oratory in the side of the cliff shortly after Christ's Crucifixion. In 1166 the body of Amadour was found in an opening in the massive rock near the entrance to the present Chapel of the Miraculous Virgin. The body had not decomposed, and it was presented for veneration. Reports of miracles followed. No one is sure who this holy man was. Many think it was Zacchaeus, the rich publican of Jericho who was converted by Christ. Zacchaeus, according to this tradition, journeyed to the part of Gaul which is now the Limoges area to spread the Gospel, and died on the rocky cliff where he had prayed and lived alone.

The chapel is about halfway up the side of the cliff. An elevator ascends to the chapel/church level from the valley floor. A series of wayside shrines, making a Via Crucis, is along the path which zigzags to the top of the cliff. At one point is a grotto with a Nativity scene, simply done—some hay, and the solitary figures of the Infant, Mary and Joseph.

This is the Lot region, an area of grottoes and underground passages much like the nearby Dordogne valley with its Lascaux caves. It is an area, too, where the baker's wife delivers bread in a rattly Citroën 2-CV, slipping a fresh loaf in the gate or atop the stone fence at each house, like a newspaper delivery boy in Southwest U.S.A. The baker's wife on her rounds also provides news of the village to those who come to the door to meet her.

It is a friendly area, too. For years it has been the custom of the mayor of Roc Amadour to arrange a dinner, from soup to tarte aux pommes, for all residents of the village who are in the Third Age. The First Age are those under 21; the Second Age, under 60; the Third Age, the others. The dinner is usually in the off-season, in February, and is at a different hotel each year. It starts around noon, and continues into the evening when there is music for dancing after some speeches. About 80 or 90 Third Age residents attend.

TRANSPORTATION: Roc Amadour is 30 miles south of Brive, via Highway N-20 to Payrac and then west on N-673. Brive is a main rail junction. There are some through trains to Roc Amadour from Paris and Toulouse.

HOTELS: *Hôtel du Château,* across from the castle, is comfortable. An unpretentious hotel is at the railroad station.

BRITTANY

Neither the sites nor the folklore of Brittany's ancient pilgrimages have been altered by the 20th century. Each village is the scene of a *pardon*, a traditional way the Bretons ask a favorite saint for forgiveness of the sins they have committed during the year. The religious ceremony takes place in a chapel or church. When it is over, the *gavottes* are danced throughout the village, Breton bagpipes skirl, and oldtime songs are sung by a new generation of voices. Often, young men put on a show of wrestling matches and gymnastics. There are normal *pardons*, and there is also a *grand pardon*, something extra-special.

St. Yves, the "poor man's lawyer" and a patron saint of Brittany and of lawyers, is honored on May 19 at Tréguier (35 miles from St. Brieuc). St. Jean-du-Doigt has a *pardon* with bonfires on June 23 and 24 (50 miles from Brest). St. Anne, the mother of Mary, is honored in a granite chapel isolated in the moors near the sea at Ste. Anne-la-Palud on the last Sunday in August (15 miles from Quimper). A major *pardon* takes place at Ste. Anne-d'Auray on July 25 and 26 in honor of St. Anne, who is known as "The Holy Grandmother of Brittany" (10 miles from Vannes).

On the second Sunday of July the people of Brittany follow the 7½-mile-long mountain route at Locronan along which a 5th-century Irish hermit named Ronan used to walk before breakfast in bare feet as a penance (40 miles from Brest).

A noted *pardon* is the one for St. Eloy on June 24 in Landerneau (12 miles from Brest). An old French song keeps alive the memory of this onetime bishop. In Brittany, they call him "Sant Allar" and entrust their horses to his care. Bretons make the rounds of the chapels dedicated to him on horseback. At each place they leave an appropriate offering: a beribboned horsetail, or a bunch of real horsehair from the mane of their animal.

NORMANDY

Caen was the capital of William the Conqueror. It is more immediately known for its part in the Battle of Normandy when the greatest invasion army ever assembled landed on the beaches near Caen to begin the liberation of Europe. A worthwhile detour is to Bayeux (*Hotel Lion d'Or*), the fine-lace town and home of the ancient Queen Mathilda tapestry. The 9-centuries-old embroidered tapestry retraces the principal episodes in the conquest of England by William, the duke of Normandy.

MONT ST. MICHEL

A bishop from the nearby coastal town of Avranches reported in the 8th century a vision of St. Michael. He built an oratory on the point of land where the sea surges against the Norman and Breton shorelines. Since then, men and nature have made the "Mount of St. Michael" a wonder of the world.

From the 13th to the 16th centuries, monks judiciously added to the magnificence of their monastery, pyramiding it with artistic and architectural skill on the mountain of rock which is the island. The ocean swirls around Mont St. Michel, and its tides climb up the abbey walls, creating an island of the small mass of land. When the waters recede the island becomes a peninsula.

The most interesting time to visit Mont St. Michel is during the high tides. One can watch the waters arrive to circle the monastery, and cut it off from all dry land. The waters race in fast. A copy of the Table of Tides can be obtained at local tourist offices in Normandy and

Brittany. An overnight stay on the island is always a memorable experience. The major pilgrimage to Mont St. Michel is on Sept. 29.

TRANSPORTATION: Mont St. Michel is 200 miles west of Paris. There is direct rail service.

HOTELS: The traditional stopping-place is *Mère Poulard*. Another fine place is the *Guesclin*.

LISIEUX

One of the ex-voto offerings on the walls of the chapel holding the reliquary of St. Teresa of Lisieux records the visits of Amelia of Portugal in May and September 1923, and the queen's thanks for a "cure obtained by her intercession." Dozens of other ex-voto tablets are on the chapel walls: some from prominent personages, others from people as anonymous as a Normandy farmhand. After Lourdes it is the most visited shrine in France. In 1973, at the centenary of the French Carmelite's birth, there were 1.5 million visitors.

Teresa was born at Alençon, 60 miles south of Lisieux, at 42 rue St. Blaise, on Jan. 2, 1873. Her father, Louis Martin, was a jeweler. There were 7 girls and 2 boys in the family. She was the youngest child. When her mother died the family moved to Lisieux because her father's brother-in-law was a pharmacist near the cathedral and, therefore, an important person in the town. Lisieux has a population of 30,000. It is a town of agriculture, canneries, slaughter houses and some light industry.

Teresa was 9 when her favorite sister, Pauline, entered the Carmelite convent at Lisieux. She was saddened at the departure of her sister, and subsequently suffered several bouts of sickness. In the garden of her home one day, when she was 14½, she confided to her father that she, too, wanted a religious life. He reached over and plucked a white flower, telling the child that God had protected and cared for her the way He had for the little flower. She has become known as "The Little Flower" from this casual incident.

The prioress of the Carmelites said she was too young, so she and her father visited the bishop at Bayeux. He declined to overrule the prioress. There were already family plans for a pilgrimage to Rome— her father, Céline her younger sister, and herself. In Rome she asked Leo XIII: "In honor of your jubilee, Holy Father, please allow me to enter the Carmel at the age of fifteen." The Pope, advised by a priest in the group that the matter was under study, responded: "You will enter it if it be the will of God." Three months after her 15th birthday she became a Carmelite.

At Easter, when she was 23, she contracted tuberculosis. During the onset of the disease she had stuck to her rigorous program of prayer and fasting. Shortly before her death, she said: "I will pass my heaven in doing good upon earth. After my days on earth I will send down a shower of roses. All the world will love me." She died on the evening of Sept. 30, 1897. She was three months from her 25th birthday. Her last words were: "Mon Dieu, je vous aime." She had kept a diary. When it came time for the prioress to send a circular letter to other Carmelite convents, as traditional, informing them of the death of a Sister and giving some details of her life, she used the diary, calling it *Histoire d'une Âme*, "History of a Soul." Soon the diary was published around the world as a classic piece of spiritual literature. She was beatified on Apr. 29, 1923 and, 2 years later, canonized (May 17, 1925). Four of her sisters were still alive. She had been dead just 27½ years. No relatives live in the town today.

Her shrine is not an elaborate sanctuary. It is the same Carmelite convent where she was a cloistered nun for 9 years on the rue du Carmel in the center of Lisieux. In the outer courtyard are the tombs of her three sisters, all Carmelites from the same convent: Mother Agnes of Jesus (Pauline), 1861–1951; Sister Marie of the Sacred Heart (Marie), 1860–1940; and Sister Genevieve of the Holy Face (Céline), 1869–1959. A fourth sister, Léonine, who died in 1954, is buried at the Convent of the Visitation in Caen.

The big ceremonies take place in an immense basilica a few blocks away on the Avenue Sainte-Thérèse. On Sept. 30, the anniversary of her death, there are processions between the Basilica and the Convent of the Carmel. Nineteen cloistered nuns are at the convent, and four externs, Sisters who are free to handle essential outside tasks, such as answering the door, shopping, and so on. There cannot be more than 25 nuns in a Carmelite convent.

In summer a chaplain is always present at the Carmel Convent Church and at the basilica; in winter, only at the Carmel.

The chaplain's office at the Carmel is a glass-doored room at the back of the church.

"We wish to create a silence so people can pray," the chaplain on duty says. He is dressed in a dark suit. A small silver cross shines from the lapel of his jacket. "We must remember that this is a convent of Carmelites. A church is made for praying."

The saint's chapel is a few yards from the chaplain's office. A waxed image of the saint is in an enormous gold-framed glass reliquary. The effigy is clothed in the Carmelite habit, and the feet are shoeless. The bones, found when her tomb was opened in the city cemetery, are underneath the reliquary.

"She thought of living her life in simplicity, not in marvels," the chaplain says. "She put her accent on the love of God, on the misericordia of God. At the end of her life—in the last year of her life—she went through a spiritual crisis. She had said earlier that she did not think atheists were sincere. But she learned that disbelief is a reality."

The family home is in a tiny street, just off the boulevard that leads to Trouville. It is a two-story house. Some rooms, such as the kitchen and dining-room, are furnished with articles from the time of the saint.

TRANSPORTATION: Lisieux is 110 miles west of Paris. Frequent train service.

HOTELS: *Regina, Capucines* and *Maris Stella* are comfortable. The *Hermitage* is medium-priced.

LOURDES

The French have an ancient Latin saying to describe France's traditional devotion to the Madonna: *Regnum Galliae, Regnum Mariae*, Kingdom of Gaul, Kingdom of Mary.

If Gaul is Mary's kingdom, then this town of the Pyrenees is certainly its capital.

Lourdes is singularly impressive at two times of the year. One is the traditional summerpeak for Europeans, Aug. 15, which is the Marian feast of the Assumption. On that day 100,000 or more people throng Lourdes. The size of the crowd, the diversity of their languages, the variety of their backgrounds will impress any observer.

Another impressive time at Lourdes is on a winter's night, when a breeze off the snowy slopes of the Pyrenees makes the candles in the grotto shiver. At night in winter the streets of this town of 18,300 residents are deserted.

Yet, at any time of a winter's night if one wanders through the hilly streets of Lourdes, walks across the vast esplanade which covers the 650-foot-long underground Basilica of St. Pius X, and circles around the Rock of Massabielle, he will find people kneeling, praying and meditating at the grotto where Bernadette Soubirous saw the Madonna 18 times. There will be nuns there, but also civilians—old and young, in pairs and alone, French and foreigners. One winter's night a Lamborghini *Spada* sports car was parked at the entrance to the esplanade.

Lourdes has always been a meeting point. It was the home of the Celts and of the Iberians, and in 58 B.C. was occupied by the Romans. On his way back from Spain in A.D. 778 after his rearguard had been routed at the Roncesvalles Pass on the other side of the Pyrenees (see Index), Charlemagne laid siege to Lourdes because it was held by the Saracens. His strategy was to starve the Moslem invaders into submission. But the legend is that a tremendous eagle, holding a trout in its beak, flew over the encampment of the Arabs, and let the fish fall among them. The leader of the invaders from Africa had the trout brought to Charlemagne as proof that they had plenty to eat. Charlemagne, convinced, raised the siege. Later, the leader of the Saracens became a Christian, and was baptized, taking the Latin name "Lorus," which became Lourdes in French.

The city's history as a shrine began on Feb. 11, 1858. On that day, the 14-year-old shepherdess Bernadette saw the marvelous, smiling Lady for the first time. Bernadette was the child's name in the patois of the region. Her actual name was Bernarde-Marie. She was born on Jan. 7, 1844, the oldest of 9 children of a miller. Five brothers and sisters died at an early age. The business of Bernadette's father had failed. The house they moved into was called Le Cachot (The Dungeon), because until 1824 it had been the prison of Lourdes.

Le Cachot is a two-story building, but the living space available to the family was only one room in the basement. Six people used it: the parents and 4 children. From here Bernadette went to the grotto, near the Gave River, where the Madonna awaited her. . . .

On Feb. 18, four days after the first Apparition, Bernadette sees the Lady again, and is told: "I do not promise you to be happy in this world, but in the other." On Feb. 20, Bernadette is taught a prayer. The following day, the Lady says: "Pray for sinners." On Feb. 24, the child is advised: "Repentance, repentance, repentance." The bursting forth of the spring water occurs the day after. On the next to the last day of the month the Lady speaks in patois, and says: "Go tell the priests to build a chapel here." The messages are repeated in other Apparitions, with the Lady adding that she wants people to come here in procession. On Mar. 25 the Lady identifies herself with the words in patois that are now over the grotto: "I am the Immaculate Conception." The last two Apparitions are Apr. 7, 1858 and July 16, 1858.

The series of Apparitions had begun the month after Bernadette had entered the school operated at Lourdes by the Congregation of Sisters of Charity and of Christian Education of Nevers. On June 3, 1858—between the last two Apparitions—she made her First Communion in the school chapel.

With the exception of Rome, Lourdes is visited by more pilgrims than any other shrine in Christendom. In the Marian Year of 1958 there were 4,812,400 visitors.

Father Jean Raymond, A.A., a husky, middle-aged priest, says there are several aspects of the Lourdes Apparitions which "impress" him. He was born at Argelès-Gazost, a village 8 miles from Lourdes. But he has not spent his long life as a priest and a member of the Congregation of the Assumptionist Fathers in the Pyrenees. In 1954 he was called to Paris to serve as national director of the Association de Notre Dame de Salut, a laymen's group. Now he is back in the Pyrenees, and directs the information bureau at Lourdes.

What impresses him about *these* Apparitions?

"For one thing, Bernadette always remained poor. She refused money from pilgrims. This is impressive. The bourgeoisie was shocked by the patois language of Bernadette. She was asthmatic. The people would have preferred a more cultured messenger than such an uneducated adolescent. Not only was her family not cultured, but it was not financially or materially wealthy. It practiced religion, but not deeply. Bernadette maintained this poverty. She remained in that condition. She did not become a parvenue. She did not try to profit in any material way.

"Second, the message is very simple, very clear: the prayer and the penitence. You must pray. You must realize you cannot do everything yourself. God waits for you to ask His help in prayer. You must always pray for sinners, for those who don't pray any more, who don't dare to pray. You must pray for them out of a kind of solidarity, not out of pity.

"There's the element, too, of repentance. Use the water. Repent, and see how your own life has changed, see if something is *your* fault. Then, use the water as a purification, as a symbol of a clean conscience.

" 'Build a chapel' is not new in Apparitions. But here the Virgin repeated 'Build a chapel' three or four times. That is what surprises me. Build this church, not as a monument for Her but as a point of assembly of people, an international assembly point."

After the Apparitions, when crowds began swarming around Bernadette in the streets of Lourdes, the mayor and the curé asked the Sisters at the school-hospice to take her in as a boarder. In 1866 she was accepted as a postulant by the Congregation in Lourdes. On May 21 of that same year, the liturgical devotion at the grotto officially began with the first Pontifical Mass in the just-completed crypt of a church that was being built.

Was that the first pilgrimage?

"No. The first pilgrimage was two years earlier, on Apr. 4, 1864, for the unveiling of the statue of the grotto. In 1866 Monsignor Laurence, the bishop of Tarbes, named a small group of priests to serve the pilgrims. He had a great devotion to Mary. He had made it his policy to use the Marian devotion as a means of restoring his diocese which, like all France, had been shaken by the Revolution and the Napoleonic era. The bishop bought back convents and sanctuaries which had been seized by the government, and sold or given to others. At one 16th-century sanctuary, Garnaison, not far from Tarbes, he installed a team of priests who were specialized in preaching missions everywhere they were needed. These priests were very qualified. When the Apparitions of Lourdes took place, Bishop Laurence sent these priests here to receive the pilgrims, to hear their Confessions, to distribute Communion.

"Also, in the year 1866–67, the railroad was extended to Lourdes from Tarbes [12 miles northeast] and from Pau [25 miles northwest]. This was done independently of the Apparitions. One month after the Pau line was built, there was the first pilgrimage by train. A curé of Bayonne brought the pilgrims. The railroad recognized at once this was good business, and set aside a dozen trains for Lourdes. In 1867 there were twenty-eight thousand pilgrims." . . .

On July 4, 1866 Bernadette leaves Lourdes for the motherhouse of the Congregation at Nevers in Burgundy, and five days later takes the veil under the name of Sister Marie-Bernarde. She is assigned as a nurse assistant, and later as sacristan in the convent chapel.

What was Rome's reaction?

"That was another reason for the success of Lourdes. All popes from Pius IX onward have shown sympathy for Lourdes.

"In 1854 Pius IX had proclaimed the dogma of the Immaculate Conception, and four years later the Virgin tells Bernadette: 'I am the Immaculate Conception.' When Pius IX heard of the Apparitions, he accepted the proofs and the report of the bishop very happily. They seemed to be a confirmation to him, a sign.

"Pius X in 1904 gave the bishop of Tarbes the right

to add 'of Lourdes' to his title. That was a sign of papal sympathy. In 1933, the Jubilee Year of the Redemption (Christ's death), Pius XI accepted that the closing of the celebration be at Lourdes, and delegated Cardinal Pacelli (later Pius XII) to preside at it."

So, the number of pilgrims kept rising?

"Well, not just like that. Till 1871 there were about thirty thousand a year. All regional pilgrimages. In 1872 Lourdes passed to its national period. There were one hundred and nineteen thousand pilgrims that year. For a village of four thousand inhabitants this was enormous. It was an extraordinary period of life, of dynamism. France had lost the war with the Prussians, the country had been occupied by the Germans. There was a rebirth of patriotism among the religious and nonchurchgoers alike. Each one interpreted events on his own. Some took the Bible literally, with Christ saying if you abandon Me, I shall abandon you. People said, '*See?* We didn't go to church, and keep His commandments. Look what has happened.' In October 1872—the sixth, it was, the feast of the Rosary—there were a dozen bishops here and all the dioceses of France, almost, were represented. Twenty-five thousand pilgrims. This was a great surprise. Till then, bishops had remained on the sidelines, prudent.

"Then in 1873 the first formal national pilgrimage was started."

Bernadette spent 13 years as a nun, dying at the age of 35 on Apr. 16, 1879 in the infirmary of the convent at Nevers. As she was dying a nun began reciting the *Ave Maria* at her bedside. Bernadette answered: "Holy Mary, Mother of God, Holy Mary, Mother of God, pray for me, a poor sinner, a poor sinner." Her body was uncorrupted when exhumed after 46 years, in 1925, at the time of her beatification. She was canonized or Dec. 8, 1933.

Did the sick come to Lourdes from the start?

"The sick were not wanted here as such in the begin

ning. They came by themselves, or their families brought them. The national pilgrimage of 1873 that I mentioned—that was organized by the Notre Dame de Salut Association in Paris. This association had been established by Parisian bourgeois women to help workers who had no money, and to pray for France. It was founded in 1871 after the Franco-Prussian War. Meanwhile, a general committee for pilgrimages to La Salette (see Index) had been formed by Father François Picard, an Assumptionist, who later became superior general of our Congregation. He was also made director of Notre Dame de Salut. In 1872 he organized a pilgrimage to La Salette, and one for Lourdes the following year. He asked the ladies of Notre Dame de Salut to help him with the pilgrimages.

"One person was cured on the national pilgrimage to Lourdes in 1873, and this impressed the women. 'We aid the poor with money; perhaps if we bring the sick poor to Lourdes they will be aided, too.' That was their feeling, and they proposed this to Father Picard. He was not in agreement. He did not say No, but he didn't say Yes. One sick person, he felt—*ça va*. Two, perhaps. But more, *impossible*. What will we do with them? The women were insistent. He said, all right, if you bring them, it is on your own responsibility. The women took the challenge. They brought fourteen sick people to Lourdes the following year. That was 1874. It was an adventure. They cared for them, housed them, carried them. One of the fourteen sick was cured. This was a triumph for the women. The director gave in. He said: 'We officially accept the sick.'

"In 1875 a hospital was already established to receive the sick—with carriages for transporting them from the station, stretchers, and so on. This developed fast. By 1880 almost one thousand sick pilgrims were coming a year. In 1881 Father Picard formed the *Hospitalité* of Notre Dame de Salut, with men and women volunteers, swimming pool assistants, therapists. The number of sick pilgrims a year increased eventually to sixty-four thousand, with two-thirds of them cared for in the two hospitals here, and the remaining—the blind, mostly— in hotels."

And the investigation of the cures?

"That was done right at the beginning, too. In 1878 the bishop nominated a commission of doctors to examine the reported cures, and determine whether they were supernatural or not. The commission reported, and from this came the idea of a *commission permanente.* Dr. Henri Vergez, the first doctor in the investigations, continued this work till his death in 1883. In that year a Belgian doctor from Louvain, Dr. de Saint-Maclou, took up residence at Lourdes and established the Bureau des Constations Medicales. Today, there is only one permanent member of the bureau, the president. But all doctors are automatically members of the bureau if they wish, no matter their religion, their nationality, or whatever. Whenever a case (of a reported cure) is being considered, any doctor can sit in and ask any question, or see anything, and vote like everyone else."

Does the bureau investigate all cures?

"No, only those cases where the complete medical records are available. I mean *everything.* If a person comes to the bureau and says he has been cured, and he seems to be serious, he is asked to return with his doctor and his full medical case history. If even one X-ray, or one page of the chart is missing, the case is no longer considered."

What made Lourdes international?

"American, Canadian and English soldiers knew Lourdes during the war. That was one reason. Also, it was the start of the era of international travel. In 1948 the Pax Christi organization made an international pilgrimage to Lourdes—all Europe was represented, Germany included. This was impressive because it sought peace among all men. In 1958, for the centenary of the

Apparitions, twenty countries were represented in an international group of members of Parliament. There have been all kinds of international groups: polio victims, widows, even motorcyclists. In 1973 there was a pilgrimage of three hundred motorcyclists in leather jackets from two or three countries. They were *impeccables!*

"Another reason for the internationalization is that in the early periods all foreigners were kept a bit apart involuntarily. Services, for instance, were in French and Latin. Now, at the communal Mass on Wednesday the group in majority will say the Gospel in their own language—English, German, or whatever. And in the processions the invocations are not just in French, but in many languages. People are made to feel at home."

At St. Michael's Gate, at the entrance to the esplanade, the hours of the various services—Mass, Confession, Adoration, Rosary—are detailed on signs in 7 languages. At the hospice where Bernadette went to school, a history is typed in many languages. The same information arrangement exists at Le Cachot, the house where Bernadette was living when she saw the Apparitions. The languages include Vietnamese, Ukrainian and Japanese.

The Congregation of Sisters which Bernadette joined at the age of 22 acquired Le Cachot in 1926, and it is a pilgrimage site. Several Masses are said there daily, and a Sister-guide is present.

Are the cures increasing like the pilgrims?

"No. The number of cures, as a matter of fact, has been dropping. Today, there are different kinds of miracles. The courage to return to one's daily life despite a great physical handicap, to think of other than physical health, to think also of intellectual or spiritual health—these are miracles, too. Some still think of physical health, and of a corporal cure. But this sentiment has been replaced, I feel, by spiritual cures. A miracle after all is a sign. Perhaps the miracle of physical cures has run its course, and we are now in the time of other signs."

And the future of Lourdes?

"The next stage is coming in a few years. We hope so. We plan to make a large simultaneous-translation room to permit people from different groups to talk among themselves in many languages. That is the direction in which we are heading. To help groups from different countries meet and exchange ideas without any language barrier."

TRANSPORTATION: Lourdes is 500 miles southwest of Paris. There is direct rail service to Paris.

HOTELS: *Gallia-Londres*, *La Grotte* and *Imperial* are excellent. Medium-priced hotels include *Ambassadeurs*, *Excelsior*, and *Belge-Madrid*.

NEVERS

The body of St. Bernadette has lain in the chapel of the motherhouse of her Congregation at Nevers, 150 miles south of Paris, since Aug. 3, 1925. It is intact. The face and the hands are covered with a thin mask of wax, a sign outside the chapel explains in several languages.

"When she died," a nun says, "the bishop told the mother general of his desire that she not be buried in the local cemetery. It was intuition or prudence on the bishop's part. There was an oratory already in the gardens of the convent, and a cave was built to place her casket there."

The nun's face is white and radiant. She explains that she took the religious name of Margaret-Mary because of her devotion to the Sacred Heart.

"When I came here," Sister Margaret-Mary says, "Bernadette was still in the oratory, and we postulants prayed there on Sundays. She remained in the cave of the oratory for forty-six years—1879 to 1925, when she was beatified on June 14. A short time later, she was brought into the chapel."

Sick pilgrims arriving on stretchers at Nevers are met at the train by Chevaliers of Bernadette. There are 40 chevaliers (knights), and they are appointed by the mother general. One chevalier is Georges Fafart, a white-haired man in perfectly cut tweeds who was born in Paris 75 years ago, and till his retirement had worked for a bank in Hong Kong. His father had retired in Nevers, and spent the rest of his life as a Chevalier of Bernadette. He retired in Nevers, also, and became a chevalier, using his father's armband. It is made of blue cloth, and has a white cross. At the center of the cross is a medal of St. Bernadette.

TRANSPORTATION: Direct trains from Paris.

HOTELS: *Terminus, Moderne* and *Métropole* hotels are near the railroad station.

PARIS

Paris is the gate to all of France, whether one travels the highways and sleek auto-routes issuing from its edges, or remains within its boundaries. It is a city which merits the French word *unique*.

Opinions differ as to the origin of the name Montmartre. Some say its source is a temple of Mercury which once topped the little hill in the north of Paris, Mont de Mercure. Others trace the name to the beheading of St. Denis, the first bishop of Paris, in the 3rd century. He and two companions were killed on Montmartre, and it has been traditionally known as the Mont des Martyrs. St. Denis is said to have carried his head to the point north of Paris, now known as Saint-Denis. (*Métro* to Porte de la Chapelle, and then Bus No. 153.) A Gothic-style basilica was built in the 12th century on the site of his grave in the town of Saint-Denis. The basilica was the traditional burial place for the kings and queens of France, and the young princes and princesses. The tombs were emptied during the Revolution.

From his Montmartre window Utrillo looked across to the enchanting Place du Tertre and the lofty Basilica of Sacre Cœur, built in 1873 when France was dedicated to the Sacred Heart. A cable-car makes the climb to Sacre Cœur, and there is a long stairway leading to it as well. Two windmills remain on the hill. One near the corner of the rue Girardon and rue Lépic was used by Renoir as the subject for his painting, "Moulin de la Galette."

Young and old, French and foreigners, men and women are in the constant stream of visitors to the Chapel of the Daughters of Charity in the rue du Bac on the Left Bank. It was there that the Madonna appeared in 1830 to one of the Sisters, Catherine Labouré. She was born in Burgundy, at Fain-les-Moutiers, on May 2, 1806, the ninth child of a farm family with 11 sons and daughters. She joined the Congregation of nuns founded by St. Vincent de Paul and after three months in the novitiate was assigned to rue du Bac. Just before midnight on July 18, 1830, the eve of the feast of St. Vincent de Paul, a child whom she later thought might have been her guardian angel awakened her and led her to the chapel where she saw the Madonna. She spent two hours in the chapel in conversation. When she confided the experience to her confessor, he was skeptical. Then, on Nov. 22, 1830, during evening meditation in the chapel with the other Sisters, she saw the Madonna again, receiving instructions this time to have a medal struck in the likeness of the radiant Apparition. She again told her confessor, but he remained skeptical. Two years later, however, the priest had the medal made, as Catherine Labouré described it, after he had conferred with the archbishop of Paris. Devotion to the medal was almost instantaneous, but its origin was not revealed. No one except the priest knew of Sister Catherine's role, and he soon died. She, meanwhile, was assigned to her Congregation's Enghien hospice on the Faubourg St. Antoine in Paris, working in the kitchen, then in the chickenyard, and eventually at the door for 46 years. In 1876, certain that she would not live until the new year, she confided her long-kept secret to the mother superior. On the evening of Dec. 31, 1876 she died. News of her visions spread, and miracles were reported. The medal came to be known as the Miraculous Medal. On March 21, 1933 her body was exhumed and found intact. Even the robe had not changed. She was canonized on July 27, 1947 and is buried beneath the Altar of the Apparition in the chapel at 140 rue du Bac.

France's popular saint of charity, St. Vincent de Paul, founded the Daughters of Charity and also the Lazarist missionary priests. The body of "Monsieur Vincent," as he was called, is conserved in a silver reliquary in the Lazarist chapel at 95 rue de Sevrès, a few steps from the Miraculous Medal shrine. The house where he was born at Ranquine, near Bordeaux, is open to visitors. He is also remembered at the Cathedral of Notre Dame in Tarbes (north of Lourdes), where he was ordained subdeacon and deacon.

Another Paris landmark, the Church of St. Joseph-des-Carmes, is closely linked with the saint of charity. In the church crypt is the tomb of Frederic Ozanam, founder of the St. Vincent de Paul Society.

St. Genevieve, the holy woman associated with the conversion of France's first king, is honored in the Church of St. Étienne-du-Mont on the Left Bank. Through her intercession Clovis, pagan king of a tribe of Franks, accepted Christianity and was baptized in A.D. 496.

Napoleon is buried in a chapel in the Church of St. Louis des Invalides. There is a death mask, along with some of the stones which covered his grave at St.

Helena. The Requiem Mass of Berlioz was heard for the first time in the Church of St. Louis.

Although Père Lachaise cemetery is named after Father François d'Aix de Lachaise, a 17th-century Jesuit, he is not buried there. Père Lachaise was a confessor to Louis XIV, and he lived in a house which was on the site of the present cemetery. People visiting the Jesuit got in the habit of saying they were "going to Père Lachaise." When the cemetery was built, the name stuck. It is the largest cemetery in Paris. Its fame, however, is due not to its size, but to the number of celebrated people who have been buried there: Sarah Bernhardt, Oscar Wilde, the founder of the French Communist party, and so on.

The men who founded the city of Paris 20 centuries ago were from the tribe of Parisii. They installed themselves on the Ile de la Cité, and hoped that the waters of the Seine would shield them from unwelcome elements. Lutetia was the name of the little town. Time altered the name to Paris. The Ile de la Cité holds the Palais de Justice (Law Courts), the Conciergerie (once the prison of Marie Antoinette, among others), the Sainte-Chapelle (the chapel with lovely stained-glass windows built by France's king-saint, Louis IX, in the 13th century), and the Cathedral of Notre Dame. Adjoining this island is a smaller one named after the king-saint, Ile St. Louis.

TRANSPORTATION: Paris is an international air and rail center.

HOTELS: *Sheraton, Méridien, Plaza Athénée, Georges V,* and *Hilton* are among the leading hotels. *Novotel Bagnolet* is distant, but not high-priced.

POINTS OF INTEREST: *Rheims,* the capital of the champagne district, 95 miles east of Paris on Highway N-3, contains the schoolroom where the Second World War armistice was signed and the cathedral in which France's kings were crowned. The cathedral is known, too, for its sculpture of the Smiling Angel. *Beauvais*, 48 miles north of Paris, has the world's tallest Gothic cathedral, and its walls are lined with ancient tapestries. At *Fontainebleau*, 39 miles south of Paris, is a 2,000-room palace, and nearby is *Barbizon*, the village favored by Robert Louis Stevenson and 19th-century artists.

5
Germany

THE GERMANIC TRIBES first began appearing along the fringes of the Roman empire in the 2nd century B.C. and, evolving first into compact, capable states and then into a nation of states, became a permanent, dominating influence on all facets of the development of Europe, from geopolitics to international religion.

Waging war was a predominant characteristic of the Germanic peoples and, logically, the gods they prayed to were warlike, such as Woden (or Wodan), their chief deity. The worshiping of the gods of war called for rites at which prisoners were offered in supplication in a thoroughly destroyed form, and then solemnly buried in marshes and bogs. Nerthus, the goddess, and other deities of fertility, were also venerated. Likenesses of the gods and goddesses were borne among the people in great carts in processions of dignity and grandeur. The prophetesses who were consulted by warrior chiefs and rulers had enormous influence.

In their conquest of Gaul the Romans subdued or fought back remnants of the Germanic tribes which probed south of the Danube and west of the Rhine. East of the Rhine remained the stronghold of the

Germanic tribes. By the 5th century the Franks, one of the largest of the tribes, crossed the historic dividing line and raced across Gaul. The Franks produced giants of leaders, particularly Charlemagne who brought together into an empire some of the eastern tribes with those west of the Rhine, and journeyed to Rome to have himself crowned emperor by the Pope on Christmas Day in A.D. 800.

Otto I (A.D. 936–973) grandly bestowed upon himself the title of "Emperor of the Romans," and the various Germanic tribes were said to be part of the "Holy Roman Empire of the German Nation." To consolidate these titles the successors of Charlemagne followed his precedent of coronation by the Pope. Yet while bringing strength the papal act also brought the emperor into the web of conflicts entangling church and state across Europe. Soon the emperor seemed to be giving more concern to what was taking place in Rome than in the principalities of his kingdom. German princes were turning more independent. The Reformation and, then, the Thirty Years' War added to the independence of the princes, affording them new bargaining power. The Holy Roman Empire came to an end in 1806 with the French Revolution and the Napoleonic wars, but the Reformation had long before removed most of the German states from the spiritual aegis of Rome.

Today, a little more than half of the people of Western Germany are Protestants; 44 percent are Catholic. Practically no Jews are left in the country. The Rhineland and Bavaria, in particular, clung to their Catholicism throughout the Reformation.

The outstanding religious figure of all time in Germany was Martin Luther, who was born on Nov. 10, 1483 in Eisleben, now in East Germany, west of Leipzig. He had no deeply simmering urge for reform. He was intent on finishing his law studies at the University of Erfurt when on July 2, 1505, while returning from a visit with his parents, he was thrown to the ground in a thunderous storm. Fear-stricken he cried out to St. Anne for holy protection, making a promise to enter a monastery if she brought aid. Fifteen days later he joined the Augustinians at Erfurt and on May 2, 1507 celebrated his first Mass.

Luther's father did not approve of his son's decision to take on the religious life. When Luther declared that he had received a call from God, his father demanded: "How do you know it is not from the devil?" Which supernatural force, God or devil, was exerting influence was a perennial question in the medieval mind.

While Luther was pondering the depths of the religion and the God he served, he was assigned to lecture on the Scriptures at the University of Wittenberg (in East Germany, north of Leipzig). He also became a parish priest, and this experience introduced him into the system of indulgences in vogue among people seeking to provide spiritual help for themselves and for dead relatives. Luther was puzzled and disturbed that indulgences apparently could be obtained from the Pope, transferred like spiritual credits from one person to another, and applied to future or past accounts. The fact that those receiving indulgences were expected to make a contribution of money to the church aggravated his attitude.

On Oct. 31, 1517 Luther attacked the indulgence system in a manifesto known as the Ninety-Five Theses. They charged papal venality and exploitation, declared that the Pope has no jurisdiction over purgatory and that, even if he did, he should free its inhabitants without any assessment of fees, and denied the concept that indulgences can be accumulated in a treasury of spiritual merits. For him, the treasury was the Gospel.

Rome summoned him for an explanation. Cardinal Cajetan questioned him at an imperial Diet in Augsburg in October 1518.

The election of a new emperor—the choice fell upon

Charles V—slowed the inevitable climax. There was a new summons in the fall of 1520, with a 60-day deadline to submit ending Dec. 10. Luther in the interval produced a comprehensive program of reform: redimensioning of the Papacy into a spiritual power exclusively, marriage of the clergy, separateness of the powers of church and state, national rather than Roman handling of finances, reduction of the sacraments to Baptism and the Holy Eucharist, and a redefinition of the Mass. On the last day for his submission Luther burned the Papal Bull. He was put on trial at the Diet of the empire in Worms in the winter of 1520–21. Again he affirmed that he did not accept the authority of Popes and Councils, declaring that his conscience was a "captive to God."

The Edict of Worms condemning him as a heretic and a subversive to the state was issued by Charles V. Luther's political protector, Elector Frederick the Wise of Saxony, managed to hide him in the Wartburg, an island castle, and he remained out of public view for a year.

His words of reform were already being turned into acts by the people.

He married a nun, Kartharina von Bora, in 1525, and they had 6 children. The emperor, Charles V, seemed to be too occupied with other matters to concern himself with Luther. Till his death on Feb. 18, 1546 in Eisleben, Luther wrote prodigiously. Among his publishings in the last days was the hymn "A Mighty Fortress Is Our God."

TRIER

A Latin inscription on a building in the marketplace says that Trier existed 1,300 years before Rome. This is easily arguable. But no one will argue with Trier's description of itself as the oldest town in Germany. It was founded by the Romans under Emperor Augustus about 15 B.C. Martin, the 4th-century bishop of Tours (see Index) lived and worked in Trier. Early Christian martyrs were buried here and, nearby, at Santa Maria ad Martyros on the Moselle. Pilgrims came to the grave of Trier's first bishop, St. Eucharius. Constantine the Great's father, Constantine Chloros, resided in Trier as the Western emperor of the Roman empire. Constantine's mother, Helena, brought back from the Holy Land the Holy Tunic of Christ, part of the True Cross, and the bones of Matthias, the apostle elected to replace Judas Iscariot. Karl Marx was born in Trier on May 5, 1818.

THE HOLY TUNIC

Over the centuries the determination of when the Holy Tunic was to be exposed to public view became the high point of the life of Trier's bishop. It has not been shown often. The last times were in 1933 and 1959. Monsignor Weyand saw it on those occasions.

"It has been exhibited only two or three times a century," he says. "Otherwise it would have been destroyed by now. It is all enveloped in silk wrappings, and sewn to a cloth to keep it together."

Monsignor Weyand is a heavy-set, congenial priest who handles administrative matters for the Cathedral of Trier and its diocese.

"The Trier diocese is so big that if I took its diameter, and extended it toward France it would reach beyond Notre Dame of Paris. There are one thousand parishes. In the Peace of Lunéville, Napoleon decided he wanted the left bank of the Rhine, and to placate princes on the other side of the river he decided to confiscate church property if it was not part of a parish. Napoleon had a special idea about the church."

Constantine the Great, the first Christian emperor,

initiated a vast architectural complex for his palace in Trier. The original buildings of the cathedral and of the palace are from his time. Only the cathedral, however, is used by the Catholics. The Lutherans use the audience hall of Constantine's that had belonged to the palace. In the past it had been part of the palace of the Prince-Elector of Trier, the archbishop. In 1801 the audience hall fell to the state in the secularization effected by Napoleon, and later it was given to the Protestants. The actual palace, the living quarters, now houses the district government.

In a real sense Trier cathedral is the oldest in Germany. Part of its walls are from Constantine's time, and old bricks are woven into its fabric. It has recently been restored.

"The foundations had weakened," Monsignor Weyand says. "They are on wooden poles going back to the fourth century, and many holes were in the walls. We were afraid the entire structure would collapse."

Has the age of the Holy Tunic been authenticated?

"There are many hints to indicate that if the Holy Tunic exists at all it is here, since Helena was the empress of the empire. She brought the Holy Tunic back from Jerusalem, and placed it in a sanctuary. As for the age of the Holy Tunic we know it is correct, but that does not prove it is the authentic garment. We don't stress the point, but people think it is the tunic of Christ."

What are the plans for exposing it again?

"That's hard to say—maybe not for several years. Many people are skeptical, so why make a fuss? The general plan now is to have the Holy Tunic enshrined permanently in a reliquary-like case, without of course the vestment itself being exposed."

Monsignor Weyand says that the relic of the True Cross has not been shown for 10 years. It is kept in the cathedral treasury.

THE APOSTLE MATTHIAS

The relics of Matthias are in an alabaster sarcophagus in front of the main altar of the Benedictine Monastery Church of St. Eucharius, 2 miles from Trier's classic landmark, the Porta Nigra, the 2nd-century City Gate.

"It was not until A.D. 920 that the Benedictines established a monastery here," says a young monk named Hubert. He has a short brown beard and a mustache, and is a deacon. "But centuries before the Benedictines, a group of religious people lived here. This site was a cemetery in Roman days, and was holy to the early Christians because the first two bishops of Trier, Eucharius and Valerius, were buried here.

"During the secularization of 1802–3, the monastery was suppressed, and the abbey church was made a parish church. The people were always looking for the Benedictines to come back, and they did in 1922. There was a new settlement from the Abbey of Seckau in Carinthia [Austria] and Maria Laach [see Index]. They have been here since, except during the war. In 1941 Hitler made the monks leave, figuring the religious life was dangerous to his regime. Two of the monks were sent to concentration camps for alleged political activity. In 1945 the monks came back. Some had died in the meantime. There were economic and financial difficulties. This was postwar Germany, remember, and there was a plan to move to literally greener pastures at Tholey in the Saarland. But after long discussions, the abbot went there with a big group of monks, and a small group remained here.

"We're glad to be here. It is good for Benedictines because it is in a city, and thus civilization, and we have plenty of land around the house, so it is quiet for retreats. In the evening we have Vespers and the

Eucharist together. That is the best time for the people of the parish."

The evening services are at 6:30 P.M. and a few minutes after they end, the monks have dinner. In the refectory the prior sits at the center table of blond oak which forms the horizontal bar in an inverted U of tables. The prior is slender and in his early 30s. Next to him is an aged monk who might have been one of the concentration-camp prisoners of the Nazis. The 15 other monks in the community, and 3 or 4 civilian guests, sit at the long tables at the sides of the refectory. The prior looks around from the head table to see if everyone has been seated, and taps a bell. Everyone reaches for his napkin, and begins to eat. The monks have white linen napkins; the guests, paper ones. The meal consists of a platter of cold cuts—thin slices of beef, wurst, and salami; a bowl of white parsnips; slices of cheese on a plate; three types of bread—rye, white and pumpernickel; and a highly aromated tea drunk without milk.

Hubert, the deacon, sits at a small table beside the main one, and from a lectern, begins to read aloud a book about the Vatican. For 15 minutes he reads continuously while the monks eat. When the prior observes that everyone has finished eating, he taps the bell. The reading halts, and the monks and their guests rise from the tables.

In the vaulted corridor outside the refectory the prior greets each of the guests. In reply to the question of a woman guest he says that the big feast at the monastery is Feb. 24, just after the Ascension. "In the Acts of the Apostles," he says pleasantly, "after Christ ascended into Heaven Matthias was elected to replace Judas Iscariot."

After chatting with the guests a few minutes the prior looks at a watch which he has on a long cord inside his black robe, and excuses himself, saying he has a meeting at 8:15 and must prepare for it.

A guest remarks that he has never seen women in a monks's refectory before. Hubert laughs.

"It's probably the only monastery in Germany where women are allowed," he says. "But why not? It's the times." He says that the visitors are relatives of individual monks.

TRANSPORTATION: Trier is in the Moselle valley, 90 minutes from Coblenz by train.

HOTELS: Top hotels are *Porta Nigra* and *Constantin.* *Park* and *Monopol* are moderately priced.

POINTS OF INTEREST: The Liebfrauen (Our Lady), the first Gothic church in Germany, now a Protestant church; the Karl Marx Museum in the house at 10 Brueckenstrasse, where the founder of modern socialism was born a century and a half ago; the 17th-century Marian shrine in Blieskastel, a town founded by the Romans in the 3rd century.

FULDA

Josef Schrimpf, the sacristan at the cathedral in Fulda, watches as a priest accompanied by two acolytes leaves the sacristy to celebrate Mass at the altar of St. Boniface, the apostle of Germany.

"Mass has been said on this site every day for twelve centuries, right through the Reformation," the sacristan says. He is tall, somewhat thin, and white-haired, and wears glasses. He has been sacristan at the cathedral for 35 years.

Since 1867, the German bishops have been holding annual episcopal conferences at Fulda, recognizing it as the spiritual center of Germany.

Many Masses are celebrated each morning at St. Boniface's altar in the crypt. An elaborate relief is at the face of the sarcophagus which forms the altar table. It shows Boniface in his robes and miter, with his burial tomb half opened. As apostle of the Germans he is looking out to see what is going on with his people. The actual bones of Boniface are in a copper case behind the sarcophagus, and are not visible.

"June the fifth is his feast day, the anniversary of his martyrdom," the sacristan says.

Boniface was born at Crediton in England in A.D. 680 and baptized with the name of Winfried. After becoming a Benedictine monk and priest, he set out to convert the pagan Frisian tribesmen in what is now the Netherlands. His mission, crossed by war and the hostility of the pagans, was not successful and in A.D. 718 he traveled to Rome to receive the spiritual blessing and encouragement of Pope Gregory II. The Pope received him on May 14, the anniversary of Boniface, an early Christian martyr, and decided that would be the English monk's name from then on. . . .

Boniface begins his missionary work in Thuringia, preaches in Hesse and in A.D. 722 is summoned to Rome where he is consecrated a bishop. He returns to Germany to organize the church there, destroying idol temples—such as an old oak tree dedicated to the pagan god Donar—and raising churches on the sites. In A.D. 738 Gregory III makes him Apostolic Delegate for Franconia. When he is nearly 75 years old, he returns to Friesland, his first mission land. He is about to administer confirmation to some newly baptized Christians when a band of pagans arrives, carrying clubs and spears. On Pentecost Sunday, June 5, 754 he is killed at Dokkum with 52 of his companions. (See Index.) His body is brought to Fulda where he wanted to be buried.

"There was already a Benedictine monastery here then," the sacristan says. "It had been founded by Sturmius, a disciple of Boniface. Right where the cathedral altar now stands, Sturmius placed the first cross in A.D. 743, founding the city. Sturmius had come from Bavaria. He died here on Dec. 17, 779. There were four hundred monks here at the time.

"Fulda has had four saints," the sacristan continues, "two others besides Boniface and Sturmius. One was a woman from England, Lioba, who was abbess of the Tauberbischofsheim convent, south of Würzburg. She was a cousin of Boniface, and is buried at Petersberg, a suburb of Fulda.

"The fourth saint is Rabanus Maurus, a famous teacher in the School of Fulda. He was called *magister Germaniae,* teacher of Germany. He became the fifth abbot of the abbey here, and then archbishop of Mainz where he was born in 780. He was a great assembler of relics and probably was the one who had St. Valentine's reliquary brought from Rome. It's at the side altar at the front of the cathedral. He was also a great writer of hymns. He wrote *Veni Creator Spiritus,* which is still sung today in Protestant and Catholic churches."

Fulda had abbots originally, then prince-abbots, then prince-bishops, and in more recent times bishops.

"As prince, the abbot of Fulda had a castle which he used for the administration of his secular domain. He had property in Italy, and on the Rhine, and in many parts of Germany. Noblemen on entering the monastery would turn over their property to it. In 1803 everything owned by the monastery was secularized. The older monks were put on pension; the others sent to parishes. The monks never returned to Fulda."

The present cathedral was built between 1708 and 1712. The previous one from Carolingian times had been the largest church north of the Alps.

"When they built this cathedral, it was the time of Baroque. So they destroyed the old one for a new one in Baroque. Not everyone can stand Baroque."

Fulda is called the Baroque City. There is a Baroque Hall in the former castle of the prince-abbots. The Orangerie encloses delightful gardens, and the Roman goddess of flowers, Flora, is represented on a lavish vase, holding in her hand the golden fleur-de-lys, emblem of a former prince-abbot.

The municipal administration of Fulda now occupies the former castle of the prince-abbots. It is redoing many of the rooms, and opening them to the public. The rooms are extremely large, including the bedroom which is about the same size as the audience room. The rooms are decorated with pieces of Fulda porcelain, of paintings, and of other objects of art. One of the prince-abbots had started a porcelain manufactory in 1764. It was shut down during the secularization of church property.

A summer residence of the prince-abbots came into possession of the Prince of Hesse after the secularization. It is now a museum, and is on the outskirts of Fulda.

St. Michael's Church on a hillock alongside the cathedral is virtually a museum now, too. It was built in 820. It has three floors, and the interior is circular. At the center of the main floor is a single column which represents Christ. Eight columns, for the Beatitudes, are on the second floor. The top floor has thick walls, but no columns.

TRANSPORTATION: Fulda is 72 miles northeast of Frankfurt. Inter-City express trains connect the two cities.
HOTELS: *Europa* is the leading hotel. *Goldener Karpfen, Lenz* and *Kurfürsten* are a bit less expensive.

COLOGNE

In front of the cathedral are some solid, massive blocks of stone remaining from the Roman North Gate which was built at the founding of Cologne in A.D. 50. The typical old Roman stones are particularly impressive here because so much of the area around the cathedral was destroyed in the Second World War. One new structure is the Romano-German Museum, a low-profile contemporary composition of marble and glass at the side of the cathedral. The most precious possession is its large mosaic dedicated to the Greek god of vegetation and wine, Dionysos. There are human figures, birds, animals, flowers—all depicted in festive patterns of small stones.

THE THREE MAGI

In the Middle Ages Cologne became a major point of pilgrimage for all Europe, and was the goal of monks and emperors alike. The object of pilgrimage was the resting-place of the Three Wise Men: Balthasar, Melchior and Kaspar. The bodies had been brought from the Holy Land to Milan during the Crusades, and then translated to Cologne in 1164 by Emperor Frederick Barbarossa's chancellor. Their trinity of crowns is represented in the coat-of-arms of the city.

The remains are in three gold caskets, formed like a miniature Roman basilica. Two caskets are side by side, and the third is superimposed on them at the center. The group of caskets is 5½ feet high and 7 feet long. It was built by a master goldsmith, Nicholas of Verdun, around the start of the 13th century. It is studded with precious stones, antique jewels and overlayings of fragile enamel work. The threefold reliquary is in a large glass case immediately behind the main altar of the cathedral.

"On the feast of the Three Wise Men, on January sixth, there is a big ceremony in the cathedral," a robed man who identifies himself as a *kirchenschweizer* says. He wears a long red robe and a black silk hat similar to the kind worn in the Middle East by bishops. He is more a custodian than a guide. He tells about the unusual Corpus Christi "ship procession" on the Rhine each June.

"It is a large Eucharistic procession through the city, starting from the cathedral with the monstrance, and continuing along the river. The bishop leads the procession. At Mühlheim, a suburb of Cologne on the right bank of the Rhine, he goes aboard a ship. Hundreds of large and small boats take part. It begins about nine A.M. and lasts all morning."

DUNS SCOTUS AND FATHER KOLPING

Blessed John Duns Scotus, the 13th-century Franciscan friar of Scotland, and the German priest, Father Adolph Kolping, who started an apostolate among young apprentice workers in the last century, are both buried in the 13th-century Church of the Minoriten (Friars Minor).

The first Franciscans arrived in Cologne about 1221 from Britain. Their cloister was a house of studies for the Order, and a foundation stone for the University of Cologne. One of its stars was Duns Scotus who was born about 1265, entered the Franciscans in England, and taught philosophy and theology at Oxford and the Sorbonne before coming to Cologne. He was a pioneer theologian in his teaching about the Madonna. His remains are in a white stone sarcophagus at the Gospel side of the church. A life-sized replica of him in a Franciscan habit is on the lid. He holds in his left hand a book inscribed with the Latin words for the theological argument of the doctrine of the Immaculate Conception: *decuit, potuit, fecit* (it was fitting, it was possible, it was done). There is also his famous epitaph: *Scotia* (Scotland begat me); *Anglia* (England took me in); *Gallia* (France taught me); *Colonia* (Cologne holds me).

During the secularization of 1802, the friars were expelled from Germany. In 1849 municipal authorities presented the church to the archbishop of the Cologne diocese, and the cloister was replaced by a building for the new Wallraf-Richartz art museum. In 1862 the archbishop put Father Kolping in charge of the church.

He was a vicar at the cathedral at the time, and he used the church for his apostolate. He is buried in the floor in front of the altar on the Epistle side.

The church was bombed in 1942–43. The Kolping Society, aided by the friars—and in particular the provinces of the Order in the United States—financed the church's rebuilding. In the Marian Year of 1954, the centenary of the proclamation of the dogma of the Immaculate Conception, the friars returned to Cologne.

"When the Franciscans came back," says Hubert Tintelott, a smiling, personable and thoroughly contemporary young man, "an arrangement was made with the Kolping Society which had taken over the church. The friars are now back at the church but it still belongs to the cathedral—the diocese, that is."

The Kolping Society headquarters is in a building across the square, Kolping Platz, from the church. In 1974 the society celebrated its 125th anniversary.

"It was founded on May 6, 1849 when Father Kolping spoke at the St. Columba parish school, just down the street from the Minoriten church," Hubert says. "That was the same day Karl Marx was speaking in the Gürzenich, the big hall of Cologne which is used for concerts, carnival doings, things like that. Karl Marx had four hundred listeners; Father Kolping only eight."

Hubert is the general secretary of the Kolping Society. He is only the second layman to be general secretary—the job going to priests, usually. And, at 26, he is definitely the youngest. "Some think I'm too young," he says, and smiles. He heads an organization that is now represented in 17 countries, including the U.S.A. and Canada, and has 300,000 members, from 14 years of age on up.

Father Kolping was born in Kerpen, 20 miles west of Cologne on Dec. 8, 1813. His birthplace, a single-story brick farmhouse, is now a museum. At first Kolping was a shoemaker and some of his cobbler's tools are exhibited. Kolping was 26 when he began his studies for the priesthood, and was ordained in 1845, working first as a chaplain in Wuppertal, 30 miles northeast of Cologne.

"Our purpose," Hubert says, "is to help all young workers, to aid people in the Third World, and to support the aims of the church as a whole, and try to help members be good Christians, good family members, and worthwhile contributors to the community.

"We are also trying to use the international framework of the society to help increase understanding of the peoples and problems of the various nations, and thus we hope to contribute to peace of the future. We encourage our members to visit foreign countries, and the Kolping members there. More of our American members visit here than even from Austria, which is next door.

"Formerly only men were in the society," Hubert says. "Women got into it through the United States. In the Second World War American women entered as members, and afterwards the concept of female participation spread to the other countries. After the war, American women members promoted the sending of CARE packages to Germany."

Every Wednesday morning at 8 o'clock a Mass is celebrated at the altar of Father Kolping's grave for all dead members of the Kolping Society. There are also Masses on the anniversary of Father Kolping's birth, Dec. 8; the day he became a priest, Apr. 13, 1845, and his death, Dec. 4, 1865.

OUR LADY IN THE RUINS

Near the St. Columba parish school in Brueckenstrasse, 100 yards from Kolping Platz, is the Marian shrine of Our Lady in the Ruins. It is a small chapel in which a life-sized statue of the Madonna and Child is venerated. The chapel had been part of St. Columba Church. But the church, and surrounding houses, were bombed out in the Second World War. After the bombing the statue was found in the ruins. Except for some slight damage to the left arm of the Child, the statue was intact. It had been in the chapel since 1450, and has been reinstalled there. Now the chapel is a popular drop-in point for people of Cologne. The chapel continues the tradition of St. Columba's being the oldest parish church in Cologne, built in the 12th century.

TRANSPORTATION: Cologne is on the main north-south rail line. It is served by Cologne/Bonn international airport.

HOTELS: Leading hotels are *Dom, Inter-Continental,* and *Eden. Europa* and *Mondial* are less expensive.

POINTS OF INTEREST: The Benedictine Monastery of Maria Laach is 11 miles west of Andernach, which is between Cologne and Coblenz. The name "Maria Laach" means Mary of the Lake. The monastery is a center of liturgical activity, and is one of the most architecturally imposing abbeys north of the Alps.

AACHEN

Charlemagne, king of the Franks and after A.D. 800 emperor in the West, made Aachen (in French, Aix-la-Chapelle) an international crossroads. In the days of the Roman invasion Aachen was the barracks town of Rome's Sixth Legion. It was Charlemagne's headquarters from 789 until his death in 814. The Aachen skyline is identified by the octagon-shaped dome of the imperial chapel he built. His chapel—thus, the origin of Aachen's name in French, Aix-la-Chapelle—was an international project. Marble and granite came from Rome, Ravenna and Trier; the artisans, from all parts of his wide domain. The tomb of Charlemagne is believed to be under the dome. In the 14th century the chapel of Charlemagne was expanded, making it one of the most sumptuous works of Gothic art in the West. About the same time, Charlemagne's palace was made into the

Town Hall. It has an elaborate imperial room in which coronations used to take place. Approximately 30 emperors were crowned in Aachen. In the cathedral is the imperial chair on which they were enthroned. Seven famous relics are shown periodically in the cathedral. All are associated with the Crucifixion: the dress of Mary, the crown of thorns, and so on.

Water has always lured people to Aachen. The Roman legionnaires used the waters from its mineral springs to line out a network of military baths. The waters are the hottest in Europe, reaching nearly 170 degrees Fahrenheit.

TRANSPORTATION: Aachen is on the main west-east rail line. It is 50 miles west of Cologne.

HOTELS: The *Quellenhof* is one of the leading hotels. The *Berliner Hof* and *Central* are moderately priced.

KEVELAER

Kevelaer, a town of 22,000 inhabitants north of Cologne, lives partly from agriculture but mostly from the manufacture of religious articles and materials. The devotional goods, made in many small ateliers, are sold throughout the world.

"In the seventeenth century," Father Radbert, a thin-haired Benedictine monk, says, "there was no town of Kevelaer, only a small settlement of about three hundred residents. Two main roads crossed a few hundred yards from the settlement, the Rheinstrasse and the Maasstrasse, named after the Rhine and Meuse rivers which flank the north-south highway.

"A large wooden crucifix stood near the crossroads, and it was there that Hendrick Busman, a wandering merchant, used to pray on the way from Weeze to Geldern. At Christmas time in 1641 he heard a voice bidding him to build a chapel near the crucifix. Some weeks later two Luxembourg soldiers came to the man's wife with a pair of small paintings they wanted to sell.

The soldiers happened to be in the area because of the Thirty Years' War. The paintings they had were of the statue of Our Lady, Comforter of the Afflicted, which is in the cathedral in Luxembourg City.

"Hendrick Busman's wife did not buy the paintings because they were too expensive, she thought. That night she had an Apparition in which she saw a chapel and the picture of Our Lady which the soldiers had. On the night of the Apparition, a watchman had noticed the Busman house illuminated in a strange way, and he told Hendrick Busman about it. Busman related the watchman's story to his wife, and she told him about the Apparition. He had not said anything previously about the voice he had heard when he was praying at the crossroads, but now he informed his wife about it.

"Intuitively the woman knew that the soldiers had brought the pictures to an officer of the Luxembourg forces, and she went with her husband to the officer, saying they wanted one of the paintings. Without any fuss he gave them one. They had it mounted on wood and installed in a Carmelite monastery in Geldern, ten kilometers away, while they set about building a chapel at the crossroads. People began coming to pray at the shrine in the Carmelite monastery, and the friars wanted to keep the painting. But the Busmans said the chapel at Kevelaer was finished, and it had to be there. The painting was placed in the chapel on June 1, 1642."

It is a small painting, 3 by 4½ inches, on a copper base, and set in a large frame of gold and silver. Passersby peer at the miraculous image through an opening in the chapel wall. A candle called the Light of Peace shines over a plate held by three doves representing the Marian sanctuaries of Lourdes, Altötting and Kevelaer.

"In 1949," Father Radbert says, "a Light of Peace was illuminated and brought on foot to each of the three shrines. Every Saturday a Peace Mass is celebrated at each shrine."

Originally, Oratorian Fathers administered the shrine. In 1801, during the secularization, the shrine was turned over to priests of the diocese. Father Radbert is assigned to the shrine temporarily.

What about the second painting?

"That's believed to be the one in Natal, South Africa. A missionary group in South Africa when it was establishing missions there in the nineteenth century named each one after a Marian shrine of Europe, including Kevelaer. It was known by tradition that a farm family near Kempen, thirty kilometers from here, had the second image. It was located and brought to the Kevelaer Mission in Africa. So now, the two places are spiritually connected."

Father Radbert says Hendrick Busman's story is not just a web of legend and folklore.

"On February 13, 1647, a little over five years after the event, he appeared in person at the Synod of Venlo, in the Ter Weide Monastery, and related his story in the presence of priests, laymen and doctors. Thus, it could be checked with people who were still alive and in a position to know the facts."

TRANSPORTATION: Kevelaer is near the Dutch border, and is 20 miles from Nijmegen; 60, from Cologne. All trains do not stop at the Kevelaer station.

HOTELS: *Goldener Apfel* is the largest and best. Others are *Gold-und-Silber Schlüssel* and *Weisses Kreuz*.

MUNICH

Bavaria is Catholic and remained so through the Reformation. The name in German for its capital, Munich, is München, or "monks." In olden days it was customary to say *zu den München*, "at the city of the monks." A monk as symbol of Munich is represented in a statue atop the City Hall. Munich is an exuberant,

lively city. There are more than 200 churches. The best
known, and most easily recognizable because of its twin
towers, is the Frauenkirche, Cathedral of Our Lady. It
contains royal tombs and those of bishops, as well.

OUR LADY OF ALTÖTTING

Altötting is the religious center of Bavaria. Each
newly ordained priest of Bavaria makes a pilgrimage to
the shrine of Our Lady of Altötting.

The name Altötting means, more or less, "Old Odo's
town." Duke Odo, in the 8th century, ruled a tribe of
pagan people who had migrated from Bohemia. St.
Rupert, the bishop of Salzburg at the time, traveled
into the region to bring Christianity to Odo and his
people. The duke was impressed by the sincerity of
Rupert who, although a bishop, worked as a missionary,
and he agreed to be baptized. The tradition is that the
baptism took place in the octagon-shaped chapel at the
center of the main square at Altötting.

Rupert had brought a statue of the Madonna with
him on his mission, but no one knows what became of
it. The present statue in the shrine has been there since
around the start of the 14th century. The main pilgrimages began in 1489, and that is the year officially considered as the birthdate of the devotion to Our Lady of
Altötting.

One day in 1489 a 3-year-old Altötting boy wandered away from his home. When his mother located
him, his body was being lifted from the Mörnbach
River. As the distraught mother bent over the motionless form of her son, she heard the church bells from the
chapel in the square. She picked up her child and
rushed with him to the chapel, stretching him before
the statue of the Madonna while she knelt in prayer.
After a few minutes she looked at her son, and saw him
move. He was not dead. Exultantly, she turned again in
prayer toward the statue, this time with words of

thanksgiving. It is said that the happy mother detected a faint smile on the face of the Madonna—the same "Smiling Madonna" that has greeted millions of pilgrims for nearly 5 centuries.

For 25 years Henry Becker has been editor of the *Altöttinger Liebfrauenbote,* "The Altötting Messenger of Our Lady." He is of medium height and getting a bit heavy. His face is wrinkled, perhaps because he smiles a lot and is extremely friendly. He rambles around the room assuredly. The floors are uncarpeted, showing the golden pine wood that matches the walls. Bookcases reach almost to the ceiling at one side of his desk.

"I began in Berlin," he says casually. "A long time ago. I think I am the oldest editor in Germany. I worked on the most famous Catholic newspaper in Berlin till Hitler. He stopped it, and all the Roman Catholic newspapers in Germany, in 1935."

An arcade surrounds the Holy Chapel. Its walls and ceiling—every inch of space—are crammed with paintings telling personal stories of cures and of escapes from injury in accidents, such as a boat sinking in the Danube in 1631 and a train wreck in Belgium in 1954. The Bavarian football team was not injured in the Belgian train wreck, and the members presented the painting as an ex-voto offering.

Men, women and children are circling the chapel, walking through the arcade carrying heavy crosses. The crosses were carried to the shrine by pilgrims, as an offering of penance, petition or thanksgiving, and left in the arcade for the use of others. One cross is legendary. It is a huge oak cross that weighs 100 pounds, and was made by a young carpenter named Franz Stocker who carried it to Altötting in May 1887 from his hometown of Prien, 30 miles away. A load of wood had fallen on him and after several operations he was infected with tetanus. His jaws became firmly closed and his muscles were rigid. Unable to communicate and showing no movement of his body, the man feared he would be considered dead, and buried alive. He made a vow to carry the biggest cross he could make to the shrine if he were saved. An attendant recognized his predicament, massaged his muscles, and he soon responded to treatment.

"There are very many young people among the pilgrims," Henry Becker says. "The young people like to come on foot. We have many foot pilgrimages. Ten years ago a new foot pilgrimage began in a town in the Hallertau region, north of Dachau. That's an area where hops are grown. That first year the crop was bad because of the weather, and the beer production suffered. They came here to plead to Our Lady, walking one hundred kilometers. There were six of them that first year. Last year there were five hundred.

"The oldest foot pilgrimage is from Ober-Pfalz, north of Regensburg. It goes back to 1680. There are always six hundred of them, at least. They are on the road five days."

Do they spend the night in hotels? The question seems to be absurd.

"Not at all. They sleep in barns, out in the fields. They have never missed a year. Even in Hitler times they came. The most dangerous time was in 1945 when the war was being fought around Altötting. There were about ten in the pilgrimage that year. They reached the Inn River, and were stopped by the Americans. An officer said all the bridges had been blown up and a crossing was impossible. 'We have to go to Our Lady,' they insisted, and the officer had a bridge set up for them."

The miraculous statue is above the altar in the original octagon-shaped chapel. The Madonna is standing. She holds the Child in her left arm, and a scepter in the right. The statue is 26 inches tall. Except on Ash Wednesday and Holy Saturday the statue is dressed in rich-looking robes trimmed with gold braid, and laced with pearls and precious stones.

A life-sized solid silver statue of a young boy kneeling in prayer represents the son of Emperor Charles VII, the 18th-century ruler. The child, when 10, had become gravely ill, and his father brought him to the shrine. In thanksgiving, the emperor donated the statue, which is called "The Silver Prince." Not visible is a message of thanksgiving written in his own blood by Duke Maximilian, the leader of the Bavarians in the Thirty Years' War against the Protestants. On his return from his victory at White Mountain, near Prague, in 1620 Maximilian came to Altötting, and said a prayer of thanksgiving. He presented the shrine with a silver case, and it was placed under the tabernacle. Years after his death it was discovered that the case contained the message written in blood. It is still under the tabernacle. The message reads: "I give myself over to you, as your slave, and dedicate my life to you, Blessed Virgin Mary. This handwriting in my blood testifies to this. Maximilian, the greatest of sinners."

"The large lay people's group here," the editor says, "is the Marianische Männer Kongregation, the Men's Marian Society. There are sixteen thousand members, all men, from Altötting and the surrounding area. All are farmers."

Across the centuries the shrine has been under the care of most of the major religious orders. In the secularization campaign of 1803, when religious orders were expelled and dispersed, the Capuchin friars of Germany were sent to Altötting. The aim was to force the death of the Order. The friars were permitted only to say Mass. They could not perform any other religious activity.

"No, we haven't died," Father Frans says. Even with the beard that Capuchins in Europe still wear, the amusement on the friar's face is evident. He was born in the Sudetenland in 1935 and lived out the war there until, at the age of eleven, he was expelled with his family and the other Sudeten Deutsch.

A saint has come from the ranks of the Capuchin friars at Altötting—Brother Conrad, long the door-keeper at the cloister. Each morning for 41 years Brother Conrad served the 5 o'clock Mass in the Holy Chapel. The second-floor cloister room which was Brother Conrad's cell is recognizable from the street. A box of red geraniums is on the windowsill.

In a corner of the cloister is St. Peter's Chapel, known too as "The Tilly Chapel," for the head of Duke Maximilian's army in the Thirty Years' War. A small section of Marshal Tilly's coffin is covered with glass. That was Napoleon's doing. When he was at Altötting in 1805, he wanted to see the remains of the 17th-century soldier.

The treasury room in the parish church contains a 3-foot-high Golden Horse, created in Paris in 1392. The art object is of solid gold, coated with delicate enamel work and dotted with jewels. It shows King Charles VI of France kneeling before the Madonna while a servant holds his royal crown, and an equerry reins his horse. The boots on the equerry are of two different colors—a custom in ancient Burgundy.

"Yes, that's a scratch you see," Father Frans says. "Napoleon wanted to make sure there was gold underneath the enamel."

Another cabinet is filled with hundreds of rosaries. Some are centuries old. The friar believes it is the largest collection of rosary beads in the world.

He points to a tiny Madonna statue, no more than a foot high. It was used by St. Peter Canisius when he visited the shrine in 1571 with a group of pilgrims headed by Count Fugger of Augsburg, a member of the family of medieval bankers. The lady's maid of Countess Fugger had claimed to be possessed by an evil spirit which said it would free her only if she made a pilgrimage to Altötting. Canisius, a former General of the Jesuits, blessed the woman with the statue, and a short time afterward she said the demon had vanished.

Canisius traveled much in Germany in these years, marshaling the Counter-Reformation forces. At Cologne he established the first house of the Jesuits in Germany.

TRANSPORTATION: Altötting is 60 miles east of Munich. Several trains a day from Munich.

HOTELS: Moderate-priced hotels include *Wienerwald, Twelve Apostles* and *Altöttingerhof.*

PLACES OF INTEREST: The Benedictine monastery founded in A.D. 731 at Niederalteich. Long before the Second Vatican Council it was noted for its ecumenical work with Protestants and Orthodox. It has both Latin and Oriental rite chapels.

DACHAU

Young people, particularly Americans, journey to Dachau, a dozen miles northwest of Munich, to reflect and meditate at this place where so many people were imprisoned, tortured and killed because of their religion—not centuries ago, but recent enough to be remembered by relatives, friends and total strangers.

"Never Again" is inscribed in immense letters—like a shout—on the memorial at the burial place of the *Unknown Concentration Camper.* A mesh of barbed wire bespeaks one long tale of ferocity.

Protestants and Catholics have built houses of prayer on the emplacement of what was the Nazi concentration camp that was already known to Americans, and others, long before the entry of the United States into the Second World War.

In 1964 a community of Catholic Carmelite nuns established a cloister and chapel at the Dachau campsite. The community started with six Sisters, and has grown to a score.

Before the establishment of the Carmelite cloister Bishop Johannes Neuhausler, a prisoner at Dachau during Nazi times, built a small memorial Chapel of the Agony of Jesus Christ in connection with the Eucha-

ristic Congress in Munich in June 1960. Two years later
Mother Maria-Theresa asked Cardinal Julius Döpfner,
the archbishop of Munich, if she could be given two old
barracks for herself and a few Carmelites so that they
might settle at Dachau. She and the other nuns wanted
to do penance for the crimes of Dachau, and pray for
the reconciliation of people. The cardinal said there
should be a new building, and a fund-raising drive was
launched in which 3½ million marks was collected
from small and large benefactors.

At the time of the Nazi *putsch* in the Munich beer
hall in 1933, Bishop Neuhausler was at the cathedral.
He was 45.

"On the first day after the beginning of Hitler's government," he says, "Cardinal John Faulhaber said to
me: 'We will have a very difficult battle with Hitler,
and for this reason it is very important that one person
alone be assigned to gather information about the
National Socialists, and to pass on my instructions to
the priests of the diocese.'"

Bishop Neuhausler was given the assignment.

"This started in 1933, and went on till 1941. Every
year if possible I went to the Holy Father, and gave
him personal information, and sent him every second
week a letter and documents."

He was arrested in 1941.

"I was imprisoned ten days in Munich, then brought
to Berlin, and was kept in a hard solitary cell for three
months with little food, and difficult interrogations.
Then I was taken to the Saxen-Hausen concentration
camp for two months, and then to Dachau as a 'special
prisoner' together with Pastor Niemoeller and another
priest from this diocese named Höck. I believe the
reason I am living is that I did not know why my very
dangerous situation was all at once changed.

"Ten years after my liberation I got the information
from the Protestant *probst*, Dr. Asmussen, in Schleswig-

Holstein. He came to me, and one of his questions was: 'Do you know why you were brought together with Niemoeller to Dachau?' I can give you the reason. In 1941 there was a rumor that Pastor Niemoeller had an inclination to become a Catholic, and the Gestapo said that would be good for Hitler because in this case all the reputation of Niemoeller in the Protestant world would end—if an important man like him became a Catholic. So the Gestapo decided to help Niemoeller become a Catholic, and they put him with two Catholic priests, you and the other one. That's why you were at Dachau.' "

Bishop Neuhausler pauses reflectively.

"It is true we [he and the other priest] had a very good connection with Pastor Niemoeller. We read every day the Holy Bible together. But we did not speak about differences in the Catholic and Protestant churches. We behaved as Christians together."

In the Catholic chapel attached to the Carmelite cloister is a Madonna statue that had been in the priests' quarters at the concentration camp. A priest comes from Munich to say Mass in the chapel daily.

A former inmate of Dachau, Prisoner No. 26661, lives at the concentration campsite. He is Evangelical Minister Christian Reger. He has been living there since his wife died in August 1970. He is the custodian of the Lutheran chapel, a few dozen yards from the Carmelite cloister, and holds services there for visitors. The Protestant memorial was built in 1965.

Minister Reger was first arrested in 1934. He had spoken out against prejudice from his pulpit in a village in East Germany. Twice in 1937 he was again arrested on the same charge of preaching that prejudice was against the law of God. In 1941 he was put in Dachau, and remained there four years.

"I was betrayed by my organist," he says. "He played the organ in the church with the left hand, and wrote letters to the Gestapo with the other. Sixty to seventy percent of the people were betrayed by German elementary schoolteachers. On the one hand, there is the political German legend of enthusiasm, and on the other, personal ambition—and these two together made a big fire, and had many victims."

He smiles when he recalls the words of a young Gestapo officer just before the war ended:

"Even if you return alive, Europe will have no need of churches any more."

TRANSPORTATION: Direct train service from Munich.

OBERAMMERGAU

A plague that ravaged Europe in 1633 made the residents of the Bavarian town of Oberammergau the best-known amateur actors in the world. When the plague reached the alpine town south of Munich the burgomaster and notables of the community gathered in the village church and solemnly promised to present the Passion of Christ in dramatic form regularly if the people were spared. Deaths from the plague ended, and each 10 years since, the Passion Play has been staged, with villagers playing all the roles. The first year there was only one performance and the village church was large enough. At the most recent presentation in 1970, nearly a half million persons were present at about 100 performances. Visitors enjoy meeting shopkeepers, hotel owners, restaurant waiters and other townspeople who have been identified with a particular Biblical personage because of their roles in the Passion Play.

TRANSPORTATION: Oberammergau, south of Munich, is reached by rail.

HOTELS: The main hotels are the *Wittelsbach* and *Alois Lang*. *Friedenhöhe* and *Turmwirt* are moderately priced.

CONSTANCE

In 1414 Emperor Sigismund arranged for the convocation of the strangest General Council in the history of the Catholic Church. Along with 185 bishops, several hundred theologians, nearly 20,000 ecclesiastics of various ranks and missions, princes, public authorities of all kinds—close to 100,000 people in all—assembled at this town on the lake of the same name. The Council Fathers had to act on a schism splitting the church over who was its head, the successor of the apostle Peter. Three men claimed the Papacy.

The emperor took another action which, while seeming at the time to be a matter of routine, resulted in having profound effect on the church. Sigismund issued a safe-conduct guarantee to Jan Hus, who had been ordained as a Catholic priest, to come to Constance and explain his views which already had caused him to be excommunicated several times. Hus was born in Husinec in Bohemia in 1371, taught at Prague University in 1396, and after ordination in 1402 was appointed a preacher at the Bethlehem Chapel, the focal point of the Czech reform movement. The teachings of John Wycliffe, the English religious reformer of the 14th century, had filtered to Prague and some, but not all, were accepted by Hus. The archbishop prohibited Hus from further preaching and, when the order was rejected, excommunicated him. Hus was summoned to Rome and when he did not appear was excommunicated once more.

Reassured by the safe-conduct promise of Emperor Sigismund, Hus set out for the Council of Constance.

Hus arrived in Constance on Nov. 3, 1414, and found accommodations on the second floor of the house of a baker's widow, Fides Pfisterin. It is a three-story narrow building finished in gray stucco, and with two

windows at each floor. On the façade is a relief of his
head—capped, bearded—and an inscription in Czech
and German identifying him as "The Bohemian Reformer." About the time of the formation of the republic
of Czechoslovakia a half century ago, a Czech man
bought the house. In his will he gave the property to
the Konstanzer Hus Gesellschaft und Verein, a nonprofit organization of Prague. It has been made into a
museum.

From the house of the baker's widow on Nov. 28,
1414 Hus was led to prison, accused of supporting
Wycliffe.

His prison was a room in the tower of Constance's
Dominican friary. The monastery had been founded in
1235 and was suppressed at the start of the 19th century in the secularization of Napoleonic times. Some
years before that, in 1785, a family of French religious
refugees named Macaire de l'Or arrived in Constance
and set up a calico-printing atelier. A later generation
acquired the former Dominican cloister and on July 8,
1838 Count (Graf) Ferdinand von Zeppelin was born
there. Graf Zeppelin, a pioneer of air travel, turned the
old cloister into a hotel in 1875. It is named the *Insel*
(Island) because it rests on an island-like sliver of land
a few dozen yards from the Constance shore. Hus was
imprisoned in what is now Room 108. A false ceiling
has been built, and except for the roundness of the
room itself there is no indication of a tower. It appears
to be a cosy neatly appointed sitting-room, about 8 feet
in diameter, with a small table and some chairs, a setting ideal for breakfast or an evening drink as one
watches the gulls and ducks on the lake. Three small
windows have been added. In Hus's time it was win-
dowless. The bedroom, separating the round room from
the corridor, is tremendous in size.

The main street bordering the former monastery is
Konzil (Council) Strasse. The building in which the
Council of Constance met in 1414 faces the lake about

200 yards from the Hotel Insel. A pathway, the Suso-steig, connects the two historic structures through a park. The pathway is named after Heinrich Suso, a 14th-century mystic and Dominican friar who lived in the old monastery. He is known as the last *geistlichen minnesänger*, a singer of spiritual love.

A high sloping roof of tiles crowns the Council building. The two lower floors are finished in gray stucco, but stone buttresses point to age. The upper floor is paneled in wood, and there are small dormer extensions. The building is now the property of the municipality, and is leased as a restaurant. Inevitably, it is called the Konzil Restaurant.

Between June 5 and 8, 1415 the crucial interrogations of Jan Hus took place in the Council building. He was condemned to death as a follower of Wycliffe, and burned at the stake on July 6, 1415. He was burned "before the door of the city," but no one knows where. There is no grave.

The American Sokol Organization, on July 13, 1962, installed a plaque to Jan Hus on the main floor of the house where he had lived in Constance. It says: "The flames that consumed his body released a spirit, a paragon of virtue for humanity to emulate."

Reinhard, a German customs agent, speculates that Hus might have been killed at or near the spot where a friend and disciple, Hieronymus of Prague, was burned on May 30, 1416. The site is near a crossing point into Switzerland, and just a few hundred yards from the house of the baker's widow where Jan Hus lived.

The customs man, Reinhard, is on his way to work. He is about 50 and burly. He wears a leather coat and dark shirt. He has no hat.

"When I was visiting the Palazzo Vecchio in Florence on my vacation last year," he says, "I saw a coat-of-arms of the city of Constance. That was very interesting."

The Evangelical church of the parish is a few blocks

from the Hus Museum. The parish is named after Luther and Ambrosius Blarer. Blarer, once a monk in the former Benedictine monastery at Alpirsbach in the Black Forest, had been a sympathizer of Luther's.

"On July 6 each year, the anniversary of the burning of Jan Hus," the pastor of the church says, "many Czechs come here—Communists and anti-Communists. The Communists say: 'He belongs to us.' The refugees say: 'He belongs to us. You are Communists. We are democrats.' This makes it difficult for the Germans. They are told to stay out of the argument. 'He doesn't belong to you Germans,' the Czechs say. 'You burned him.'"

The pastor is told that a woman in Bonn remarked that the burning of Jan Hus might be one reason why there has always been tension between Czechs and Germans. He is not sure about that.

"I and my family were in Prague for eight days last year, and we were well received."

TRANSPORTATION: A direct car on German express trains serves Constance.

HOTELS: *Insel* is the finest. *Seeblick, Hecht* and *Barbarossa* are comfortable, medium-priced.

WORMS

Martin Luther made his first move in 1517 when he published his Ninety-Five Theses describing church practices he felt needed reforming. But the city of Worms became the birthplace of the Reformation four years later when, before a Diet convoked here by Emperor Charles V, Luther defiantly refused to recant.

Worms is an old city of the Celts, of the Romans, of the Vandals, of the Huns, of the Franks, and eventually of the Hapsburgs. It was a Hapsburg emperor who called the Diet of Worms in 1521. Bishop Victor presided over the church in Worms in A.D. 346. Europe's oldest Jewish cemetery and Germany's oldest synagogue are in Worms. Like Heidelberg and some other cities, Worms was heavily damaged by the French in 1689. The bishop's palace, where the Diet took place, was damaged at that time, and finished off in the French Revolution a century later. There is a small park now where the palace had been alongside the cathedral, and a memorial tablet which says: "Here before Kaiser and Reich stood Martin Luther."

Among the old pieces of sculpture in the cathedral is a representation of "Daniel in the Lions' Den." The Burgundians occupied Worms for a time, and they liked to honor the prophet Daniel in their churches.

THE LUTHER MONUMENT

Martin Luther is honored, and remembered, in an immense monument in the Schloss Garden, a parklike area along the Luther Ring, the main downtown thoroughfare. It is in the form of a square, with each side a bit more than 40 feet long. The monument presents Luther along with religious and political figures of the Reformation.

Luther himself towers above everyone in an 11¼-foot statue on a pedestal at the center of the monument. He is shown dressed as a preacher, holding the Bible in his left hand and resting his right fist across it. Inscribed in large letters on the face of the granite pedestal are the words known by millions: *Hier stehe ich, Ich Kann Nicht Anders. Gott Helfe Mir. Amen.* (Here I stand. I cannot do otherwise. God Help Me. Amen.)

Seated at his feet are figures of Reform: Girolamo Savonarola, the prior of the Dominican Monastery of San Marco in Florence who was burned as a heretic in 1498; Jan Hus, the Czech preacher burned in Constance in 1415; Peter Waldo, the 12th-century Lyons merchant who founded the Waldenses, a group that was to practice and preach poverty; John Wycliffe, English precursor of the Reformation.

Along the base of the pedestal are reliefs portraying highlights of Luther's life: his appearance before Emperor Charles V on Apr. 17–18, 1521 at the Diet of Worms; the traditional affixing of the Ninety-Five Theses on the door of the Wittenberg Castle church on Oct. 31, 1517; his distribution of Communion in both species; his marriage; his Bible translation and preaching.

Framing the main statuary group are statues of the Peace of Augsburg, a majestic handsome woman holding a large palm leaf, who represents the Protestants presenting their Confession of Faith to Emperor Charles V in Augsburg on June 25, 1530; the Protesting Speyer, a woman symbolizing the protest made by people—subsequently called *Protestants*—at the Diet of Speyer in 1529 against an imperial council decision forbidding the continuation of the Reformation work; Magdeburg in Mourning, a sad-faced woman reflecting the sorrow for the looting and sacking of Magdeburg in 1631 by Marshal Tilly (see Index) of the Catholic army in the Thirty Years' War. Edging the base of the outer frame of statues are the coats-of-arms of more than two dozen cities, from Riga to Leipzig, which had a role in the Reformation.

THE JEWISH CEMETERY

The Jewish cemetery, a few hundred yards from the site of the Palace of the Diet of Worms, was closed in 1937 because no room was left for any more graves. A section at the side of the Christian cemetery was established, and Jewish burials have been there since. It is the oldest Jewish cemetery in Europe. The gravestones, shaped like miniature windows from Gothic cathedrals, slant backward, weighted down by time and weather. The caretaker lives in a two-story house near the en-

trance and the family's two little girls, Esther and
Sabine Hartenbach, are usually somewhere near. So is
their tan-striped cat. Eleven-year-old Esther says her
mother usually makes the guided tour of the cemetery,
but she can give it herself, too. Esther, a year older than
Sabine, is blonde and likes to practice the English she
learns in school. "But talk slowly," she says.

THE SYNAGOGUE

Christian Barth, a hefty medium-tall man in his early
40s, is an electrician by profession. It is his wife who is
the caretaker of the synagogue. But he helps her when
he is not off somewhere on a job. They live in an old
building on the narrow Judengasse, the Street of the
Jews. The synagogue is a few dozen feet away, set back
in a small U-shaped square called Hintere Judengasse,
Behind the Street of the Jews. It is a two-story building
of large red stones, and topped by a pyramid roof of
slate shingles. Often in the early 1900s it was burned
and damaged—the last time in 1938. It was rebuilt
along the old lines, and reconsecrated on Dec. 3, 1961.
It is the oldest synagogue in Germany.

"The men's synagogue was built first in 1034," Christian Barth says. "In the olden days, women either used
the upper floor of a synagogue or, as in Worms, did not
go to the synagogue unless they had their own. In 1213
the women's synagogue was built next to the men's.
Between the two synagogues was a wall with a little
window, and a woman stood at the window and translated what the rabbi said. The women talked the
language of the area, or Yiddish—but not Hebrew.
Only the men spoke Hebrew. The women stood at this
time, too. There were no benches in the synagogue for
them. In the eighteenth century this was changed, and
benches were added for the women."

He talks about the holy man and scholar Rabbi
Salomon ben Isaac, who is known as Raschi. It is an

acronym, Christian Barth explains—Ra, for rabbi; sch, for Salomon; i, for Isaac.

"Raschi was a teacher and a Torah commentator in the eleventh century. He was born in Troyes [France] in 1040, and died there in 1105. He taught in the school here. He was a great commentator, and his commentaries were used in synagogues around the world—and still are. In 1624 a small *yeshiva* [school] was added to the synagogue and named in his honor, Raschi Jeschiba."

And the Raschi Door down the street?

"No. The door was part of the old wall of the city that was built by the Romans in A.D. 240. People later named it after Raschi out of love. That's all."

There are services at the synagogue on high holidays, but not otherwise.

"You need ten men for the services," the electrician says. "Before 1930, there were three thousand Jews in Worms—ten percent of the population. Now there are three Jewish families here, and they belong to the community of Mainz, fifty kilometers away. Since you should not drive on the sabbath, it is better for three families from here to drive to Mainz than for the one hundred families in Mainz to drive here."

LIEBFRAUEN CHURCH

The Church of Our Lady (Liebfrauenkirche) has been a pilgrimage site since olden times. It is a mile from the Luther monument. Gravestones with Christian symbols of the 5th and 6th centuries have been found in the area. From the old days, wine produced from the neighboring vineyards was associated with the Church's name—Liebfraumilch. The church owned some of the vineyards. Acres of vineyards still reach to the door of the church.

TRANSPORTATION: Worms is 40 miles southwest of Frankfurt. Fast train service from Frankfurt.

HOTELS: *Dom* is the leading hotel. *Europäischer Hof,*
Central and *Malepartus* are less expensive.

FRANKFURT

Berlin was the prewar capital of Germany; Bonn was
chosen as the capital of postwar West Germany; and
Frankfurt, bustling and booming, is the unofficial capital. During the time of Luther, Frankfurt became a
major center of the Reformation. Goethe was born here,
and his house is now a museum. Gutenberg was born in
Mainz. Rhein-Main airport was the focus of the American Airlift which broke the Berlin Blockade a little over
a quarter of a century ago.

CANAAN

Fifteen miles south of Frankfurt along Bundesstrasse
3, the main highway, a remarkable group of Protestant
women have established a remarkable center of prayer
and spiritual retreat. They call it *Canaan,* giving their
home on the outskirts of Darmstadt the biblical name of
the Promised Land of the Israelites. A banner at the
entrance proclaims: "Built solely with the help of the
Lord who made heaven and earth—through faith in
Jesus Christ." The women, members of the Marian
Sisterhood of Nuns (Marienschwesternschaft) started
in 1948 with 30 marks, about $10. Today, they often
have less than that in their cash box. But they never ask
for money, or conduct fund-raising drives. They are
convinced that God will always answer their prayers.
The Sisters have built a 1,100-seat chapel where they
present their own religious plays; accommodations for
people who come to make 10-day retreats and a con-
valescent home named for St. Francis of Assisi, where
aged and invalid people live as a family.

The community developed from Bible lessons which
a young university woman began giving in the attic of

her parents' home in Darmstadt, with the help of a friend, in 1935. The two women kept the Bible classes going during the war. On Sept. 11, 1944 Darmstadt was almost wiped out in an air raid that killed 12,000 people and left 70,000 homeless. The family house with the attic classroom had been damaged, too. The two teachers—later to be known as Mother Basilea and Mother Martyria—thought the Bible classes were over. But the former students began returning, one by one.

About 100 nuns are in the community. They are totally ecumenical in spirit and action. When they pray for the president of the Protestant churches of Germany, they pray also for the Catholic archbishop-primate. They pray for success for the Protestant charity organization, and for the Catholic Caritas. Some guest rooms in the retreat-house are named after Protestant figures, such as John Hyde and George Mueller; others carry Catholic names: the Curé of Ars, Teresa of Avila. Each Friday evening, at the start of the Jewish sabbath, they light a 7-branched candlestick.

"Lord," they pray, "let the Sabbath of Israel come, the Sabbath of the World and of all peoples, the Sabbath of the Last Day when you, God, will be all in all, and the habitation of God will be with men."

TRANSPORTATION: Frankfurt receives flights from New York, Chicago, Boston, Philadelphia and Los Angeles.

HOTELS: *Inter-Continental* and *Frankfurter Hof* are among the top hotels. *Esso* and *Monopol* are moderately priced.

6

Great Britain

ENGLAND WAS a pre-Christian country. Pagan tribes that spoke Celtic lived in what is now England 3,000 years ago. Ten centuries later the Romans began a rule that lasted for almost 500 years, becoming Christians in the meantime.

Today, England is a post-Christian nation, a land of former believers. At least, that is what Cardinal John C. Heenan, the Catholic archbishop of Westminster, believes. He says that few people are members of any church. He makes the point, however, that the English are not atheists, are not immoral and are not irreligious.

The "nationalization" of Henry VIII, which happened to coincide with the Reformation, snuffed out the Catholic Church formally, and it was not until 1850, 3 centuries later, that its hierarchy was restored.

In Scotland, things were a bit different. For 3 centuries after the Reformation no Catholic diocese existed there. It was only in 1880 that the Catholic hierarchy was restored, and that bishops were appointed rather than episcopal vicars. But unlike in England, the people of Scotland practice the religion brought to them by the Reformation. Their Reformer was John Knox of

Edinburgh. The Scots were determined that the new religion established in England by Henry VIII should not encroach upon their right to freedom of conscience, and they exacted covenants that were respected. Their Presbyterianism took hold, too. In the Hebrides and other parts of the north, the sabbath is austerely sacred. Everything shuts down after church on Sunday. The people literally draw the blinds on their windows, and pass the day in prayer and contemplation. While Presbyterianism prevailed in Scotland, a number of denominations of Protestantism proliferated in England, including Methodism, founded by John Wesley.

Christianity came to England about the same time that the Roman emperor, Constantine the Great, decided to become baptized. There was an archbishop of Canterbury, Restitus, in A.D. 314. Not long after this, Germanic tribes, the Angles and the Saxons, succeeded the Romans, giving England its name and making the term Anglo-Saxon a descriptive part of the evolving English language. The Vikings marauded across the land in the 8th century, pillaging and subjugating, and in 1066 the great Norman Conquest brought the Continent to England. In the 12th century, England literally made Europe a part of it by conquering Normandy.

The 12th century was crucial. The British empire was in its beginnings, reaching from Scotland to the Pyrenees. Henry II, husband of the fabulous Eleanor of Aquitaine, came to the throne in 1154. At Canterbury, his friend and appointee Thomas Becket was the archbishop. Ten years into the rule of Henry II, the Constitution of Clarendon brought to the fore a sharply familiar point of controversy—whether the clergy should be tried in ecclesiastical or royal courts. Becket's objections were so deep, so vociferous that he went into exile. On his return he sought to patch up this conflict about fundamentals in the relations between church and state. He was unsuccessful, and on Dec. 29, 1170 he was murdered in his cathedral at Canterbury by assassins sent by his king. He told them: "I am ready to die for my Lord, that in my blood the church may obtain peace and liberty."

Becket's words prior to his death fired the spirits of people across Europe. Physical courage they had known about. It was the example of spiritual courage that heartened them—a high-ranking figure in the church who had refused automatic, total subservience to a monarch. His burial place in the cathedral at Canterbury became a goal of pilgrims from all Europe. This lasted for 4 centuries until brutally halted by Henry VIII after he had ordered the hanging of his own lord chancellor, Sir Thomas More, on another point of principle dividing king and church. Henry VIII had the shrine in Canterbury Cathedral destroyed and interdicted all pilgrimages with a royal proclamation of Nov. 6, 1538.

The reign of Henry VIII split the church into its worst schism since the 11th century, again with the spiritual supremacy of the bishop of Rome as the issue.

Henry VIII's personal problem—which escalated into a vital one for the church—was his marriage to Catherine of Aragon. He said the marriage offended the divine law because she was his brother's widow. But other points were troubling him: he wanted a male heir to the throne, and he wanted to marry Anne Boleyn. Pope Clement VII did not oblige with a dispensation. The Parliament, starting in 1529, legislated acts to correct purported abuses in the church, and individual churchmen were pressured and harassed. Soon Sir Thomas More, who as Lord Chancellor continued to serve Mass at his parish church, was brought into the controversy.

After almost 4 years of waiting for definitive word from Rome on his divorce, Henry VIII in February 1531 decided that the Pope had too much authority over the church in England. He called upon the clergy to recognize him as their supreme head, and on May

15, 1532 they made a formal submission. More resigned
as lord chancellor the following day. In this year, too,
Thomas Cranmer took office as the new archbishop of
Canterbury, and at once devoted himself to Henry's
cause. The following May, with Rome still not heard
from, Archbishop Cranmer annulled the marriage between Henry VIII and Catherine of Aragon, and 5 days
later declared valid the marriage that had taken place
between the king and Anne Boleyn 4 months earlier.
More's sole sign of protest was his refusal to attend the
coronation of Anne Boleyn on June 1.

Various charges, from bribery to treason, were soon
brought against More. He and Bishop John Fisher were
charged with not having informed Henry VIII of
prophesies made against him by Elizabeth Barton,
known as the Nun of Kent.

In 1534 Parliament gave the monarch the title Supreme Head on Earth of the Church of England, establishing thus the Church of England by statute, and
proceeding to enact a Succession Act which sought to
give reason to the abandonment of Catherine and the
denial of papal authority in the matter. A few days later
word arrived from Rome that the Pope considered the
marriage with Catherine valid. Members of Parliament
were called upon to take an oath accepting the succession provided for in the Act, and commissioners traveled through the country administering a similar oath to
the people.

Bishop John Fisher and Sir Thomas More were called
to Lambeth Palace (residence of the archbishop of
Canterbury) on Apr. 13, 1534 to take the oath. They
refused. They were given time to think it over. Finally
Bishop Fisher spoke up. He pronounced himself against
the new title of the king as Supreme Head on Earth of
the Church of England, and was condemned to death
on June 17, 1535. More remained silent until after
being found guilty at a trial on July 1. Anne Boleyn's
father, uncle and brother were among his judges. When

the guilty verdict was in, More declared that for a secular prince to claim supremacy would deny divinely given authority of the Pope and threaten the church's unity. "No more might this realm of England refuse obedience to the Holy See of Rome than might the child refuse obedience to his own natural father," he declared. He was taken to Tower Hill on July 6, 1535 to be hanged. His last words were:

"I die in and for the faith of the Holy Catholic Church—the king's good servant, but God's first."

From 1535 to 1544, under Henry VIII, 35 members of the clergy were killed, and 5 laymen (including 1 woman).

The new lord chancellor, Thomas Cromwell, busied himself with the suppression of monasteries and convents, and in transferring the property to the king who in turn sold some, and made grants of others to noble families to reward old friends and win new ones. Cromwell's reward was some of the confiscated land, and the title of Earl of Essex in 1540. Later that year he was executed for treason on Tower Hill.

At the time of Parliament's swift passage of the Suppression Act of 1536 more than 10,000 monks, friars, canons and nuns were living in over 800 monasteries, convents and cloisters in England and Wales. Four years later, all these religious buildings had been closed in stages—the technical term was "dissolution" —and the occupants were dispersed.

Jane Seymour succeeded Anne Boleyn, but she died giving birth to the son that Henry had wanted. Then came Anne of Cleves, Catherine Howard and Catherine Parr. Catherine Parr survived him.

The spiritual-supremacy issue had been the cause for charges of treason and death under Henry VIII. Under Queen Elizabeth I, his daughter, two more treasonable offenses were added. In 1585, after Elizabeth had been reigning 27 years, Parliament made it high treason for a priest ordained by the authority of Rome to be in

England. Laymen who gave shelter to a priest were punishable by death. Between 1570 and 1603, in the reign of Elizabeth I, 188 persons were put to death because of their religion—125 members of the clergy, 63 laymen. In the 17th century, during the reigns of James I and Charles II, there were 74 other deaths.

Protestants were martyred, too. In the 16th century, 41 people of Kent were burned at the stake in Canterbury during the reign of the Catholic Mary, Queen of Scots.

The renaissance of Catholicism came with the arrival of Irish immigrants in the 19th century, young people headed for jobs in the coal mines of the north. Literally, in the past century, the Irish have built Britain's highways, steel mills and nuclear power stations, and have rebuilt its Catholic Church. The busiest church in Britain is the Church of the Sacred Heart in London's predominantly Irish Kilburn district. Sunday Mass attendance is 80 percent.

JOHN KNOX OF SCOTLAND

There has been some controversy about the exact date, and even the place, of John Knox's birth. But no one questions the deep influence he had on the social, political, educational and religious life of Scotland in the 16th century. He more than any other person led his fellow Scots through the Reformation of 1560. He studied at Glasgow and St. Andrews universities, and was ordained as a Catholic priest. He grew up at a time when the teachings of Luther were being heard, when men were being branded as heretics and burned at the stake—like Patrick Hamilton, in 1528, the first Protestant martyr; when others fled for their lives into exile, like George Wishart. Knox himself, as he turned toward the Reformed faith in 1542 and was declared a heretic, fled first to southern Scotland and then to the castle at St. Andrews which members of the new religion captured in 1547. Catholic French forces arriving by sea helped the Scottish government seize the castle. Knox and the other Protestants were taken prisoners. Treated as a heretic he was kept captive for 19 months, assigned to manning the oars on French galleys. After being freed he went to England, and Archbishop Cranmer of Canterbury assigned him to preach at Berwick. Later he became chaplain to King Edward VI at Westminster.

When Mary Tudor came to the throne, Knox headed for the religious safety of the Continent, meeting up with Calvin in Geneva. He served as minister to religious refugee congregations in Dieppe (France), Geneva and Frankfurt, returning to Scotland in 1559 as the Reformation movement reached its climatic turning point. With five others he drafted the Confession of Faith of 1560 which Parliament accepted. He was made the minister of Edinburgh, and St. Giles was his church. In the late summer of 1572 he went into the pulpit at St. Giles to condemn the Massacre of St. Bartholomew's Day. He died on Nov. 24, exactly three months later. At the burial of John Knox in the churchyard of St. Giles on Nov. 26, 1572 the Earl of Morton, the newly elected Regent of Scotland, declared: "There lies he, who never feared the face of man."

HADDINGTON

"On the four hundredth anniversary of John Knox's death in 1972," Don Ross says, "the local people of Haddington had a memorial service in St. Mary's Church. But there was no wreath-laying. The people did not know where to go to put a wreath at his birthplace."

Don Ross, an amiable, helpful man in his 30s, is an information officer for the Church of Scotland.

Haddington is a modern *burgh,* 17 miles directly east of Edinburgh along the East Lothian coast on the A-1

Highway. It is a lovely market town. John Knox was born here about 1514, and knew St. Mary's Church as a boy. It was built as a parish *kirk* about 1134 as a replacement for an older one. In the fighting involving English, French and Scots in the middle of the 16th century the church was damaged, and Haddington was an English garrison town for 18 months. A few miles from Haddington, Catholic Cistercian monks have just completed a new abbey, 20 years a-building. Don Ross says the monks are "very hospitable."

"This is an interesting area to visit," Don Ross points out. "The Duchess of Hamilton, or Lady Lothian as she is also called, is still in residence. Her husband, the Duke of Hamilton, is the keeper of Holyrood Palace. St. Mary's Church is on the remains of a medieval community known as the Lamp of Lothian, and the term is being revived by the duchess in a great arts project."

TRANSPORTATION: It is a 30-minute bus ride from Edinburgh.

ST. ANDREWS

St. Andrews is essentially a university town—the university where Knox came under the influence of Wishart. There is no industry, and this makes it the finest university town in Scotland. The students wear red robes—the first year, around the shoulders; the second year, a little further back on the shoulders; and so on, so that one can tell what year a student is in. St. Andrews Cathedral had been an Augustinian monastery founded in A.D. 1144, and was one of the largest churches in Britain. There are early Christian stones, medieval relics, and a sarcophagus of the 9th or 10th century said to be unequaled in Western Europe.

TRANSPORTATION: St. Andrews is 50 miles from Edinburgh. Trains to Dundee or Leuchars; then, bus.

EDINBURGH

It is a stunningly beautiful city, in part because of its architecture; partly, too, for its natural situation. It was built originally atop a plateau creased in prehistoric times by a glacier, and streets and alleys with long stairways stream like rivulets along the sides to the New Town built in the 18th century. Most of the city's ancient history is in the Royal Mile, extending from the castle to the Palace of Holyrood. The oldest religious building in Scotland is St. Margaret's Chapel atop Castle Rock. It was built in 1076 by the Saxon Queen Margaret, great-niece of the king-saint Edward the Confessor. Queen Margaret was known as a pious woman. One of the streets in the Royal Mile is Canongate. It should be spelled Canon*gait* because its name comes from the walk the canons of Holyrood Abbey used to take to the castle. The Abbey of Holyrood, now a magnificent ruin, was established in 1128 by David I, king of Scots.

JOHN KNOX'S HOUSE

John Knox was named the minister of Edinburgh in July 1559, taking over the assignment in the following spring. The house identified as his residence is halfway along the Royal Mile and bulges into the street, involuntarily causing the notice of pedestrians and motorists alike. It is a stone dwelling of several floors, with timbered galleries, and is the oldest house of its type in Edinburgh. An inscription over the ground-floor window says: "Lufe God abufe al and yi nyghbour as yi self." The house is now a museum with many items associated with John Knox. Across the street from John Knox's house is a Museum of Childhood, with toys, books, costumes and other articles intended to tell historically about children. An experimental theater, the

Netherbow, is alongside the house. The Nether Port Bow had been the eastern entrance to Edinburgh, and the heads of criminals would be impaled on spikes above the gateway. St. Giles's Cathedral can be seen from the windows of the house where the Reformer lived.

St. Giles's Cathedral

On the right side of the cathedral exterior is a bearded statue of John Knox, with an inscription stating that south of the spot had been the St. Giles *kirkyard* where John Knox was buried. The old churchyard has been transferred into a paved square in front of Parliament House where the Scots Parliament met from 1639 until the Union of Scotland and England in 1707. Even during the physical transformations in the area a stone had marked the place in the ground where Knox had been buried. In recent times the stone was brought inside the cathedral, and the site of Knox's grave is now indicated by a yellow square.

Inside the cathedral a bulky balding man in a rumpled suit sits comfortably at the end of a long table in an office just off the Albany aisle. He identifies himself as an officer of the church, and talks like its historian.

"This has been Catholic once: Anglican twice; three times, Presbyterian," he says.

"There's been a church on this site since A.D. 984, a church built by a religious community called Lindisfarne because they came from the island of Lindisfarne in Northumberland. It has not been a cathedral since 1688, when it was Anglican. Presbyterians do not have cathedrals. Its proper name is the High Kirk of St. Giles."

One group of stained-glass windows shows the life of Christ. The church officer says this is the fourth set of windows.

"They have been destroyed three times—in 1385 by Richard II of England; then by Cromwell; and again during the Reformation when the church was ransacked."

The stone from Knox's grave rests on a pedestal at the entrance of the Moray Aisle Chapel. A smaller stone, nearby, is marked "1559."

"It was given by the mayor of Dieppe," the church officer says. "It had been in the St. Magdalene Chapel at Dieppe where Knox preached on his way back to Scotland from Geneva."

A few feet away is a bronze plate engraved with the name "Janet."

Janet?

The church officer chuckles.

"This is John Knox's church, but it is also hers, Genny Geddes. Her proper name was Janet, but everyone called her Genny. That plaque is where she usually sat. She is the one who threw the stool. She would bring her own stool to sit on because the church had no benches or chairs then. Genny sold vegetables and herbs outside the church door. She threw the stool when King Charles II was on the throne. He was a Stuart, a Roman Catholic, but to get the throne he had to become an Anglican. He thought of making Scotland Anglican, too. It was half Catholic and half Presbyterian at the time. So he sent Dean Hannay to Edinburgh to make it Anglican. Dean Hannay was reading the English Prayer Book one day when Old Genny came in for her prayers. When she heard him reading the Lauds liturgy from the Anglican service she thought he was saying Mass. 'Nae man will dar say Mass in my lugs'—*lugs* is an old Scottish word for ear—she cried out, and threw her stool at Dean Hannay. That started a riot, a whole series of them, for that matter, called Geddes Riots. They lasted fifty years, but they gained for Scotland freedom of religion. The stool is in the

Museum of Antiquities on Queen Street, along with the
pulpit—the wooden one—of John Knox."

A plaque on the fifth pillar along the center aisle
recalls the incident.

"To James Hannay," it says, "dean of this cathedral,
1634–1639. He was the first and the last who read the
service book in this church. This memorial is erected in
happier times by his descendants."

The Thistle Chapel looks old, but it was completed
only in 1911. It is the chapel of the Most Ancient and
Most Noble Order of the Thistle, Scottish chivalry's
highest order.

"To be a Knight of the Thistle you must be a Scots-
man or of Scottish descent," the church officer says.
"There are only sixteen knights at one time. It is a life
honor. The monarch does the installation of new
knights herself. She comes to the cathedral at least once
a year—in June or July—and when she does she sits in
the Preston aisle."

A memorial tablet in the center aisle honors a Reformation figure.

"To John Craig," the inscription says, "for many
years a Dominican friar who in Italy embraced the
Reformed faith and was by the Inquisition at Rome
condemned to be burnt. Escaping to his native country
he became assistant of John Knox at St. Giles, and
minister to the king's household. He was the author of
the King's Confession or National Covenant of 1581.
He died in Edinburgh in his 89th year."

The Covenant was signed at Linlithgow Palace and
is in the chapel just before the Thistle Chapel, spread
on a stand covered by glass. The tiny handwriting is
hard to read, and so are the signatures. The church
officer says the names were signed by the people in
their blood.

"By the Covenant they undertook to insist on a
church separate from the Catholic and the Anglican
ones."

GREYFRIARS KIRK

At the corner of High Street and George IV Bridge Road, a few blocks from St. Giles, three brass plates in the roadway identify the site of the last public execution. It took place in 1864. Two hundred yards along George IV Bridge Road is the post-Reformation Greyfriars Church, dedicated in 1620 on the site of a Franciscan friary which had existed from 1447 to 1560. The Greyfriars Kirk is a historic church. (The friars originally wore gray habits—thus the name.) A Martyrs Monument is in the northeast corner of the churchyard, and there are graves of famous Scotsmen, including the father and several members of the family of Sir Walter Scott.

In 1858 John Gray was buried in the grave marked with a red granite stone on the right-hand side of the churchyard. His dog, a terrier named Bobby, began a faithful watch at its master's grave from the time of his burial until its own death fourteen years later. Known therefore as "The Greyfriars Bobby," the dog is represented on the drinking fountain across from the entrance to the churchyard and also above the doorway of a nearby public house called "Bobby's." The water in the drinking fountain, an inscribed plaque says, was turned off in 1957.

TRANSPORTATION: Edinburgh is connected to London by fast, frequent trains. Flight time between London and Edinburgh is 1 hour.

HOTELS: The leading hotels are *Caledonian, George, North British,* and *King James. Forth Bridge's Motel* and *Esso Motor Hotel* are medium-priced.

DUNFERMLINE

The Abbey of Dunfermline is associated with Macbeth, the early days of Christianity in Scotland, and the pious Saxon princess Margaret whose chapel is on the summit of Edinburgh. Princess Margaret, a refugee who fled to Scotland because of the Norman Conquest in 1066, married Malcolm III whose father, Duncan, the first king of all Scotland, had been slain by Macbeth. The marriage was celebrated in Dunfermline in a church of some holy men known in Gaelic as *Kele-dei*, "devotees or servants of God." Such clerics were called by the Anglicized term *Culdees*. Margaret made a promise to establish a new church. It was started in 1072, and dedicated two years later to the Holy Trinity. Margaret died in 1093. Either before her death, or shortly afterward, Benedictine monks settled at Dunfermline. After occupying the monastery for 97 days in 1303, an English army under Edward I destroyed most of its buildings. King Robert the Bruce helped in the reconstruction, but in 1385 the monastic buildings once more were destroyed—this time by an English army led by Richard II. Again they were rebuilt. At the Reformation the monastery was destroyed once and for all. A record of those days says: "On the 29th March, 1560, the whole lords and barons that were on this side of the Forth passed to Stirling and, on the way, cast down the abbey of Dunfermline." They left the church standing, and it was used for public worship until a modern one was built in 1821.

TRANSPORTATION: It is a short drive from Edinburgh on Highway A-90 across the Firth of Forth bridge.

GLASGOW

Glasgow prides itself on its 12th-century cathedral and its university founded by the Pope five centuries ago. In Ayrshire are shrines of Robert Burns, such as the thatched cottage at Alloway, where he was born in 1759. A memorial to David Livingstone, the African missionary-explorer is at Blantyre. The Jesuit martyr

Blessed John Ogilvie might have been buried in the cathedral, but no one is sure. He was born in 1580 at Drum, near Keith, in Banffshire, the son of a noble family of Protestants. He became a Catholic, and after a long exile in Europe he was given permission by his Jesuit superiors to return to Scotland as a missionary, even though it was a time of great persecution. His mission, as he put it, was to "unteach heresy," and he said Mass privately for a number of people in Glasgow and Edinburgh. He was betrayed and arrested, and after a long interrogation which involved many nights of enforced sleeplessness he was hanged on the morning of Feb. 28, 1615. The scaffold was set up at the Glasgow Cross, the point where High Street and Argyle Street meet.

TRANSPORTATION: Glasgow is on a direct rail line with London.

HOTELS: The leading hotel is *Albany*. *Central* and *Royal Stuart* are not as expensive.

IONA

Columba, an Irish monk, exiled himself from his native land to this tiny island off the west coast of Scotland in the 6th century A.D. to do penance for the part he had played in promoting a tribal war. In 563 he founded a monastery which became a key center for the spread of Christianity throughout the northern part of Britain. The graves of many early-day Celtic and Scottish kings are at Iona. The monastery itself was suppressed during the Reformation.

A modern community of Church of Scotland ministers and laymen have rebuilt the abbey, and made it into a retreat center. Their building was started by Lord MacLeod Fuinary, a parish minister in Glasgow in the 1930s. It was a time of economic depression, and he decided to engage men in work to repair the historic abbey. The work continued till the 1960s, and in the meantime a community, peace-oriented, evolved. In summer, services in the morning and evening are attended by ministers who reside at the abbey and by young people who stay at the international youth camp, a series of long wooden huts which provide shelter for as many as 500 visitors. The island is 3 miles long and half that in width.

TRANSPORTATION: From Glasgow take Highway A-82 along Loch Lomond, a lovely route, as far as Tyndrum. From Tyndrum proceed west on Highway A-85 to Oban. At Oban, take a car ferry called *Columba* to Craignure which is on the large island of Mull. One can leave his car at Craignure and take a bus for a 35-mile journey through some of the loveliest parts of Mull to Fionnphort. At Fionnphort there is a short ride on a passengers-only ferry to Iona.

HOTELS: *St. Columba* and *Argyl* on the isle of Iona are small, inexpensive places to stay.

NORTHUMBRIA

The Roman emperor Hadrian, when he visited Britain in A.D. 122, ordered the construction of a lengthy wall along the northern boundaries of the empire. The wall, with mile-castles set out at each mile, extended from Newcastle to the Solway Firth, which is just south of the border between England and Scotland. By the time of the departure of the Romans from Britain around A.D. 410 Christianity was firmly established. But a new barrier, more formidable than a wall, arose to cut off the Christians. Heathen Germanic tribes invaded the island, imposing their own customs and sealing off the Christians from contact with the Christianity of Europe. For a century and a half a Celtic Church developed on its own. Then, at the end of the 6th century, monks from Iona traveled across Britain to

Northumbria and in A.D. 597 St. Augustine (known as the Apostle of the English) arrived from Rome. Different liturgical customs, different calendars were coordinated. The joining of the European and Celtic forces of Christianity, spiritually and physically, strengthened both and facilitated the conversion of the pagan invaders and their descendants.

LINDISFARNE

Northumbria early in the 7th century reached from the River Humber to Edwin's burgh (Edinburgh), which took its name from King Edwin. Christianity's progress was slowed by the slaying of King Edwin in a battle with a barbaric chief from the Midlands (Penda) and Cadwallon, a Welsh king. Oswald, the new Northumbrian leader and son of Edwin's predecessor, was a young Christian who had been educated by the Irish monks at Iona. In a battle at Heavenfield, near Hadrian's Wall, about A.D. 634 Oswald defeated Cadwallon. The Annals of Iona relate that before the battle Oswald implanted a wooden cross alongside his camp, and called upon his warriors to kneel and pray before it. After victory, Oswald appealed to the monks at Iona to help him reestablish Christianity in the kingdom of Northumbria.

In A.D. 635 St. Aidan, a bishop from Iona, established the monastery at Lindisfarne, a tiny island just north of Bamburgh where Oswald had his castle. Because of its influence on the Christianizing of other kingdoms in England, Lindisfarne became known as the Holy Island. The Lindisfarne Gospels were written to honor St. Cuthbert who died in 687 after serving as prior.

St. Wilfrid, a nobleman educated at Lindisfarne, established monasteries at Ripon and at Hexham. From Ripon, Wilfrid subsequently sent Willibrord and a dozen other monks to the Low Countries. In the following century the scholarly monk Alcuin of Lindisfarne became a counselor and a schoolmaster for Charlemagne and his empire, making for an enormous influence on the revival of Christianity in Western Europe. Between A.D. 793 and 796 Viking invaders from Denmark plundered Lindisfarne and other religious settlements as far west as Iona. In 875 the monks were forced to flee. They took with them the Lindisfarne Gospels and the coffin of St. Cuthbert. After resettling temporarily at Chester-le-Street they definitely reestablished the episcopal see at Durham in A.D. 995. A century later, on the banks of the river Wear, a splendid cathedral was built over the grave of St. Cuthbert. Benedictine monks from Durham rebuilt the monastery at Lindisfarne in 1082, after the Norman Conquest. It was destroyed with other monasteries in the Reformation.

TRANSPORTATION: A causeway from Beal, 15 miles south of Berwick-upon-Tweed, connects the mainland with the Holy Island during low tide.

THE VENERABLE BEDE

In an age of intellectual giants the monk named Bede ranked above his colleagues in scholarship. He was born in Northumbria in A.D. 672. He was associated with the Holy Island of Lindisfarne but primarily with St. Paul's at Jarrow, and to a lesser extent with St. Peter's Monastery at Sunderland. Much of the history of this golden age of Christianity is known through the Venerable Bede because he, literally, was the first English historian, producing *Ecclesiastical History of the English People.* He wrote on everything he knew, and he seemed to know everything—astronomy, mathematics, Holy Scripture. Bede died at St. Paul's Monastery in A.D. 735. The bones of Bede were carried from Jarrow about 1022, and interred in the cathedral at Durham.

St. Paul's Monastery was rebuilt, starting about 1075, but it was confiscated during the Reformation, on Dec. 31, 1540. The chancel of St. Paul's Church is believed to be from the original structure of the 7th century. There is a chair which, according to tradition, was used by Bede. Jarrow is just a few miles from the eastern side of Newcastle-upon-Tyne. After 1,300 years St. Peter's Church at Sunderland, near the coast east of Newcastle, is still in use. Its west wall is from the original Saxon construction of the 7th century.

TRANSPORTATION: Newcastle is on the direct main rail line to London, Edinburgh, and Glasgow.

HOTELS: *Gosforth Park, Airport* and *Magnum* are the leading ones. Throughout Northumbria is a chain of moderately priced *Swallow* hotels.

POINTS OF INTEREST: Within easy radius of Newcastle are the Norman castle at Bamburgh on the site of King Oswald's 7th-century headquarters; the 7th-century Anglo-Saxon church at Escomb; the cathedral built at York on the site of King Edwin's baptism of A.D. 627; the original crypt of St. Wilfrid's Church of the 7th century enclosed in the cathedral at Ripon; the 13th-century parish church at Hartlepool on the site of St. Hilda's 7th-century abbey; near Chollerford, site of the pivotal Heavenfield Battle, marked by a cross, which was won by Oswald in 634. Remains of Hadrian's Wall, and other Roman ruins, lie west of Newcastle.

CANTERBURY

While Northumbria was developing as a center for the spread of Christianity through northern England in the latter part of the 6th century, a complementary current was flowing through the south from the court at Canterbury of the king of Kent, Ethelbert. Benedictine monks arrived at the court in A.D. 596, sent by Pope

Gregory I from his own St. Andrew's Monastery on the Coelian Hill in Rome. The dispatch of the monks formally launched the English mission although there had been Christians in Britain earlier, at least from the end of the 3rd century. In A.D. 314, for example, three British bishops sat in the Council of Arles (France). But the withdrawal of the Romans and the ferocity of the invading Germanic tribes discouraged the spread of Christianity until the arrival of the new Romans.

CANTERBURY CATHEDRAL

St. Augustine arrived in England in A.D. 597 from Rome and, the Venerable Bede writes, when the episcopal see was established at Canterbury he took possession of a church "which he was informed had been built in the city long before by Roman believers." In the 10th century Odo, as archbishop of Canterbury, had the body of St. Wilfrid translated from Ripon, in Northumbria, so that it could be enshrined in the cathedral.

Following the murder of Archbishop Thomas Becket in his own cathedral in 1170, pilgrims made it their goal for almost 4 centuries until Henry VIII ordered the dissolution of its monastery. In response to the king's order Archbishop Cranmer on Mar. 20, 1540 presided at the surrender of the monastery. Twenty-eight of the monks agreed to stay on in the new Reformation foundation. The others were pensioned or sent off. The following year a royal charter was issued, establishing a secular college to replace the monastery.

The cathedral area, like the city of Canterbury itself, retains its medieval aura. The cathedral is within a ring of ancient stone walls, buildings and towerlike gateways. Among the general regulations posted at the entrance is one asking visitors to "pray during their visit for the cathedral and for those who work and worship in it."

Around the cathedral are small houses of various

styles which are occupied by retired canons, staff members, vergers, and so on. A robust man in overalls points to a house and says: "The old bloke in there has been there for fifty or sixty years. He goes to the prisons and helps them write letters—things like that. The church encourages him in this work."

One set of buildings is in a close, a zone enclosed by a stone fence. Inside are modern two-story brick buildings. Some are rented to private individuals for rents of about 25 pounds a week.

"Last week one bloke died, and he left thirty thousand quid. So he could afford to live there," the man in the overalls says.

At the end of the cathedral grounds is another close, with a high arched entrance. The open greensward had been the bowling turf of the monks. A mulberry tree at one corner was one of many planted by Huguenot refugees from France in the 16th century who used the silk from it in weaving a special cloth called Canterbury muslin.

In the courtyard of an old-looking building behind the cathedral a husky, light-haired man of about 40 is removing packages from a black station-wagon. A couple of teenage boys help him carry the packages into the building which, in a pleasant, friendly way, he identifies as the former refectory of the monks.

"It is now a boardinghouse for sixty of the boys at King's School," the man says. He is the house-master. "King's is said to be the oldest public school in England. It might go back to the school founded by St. Augustine in the sixth century. This boardinghouse is called Meister Omer's House."

Meister Omer?

"The title *Meister* signified an educated man with a degree. Omer? That possibly is from St. Omer, a town on the French side of the channel, where he came from, perhaps—the way you might say 'Professor London.' Meister Omer was a layman who looked after the monastic properties. Part of this building goes back to 1290. Another section is a little more recent.

"On the ground-floor of the old part is a space for a twenty-two-foot wide fireplace in the room that was a kitchen when the monks ate here. That filled-in section on the first floor, the size of a doorway—which you can see from the outside here—was, they say, the entrance to Meister Omer's quarters. He lived just above the kitchen, and had to use a ladder."

One monastic work still visible is the fresh-water system devised by Wilbert, the prior of the monastery in the 12th century. From a conduit house on high ground a mile away water passed through a series of sediment-settling tanks on its way to the water tower and into a large basin.

At the entrance to the cathedral is the ship's bell from *H.M.S.Canterbury*, presented by the Admiralty after the vessel was decommissioned in 1934. It is struck daily at six bells (11 A.M.) "in remembrance of all who face perils of waters in the discharge of their duties."

Several men in loose-fitting black robes are standing near the entrance. They are Canterbury residents who volunteer their time as honorary chaplains to assist visitors. A big-built man around 50 with cropped graying hair says that everyone asks about Thomas Becket.

"The archbishop of Canterbury when he enters the cathedral today," he says, "still comes in through the same palace corridors walked by Becket when he was going to Evensong on December 29, 1170. Becket knew he was a marked man. But he did not think he would be killed in his own church. The people knew the four strange knights were in town, and the monks sought to persuade Becket to remain in the palace. But he wanted to go to Evensong.

"Just as vespers were to start, the four knights burst into the cathedral, shouting 'Where is the archbishop? Where is the traitor?' The monks with Becket fled, and he could have, too. Instead he approached the knights, saying 'Here I am. No traitor, but archbishop. What seek you?' 'Your life,' one answered. 'Gladly do I give it," he said, and bowed his head. They knifed and axed him to death.

"After killing him the knights intended to secrete his body, but the monks seized it and brought it to their crypt. Four years later a fire destroyed a large part of the church, and in the restoration a Trinity Chapel was added at the front. When the restoration work was completed in 1220 the monks brought Becket's body from the crypt, and installed it in an elevated shrine in the new Trinity Chapel. The chapel was raised above the level of the rest of the church so that from the entrance—almost six hundred feet away—the shrine was visible.

"In 1538 Henry VIII ordered the destruction of this and all other shrines, saying that people should not worship saints, but should give homage only to God. No trace of the body or the shrine remains, but the site is still a holy one, and other holy men are buried in the chapel today—like the first archbishop, St. Augustine."

The famous Canterbury Boys' Choir has been recently transformed, creating quite a stir throughout Kent.

"For centuries," the honorary chaplain says, "there was a choir school, with sixty-eight boys ranging in age from eight to thirteen or fourteen. Increasingly, it became expensive and difficult to maintain such specialized, high-level education for them, and it was decided to end the school. The choir continues, of course, but now with only thirty-six boys living on the grounds, and for their education they are taken each day by minibus to St. Edmond's School in town. The decision to end the choir school caused a great rumble. It came fast, without too much advance warning, and people who had been happy that their son had been accepted in the school—it was snobbish, you know, but in a good sense—these people suddenly faced a great disappointment."

And the archbishop of Canterbury?

"His office is in Lambeth Palace in London, but he seeks every occasion to come to Canterbury. It is the dean who runs the cathedral, and the archbishop visits it by invitation only. Even for Christmas, Easter and Whitsun an invitation is extended to him in advance to preside at the services. You see, *dean* is an old Saxon title for the superior of the monks at a cathedral. The archbishop, technically, was the abbot but he had so many duties in his diocese that in Catholic times complete responsibility for the cathedral was given to the dean."

Evensong is simple, impressive.

A verger in a black cassock carrying a silver stick, the *verge,* leads the dean and the canons to their stalls which are set in a row at the back of the church, facing forward down the long middle aisle. The dean and the canons are in black robes, and white surplices which reach almost to the ankles. Stoles hang around their necks. Military campaign ribbons are sewn to the stole of one canon. Four banks of pews are at each side of the nave in long lines. A soft light shines above the Matutinal Altar at the other end of the cathedral, where the Trinity Chapel had once stood. Many of those at Evensong are young people: boys with long hair and beards; girls in jeans. The canons conclude the prayers with the *Magnificat* and then the *Credo,* announcing as they do each evening their belief in "the holy Catholic Church."

St. Augustine's Abbey and College

Monks from Rome founded St. Augustine's Abbey in A.D. 598. In the dissolution of the monasteries in the 16th century, stones from the chapel were used to remodel the Abbey into a royal residence, but the new use was not successful and the entire complex soon fell into ruins.

St. Augustine's College was started in 1848 on the site of part of the old abbey as the first missionary training college of the Church of England. War damage closed it in 1942. It was reopened in 1969 as a college for students for the priesthood.

Between the abbey ruins and the cathedral are new modern buildings of a teacher training college, a government undertaking. They contrast too sharply with the soft setting of Gothic architecture and vivid green grounds. A spry, aging man in a cap, handling some tools in a shed, looks quizzically at the new development.

"When I first came to work for St. Augustine's in 1929," he says, "there was a cowshed over there." He gestures in the direction of a green lawn along a ruined wall of the abbey. Pointing to a playing field, he continues: "And a pigsty there."

The man lets his mind ruminate on the scene.

"In the sixties," he says, "the church, apparently needing the money, sold the large piece of land toward the cathedral to the government for the teachers' college—schoolteachers. They have no proper roof on any of the buildings. They all have pitched roofs. There's always repair men around them. I see a scaffold going up almost every day."

St. Margaret's Church

There has been a church on the site of St. Margaret's since Saxon times. Part of the present structure remains from the 12th century. The stones in its outer walls look like oyster shells. Until A.D. 1271 it belonged to St. Augustine's Abbey, and each time the abbot passed he was saluted with a peal of the church bells. St. Margaret's now is used as a church and institute for the deaf and dumb of Canterbury and East Kent.

St. Dunstan's outside West Gate

St. Dunstan's, named after an early-10th-century archbishop of Canterbury, has been since the Reformation an Anglican church. Although now part of the Church of England, it is a shrine for two English saints, Thomas Becket and Sir Thomas More, who were killed because of their conviction of papal supremacy in matters spiritual.

It was at St. Dunstan's that Henry II, six months after ordering the death of the archbishop of Canterbury, doffed his royal robes, donned the sackcloth of a penitent, and set out to walk to the cathedral to pray for forgiveness.

Thomas More's head, retrieved by his daughter Margaret Roper who had married into a Canterbury family, is conserved at St. Dunstan's.

"Thomas More was a remarkable man," says the curate. He is youngish, with a mustache, rather long dark hair, and glasses. He wears a long cape. "Thomas More actually bothered to have his daughter educated, a thing not ordinarily done in those days. He did the educating himself, and with the help of friends—such as Erasmus—who were passing through London."

"The story is that, like others executed, his head was stuck on a pole on London Bridge as a warning to everyone else to behave. It stayed there fourteen days. Margaret, his favorite daughter, was married to William Roper, a grandson of John Roper who added the St. Nicholas Chapel, or Roper Chapel, to St. Dunstan's in 1402. She went down the Thames to London, bribed someone to remove the head from the pole and toss it to her in the boat in the river. She brought it back to Canterbury, and it was buried with her. She actually served six months in prison for this, and this seems to confirm the story. When she was released from prison, she was allowed to keep the head. The head was found when her grave was opened in the nineteenth century."

Thomas More's head is in a lead casket in the Roper vault below the floor of the St. Nicholas Chapel.

A stained-glass window honoring More was dedicated in the chapel on June 14, 1973, in the presence of the archbishop of Canterbury. It was donated by two Catholics (an American and a Viennese) and by the Church of England vicar of St. Dunstan's. The American was Alfred J. Blasco, representing members of St. Thomas More Catholic Church in Kansas City, Mo.

At a prie-dieu in the chapel is a copy, for visitors, of St. Thomas More's prayer:

"Thank you, dear Jesus, for all you have given me, for all you have taken away from me, for all you have left me. Amen."

ST. THOMAS'S CHURCH

St. Thomas's is usually referred to as the "Catholic church" because it is the only Catholic church in Canterbury today. It is dedicated to the canonized archbishop.

Two reliquaries over the altar contain relics of Archbishop Thomas Becket: a piece of bone, a little more than 1 inch long in one; a tiny fragment of bone and a 1-inch square swatch of cloth from his vestments in the other. His fellow monks obtained the relics when his shrine was destroyed. Eventually, the relics arrived in Belgium. They were solemnly presented to the church on Sept. 20, 1953 by the Benedictine prior of Belgium's Chevetogne Monastery (see Index), Father Thomas Becquet, a collateral descendant of the saint.

St. Thomas More is honored each year on his feast (June 22) in an ecumenical service held in conjunction with St. Dunstan's. The service takes place at St. Dunstan's because part of the ceremony involves placing a wreath at his shrine by the parish priest (pastor) of St. Thomas's and the vicar of the Anglican church. A wreath is also placed at St. Thomas More's shrine on May 12, when a procession marks the anniversary of the hanging and quartering in 1538 of St. John Stone (one of the Forty English Martyrs canonized by Pope Paul), an Augustinian friar from Canterbury. He was sentenced to death for refusing to take the "supremacy oath." After the wreath is laid at St. Dunstan's the procession is joined by the Catholic archbishop of the diocese, and it continues through the town to the Dane John where Father John Stone was hanged.

DANE JOHN

Dane John is a mysterious-looking cone-shaped mound just inside the city wall. A wrap-around spiral path leads to its peak which is almost as high as the cathedral tower. Plaques along its side are replete with lengthy historical notes, relating how various citizens contributed at different times over the centuries for the fence, or the paving, or some other physical improvement. None mentions that this was where the Augustinian friar, John Stone of Canterbury, was hanged and quartered. Two open-air Masses are said here each year: one by the parish priest on the anniversary of the execution, May 12; the other on June 22 by Augustinian friars from Hythe. The origin of the name Dane John is as much of a mystery as the mound itself. It could be from the French *donjon*.

PROTESTANT MARTYRS

A memorial to 41 Protestants of Kent who were burnt at the stake in the reign of Mary, Queen of Scots (1555–58), is along Martyrs Field Road. The memorial to the Kentish martyrs, a column of marble topped by a cross, was erected by public subscription in 1899 on the spot where they were killed. An inscription says:

"For themselves they earned the martyr's crown; by

their fidelity they helped to secure for succeeding generations the priceless blessing of religious freedom."

Names of the 41 martyrs are listed on the memorial. The list includes two vicars (from the Kentish towns of Adisham and Rolvenden) and, among the civilians, some women. One woman is identified as "Bradbridge's widow"; another, as "Wilson's wife."

TRANSPORTATION: Canterbury is almost due east of London. Train service is frequent.

HOTELS: The *County Hotel* is traditional.

OXFORD

In its 7 centuries Oxford has been a center for 3 main streams of religious thought. John Wycliffe, the scholar-priest, taught in the 14th century that Christianity should rest solely on pious meditation on the Scriptures, and that the church should return to its original state of poverty. In the 18th century John Wesley was the inspired genius of Methodism. A century later, Newman launched the Oxford Movement.

NEWMAN

John Henry Newman was born in Old Broad Street, London, on Feb. 21, 1801. In 1822 he was made a fellow at Oriel College in Oxford and for the next two dozen years was active in the university city's religious life, first as an Anglican minister and then as a Catholic. The Church of England was in a crisis, and not taken seriously. There was talk it would be disestablished. If that happened, clergymen asked, where would that leave them?—by what authority would they be able to continue preaching? On July 14, 1833 a colleague of Newman's, John Keble, issued a challenge to those attacking the church. "I have ever considered and kept the day as the start of the religious movement of 1833,"

Newman later wrote. He hit upon the idea of publishing tracts about specific issues. Tract No. 1 started the Oxford Movement. Colleagues helped Newman with writing some of the tracts. Every Sunday he himself continued to preach at St. Mary the Virgin Church. The series of tracts eventually dealt with the biting question of the relationship of the Church of England to Rome. Newman's interpretation brought charges that he was a traitor to Anglicanism. Newman resigned from St. Mary's on Sept. 19, 1843. His entry into the Catholic Church a little over two years later was predictable. After studies in Rome, he was ordained a priest there on May 30, 1847. He was encouraged to continue in England the apostolate of preaching, prayer and sacraments instituted by the 16th-century saint of Rome, Philip Neri. On Feb. 2, 1849 he opened a Chapel of the Oratory in Birmingham.

TRANSPORTATION: Oxford is 60 miles west of London. The train route is by way of Reading.

PLACES OF INTEREST: In Broad Street, an iron cross in the road marks the spot where Lattimer and Ridley, Anglican martyrs, were burned. The library of the Baptists' Regent's Park College has a number of mementoes of William Carey.

BIRMINGHAM

St. Philip Neri established the Congregation of the Oratory in Rome in 1575. Newman, the first English Oratorian, spent the last years of his life developing the Birmingham Oratory. He was elected a cardinal in 1859, and died on May 12, 1879. His burial place was at Rednal. His successors at the Oratory decided to build a new and larger church as a memorial to him, and it was consecrated on June 23, 1920. On the grounds of the Oratory is St. Philip's Chapel, built in

1858, which was used much by Newman in the early days of his work.

TRANSPORTATION: Inter-City train service from London.

WALSINGHAM

The Marian devotion in this Norwich town is linked to the Holy Land in two basic ways. First, a replica of the Holy House of Nazareth was built here in the 11th century. Second, as in the Holy Land, the devotion to the Madonna is maintained by different representatives of Christianity—in this case, by Anglicans and Catholics. The devotion began in 1061 when a woman named Richeldis de Faverches, after receiving a vision of the Madonna, is said to have been "led in spirit" to the Holy Land and there shown the house at Nazareth where Christ grew up. The woman was asked to build one like it at Walsingham. She built a wooden, Saxon dwelling. Pilgrims were numerous, and a priory of Augustinians was founded in 1153 to assist them. After Henry VIII's establishment of the Church of England, the priory was dissolved, and the Holy House destroyed by fire.

Devotion was revived on Aug. 20, 1897 when a small group of pilgrims visited the Slipper Chapel, the last of several wayside chapels from the old days. It is a mile outside Walsingham. The name apparently comes from the custom of medieval pilgrims to remove their shoes at the wayside chapel, and walk barefoot the rest of the way to the shrine of the Holy House.

An Anglican woman, Charlotte Boyd, took steps to acquire the chapel, planning to restore it for a community of Anglican nuns. While the negotiations for the chapel were going on, Miss Boyd became a Catholic. In 1896 she presented it to the Benedictine monks at Downside Abbey, near Bath. (The nuns joined the

Catholic Church in 1913, and established a Benedictine community at Talacre Abbey in Flintshire.)

The Benedictine monks made no special use of the chapel and handed it over to the diocese of Northampton. In 1933, when Bishop Laurence Youens was consecrated as head of the diocese, he announced his intention to restore the ancient devotion to Our Lady of Walsingham. On the feast of the Assumption in August 1934, the Cardinal-Primate and most of the bishops of England led more than 10,000 pilgrims to a Benedictine service at an open-air altar across from the chapel.

Coincidental with the development of the Catholic shrine, the Anglicans built a magnificent church in Walsingham in 1934 to encourage the ancient devotion. There is a joint pilgrimage each year from the Slipper Chapel to the Anglican shrine. The directors of the Catholic and Anglican shrines walk together each Whit Monday in the main Anglican pilgrimage and, in July, in the Union of Catholic Mothers pilgrimage.

TRANSPORTATION: By train to Norwich or King's Lynn—both 27 miles from Walsingham—and then bus.

HOTELS: Historic inns are available, such as *Falcon House* (where it is said Erasmus stayed in 1511).

LONDON

There are many Londons—of finance, of royal pomp, of art, of religion, and so on. Even the London of religion has many facets, offering particular points and places of sacred interest to specific religious groups. As a result there are the Londons of the Wesleys, of Spurgeon and the Baptists, of the Jewish people, of the Society of Friends (Quakers), of the Anglicans, of Catholics, of the great cathedrals (St. Paul's, Westminster) which really belong to everyone. The various Londons of religion, like the nonreligious Londons, often meet. The religious leaders have hoped for such encounters, deeming them natural and necessary. John Donne, dean of St. Paul's, wrote that no man is an island. John Wesley, the founder of Methodism, regarded the world as his parish.

THE NONCONFORMISTS

"I have three hundred ministers here," Arthur Murphy, the gaunt Cockney caretaker in a cap at Bunhill Fields Cemetery says. "He [John Wesley] has five thousand, but they are under his church."

Bunhill Fields, the burial grounds of many Baptist leaders of the 17th and 18th centuries, is in City Road, across the street from the Wesley Chapel, "the cathedral of Methodism." (*Underground station: Old Street.*)

"At the time the chapel was built in 1777, there was no City Road, and the entire area was a graveyard," Arthur says. "The Nonconformists and Methodists were not allowed to be buried anywhere else."

It is perhaps a city-block square. Some high-rise office buildings now stud the neighborhood. A path runs through the center of the cemetery from Bunhill Row, and local residents criss-cross it. In the summer, roses bloom in parts of the graveyard and girls from the offices like to eat their lunch here, Arthur says.

The most famous grave is covered by a large stone memorial. A life-sized figure of John Bunyan lies atop a high stone which portrays on one side a plodding pilgrim bearing a backpack and clinging to a staff to aid his progress. The other side of the stone shows the same pilgrim kneeling before a cross, with his pack resting behind him on the ground. Bunyan died Aug. 31, 1688 at the age of 60.

A local resident, a slender, pleasant man about 40, says he always salutes John Bunyan with a cheerful "Good morning, John" as he passes his grave on the way to work each day.

The only two crosses in the graveyard are for Bunyan and the Rev. William Hooke, born in Southampton in 1601, who taught at the First Church in New Haven, Conn., from 1644 to 1656.

A 15-foot monument marks the grave of Daniel Defoe, author of *Robinson Crusoe*. The *Christian World* newspaper raised funds for the memorial by appealing to English boys and girls. It was erected in 1870. A few yards away a darkened tablet says: "Nearby lie the remains of the poet-painter William Blake, born in 1757 and died in 1827, and of his wife, Catherine Sophia, 1762–1831."

Arthur points out the gravesite of Mrs. Susanna Wesley, near the John Bunyan memorial. The tombstone says:

"Late widow of Rev. Samuel Wesley, late rector of Epworth in Lincolnshire. She died July 23, 1742 at age 73. She was the youngest daughter of the Rev. Samuel Annesley, ejected by the Act of Uniformity from the rectory of St. Giles's, Cripplegate [London]. She was the mother of 19 children of whom the most eminent were the Revs. John and Charles Wesley, the former of whom was under God the founder of the Societies of the People, called Methodists."

WESLEY'S CHAPEL

John Wesley was born in Epworth in 1703. The Old Rectory, the family home, is preserved by the World Methodist Council which acquired it from the Church of England in 1954. His father, a Church of England priest, administered to him his first Holy Communion, and the chalice used in the service is in the parish church. The communion rail of the parish church at the time when Samuel Wesley was rector and his son John curate is in Epworth's Wesley Memorial Church that was built in 1888.

Both John and Charles Wesley were undergraduates

at Christ Church, Oxford. A portrait of John Wesley is in the dining hall at Christ Church. On graduation, he was appointed a fellow at Lincoln College, Oxford, and his rooms there can be seen. He was ordained a priest in 1728. The two brothers spent most of 1736 and 1737 in Georgia, then a colony, as missionaries. In 1738 John Wesley experienced the "evangelical conversion" that encouraged him to become a tireless missionary-on-horseback in his own country. A few days earlier Charles Wesley had a similar evangelical experience. Followers had already gathered around the two brothers, joining with them in the methodical rule of life of preaching, of regular readings, of fastings, of prison visits, and of the sacraments. The original intention was to serve the Church of England by forming "societies" within it. But a separate Methodist movement was inevitable.

In 1739 John Wesley erected in Bristol the first Methodist place of worship, calling it the New Room. Its Holy Communion Table, pulpit and benches are from the beginning days. John Wesley used the New Room as a training center for ministers. He lived in quarters upstairs and through a window could watch preachers in the chapel pulpit. Charles Wesley, known for his many hymns, lived at 4 Charles Street in Bristol from 1749 till moving to London in 1771.

A plaque in Northumberland Street in Newcastle-upon-Tyne identifies the northern headquarters and a school for orphans established in 1743. A museum with portraits of early-day Methodist preachers and other memorabilia is at Brunswick Chapel, the home of Newcastle's Orphan House Congregation after 1821.

On Apr. 21, 1777 John Wesley laid the foundation stone for the Mother Church of World Methodism, Wesley's Chapel, opposite the Bunhill Fields Cemetery, in London. A year later he acquired the next-door house, at 47 City Road, and used it as his home for the rest of his life. He preached his last sermon in Wesley's

Chapel on Feb. 22, 1791 and died a few days later. He is buried in the small cemetery behind the chapel.

A block from Wesley's Chapel graveyard a memorial tablet at 19A Tabernacle Street indicates the location of the Foundry ("a vast uncouth mass of ruins") which John Wesley made into his headquarters from 1739 to 1778. The first Methodist bookroom was established at the Foundry, and his mother died there on July 30, 1742.

Wesley's Chapel was opened on Nov. 1, 1778 to continue the work begun at the Foundry. The house where he lived next to the chapel is now a museum. There is a fascinating assembly of articles relating to John Wesley: a walking stick with a knobby handle, his robe and brass-buckled shoes, his black leather study chair with a T-shaped wooden back which curls forward at the edges, his umbrella.

"Umbrella styles have not changed much," the custodian says amiably. He is a middle-aged man with glasses. "The only thing is, there is no curved handle on his umbrella."

On the first floor a portrait commemorates the union of the Methodist churches. A message to the Methodist Conference (the governing body of Methodism) from the king of England, George V, on Sept. 21, 1932 said: "I congratulate the uniting Churches on the attainment of this happy result. They may well see in it a token of divine guidance and blessing, welcome it as marking one step towards the unity of all Christian people."

John Wesley's first London Society was established at 28 Aldersgate Street shortly before his conversion there on May 24, 1738. At No. 13, on a narrow side street called Little Britain, is the site of the house of John Bray where Charles Wesley was converted three days before his brother.

Charles Wesley is buried in the yard of Marylebone parish church on Marylebone High Street, not far from the Planetarium. He died in 1788. It is a city-style graveyard, fenced off from the sidewalk, and small. Some old tombstones are set in the walls. There are a number of wooden benches—3 or 4, anyway. Also buried here are his wife, Sarah, who died in 1822 at the age of 96; his son Charles who died in 1834, at 77; and Samuel, the couple's second son, a composer and organist, who died in 1837 at 74. Susanna Wesley, the mother of John and Charles, was married in the old Marylebone parish church. The house where she was born on Jan. 20, 1669 is in a cul-de-sac, Spital Yard, just off Bishopsgate and the start of Petticoat Lane. The small building, known as Annesley House (her maiden name), is now used by the Methodist Women's Fellowship.

JEWRY

"The ideal way for a visitor to spend a Sunday morning," says Barry, a young university student, "is to see the Bevis Marks Synagogue, browse around in the market at Petticoat Lane, and have lunch at Bloom's."

Barry is one of the young people from the Inter-University Jewish Federation which has a small, cramped office in the Hillel House of B'nai B'rith near Euston Station. Barry and two young women are in the office collating some mimeographed material about the federation and its cultural programs. The first thing one of the young women asks is: "How would you like your tea—with lemon or milk?"

"The Bevis Marks Synagogue," Barry says, "was built by the Sephardic community of Spanish and Portuguese Jews who came in the middle of the seventeenth century. It is still in use. These were the Jews of the Resettlement. This is the oldest synagogue on English soil except for the long-forgotten one in Lincoln where there's no community any more. It is only in the last few years that they have installed electricity. Candelabras are still used on high holy days."

Jews of the Resettlement?

"Yes. Or, they're also called Post-Expulsion Jews. Around the thirteenth century massacres of the Jews began, and in 1290 they were expelled by Edward I. In 1650 Oliver Cromwell invited the Jews to build a house of prayer. It was not until 1858 that the first Jew was allowed to enter Parliament—Baron Lionel de Rothschild. In 1885, his son Nathaniel was made a peer.

"That whole part of the East End, starting near the Bank of England, and reaching up to Bevis Marks and the Petticoat Lane market used to be where the Jews lived. On Old Jewry, a street at the back of Threadneedle Street—now there are banks there—the first synagogue in the city is supposed to have stood. And the church for the Corporation of London, just down from the Bank of England, is called St. Lawrence Jewry because of the number of Jews who lived nearby until their expulsion in 1290. [*Underground station: Bank.*] The Petticoat Lane market used to be a Jewish market. That's why it is on Sunday, instead of Saturday, because Saturday is the sabbath."

Around the corner from Barry's office is Woburn House in which the headquarters of the United Synagogue are located. The United Synagogue is the largest of five main synagogal organizations and represents about 150,000 Orthodox Jews in 80 synagogues of Greater London. The United Synagogue was established by an act of Parliament of July 14, 1870 and its chief rabbi is recognized by the monarch.

The Jewish Museum is also in Woburn House. The museum was set up by the Jewish Memorial Committee in memory of Jewish casualties in the First and Second world wars. A splendid assortment of religious articles is exhibited. The choice item is an elaborate, carved Ark which found its way to Kent from a synagogue in Venice. Viscount Bearsted's family bought it, and presented it to the museum.

The site of the first synagogue after the Resettlement

(1657–1701) is at the end of Cunard House on Cree-church Lane. (*Underground Station: Aldgate.*) Its successor, Bevis Marks, is in the next street, called Bevis Marks. There is an arched doorway with a sculpted abstract design in the mantel. An unobtrusive inscription in Hebrew and the date of construction, 1701, are over the doorway. There is no other indication of the synagogue's identity. Even a little sign at the door uses vague terminology: "When closed please apply to Vestry Office in Heneage Lane, next turning." Three large arched windows with small panes are in the streetside wall of the synagogue, but they are above the level of passersby.

The main Ashkenazi house of prayer, the Great Synagogue, had been nearby at Creechurch Lane and Dukes Place until bombed out in the Second World War. It has been rebuilt at Marble Arch.

A block away, on Aldgate High Street, is the church of St. Botolph-without-Aldgate. There are large mulberry trees in the churchyard. A sign says:

"For a thousand years a church has stood here outside the Old Gateway [Ald Gate] in the City Wall and beside the bridge which crossed the City Moat [Hounds Ditch] so that travellers leaving or entering the City would pause here to pray. It was dedicated in the name of St. Botolph, a 7th century Suffolk man who built a Benedictine abbey near Aldeburgh. He loved to help travellers on their way, and after his death he became venerated as a sort of English St. Christopher.

"Twentieth century traveller, whatever your race or religion, St. Botolph as patron saint of travellers bids you welcome to his church in Aldgate."

THE WREN CHURCHES

The Great Fire of 1666 destroyed 88 parish churches in the City, the ancient center of Greater London. Sir Christopher Wren, a complete man—architect, painter, mathematician, lawyer, astronomer—rebuilt 51 of them and they are known as the "Wren Churches." All except a few are in the City, an area about the size of midtown Manhattan and often called the Square Mile. All the Wren Churches have been part of the Church of England communion since the Reformation.

Wren's network of churches begins at Temple Bar, a mammoth sculpture topped by a griffin at the upper end of Fleet Street, the western boundary line of the City. A few dozen yards from the entrance to the City is one of Wren's "island" churches, St. Clement Danes, surrounded by traffic. "Oranges and lemons, say the bells of St. Clement's," according to the nursery rhyme. "When will you pay me? say the bells of Old Bailey. When I grow rich, say the bells of Shoreditch."

A gatehouse, built on Fleet Street by Wren, opens to the Temple, a vast enclosed area of greenery, antiquity and historic buildings which had belonged to the Knights Templar in the Crusades. Lawyers adopted it because it was near the City and the courts. Charles Lamb was born in the Temple. In Middle Temple Hall Shakespeare presented his *Twelfth Night*. Wren designed some of the house doorways in King's Bench Walk, a pleasant square of brick dwellings near the 12th-century Temple Church.

The Embankment, the riverside roadway on the Thames side of the Temple, was Wren's idea although it was not carried out till a century ago. Blackfriars Bridge, 100 yards downstream from Temple Avenue, takes its name from the nearby district in which the Dominican friars established a large priory in the 13th century. Upper Thames Street is bordered with many of Wren's works. Several are on the street just above, Queen Victoria Street. His St. Andrew-by-the-Wardrobe Church, at the corner of Wardrobe Terrace, gets its name from the master of the king's wardrobe (a post abolished in the 18th century) who lived in the neighborhood. Nearby is the College of Arms, which many think Wren built. It is the official registry of coats-of-arms and of pedigrees. Washington, after the Revolution, wrote to the college about his pedigree. Lee, Penn and others are on record with it. Across from the college is St. Benet Welsh Church, one of the best preserved of the Wren churches. As the name suggests, services are in Welsh.

St. Nicholas Cole Abbey is across the street from the international headquarters of the Salvation Army. It is assigned to the Bowyers Guild, descendants of the men who made the bows and arrows for the archers of Crécy and Agincourt. There is a fine view of St. Paul's Cathedral from its back door. St. Michael Paternoster Royal Church was founded by Dick Whittington when he was mayor in 1397 and rebuilt by Wren after the fire. It contains some 17th-century ironwork pieces: a hat rack, a sword rest for the visiting Lord Mayor, and a mace rest. Near London Bridge is the 202-foot-tall Doric column known as the Monument, which Wren erected as a memorial of the Great Fire. Its height is said to be the exact distance in feet from the bakehouse in Pudding Lane where the fire started. There are 311 steps to its gallery.

All Hallows Church, at the start of Great Tower Street which leads back into the City, is not a Wren church, but is a great London monument. It is said that the Saxons built a church on the site in A.D. 675. Sailors heading for sea used to leave a replica of their vessel at All Hallows, and pray for a safe voyage. Some of these miniature vessels still hang in the church. All Hallows permits rubbings to be made of the 16th- and 17th-century brass memorials in the church floor. Cobbler's wax and paper for the rubbings are provided by the church at a nominal cost.

St. Stephen's is behind Mansion House, the residence of the Lord Mayor. Wren used the dome of St. Stephen's as the model for the masterpiece he put atop St. Paul's. Wren also rebuilt St. Lawrence Jewry.

Wren's St. Mary le Bow gets its name from the
arches, or "bows," of the crypt. St. Mary le Bow has
been part of British history since the Norman Conquest.
In the reign of William the Conqueror a church was
built on the site to replace one that had been destroyed
by fire. In the courtyard is a statue of Captain John
Smith. It is inscribed to: "Citizen and Cordwainer,
1580–1631. First among the leaders of the settlement at
Jamestown, Virginia, from which began the overseas
expansion of the English-speaking peoples."

"Bow bells" is part of London life. In the early days
the church's Great Bell defined the boundaries of the
City, and all born within its sound claimed the right of
being a Cockney. A German air raid stilled the bell on
May 10, 1941 but it was recast in 1956. A variation in
the response to the oranges-and-lemons nursery rhyme
is: "I'm sure I don't know says the Great Bell at Bow."

On the Ludgate Hill side of St. Paul's is a church
dedicated to a soldier, St. Martin of Tours. (See Index.) Wren designed the spire of St. Martin's to act as
a foil to the dome of St. Paul's.

St. Paul's was Wren's masterpiece. He started it in
1675 at the age of 43, and worked on it 35 years. He
watched his son place the last stone atop the dome. He
is buried in St. Paul's, and a Latin inscription above his
tomb says: "If you would seek a memorial, look about
you."

St. Paul's Cathedral

A cathedral church has been on the site of St. Paul's
since A.D. 604, seven years after the arrival of St.
Augustine in Britain. In that year St. Mellitus, the
archbishop of Canterbury, built a Saxon church which
probably replaced a Roman one of the 4th century.
Some think the goddess Diana was venerated in a
temple on the same spot before the Christianization of
Britain and the Roman empire.

An American Memorial Chapel is behind the high altar. It was presented by the people of Britain to honor Americans killed in the Second World War. Names of the American dead are in a large gilded case under glass, written as in a hand-illuminated manuscript. An inscription on the marble table holding the book says the memorial was unveiled by Queen Elizabeth II on Nov. 26, 1958 in the presence of Vice President Nixon.

Halfway down the left aisle, under one of the arches, are four marble tablets with the names of deans of St. Paul's since A.D. 1066. The first name is Wulfstan. Four tablets in the right aisle list bishops of London, starting with Restitus in A.D. 314. But after him there is a gap in the list till Mellitus in A.D. 604.

A statue of John Donne, the poet, dean from 1621 to 1631, is at the right side of the high altar.

"That's the only memorial statue on the main level of the cathedral dating from the pre-fire [1666] church," a canon on his way to Evensong says. "It had been in the crypt, in the lower part of the church, with other old memorials—many, pre-Elizabethan—but because of its interest it was brought up here. In the crypt the statue had been in a recumbent position. Now it's standing up because that was the only way to place it."

The white marble urn at the base of the statue is now smudged. "Some say the dark patina is from the smoke and flame of the fire," the canon says. "Others think it was darkened by countless hands reaching out to touch it."

A group of Japanese visitors passes in front of the John Donne memorial and listens, enraptured, as a guide talks to them excitedly. One imagines that perhaps she is quoting from his *Devotions* of 1624: "No man is an island, entire of itself; every man is a piece of the continent, a part of the main. If a clod be washed away by the sea, Europe is the less, as well as if a promontory were, as well as if a manor of thy friends or of thine own were. Any man's death diminishes me, because I am involved in mankind. And, therefore, never send to know for whom the bell tolls. It tolls for thee."

The only free-standing painting in the cathedral is "The Light of the World" by Holman Hunt. Ruskin told about it in 1854, interpreting the biblical declaration of how Christ enters a soul.

There are 627 steps to the very top gallery. Most visitors stop at the gallery at the lower end of the cupola. It is only 375 steps.

THE BAPTISTS

Charles Haddon Spurgeon, born at Kelvedon in Essex, on June 19, 1834, was probably the most celebrated preacher of the Victorian age. His sermons were models of Puritan principles interlaced with humor. He preached at the Metropolitan Tabernacle. (*Underground station: Elephant and Castle.*) He was minister there from 1854 till he died in 1892. He founded Spurgeon's College, establishing it along new lines— taking in impoverished candidates and developing them educationally. He died in 1892, and is buried in West Norwood Cemetery, south London, a few miles from Spurgeon's College.

The college had been at Metropolitan Tabernacle, but in 1923 was moved to South Norwood Hill, Croydon. (*British Railways station: South Norwood Junction.*)

"It moved into a mansion which had been the home of a man called Hay Walker," says the well-dressed, busy publications man at Baptist Church House headquarters. (*Underground station: Holborn.*) "Hay Walker was an evangelical layman who wanted the place used for Christian purposes. He was not a Baptist. The college has regular visits from American Baptist university groups. Oklahoma Baptist University, for instance, has taken it over for vacation courses.

"There's been a succession of men—ministerial candidates—from the U.S.S.R. in the last ten to twenty years. They've been sending maybe one or two a year. They are good students and stay on for several years. We never have any advance notice. They just call up on the phone and ask if we can take one or two students—or, whatever the number."

Do they pay?

"They certainly do. They are very particular about that. They do not want to be beholden to anyone."

Another college, Regent's Park, had been started at Stepney in 1810, but was moved to Oxford in 1928.

"It is one of the finest modern pieces of architecture. We are proud of it. You could almost certainly find an American studying at Regent's Park at any time—and probably an older man, too, on a sabbatical."

The Bloomsbury Central Baptist Church (*Underground station: Tottenham Court Road*) is replacing the Metropolitan Tabernacle as the principal church of the Baptists. It was remodeled in 1964, and a new Communion table was designed. It is a massive wood table of dark maple. "It takes four men to move it," the caretaker says.

PLACES OF INTEREST: The Bristol Baptist College in Bristol, established in 1679, is the oldest Baptist theological college in existence. At Tewkesbury, Gloucestershire, is a 17th-century Baptist chapel. A statue of John Bunyan, author of *Pilgrim's Progress*, is in Bedford. The Bunyan Meeting in Bedford possesses a number of items associated with him. He was a member of the Bedford meeting.

THE QUAKERS

The Religious Society of Friends (Quakers) has a Friends House opposite Euston station. It is an immense building with Greek columns. Next to Friends

House is a private garden and, when it is open, the public is invited to use it "for rest and quiet enjoyment." The Friends also have a Fellowship of Healing which is ready to "give encouragement and counsel to those who are lonely or not in good health."

A center of pilgrimage for the Friends is the Lancashire town of Ulverston, 250 miles northwest of London. While on a preaching tour in the 17th century, George Fox, a 28-year-old weaver's son, interrupted a service in the parish church at Ulverston to give his views on religion and morals, views which already had brought him persecution and imprisonment. Margaret Fell, the wife of a judge, befriended him, impressed by his piety and zeal. Judge Fell permitted him to have his "Friends" meet in the Great Hall at Swarthmoor, the family mansion, every Sunday. Judge Fell never joined the Society of Friends but Margaret Fell became an active disciple. Several thousand Friends were subsequently released from jail because of her intercession. George Fox lost his protector when Judge Fell died in 1658, and soon was imprisoned. Margaret Fell continued to invite Friends to meet at Swarthmoor, and in 1664 she too was jailed. Both she and Fox were eventually released, and in 1669 they married—she 10 years older than he. Until his death in 1691, George Fox made Swarthmoor his headquarters. His wife outlived him by 11 years. She is buried in an unmarked grave at nearby Sunbrick Cemetery. Judge Fell's grave is in Ulverston itself. George Fox is buried at the Friends burial ground in Finsbury, London.

TRANSPORTATION: Ulverston is a train journey of about 5 hours from London.

WESTMINSTER ABBEY

Westminster Abbey has been the coronation church of England's monarchs ever since William the Conqueror was crowned there on Christmas Day, A.D. 1066, by the archbishop of Canterbury. Before William the Conqueror, Saxon kings had usually been crowned at Winchester. Westminster Abbey was founded 16 years before the Norman Conquest by King St. Edward the Confessor. He was buried in it after his death in 1066, and till recent times most of the succeeding sovereigns picked it for their graves, too. Edward the Confessor was canonized in 1163, and the abbey became a place of pilgrimage. It literally was an abbey, a monastery of Benedictine monks, until, like all monasteries in England, it was suppressed during the dissolution by Henry VIII.

At the right-hand side of the entrance is a memorial plaque to Franklin Delano Roosevelt. Nearby is a Union Jack, known as "The Padre's Flag." It was used on the Western Front in the First World War, and covered the coffin of the Unknown Warrior at his funeral on Nov. 11, 1920. The Unknown Warrior is buried in the middle aisle. The Unknown Warrior was picked from among six coffins by a blind man at St. Dunstan's Church. He is buried in a coffin made of English oak, which is enclosed in French soil and covered with Belgian marble.

On the wall of the right aisle is a marble sarcophagus supported on the heads of two male figures. Its inscription says:

"The monument was erected by a disconsolate parent, the Lady Viscountess Townshend, to the memory of her fifth son, Lt. Col. Roger Townshend, who was killed by a cannon ball July 25, 1759 at age 28 as he was reconnoitering the French lines at Ticonderoga in North America."

Major John André, the Revolutionary War figure, is buried here, too. He is described as a "British soldier who was sentenced to be hanged as a spy; although captured in uniform and although pleas were made for him to be shot, he was hanged at West Point."

Geoffrey Chaucer, writer of *Canterbury Tales,* who

died in 1400, inspired the custom of the Poets' Corner, where dozens of poets, writers and musicians are either buried or are remembered with memorials. There are memorials, for instance, for Henry Wadsworth Longfellow, who is buried in Cambridge, Mass.; and for Thomas Gray, author of *The Elegy,* who is buried in the churchyard at Stoke Poges which inspired the classic poem. (For Stoke Poges take train at Paddington Station to Slough, which is nearby.) Among the graves are those of Ben Jonson, Samuel Johnson and George Frederick Handel. A memorial plaque shows Handel holding in his hand a page from his *Messiah.*

WESTMINSTER CATHEDRAL

Westminster Cathedral is the present seat of the Catholic archbishop. It was built in 1910. Until the reestablishment of the Catholic hierarchy in the latter part of the 19th century only a pro-cathedral had been used.

Bronze panels list the "chief pastors of the Catholic Church in England showing their communion with the Apostolic See of Rome." The list begins with Restitus as Archbishop of Canterbury in A.D. 314, moving then to St. Augustine in 597. The tables also list the date and place the Catholic prelates received their *pallium,* a circular band of white wool worn by archbishops since the 8th century. Most entries list the location as Rome or England, but a few show other places: Viterbo (Italy), A.D. 1207; Aquila (Italy), A.D. 1294; Avignon, A.D. 1328; "a *rue* in Ponthieu," A.D. 1334; and Bow Church, 1556.

A cathedral chapel honors a new English saint, John Southworth, one of the Forty English Martyrs canonized by Paul VI in October 1970, and a priest from Lancashire. Some biographical notes are sketched in a memorial. They say:

"He studied at Douay College [France], and was

ordained there in 1618 on Holy Saturday. Arrested on his return to England he was imprisoned for three years. In the plague of 1636 in London he worked among the sick. In 1654 he was condemned to death, and on June 28 drawn and quartered at Tyburn, near where Marble Arch now stands, the last secular priest so to suffer. His remains were sewn together and taken to Douay. When Douay was demolished in the French Revolution the coffin was lost until its accidental discovery in 1927."

TRANSPORTATION: London receives flights from Boston, Chicago, Detroit, New York, Miami, San Francisco, Honolulu and Anchorage.

HOTELS: *Inn-on-the-Park, Inter-Continental, Hilton,* and *Dorchester* are leading hotels. *Cumberland, Piccadilly* and *Trafalgar* are less expensive.

PLACES OF INTEREST: St. Albans, 20 miles north of London, colonized by the Romans and site of the martyrdom of Alban, a Roman soldier beheaded for his Christian faith in the 4th century—the first Christian martyr in England. Offa, king of Mercia, reputedly established an abbey church (now cathedral) on the site of Alban's martyrdom in the 8th century.

7

Greece

IN 1963 one thousand years of monastic life on Mount Athos was celebrated. This means that Catholic monks initiated the unbroken millennium of Mount Athos's holy life at least a century before the great schism in Christianity, the split between the Western and Eastern branches of the 11th century that resulted in Christians being classified as Latins or Orthodox. Some historians say that hermits began to settle on Mount Athos in the 9th century.

Always, the Greeks have been people of religion.

Mesopotamia and Egypt influenced Greece by way of the Minoan society of Crete 2,000 years before Christ.

In their expansion, politically and culturally, the Greeks moved to the East about 10 centuries before Christ. Westward, they roamed across the Mediterranean to the shores of southern France. The glory of Athens mushroomed to its zenith in the 5th century B.C.

The Greeks adopted the gods of others, and adapted themselves to them. In the Mycenaean religion, for instance, were gods mentioned later by Homer: Zeus,

Artemis, Demeter, Hera, Hermes, Dionysos, Paian (a title of Apollo; thus, *paeans* of joy and triumph). From the Cretans, the Greeks took Athena, the serpent goddess sometimes represented as a bird. Their gods were human in form and had personalities. Homer related how they dwelled on Olympus, like a family of superior beings able to help the lower order of men—but not completely. A man has his fate, an allotted share of time—his *moira*—and a god is helpless to take him beyond that. Zeus, for example, could not save his son Sarpedon from death. When death did come to the ancient Greeks, the body was cremated and the soul went to Hades—not a sympathetic, gentle place, either. Only close friends, relatives and favorites of the gods were meant for Elysium.

The military forces of Rome proved superior to those of the Greeks. But even in pagan times the religion of the Greeks influenced the Romans. In the early days of Palestine, after the death of Christ, Hellenization had a key effect on the newly evolving Christianity, with the Greeks forcefully fitting the very religion within their philosophical framework. It was an effect that lingers today.

From the meeting in Palestine between Greek and Roman was born a mutual antipathy, expressed in various ways through the centuries but always there. For the Latin and the Greek, there were Western and Eastern emperors in the early centuries. Constantine put the cross in his coat of arms early in the 4th century, and for the last 13 of the 31 years of his reign made himself the sole emperor, West and East, moving his headquarters from Trier, in the middle of Western Europe, to the city on the Bosphorus named after him, Constantinople. But the same Christian religion linked the patriarch of Constantinople with the bishop of Rome, and this had a cohesive effect. Although the Eastern patriarchs in Constantinople, Antioch, Alexandria and Jerusalem were every bit as autonomous as the bishop of Rome, it was at the same time recognized that he, being the Pope, was first among equals. While the Pope directly presided over the evangelization of Western Europe, Christianity was carried to the Slavs from Byzantium.

In the 4th century the Greeks gave the title *Theotokos*, literally "God-bearing," to the Madonna, and started a devotion to Mary that has continued till today among Roman (Latin) Catholics and Orthodox. In each Orthodox church and chapel of Greece Theotokos is always represented in the most resplendent form. On Mount Athos the monks consider Theotokos the abbess of each monastery and of the entire Holy Mountain for that matter. It is to her that they pray, that they tell their difficulties, that they turn for guidance. One of the most emotion-provoking heresies in the early church, Nestorianism, took its name from Nestorius after he became patriarch of Constantinople in A.D. 428. He banned use of the title Theotokos, declaring that Mary was mother only of Christ's human nature. His teaching was quickly condemned by an ecumenical council that met in Ephesus in A.D. 431. (See Index.)

Emperor Leo III in the 8th century banned the giving of any religious reverence to images of the saints, and ordered their removal from the churches. The imperial edict set off riots, and a great confrontation between church and state. The outlawing of the pictures and ikons was called *iconoclasm* from the Greek for "image-breaking." An ecumenical council at Nicaea in A.D. 787 branded iconoclasm as a heresy, declaring that the image itself (such as Theotokos) was not being venerated but, rather, the person it depicted.

Whereas questions of religion drew Greek and Latin together, the jurisdiction of its exercise was a separating factor. Leo III, the emperor with the iconoclastic tendencies, drove a fatal wedge by making it possible for the patriarch of Constantinople to take from Rome jurisdiction over churches along the part of the Adriatic shore that is now Yugoslavia. Responsibility for the missionary activity in Bulgaria was also a divisive question. These two matters were still issues in the 9th century when a dispute developed around Photius, a brilliant layman who had been made patriarch of Constantinople in a compromise effort. The dispute went on for years, with legates from Rome involved—and not always acting in concert with the Pope.

Photius was already dead 150 years when the current patriarch of Constantinople, Michael Cerularius, unloosed a strong anti-Latin campaign in 1053. He ordered the closing of all Latin churches in Constantinople and to justify his action resurrected all the Latin-Greek issues from the time of Photius. The papal legates, far from clarifying matters theologically, solemnly excommunicated the patriarch—and him alone —on July 16, 1054. Ironically, the legates were acting—if badly—in the name of a Pope (Leo IX) who was already dead, and no one as yet had succeeded him. For at least two more decades Rome and Antioch remained in communion. But the cleavage, the Greek *schisma*, was there. When the Crusaders from Western Europe rampaged through Greece, old Latin-Greek animosities were kicked up once more. The Crusaders, in a twin burst of fanaticism and mindlessness, sacked Constantinople in 1204, putting a Latin emperor and a Latin bishop in a city that had been Greek for centuries. From then on being Orthodox was a symbol of patriotism.

On May 1, 1453 the Greeks lost Constantinople to the Turks, and for centuries Greek aspirations and culture virtually were extinguished by the Ottoman empire. The Turks, Moslem to a man, changed the name of Constantinople to Istanbul. For their political convenience the Turks permitted the Orthodox patriarchate to continue to be ruled by a Greek so that he could deal with other patriarchates in their empire: Antioch, Jerusalem, Alexandria. The patriarch of Constantinople

(Istanbul) became the ecumenical patriarch in the East, and remains that today. His authority was diminished somewhat after 1830 when Greece became independent and the Greek church "autocephalous," or self-governing.

SALONIKA

Before Constantinople became the seat of the Eastern branch of the Roman empire, the emperor ruled from Salonika (also spelled Thessaloniki), a port city on the Via Egnatia, the main Roman road. The Via Egnatia remains the main street of Salonika, a cynosure for Roman ruins and memories. The Via Egnatia is straddled by the Triumphal Arch of Galerius, the pagan emperor who ordered the slaying of Demetrios, a Greek Christian nobleman and an officer in the Roman legions. Demetrios, martyred in A.D. 306, the year after Salonika was made the imperial capital for the Eastern branch of the empire, is the patron saint of the city. Each October the people of Salonika celebrate the memory of their patron saint with a series of Byzantine-style festival events known as *Demetria*. Salonika, the capital of northern Greece, is in Macedonia and is the gateway to Mount Athos.

MOUNT ATHOS

The pilgrimage to Greece's Holy Mountain, Aghion Oros, is unique for a number of reasons: permission must be obtained, the pilgrimage area is vast, no women are permitted, the pilgrimage must be made on foot or on the back of a mule because no motor transportation exists, distances between points on the pilgrimage route are measured not in miles but in walking hours, and the tradition of monastic hospitality makes the pilgrim a nonpaying guest in any monastery he chooses.

Mount Athos is the most eastern of three long fingers of land which reach into the Aegean Sea somewhat less than 100 miles southeast of Salonika. The Mount Athos peninsula takes the name from the 6,600-foot mountain at the end of the long green prong. The peninsula is more than 40 miles long and nearly 5 miles wide. For more than 10 centuries, till the end of the First World War and of the Ottoman empire, the monks on Mount Athos maintained their independence from the outside world. The new constitution of Greece in 1927 placed Mount Athos under the jurisdiction of the Greek government but recognized it as a theocratic semiautonomous republic. Each of the 20 monasteries on Mount Athos maintains a representative and a house at Karies (also spelled Karyai), the only town on the peninsula. The 20-member group of monks meets regularly to set general policy. Day-to-day administration is done by four monks who make up a Committee of Supervisors, called the Epistasis. The score of monasteries are divided into four groups, and each group names a monk to the Committee of Supervisors for a fixed term—in recent times, a year.

A pilgrimage to Mount Athos requires advance permission. Permission is obtained by acquiring three identification statements—first, from one's consulate; then, from the Greek government; and finally, from the Greek police. The first two statements (consulate and government) can be obtained in Athens, but the third is issued only in Salonika. It usually is easier, therefore, to carry out the entire permission procedure in Salonika where, by taxi, the rounds of the three key points can be made in less than two hours.

The pilgrim presents his passport at the consulate and a clerk types out, on a form in quadruplicate, a one-line entry with the name, birthplace, age, profession and passport number. The form is not even signed. A clerk at the government office asks the pilgrim how long he would like to remain on Mount Athos. She enters the number of days on the copies of the form, initials all 4 copies, keeps one and slips the others into envelopes addressed to the Aliens Police Service, to the Administration and to the Committee of Supervisors on Mount Athos. Theoretically, the pilgrim is allowed to visit each of the 20 monasteries on a one-monastery-a-day basis, and this in effect limits stays to 20 days. Most visitors remain a week, visiting 2 or 3 monasteries. At the Aliens Police Service the pilgrim presents the appropriate envelope and his passport. The return of the passport is accompanied with the actual permit, a single sheet of paper identifying the individual and affirming the authorization for him to visit Mount Athos for the number of days indicated.

Ouranoupolis, 90 miles from Salonika, is the access point to Mount Athos the year around. There are one or two boats a day—the schedule varies—from Ouranoupolis to the main port of the Holy Mountain, Dafni, on the south side of the peninsula.

There are morning and afternoon buses to Ouranoupolis, and the journey takes up to 3 hours because the first 50 miles of the route—more than half—is through mountains, and along a narrow road. Even by private car, it is slow driving, although beautiful. At Paleohorion, 35 miles from Ouranoupolis, the descent toward the sea begins and the road slips through villages with small stone houses painted white and often trimmed in blue. One gets sight of the sea at Stagira and on a hill looking out into the sea is a shining white statue of Aristotle. A warning sign made of white stones spaced across the side of a hill at Stratonion asks travelers to be careful of fire "because our trees are so small."

The hills here are filled with metals—copper, iron, aluminum—and ore-carrying vessels call at the makeshift horseshoe-shaped port to be loaded with the precious diggings. Although all this means wealth for somebody the few hundred residents of Stratonion lead an unpretentious life. Several cars are visible around the village, but mostly one sees men riding donkeys side-saddle to their front door. There are no piers in the port, and the ore-carriers sidle up to the funnel of a conveyor belt that extends out over the water some 50 yards or more.

Outside Ierissos there is a long sandy beach, and not a house in sight. Flocks of sheep and goats are the only creatures stirring for mile after mile. It has a large white church which, except for the bell tower at the right side in front, looks like a church in a New England town. An enormous modern hotel, built of stone, overlooks the sea at Trepidi, just beyond Nea Roda.

Ouranoupolis is 7 miles from Nea Roda. It is a collection of small dwellings, huddled at the seaside. There are dozens of fishing vessels and small boats along the beach. A narrow cement wharf extends into the sea. The water is startlingly clear. It has a vividly pure look. There is a small hotel with a dozen simple rooms, and an obliging manager who is balding, fortyish and chunky. He calls himself Kosta, and speaks German. When the bus arrives from Salonika, Kosta walks to meet it in the small open area near the wharf. Many of the passengers are townspeople, but Kosta at a glance knows the residents from the pilgrims. Once the bus is empty, the driver moves it near the town pump. He and the ticket collector then douse its windows and sides with buckets of water. There are only a few hundred residents in Ouranoupolis and one meets many of them —the men, that is; the women stay out of sight—in the two or three cafés which they frequent to play cards and sip *ouzo*. Kosta shows the way to the restaurant, a large square room with a dozen or so tables that have opaque plastic coverings. Fresh fish and vegetables are displayed in a glass-fronted showcase near the kitchen. The bus driver and ticket collector are in the restaurant, and they go into the kitchen to inspect the lamb stew in a black caldron.

On a side table someone has left a copy of the official

greeting addressed by the Athos community to "every visitor or pilgrim of the Holy Mountain of Athos," and signed by the Epistasis, the Committee of Supervisors. It reads:

Dear Sir—You doubtless realize that you are now travelling towards a Monastic State, the "Garden of the Virgin Mary," far from the secular world, a State where prayer, the constant praise of God, the purification of the soul and spiritual monasticism are the main pursuits in life.

This Sacred Place is not merely a historic site marked for its beautiful scenery, its stately temples, its holy relics and rich libraries. It is chiefly a place of spiritual endeavors that produced a great number of saints.

We can thus repeat that "this land is subject to miracles."

The sacred history of the Holy Mountain and its great heritage require of every visitor an adequate, becoming and dignified demeanor.

The treasures of this more than one-thousand-year-old shrine can only be appreciated by those who approach them with respect and reverence, not merely as curious visitors, but as devout pilgrims.

Orthodox Christianity, of which the Holy Mountain is the bastion and treasury of traditions, is closely bound to modesty, not only a modesty of behavior but also that of appearance.

You are consequently requested that, since you intend to visit the Holy Mountain, your appearance in general, both in regard to clothing as well as hair, should be appropriately restrained. We shall regret being obliged to refuse entrance to those who do not comply.

As promised, Kosta awakens the hotel guests in time for the 7 o'clock boat. About a dozen men in caps and work clothes are in the café at the wharf. There is coffee in small white cups, the thick Turkish style, but nothing at all to eat—not even a slice of bread. Some of the men are drinking brandy. A uniformed Greek naval chief petty officer checks papers of passengers prior to the departure of the boat. The boat is about 40 feet long. The "skipper" could be a fishing-boat captain—

black curly hair, leather jacket. He watches the goings-on from the wheelhouse and his attention soon focuses on a long, loud argument between a deckhand and a passenger about the stowage of some wooden crates and bags. The deckhand wants the man to clear the starboard passageway of the boxes and bags he had brought aboard, and move them elsewhere. In a few minutes the reason for the commotion is made clear to the other passengers. The deckhand wanted the space cleared for a saffron-colored mule, as big as a young horse, which is led aboard gingerly and tethered to the railing, with other ropes lashed in such a way as to form the outlines of a stall that can protect the animal from being thrown about in case the boat pitches or rolls during the voyage. The deck cargo, like the mule, is being transported to the monks on Athos. Some of the 30 passengers are workmen who, after a brief vacation with their families in Ouranoupolis or another nearby town, are returning to jobs at one of the monasteries for another work interval of two or three months. The workmen crowd into one of the two small rooms below deck. In the other room a uniformed policeman reads a newspaper.

Foreigners remain on deck, staring intently at the Athos peninsula. One foreigner on deck is a husky, 6-foot-4 American in a long black robe, but no hat. He has the look and easygoing geniality of a Californian, but actually was born in Cleveland in 1952. He identifies himself as Ratsko Trbuhovich, explaining that Ratsko is "Roscoe in American." He studied for six years in St. Vladimir's Seminary in Crestwood, near Scarsdale, in Westchester County, N.Y. He married a girl who was a theology student at Crestwood when he was there and for the past year they have been living in Belgrade where he has been studying at the theology faculty.

"I am glad Americans don't send young seminarians to Belgrade for study," Roscoe says, "because then they come home as fine Yugoslav village priests, not knowing the American scene or how to approach youth. It's better that they get their early study where they are going to work—in America—and then go to Belgrade for advanced studies, and to perfect their language. It's important for them to know Serbian because of many reasons. But, psychologically, in dealing with older people, it is important. We [the young] want the liturgy in English, for instance, and the older people say the only reason we want it in English is because we don't know Serbian. But if we speak Serbian, they can't say that."

The "skipper" keeps the boat close to the shoreline, moving it assuredly among clusters of reefs. Actually the sea holds no secrets. Even at depths of 20 feet the bottom is visible. The monasteries seem to be evenly divided—half on the south side of the peninsula; the others on the "Turkish side," as the Greeks say, the side where the sea becomes frenzied.

Roscoe has done a great deal of reading to prepare for his pilgrimage to Mount Athos. He is leaving his specific program to the monks of the Serbian monastery, Chilandari, to work out for him. The "Holy Monastery of Chilandari," as it is formally called, was founded by Czar Stefan Nemanja and Archbishop Ratsko of Serbia in the latter part of the 12th century.

The voyage to Dafni takes two hours, and on the way the boat makes a couple of stops at landings serving nearby monasteries. The first stop is at the landing for the Xenophontos monastery, a large building several stories high, that is attached to the side of the mountainous ridge. The monastery was established in the 10th century on the site of a chapel raised four centuries earlier to honor St. Demetrios.

At each stop a few monks, bearded and dressed completely in black, come aboard, headed for Karies to transact official business for their monastery, or to shop for it. At the last stop before Dafni almost everyone on board studies the huge monastery founded in the 12th century by St. Panteleimon the Russian. In recent times it reached its peak a century ago when the liturgy was celebrated both in Russian and in Greek, and the abbot was a Russian. But once again, as many times in the past, the monastery looks as if it is physically falling apart.

As the port of Dafni comes into view, passengers spot a white jeep coming down the mountainside, and follow its path as it heads first in one direction, then in the opposite, like a ball in a pinball machine. The jeep, driven by a policeman, arrives at the Dafni boat landing just as the passengers are about to disembark.

The Dafni port infrastructure consists of a one-room customs shed, a café, an office above the café that is used by the blue-uniformed Greek government customs inspectors, and several dingy shops. In one shop which is basically a grocery store but which also sells picture postcards, the policeman-jeep driver is in a corner wrapping the passports in a sheet of paper. After inspecting the shops the passengers turn their attention to the loading of the waiting bus with the bags of beans, sacks of potatoes and corn, and assorted wooden crates that had been carried from Ouranoupolis on the boat. The vehicle looks like an American school bus of prewar vintage except that it has the gray-blue color of the sea.

Karies is only 3 miles inland from Dafni but it is a twisting uphill route, and the journey takes nearly a half hour. The road is hardpacked gravel and stones, and the bus lurches and shudders alternately all the way. The ticket seller passes through the bus serenely, having acquired his "sea legs" long ago. He is wearing a white turtleneck that fits him loosely, a badly scarred leather jacket and a beret. A cigarette dangles from a corner of his mouth. The bus is headed only for Karies but he has in his hand a batch of three or four types of tickets, each colored differently. Apparently monks pay one fare, civilian workers another, and visitors still another.

Karies looks like a prewar Arizona copper-mining town. A few stone steps lead to the main street, about 50 yards long, which ends at the big square. The stone slabs with which the street is paved are cut from local granite and are wearing shoddily. Many pieces are missing. Several shops are at the left side of the street. They are the main source of food and miscellaneous supplies, from window glass to nails. The wooden store fronts, the beards of the monks, the absence of women, the mules with saddlebags hitched to posts outside the stores, the kerosene lamps furnishing the only light in the shops—such features heighten the impression of an American frontier town. From a doorway across from the stores a heavy tall man in shirt and dark trousers stares at the new arrivals. A handpainted sign above his head identifies the place as a hotel and restaurant. The man points down the street to a decaying building. "Police," he says.

The building down the street turns out to house another restaurant, and its proprietor seems to be a twin of the man who had pointed out the way to what is necessarily the first stop for the new arrival, the police office. The restaurant man stares from a window, letting the foreigner speak first. Police? In response to the question he gestures to a lane at the corner. A sign in the dirt lane points to "Police Aliens Service." The face of the restaurant man appears once more, this time at what is apparently the back of his restaurant. He realizes the humor of the situation, and laughs.

An office with a desk, a table and a couple of chairs is occupied by the policeman in a small two-story building that represents the Greek government presence. He hands out a mimeographed form which asks for the same information contained in the passports on the desk in front of him and, in addition, the name of the visitor's father and the visitor's maiden name. Since only women have maiden names, and since women are not allowed on Mount Athos, the question seems incongruous. No one points this out. But Roscoe, the American Serbian theology student, asks aloud: "How can I write down my passport number when he [the policeman] has my passport?" The policeman, without a word, hands Roscoe his passport.

Then the policeman asks for the two envelopes elegantly addressed in Greek which had been given by the clerk in the Greek government office in Salonika. He spends several minutes comparing the data in the passport. Everything seems to "check." The way is now clear for the final formality at the offices of the monastic government of the Athos community.

The monastic government occupies an aging building which has a wide steep stairway at the front, like a county courthouse. The building is along the only square of Karies. The square is about 150 yards long and 100 yards wide. At its center is a red brick church with faded frescoes along the outer walls. Monks pass back and forth across the square, some leading heavily laden mules. It is forbidden to ride a horse or mule through the streets of Karies. Several serious-looking civilians are walking through the square. They have a silver badge engraved with some small writing, and the large Greek letters, Alpha and Omega. They carry walking sticks, which are actually clubs. One wears a beret. They are members of the Athos community police force.

A large, almost bare reception hall is at the entrance of the monastic building. There are straight-backed wooden benches along the wall near the front window, and a long table. An Athos policeman gestures for the permit in the visitor's hand, and enters a room at the side of the hall opposite the benches. After going back and forth across the hall several times, the policeman brings a tray with a small cup of coffee and a dish of jelly. This is the sweet the Greeks traditionally offer guests to show them they are welcome.

Soon a monk comes to the door, and invites the visitor to enter the office. Paintings of religious subjects and of patriarchal-looking men are on the walls. A monk with a whitish beard is at a table which he uses as a desk. He is a kindly man of about 50 who searches for a few words in English. He makes clear he is a kind of executive secretary.

From the next room another monk, thinner but also middle-aged, brings a piece of paper, and hands it to the monk-secretary. The monk-secretary glances at it and then presents it to the visitor. It is like a diploma, and it is authenticated with a seal and two stamps. The policeman steps forward and asks for 150 drachmas. "For the stamps," he says.

The certificate, written in Greek, is described in the heading as a "permit of sojourn valid for 20 holy and venerable monasteries of the Holy Mount." It bears the name of the visitor, his nationality and the number of days authorized for the visit."

"He [the visitor] came to visit the Holy Lodge and to worship the holy and sacred doctrines of our faith," the certificate says. "Therefore we ask you [the various monasteries] to welcome him warmly, to give him as much hospitality as possible, and to assist him in the achievement of the purpose he came here for."

At the bottom of the certificate are the signatures of the four supervisors.

What puzzles the visitor is the date. How could they make such a mistake?—13 days earlier than the current date? But there is no mistake. The monks use the old Julian calendar of Julius Caesar, rather than the corrected 16th-century Gregorian calendar of Pope Gregory XIII.

The monk-secretary suggests monasteries where communication in Western languages is possible. A monk at Stavronikita speaks French. There is a German-speaking monk at Simonos Petras, and also, he adds, a Canadian. That seems to be the extent of Western languages.

In the square outside a monk hears an American visitor talking, and comes over to greet him. He has a long gray beard and talks excitedly. He says he knows America and collects an American social security pension.

"I am seventy now," he says, speaking good English.

But what makes him eligible, besides age, for American social security benefits?

"I was in the crew of an English cargo vessel and jumped ship in New York in 1929," the monk says. He says his name is Strichas. His first name is Ernest or, in Greek, Athenasios. "In 1930 I joined the Communist Party in Detroit. I had been a Communist in Greece in the Greek army, and I had my diploma from there when I arrived in the states. In 1936 I married a girl from Kiev named Vera. She was a dressmaker in New York. We had met in demonstrations and on picket lines."

How did he manage without immigration papers?

"There were thousands like us in those days without papers. Vera and I had a little girl. In 1942 we went to California and I worked in the San Pedro shipyards. I was a CIO member. We got divorced in Los Angeles in 1942. We didn't agree together. I left the little girl with her mother. She was sixteen when I left America in 1955. I saw her last then."

And before that?

"Before that. In 1942, after the shipyards job and the divorce, I went into the produce business in California. I was a truck driver. I lived with a Greek woman named Ariadni in San Diego. She was a widow. We got married there in 1951. Through her I met Bible pastors from Billy Graham's, and through her and them and Brother Garfield of San Diego, and John the Greek, a theologian of the Four Square Gospel in Los Angeles, and Father Gene Martin, a pastor in the Church of God in San Diego—through them, I came back to God."

He interrupts to call to a youngish-looking monk who is leading a pack mule through the square.

"That's an American," Athenasios says. "He's at the Russian monastery."

The newcomer introduces himself as Father Seraphim. He suggests that the visitor have lunch in the restaurant opposite the shops in the main street. They can meet there after he has finished shopping.

When Father Seraphim leaves, Athenasios continues his story about himself in America.

"After I came back to God, I studied at the Four Square Gospel Theological Institute, 1100 Glendale in Los Angeles. Aimee McPherson was dead, but her son was there. He was young then. There were five or ten pastors there. Then in 1955 Ariadni squealed on me, and the 'Immigration' deported me."

Why did she squeal?

"Because I lost interest in women—even lost interest in myself. I became interested two hundred percent in God. I had many Apparitions of God. In 1951 I had my first vision. That was in San Diego. In the vision there were two dinosaurs at the edge of one mountain and a little boy at another mountain. One dinosaur was looking up, and that is when I saw God. And He explained to me that one dinosaur was the American nation which had cured my communistic cancer, and the other dinosaur was Greece. And the little boy was there to show me that I was born again like a little boy of five. Now I am a Christian twenty years, and God would show me now as twenty-five years old. That's how God talks.

"Another time He appeared to me and showed me with whiskers. I thought the one with whiskers was my father. But He said: 'It is you. You will be a monk. You will go back to Greece, to Athos, and be a monk, and work for Me.'

"I had a little Chevrolet car and I put a box of two hundred oranges into it, and went into the San Bernardino Mountains. I took the oranges out of the car and then walked to a gold digger's shack and stayed there, fasting and praying. I lived on the oranges. They finished in twenty days, and after that I lived on water. Then, after thirty days (altogether) I came back to Great Bear Lake and San Bernardino, and went into a grocery to get something to eat. I saw my face with whiskers in a window, and I saw this was the way God wanted me, and I began going from place to place preaching. I would ask people why are they sad, why are they crying. Then, the pastor took over. And he said, 'We are crying because we do not have what he has—meaning me. If he (me) didn't have what he had—the blessing of God—he could not have gone in the mountains for twenty-one days eating only oranges and nine days [living only] on water!'

"Ariadni squealed on me in 1955, and I was arrested, and an airplane took me from Los Angeles with two Italians and one Greek to New York, and then we were put on an army boat bringing soldiers to Europe. We could go around the boat. We were not locked up. I still had my beard. I stayed with my family in Athens for some months. Then I came to Athos to meet my brother who had been a monk here eighteen years— Father Triphon.

"Then I saw it was God's will that I stay here as a monk. I was in Lavra and other monasteries, but I like to live alone. So I live with a few of my own disciples in a *kellion* which is dependent on Pantokratoros, the Russian monastery."

Athenasios accompanies the visitor to the doorway of the restaurant, and then says goodbye, explaining he has shopping to do in the stores across the little street.

The restaurant is a large square room, bare except for

a half-dozen wooden tables with no placemats or coverings. A few civilian workers are sipping wine at a table. The proprietor is the man who had been in the doorway earlier, pointing the way to the police office. He now beckons the visitor to an adjoining room where some huge pots are on a grill over a wood fire. He removes the lid from one pot. "Soup," he says, pointing to white beans in a tomato sauce. He removes another lid. "Beans," he says, and he indicates the white beans which have not been splashed with sauce. In the third pot he shows a tremendous quantity of squid. "Calamari," he says, sticking to his one-word descriptive style. He brings the food to the table himself, along with a liter of *retsina,* the resin-based white wine.

A Greek civilian sitting at the next table, neither drinking nor eating, gets a conversation going by asking, in German, "Are you German?" Because so many Greeks find temporary, high-paying jobs in Germany, Germany becomes their second world, and all foreigners for them are Germans. It turns out that the amiable civilian is a rent-a-mule operator. With a mule, he observes, it is possible to visit three monasteries a day; on foot, only one.

"Look," he says. "The Grand Lavra, the oldest monastery here, the one founded in A.D. 963 and which has so many works of art—that's over twenty miles from here, and seven hours on foot. Pantokratoros is five miles—an hour and a half on foot. Stavronikita is about the same."

In the street, Father Seraphim is tightening the saddlebags on his mule. Father Seraphim is slender, and has a small reddish beard. He was born in Pittsburgh. He speaks sparingly. When told that the calamari in the restaurant were good, he says: "No wonder. They probably were American. They import canned calamari from California." When told that Athenasios said he jumped ship in New York in 1929, Father Seraphim says easily: "That's the year I was born."

Father Seraphim does not ride his mule. He uses him only for carrying the packages of food that he bought in Karies. A few hundred yards from Karies Father Seraphim pauses, pokes in a saddlebag in search of a package of dates, and after ripping away the cellophane wrapping begins feeding the fruit to the mule. "He likes dates," Father Seraphim says. "His name is Arrab."

No female animals at all—whether mules, dogs, cats or livestock—are allowed on Mount Athos. Some monasteries have their own cattle but they are beef cattle, and not milk cows.

Besides the basic 20 monasteries there are a number of smaller monastic foundations. Athenasios had remarked that he lived in a *kellion*. This is a group of several independent houses which do not have a central church. That is its main difference from a *skete*, the type of monastic settlement in which Father Seraphim, the Pennsylvania monk, lives. A *skete* is a collection of several houses, maybe as many as a dozen or more, which are grouped around a church. Life in a *skete* or a *kellion* is more independent, especially in the matter of prayer. Whether *skete, kellion* or a hermit's cell, each monastic foundation is dependent on the nearest monastery. This is the principle of Athos.

A big monk in a high black hat and a faded robe that apparently serves as a working garment is in the yard of a house along the road. Father Seraphim knows him, and they exchange greetings and some words of conversation for a minute or two. Later Father Seraphim remarks that the monk is an expert in making ikons. Every monastery has an ikon-maker, and some monasteries conduct schools in the ancient art, accepting students.

Women have been barred from Athos since A.D. 1060 when the emperor Constantine X issued an edict of prohibition. The monks tell stories about attempted invasions by women.

"About a year or so ago," Father Seraphim says, "a couple women—they were French—walked along the sea from Ouranoupolis and when they came to the boundary of Athos they saw a fence which extended into the sea for several yards. They swam into the sea and around the fence, surfacing on the other side. Success! they thought, exultantly. A woman had entered the men-only area! But from a hut nearby their arrival had been noted, and it was not long before they were in the hands of the police. What happened to them, I don't know. A big fine, anyway, and expulsion. There's very little crime in Greece because the police do not miss a thing.

"I remember, too, there was a French woman writer who published a story about having disguised herself, and how she penetrated Athos to spend *Forty Days Alone with 1,000 Men*—something like that. She told all kinds of nonsense, like how she flattened out her breasts—real nonsense."

In 1963, at the time of the celebration of the millennium of monastic life on Athos, some roads were built along the peninsula. The only vehicle which uses them is the white police jeep. Perhaps half the monasteries are near the roads; the rest are reached only by narrow paths which often are crossed by broken trees and sprawling branches, and the pilgrim has to beat a way through brush.

A mile along the main road from Karies the Pennsylvania monk points to a small footpath at the left. A handpainted stick of wood nailed to a tree carries the word "Pantokratoros." This is the route to Father Seraphim's monastery, and to his *skete*, too. Before taking the path with his mule Arrab, the American monk says that the turnoff to Stavronikita Monastery, a mile farther along the main road, will be marked with a sign.

The road to Stavronikita is deeply rutted and not as wide as the main road. There are no telephone lines along it, either. Till 1973 there were no telephone lines at all to the monasteries. Now some are connected to the telephone system. Many monks resent the introduction of the roads and telephones by the Greek government, looking upon them as trespassers on the traditional monastic setting.

If there is a road, the police jeep can transport a sick monk to the infirmary of the one doctor at Karies. If there is no road, the monk has to be carried out on muleback. So, isn't it better to have roads?

"We don't think too much about things like that," the French-speaking monk at Stavronikita says.

Stavronikita is the smallest and the poorest of the 20 monasteries, he says.

It is laid out around an inner quadrangle with a high side facing the sea which roars even in good weather. The 10th-century tower gives it the look of a fortress. At the right of the entrance arcade, just before the courtyard, is a kind of porter's lodge where guests are received. It is a small room, neatly furnished with a polished table, a few straw-bottomed chairs, and a wall bench. There is a small pantry where coffee is made for guests over a kerosene burner.

Why is Stavronikita poorer than the other monasteries?

"It has suffered tragedy often—several times destroyed by fire, for example, and in recent years virtual extinction because of the vocation gap," the monk says. "Till three centuries ago there were many monasteries on Athos. Even a *kellion* was called a monastery in the early days. In the reorganization of the seventeenth century, Athos was divided into twenty parts, and there was a monastery in each part. Stavronikita was the last to be recognized as a monastery, and the best territory had been divided by that time, too. Stavronikita was not assigned the forest land from which you could sell lumber that would bring you money you could use to buy houses in Salonika to rent for income."

Stavronikita is a new community of monks, too. The

oldest monk is only 49. The prior is 38. There are only a dozen monks in the immense monastery. Three are priests.

"In 1968, no more monks remained here, and the monastery became cenobitic and was resettled with monks from other parts of Greece and of Athos. The cenobitic type of monastery follows the severe monastic rule. The monks eat together, live together, work together, pray together, and own all the property in common. The idiorrhythmic type of monastery is more liberal. It permits the monks to have personal property. Each monk lives on his own in a room or two. There are some things together, such as prayer. But the monks eat separately, each preparing his own food. The monks work at the monastery and are paid so that they can buy their food and clothes. Now seven monasteries are idiorrhythmic and the rest are cenobitic. Another cenobitic monastery is the Philotheon. It has many treasures, including the right hand of John Chrysostom and an ikon of the Virgin which had been thrown into the sea during the iconoclastic period, and washed up near the monastery."

But the monastery that is cenobitic—from the Greek words for "common life"—does not represent Athos monasticism at its most austere.

"If you consider all of Athos as a temple, then at its very tip is the Holy of Holies because there live the monks who are most advanced spiritually, living in a most ascetic fashion. The Holy of Holies is a desert area circling the base of Mount Athos itself. There is no fresh water. Some monks live as high as three thousand feet on the mountain, even more. They live in a *kalivi*, a small hut, and spend several hours a day in prayer."

At Stavronikita, as on all Athos, the monks not only follow the old Julian calendar but also Byzantine time. For them the day begins at sunset. This means that much of the nighttime is spent at prayer in the church, with the actual schedule varying from season to season according to the time that the sun sets.

Their day begins at 7 A.M. But 7 A.M. for them means seven hours after sunset.

"On normal days we spend three and one-half hours in the church in common prayer. Then there is one hour of Vespers in the afternoon, and a half hour of Compline, making five hours in the church in each twenty-four hours. This is a normal day. Also in our cells we have fixed hours of prayer. On Sundays and feastdays we spend up to eight and one-half hours in the church in prayer. On great feasts, like the feast of St. Nicholas, the patron of our monastery, we are in the church for fourteen hours."

Monks are summoned to prayer in the church by the sounding of a *talanton*, a long strip of heavy metal. It is struck 3 times: a quarter of an hour before start of the service; then 5 minutes before; then, at the actual start.

The church, entered from the inner courtyard, is relatively small. It is lined with a dozen or more individual stalls with high armrests on which tired monks lean, like crutches, during services. An ikon depicting Christ is at the right side; an image of the Theotokos (Mother of God) is at the left. The center doorway of the iconostasis consists of two half-doors covered by a curtain. The liturgy is celebrated behind the iconostasis after Matins each day, two hours after sunset. The only illumination in the church is from the candles.

Some monks are excused from parts of the prayers in the church during the day because of special work assignments, such as preparing meals or remaining available to greet visitors. But all attend the last hour of the day's Divine Office, Compline. At the end of Compline, each monk prostrates himself before the Theotokos ikon. Then he proceeds to where the prior is standing, a few yards away, and prostrates himself before him, rises to kiss the prior's hand, and prostrates himself once more to receive the prior's blessing.

The long table in the refectory, with benches on each side, could seat 50 monks. But not even Simonos Petras, considered a "big monastery," has that many monks. Only 40 are there.

Meals are simple: a large bowl of lentils, a plate of fresh scallions from the monastery garden, an orange from one of the citrus trees that grow on the side away from the sea, and chunks of white halvah made from sesame seeds, nuts and honey. Rooms for guests have nothing in them but a single iron bed (with sheets and plenty of blankets), a wood stove and a kerosene lamp. No matter how early in the morning a visitor plans to leave Stavronikita in order to continue his journey on Athos, the prior is on hand and asks him to delay long enough to have a cup of tea and some halvah.

Karies, any morning in the week, is like a Sunday morning in a Greek village after church. The foreigners have been on Athos for varying periods of time. Some are leaving. All are exuberant about their experiences, and compare notes.

"I wish I were here in August," a middle-aged Englishman in a jeans outfit says. "I'd gladly walk to the Holy Lavra even if it did take seven hours. I understand the monks lead a procession up to a chapel on the summit of Mount Athos on the feast of the Transfiguration. It must be an unforgettable experience."

Werner, a Berlin University student who speaks good English, says he has been having a "fantastic time." He had spent 10 days hitchhiking from Berlin to Salonika. At Salonika he bought a bus ticket to Ouranoupolis because there were so few cars headed for Athos, and the chances of a ride looked meager.

"All along they warned me I'd have to have my long hair cut," Werner says. "The ticket collector on the boat, a guy who hadn't shaved for a week it looked to me, he told me I'd have to get a haircut. But I didn't get it cut. When I reached the monastic administrative office here [Karies] the monk told me I'd have to have my hair cut, or I would not be allowed to visit Athos. Two other young Germans were there in the hall, and they showed me their new haircuts. *Man muss,* they told me.

"I was pretty depressed. I left my rucksack on the floor in the reception hall, and walked down the marble steps, and for several hours wandered around Karies and the nearby paths. In the afternoon I met a young monk of about my own age—twenty-five. He told me he had been a Jew, but had converted to Christianity. He was living on Athos temporarily with an old monk of sixty-five, but planned to go to Israel to join his brothers, and await God's direction on his next move. He reassured me, and told me to go back to the monk in the administrative office and ask him to make an exception for me about the hair. Only one monk was in the office. I told him my father had been on Athos ten years ago and had talked to me about it a lot—which was the truth. I said I wanted to visit Athos, but I didn't want to cut my hair. He gave me a certificate for five days here.

"It was great. I stayed in the house of the Jewish monk and the older monk. They raise almost all their own food, and they taught me how to make bread. They make their own wine, too, and it's good. They have nut trees, and they sell the nuts to buy flour and other things they need. But their needs are very little."

Roscoe, the American Serbian theology student, is in the group waiting for the bus for Dafni. He has not as yet visited Chilandari, the Serbian monastery, which is six hours (19 miles) from Karies. He first wants to visit Simonos Petras, near Dafni.

"The new abbot there," Roscoe says, "is a holy man from Meteora (the monastic village in central Greece). Since Meteora has become so much of a tourist attraction lately, the spiritual solitude has been spoiled and he decided to come to Athos with some disciples. From what I've heard, all seem to be college graduates, and young."

Roscoe has not as yet met the American monk, Father Seraphim of Pittsburgh. When told that Father Seraphim studied at Scranton, Roscoe nods knowingly: "He must have been at the Russian seminary, St. Thikon, at South Canaan. It's near Scranton."

Someone remarks that he heard that monks at Esphigmenon Monastery, on the north shore, were challenging the authority of Ecumenical Patriarch Demetrios I. He had ordered the deportation of the abbot and four monks for having deviated from his guidance. In defiance, the monks barricaded themselves in their monastery.

"That's not surprising," the Englishman says. "When Athenagoras as patriarch began his famous friendship with Pope John, the monks on Mount Athos did not feel hesitant to drop him from the *diptics,* the litany of persons for whom they pray daily. I understand they are just as wary of the ecumenical spirit of his successor, Demetrios."

Roscoe talks about the way the monks supplement the many hours of prayer in the church with private prayer in their rooms during the night. He laughs, really amused, when someone suggests that maybe the monks sleep instead of pray.

"That's exactly what they would like you to think because they do not want to show off and be known as someone who is praying all the time. That is why some monks prefer to live alone or in a house away from the monastery. Then, they can pray as much as they want to, and no one will think they are trying to impress with their holiness."

Before being allowed to board the boat for its return voyage to Ouranoupolis, passengers must go into a small customs shed at the head of the pier where a blue-uniformed Greek customs inspector searches their baggage.

"There are many treasures on Athos, more than in the Vatican even," Werner, the Berlin youth, says. "Besides ikons, there are old manuscripts and books, and archaeological pieces. That's why they have to be very careful."

At Ouranoupolis, Kosta, the hotelman, is bustling about. In reply to a question, he estimates there are 1,500 monks on Athos but says the population is getting smaller all the time.

HOLY DEMETRIOS

The tomb of the Greek Christian nobleman, Demetrios, who was martyred by a pagan emperor in the 4th century, is in the church named after him, a few blocks from the Northern Greece government administration office in Salonika. Throughout the day people enter the St. Demetrios Chapel to light a candle and kiss the gilt-framed silver-overlaid image of the Theotokos. A high brass candleholder, and a lower one for children, is in the entrance part of the chapel. The basin of each candleholder is filled with sand, and the visitor plants his lighted candle in an empty spot in the sand as if it was a small tree. A massive marble sarcophagus is at the end of the chapel over the traditional tomb of Demetrios, the patron of Salonika. A framed painting of the martyr is on the sarcophagus, against an easel, and each visitor kisses it after saying a prayer.

It is a spacious church. The nave is reminiscent of the great hall in the Palazzo Vecchio at Florence. Wooden chairs are in the side aisles, but the central part of the nave has no seats at all. A tremendous bronze chandelier, held by gilded chains that reach from the lofty ceiling, hangs 15 feet above the floor. The chandelier is circled by a brass ring, 20 feet in diameter, with miniature ikons of the apostles and other holy figures of the church on each side.

TRANSPORTATION: Salonika is 325 miles from Athens; 350 miles from Pythion on the Greek-Turkish border. Fast express trains connect Athens and Salonika.

HOTELS: *Mediterranean Palace* is tops; *Athos* and *Egnatia* are moderately priced.

NORTHEASTERN GREECE

The area of Macedonia and Thrace contains several sites important in religious history. *Filippi,* 15 miles northwest of Kavala, was once called the "city of Christ." Orpheus and Dionysos lived at Filippi. It was the place of exile for Thucydides. Brutus and Cassius died here. St. Paul began his evangelization of Europe at this point, building his first church here. Filippi gets its name from its founder, Philip of Macedonia. At *Veria,* 50 miles west of Salonika, St. Paul built his second church before proceeding south to Athens and, then, to Corinth. The first temple to Aghia Sophia (Santa Sophia) was raised in Constantinople, but the second is in the small town of *Fere,* east of Alexandroupolis near the Turkish border. Turkish calligraphy on the walls remains from the times when it was used as a mosque (as Santa Sophia in Istanbul). There are 11 miles of catacombs in Fere which were used by the Greeks during the Turkish occupation, but they are now sealed off. It is said that a community of 600 people and a priest lived in the catacombs. The Victory statue of Samothrace in the Paris Louvre was found at *Samothraki.* In ancient times it was a principal pagan sanctuary where mysterious rites were performed at night with the use of oil lamps. Constantine and his mother, St. Helena, are remembered in a festival at *Langadas,* 14 miles from Salonika, on May 21. The festival reenacts the ancient tradition in which the faithful "walked" on burning coals. A similar but smaller festival also takes place at the village of *St. Helena*, near Sere, 60 miles from Salonika. The Holy Apostles are honored in a festival at *Nea Fokea*, 52 miles from Salonika, on June 30.

DELPHI

Zeus, the greatest of the gods for the ancients, once released two eagles, sending them off in flight in opposite directions. Where they later met head-on, the ancients believed, was the center of the earth, the point at which the inhabited world bordered on the realm of God. This was at Delphi, a place of extraordinary natural beauty along the slopes of Mount Parnassos, with the blue Gulf of Corinth at the base and the climbing mountains of the Peloponnesus on the southern horizon. Apollo, the son of Olympian Zeus, spoke to the ancients through his Oracle at Delphi, counseling and encouraging them. He spoke through an interpreter, Pythia, his priestess, and for centuries made Delphi the greatest point of pilgrimage in the ancient world.

An oracle was the site where a deity was consulted. Originally, the responses of a deity were made by male interpreters. Later, priestesses were used, and at times they made the responses in an agitated religious state. More ancient civilizations than the Greek had oracles but Greece's were the most famous. The Oracle at Dodona is the oldest. There, Zeus spoke to men with his voice being heard through the rustling of leaves. The temple of Zeus was destroyed in a war in the 3rd century B.C. and the oracle's voice was stilled.

Apollo was the ideal god for the ancient Greeks, a powerful, masterly young man who liked music, art, poetry and medicine. He represented moral discipline and purity of spirit. From his oracle the ancients were told about the forgiveness of sin and the equality of all men before God. Some of his advice remains inscribed in the walls of the immense Doric temple that dominated the sanctuary, counsel such as "Know thyself," and "Be moderate in all things."

The ruins at Delphi are from the temple built in the 4th century B.C. after an earthquake destroyed an earlier one. Before the arrival of Apollo the goddess Mother Earth was worshiped at Delphi.

TRANSPORTATION: Delphi is 120 miles from Athens. A ferry from Egeon connects the Peloponnesus with Itea, the landing point of Apollo after being transported from Crete by a sacred dolphin.

HOTELS: *Amalia, Vouzas* and *Xenia* are the finest. *Apollo* and *Europe* are moderately priced.

POINTS OF INTEREST: A half dozen miles from Delphi is where Oedipus, on returning from the Oracle, killed his father. The Korycaean Cave, a favorite of the ancients because of its weird panoply of stalactites and stalagmites in various colors, is on Parnassos. The cave was dedicated to the god Pan and some minor goddesses. The Thyades, women from Delphi and other pagan religious centers, participated in Bacchic rites in the cave every 4 years.

OLYMPIA

For more than 1,000 years, up to the spread of Christianity in Greece in the 4th century A.D., the most renowned pagan festival of the ancient world took place at Olympia in the Peloponnesus. It was watched and presided over by Zeus from his temple in a pine grove. Zeus was represented in the temple as a seated figure in a 40-foot-high statue of ivory and gold that was one of the Seven Wonders of the ancient world.

There were early festivals at Olympia, honoring the mythical king Pelops for whom the Peloponnesus is named. But the actual Olympic Games began in 776 B.C. and continued every four years until A.D. 393 when

Emperor Theodosius I outlawed them. Later, Theodosius II ordered the various monuments of the pagan sanctuary destroyed. Only ruins remain now.

TRANSPORTATION: There are several trains from Athens daily. Buses operate between Athens and Pirgos, 15 miles from Olympia, where taxis are available. Pirgos is 200 miles from Athens.

HOTELS: *S.P.A.P. Hotel* at Olympia is the best. *Apollo, Xenia* and *Olympia* are moderately priced.

METEORA

Two dozen monasteries dating from Byzantine times are perched, somewhat scaringly, on the collection of lofty mountain crags called the Meteora Rocks in the western Thessaly region of central Greece. The Meteora Rocks are in a vast, fertile valley ringed by a number of mountains, the highest of which is Olympus. Only a few of the monasteries are still occupied. There is a museum at the Aghios Stefanos (St. Stephen) Monastery which was built in A.D. 1312. A bridge now leads across a ravine to the monastery but until recent years visitors were hauled up to it in a net. Its church has 15th-century frescoes. The 14th-century Monastery of the Metamorfosis is now reached by a staircase in the rock, but in the past the visitor had to use a rope ladder or be hauled up in a basket. It has a fine library and treasury of relics. A guest house and restaurant are open from spring to fall. To get to the Aghia Triada Monastery the visitor has to climb a spiral stairway with 140 steps. The Meteora Rocks rise in back of the village of Kalambaka.

TRANSPORTATION: Meteora is 220 miles north of Athens. Trains from Athens and Salonika to Larissa; then, bus.

HOTELS: *Xenia Hotel* and *Divani Motel* are the best at Kalambaka.

SOUNION

The ancient Greeks built the temple for Poseidon, the god of the sea, at the point of land called Cape Sounion, 40 miles south of Athens. Less than 20 columns of the ancient temple now stand at the very top of this high promontory looking across the water. The coastal route to Sounion passes numerous miles of sandy beaches. An inland route leads through small towns, each built around an imposing village church. A tourist pavilion at Cape Sounion provides both refreshments and a convenient viewpoint to contemplate the temple of the god of the sea, and part of his domain.

TRANSPORTATION: Buses at half-hour intervals leave for Cape Sounion, with one each hour taking the inland route and the other the coastal.

HOTELS: *Belvedere Park* and *Egeon* are the leading ones. *Sounion Beach* and *Triton* are less expensive.

ATHENS

The religious nature of the Greeks is quite evident, and impressive. While the monasteries are mostly in the northern part of the country, churches are everywhere in Athens and nearby villages. A few blocks from Omonia Square in Athens, one of the busiest spots in all of Greece, is a curbside shrine with a vigil light burning in it. There are a number of such outdoor shrines in Athens. In downtown Athens a funicular leads up to Lycabettus Hill and its Chapel of St. George. Most of the gods mentioned by Homer dwelled on Olympus. But Athena lived on the Acropolis, the ancient city on which her Doric temple, the Parthenon, was built in the 5th century B.C. *Parthenon* comes from the Greek for "Virgin." Athena was the goddess of wisdom, skills and warfare—the counterpart of the Roman Minerva. She carried a shield. On the Acropolis she lived with her sacred snake, her bird and her tree.

TRANSPORTATION: Athens is on the main line of planes and trains from Paris and other points in Western Europe.

HOTELS: *Hilton* and *Grande Bretagne* are among the luxury hotels. *Olympic* is splendidly situated, overlooking the ruins of the Temple of Zeus and facing Lycabettus Hill.

8
Ireland

A MAN CUTTING TURF in the Bog of Allen, 30 miles west of Dublin, replies to the question cautiously. He says there is a difference of opinion about the source of the Boyne. One landowner insists that the river begins with the brook on his property. Another claims the distinction for his land. In any case, the turfcutter observes, pointing with his *slané*, the river Boyne rises in the general area of the bog.

Irishmen from County Donegal's Lough Swilly to the McGillicuddy Reeks in Kerry identify themselves with the Boyne as much as any county Kildare landowner. The Boyne has flowed through Ireland's tumultuous history, from the Bronze Age onward.

The Bog of Allen produces most of the peat fuel in the country. Ireland's biggest cement factory is at Drogheda where the Boyne streams past the County Louth Golf Club and the thatched cottages of Baltray before supplying fresh water for the swans drifting gently on the fringe of the tameless Irish Sea. On July 12, 1690 the Catholic forces of the exiled James II were defeated by the Protestant followers of William III of Orange—ever since known as Orangemen—in the pivotal Battle of the Boyne for the crown of England. The high stone fences along farm roads in the Boyne valley are known today as "famine walls," a throwback to the Great Famine of 1846–47 when landowners often created fence-building and other make-work projects for the impoverished people. On arriving from mid-Europe the Celts established some of their first settlements along the Boyne. In pre-Christian times Druid priests massed earth into immense pyramid-shaped mounds at Newgrange and other sites in the Boyne valley, as burial places for the kings of Ireland. The pantheistic Celts, religiously responsive to wind, sun, trees, fountains, memory of dead ancestors, honored the goddess Bóand as the deity of the river Boyne. At the time of St. Patrick's arrival in Ireland in the 5th century, the Boyne's Hall of Tara was still the religious capital of the country, and the residence of the High King.

One spring night, High King Laoghaire stared in amazement from his palace at a light which flickered on the Hill of Slane, 10 miles across the Boyne valley. The bards (the favored people at the high king's court), the Druid priests, and the chieftains from the Tara pentarchy of kingdoms were as puzzled and shaken by the unknown light as the high king. All Tara at the moment was celebrating a sacred festival in which light and darkness were pivotal elements. On the night of the festival the pagan ritual demanded total darkness until the ceremonial kindling of a special fire. By coincidence Patrick had sailed down the east coast of Ireland to the mouth of the Boyne and, while the pagan feast was underway at Tara, proceeded to the Hill of Slane to celebrate his first Easter in the land which he planned to evangelize. For him and his band of companions it was Holy Saturday, and to mark the coming of Easter he lighted the Paschal Fire.

Since then, Patrick has become known as the apostle of Ireland. Yet, not that much is known about him. The enigma starts at the place of his birth. It was France or

Britain—more likely, somewhere in England or Wales. Some wonder whether his name really was Patrick. His father, a civil servant in the Roman army, belonged to a patrician family. It has been suggested that his name originated with that noble word *patrician*. As a child Patrick was seized by Irish raiders and carried off to Ireland. Years later, after his release, he traveled in Europe and in a dream received his heavenly mission to bring Christianity to the pagan land where he had served as a slave. The date often accepted for his return to Ireland as a missionary is A.D. 432. It is believed that he came ashore at Saul, in county Down (now, one of the six counties of Northern Ireland). His former slave-master, Miliuc, lived in the northeast part of the country, and Patrick hoped to begin his mission in Ireland by making him a Christian. He failed. Since Easter was approaching he and his companions considered an appropriate place to celebrate the feast. They reasoned that the Boyne valley was the place because Tara, as the seat of the high king, would be the point from which the Druid religion flowed across the kingdom.

High King Laoghaire, alarmed by the light on the other side of the valley, demanded its meaning from his priests. The explanation was not reassuring: if the fire was not at once extinguished it would never go out.

Gradually the Druid religion lost its hold. The kings of Dublin and Munster were baptized, along with most of the people in their realms. Then, the 7 sons of the king of Connaught accepted the religion of the Christians. By the time of Patrick's death at the place where he had entered Ireland 29 years earlier, he had brought Christianity to kings and subjects alike throughout the land.

St. Brigid, the patroness of Ireland, was born in Faughart, County Louth. A shrine installed there in 1933 is said to contain part of her head. A 3-inch statue of the Madonna, known as Our Lady of Graces, is venerated at St. Mary's Dominican Church in Cork city.

It is believed to have been landed on the beach by a high tide. Rory O'Connor, the last of Ireland's high kings, was buried in the ancient monastic city of Clonmacnois, County Offaly, in A.D. 1198. In County Kerry, the 15-century-old Gallarus Oratory on the Dingle peninsula is considered to be the type of stone church which St. Patrick used. Off the Kerry coast, pilgrims in olden times ascended the 700-foot finger of rock, known as Skellig Michael.

Patrick chose Armagh (now in Northern Ireland) as the city for his headquarters as bishop. His primatial see was set on a hill named after Macha, a warrior queen of fire and brilliance, who in 300 B.C. founded the great fort on the edge of Armagh. For centuries the fort was the place from which the kings of Ulster ruled. Despite the partition of Ireland by the British, Armagh has remained the religious capital of the nation. Both the Catholic Church and the Church of Ireland (Protestant) have their cathedrals in Armagh. Each is named St. Patrick's. Brian Boru, the high king who defeated the Danes after their 160 years of adventuring in Ireland, is buried at Armagh.

CROAGH PATRICK

A hotelkeeper in the county Mayo city of Westport has a friendly bit of advice for a pilgrim heading for Croagh Patrick. "You'll need a stick," he says. "The ground can get pretty slippery from the mountain mist, and there's always the chance of a bit of a shower."

Westport, the starting point for pilgrimages to Croagh Patrick, was laid out as a model town a century and a half ago by an English architect who was commissioned by the ancestor of the present (the 10th) Marquess of Sligo, whose family name is Browne. The Marquess of Sligo lives in Westport House, a Georgian mansion near the center of town. The grounds of Westport House include a zoo and a man-made lake. At one time all the land on which the town of Westport has been built belonged to the Browne family. The Marquess of Sligo still collects ground rents from the people of Westport (population: 3,000). The fee does not amount to much nowadays—a few pounds a year. But everyone pays the ground rents—St. Mary's Church, Cavanaugh's Hotel, Wimpy's Hamburger Stand, and so on.

The Holy Mountain which pilgrims have named Croagh Patrick after the apostle of Ireland can be seen from most of Mayo. It is shaped like a perfect cone, rising 2,500 feet above Clew Bay. In ancient times it was called Croachan Egli (Eagle Mountain). About nine years after his arrival in Ireland, Patrick spent the entire period of Lent on the County Mayo mountain. The year is thought to be 441. The Book of Armagh, an early 9th-century compilation of older manuscripts, says that "Patrick went to Mount Egli to fast on it, 40 days and 40 nights, keeping the discipline of Moses, and Elias, and Christ."

When Patrick arrived at the base of the mountain, near the present village of Murrisk, his chariot driver, named Totmeal, died. Patrick buried Totmeal by the sea, heaping over the grave a cairn of stones. An ancient graveyard, possibly the place where Totmeal was buried, is at the edge of Clew Bay. The graveyard is alongside the skeletonized remains of an Augustinian abbey which was built in 1457, but suppressed in 1540 in the dissolution of Henry VIII.

The Book of Armagh reports that Patrick "abode on the mountain in much disquietude, without food, without drink." The chilling Irish "damp" undoubtedly added to the apostle's disquietude. But he was disturbed mostly by the flock of black birds which filled the sky like a thunder cloud, making it impossible for him to see either heaven or earth from the mountain top. The annoying birds, he knew, were sent by the "demons of paganism" which were seeking to block his

Christianizing of Ireland. As a matter of fact, the mountain Patrick picked for his Lenten vigil of penitence and prayer was the very one which pagans considered to be the dwelling-place of the great idol Crom Dubh.

Patrick persevered. Before the end of Lent he had banished the evil spirits from the mountain, hurling them into the Demons Hollow that is now a small lake. It is also believed that the prayers of Patrick on the Holy Mountain made it possible for him to drive into the sea all poisonous serpents and reptiles. When the demon birds and evil spirits had been banished, an angel appeared and gave comfort to the harried Patrick. The angel was accompanied by birds which sang soothingly. It was then that Patrick presented his three famous petitions. The Book of Armagh lists them as: (1) May each person doing penance, even in his last hour, not be doomed to hell on the final day; (2) may the barbarian never gain dominion over Ireland; (3) may the sea spread over the land 7 years before the Day of Judgment (to save the Irish from temptations during the reign of the Antichrist). Patrick was assured that his requests would be heeded.

A natural time to make the pilgrimage would be during the same period the apostle did—Lent—and, most of all, on his feast day (Mar. 17). In early times pilgrims apparently followed this natural schedule. But on Mar. 17, 1113 a savage storm ravaged the mountain, and 30 pilgrims perished. That disaster influenced the eventual shifting of the pilgrimage season to the summer. The change is gleaned from a papal decree of Sept. 27, 1432. Eugene IV assigned the indulgence of Croagh Patrick to the "Sunday preceding the feast of St. Peter's Chains (Aug. 1) because on that day a great multitude resorts thither to venerate St. Patrick." There has been no change since. The largest number of people climb the mountain on July's last Sunday. The Irish refer to it as "Reek Sunday," using the West Country word for "mountain." Many make an all-night vigil, beginning the ascent on the evening before Reek Sunday, and receiving Communion on the mountain at dawn. The last Friday of July—called Garland Friday—is also a popular pilgrimage day.

The huge horse-drawn wagons of tinkers add to the traffic jam at the foot of Croagh Patrick on the last weekend in July. The tinkers—the Irish grandly refer to these horse-trading nomads as "the traveling people"— are the principal vendors of the reddish-brown hazel sticks which pilgrims lean on for support in climbing The Reek.

It takes the average pilgrim at least 2 hours to get to the top of the mountain. It is a much longer climb for those who do the pilgrimage barefooted.

The mountain is not one huge mass of solid rock. Shale and stones, loosened by wind and by the feet of pilgrims, slither down the slopes, noisily gravitating toward new resting places. The ascent is long and gradual to a relatively flat, wide area halfway up the mountain. The cone shape of the mountain forms at this level, and so does the most difficult part of the climb. This is a place of rest and of prayer for the pilgrims. It is one of the 3 "stations" of Croagh Patrick. The First Station is marked by a heap of stones (leacht) and is called Leacht Benain in honor of one of Patrick's disciples. The pilgrimage calls for the saying of 7 Pater Nosters, 7 Ave Marias, and 1 Credo while the pilgrim walks around the *leacht* 7 times.

From the First Station to the top of the mountain, the route is steep, slow and strewn with gravel. The Second Station, at the top, is called *Leaba Phadraig* (Patrick's Bed), with *bed* in the sense of a foundation for a cell or an oratory. On reaching the Second Station the pilgrim repeats the set of prayers he had offered at the First Station. Then he approaches the small chapel and, kneeling, makes additional prayers: 15 Paters, 15 Aves, 1 Credo. Next he walks 15 times around a circular mound at the summit, improvising his own prayers.

This interlude of prayers is followed with 7 Paters, 7 Aves and 1 Credo, all said by the pilgrim on his knees. With the prayers finished, the pilgrim walks 7 times around the *Leaba Phadraig,* praying.

The summit's surface is flat and jagged as if the tip of the mountain had been hurriedly lopped off by a bolt of lightning. The chapel is 32 feet long, 42 feet wide. There are 3 altars where Mass is said by pilgrim priests. On Reek Sunday the chapel is used only for the hearing of Confession and the distribution of Communion. In 1949 a structure of steel and plastic was installed on the mountain to shelter the priest during Mass, and since then the Reek Sunday Masses are outdoors. The shelter is 6 feet long, 5 feet wide, and 7 feet high. It is quite simple, containing not even a statue—just a small wooden altar.

For Reek Night a small generator is brought up, and the oratory is lighted. The rest of the year there is no lighting on the mountain. Michael Kelly, of Westport, former chairman of the U.D.C. (Urban District Council), does the wiring for the string of lamps. He has performed this task for 20 years or more. He remains on the mountain from midday of Saturday until he has unraveled the jury-rigged electricity setup the following day. He is now in his 70s.

The transport of the generator is the assignment of "Austie" Groden, a farmer from Murrisk. He loads the generator on the back of a donkey for the first half of the ascent. He carries it the rest of the way on his own back. Mr. Groden, now in his mid 40s, took over from his father, Michael.

All the building materials for the chapel, the shelter (in sections), the altars, the fixtures and so on were carried to the top of the mountain on the backs of mules and of men. When additions to the chapel were made in 1962, "Austie" Gannon and two other men slept on the mountain from Monday morning until Saturday evening throughout the summer—for two summers and two months of the third summer—until the job was finished.

Austie—everyone calls him that, he says—used to be in the construction business but is now retired, and lives with his wife and daughter, Maura, a teacher, in a thatched cottage beside the road between Murrisk and Lecanvey. He is tall, his hair is as white as a summer cloud on Clew Bay, and he likes his pipe. He has built a "suntrap," a glass-enclosed porch, at the front of the cottage. It holds back the chill air from rushing into the front room when the door is opened. The living-room is no more than 6 feet long, and not that wide. It is rendered all the more cosy by a turf fire. Till he retired Austie used to buy the turf, tubary, for the family hearth. Now at turf-cutting time in April he heads into a bog 4 miles away to dig out a year's supply for his house.

Austie estimates that he "goes up" the mountain at least 20 times a year. He has been making the climb since his late teens. He is 68.

"I was on the Reek before that, but I've only been going up to give a hand in the last fifty years. I went as a pilgrim the first time when I was ten or twelve years old. Then, when I was about eighteen, the curate [of St. Patrick's Church in Lecanvey] asked me to go with him. At that time Sunday Mass in the summer would be at six A.M., and Father Godfrey—he's now dead—would leave around four A.M., and he would need someone to point the way for him in the dark. So I accompanied him, and I have gone with every curate since."

In 1949 Austie Gannon was one of 4 men who carried a new statue of St. Patrick on their shoulders to the top of the mountain. The statue was lashed to a wooden frame.

For Austie there is no "typical" pilgrim.

"I've seen babes in arms on the top. I've seen old men and old women, some in their bare feet. I've seen girls of every color on the Reek—their scarves, faded by the rain, seeping colors from cheap dyes across their faces. Weather doesn't mean anything. On that morning [Reek Sunday] weather doesn't keep away anyone who meant to climb."

Even some priests, he says, do the pilgrimage barefooted.

"A former curate, Father Joe Scott—he's now in Galway—used to make it in his bare feet. Father Leo Morahan, a native of Louisburgh right near here, is now in Galway but he does every Reek in his bare feet, and hears Confessions all night."

Probably the best-known pilgrim was Father Angelus, a Capuchin missionary from Dublin, who made his first pilgrimage in 1906, and climbed every year for 44 years, missing only two Reek Sundays. In the last few years of his life, Father Angelus no longer was physically able to ascend the mountain but he journeyed to Westport each year to be there at the time of the big pilgrimage. He died in Westport in 1953 on the day after Reek Sunday. Before dying the Capuchin friar asked that his main possession, his mission crucifix, be left on The Reek. Austie fashioned a large cross of oak, affixed the friar's crucifix to it, and placed it over the main altar in the chapel.

The pilgrimage does not end at the top. The last of the 3 Stations is almost halfway down the western slope (the Lecanvey side). The Third Station is dedicated to the Madonna. Three sets of stones are grouped into circles at the Third Station. The pilgrim prays at each circle of stones, reciting 7 Paters, 7 Aves and 1 Credo; then walks 7 times around each circle, in meditation or personal prayer. After this, he completes the rite at the Third Station by walking 7 times around the entire area, which is known as Garrai Mór, the Great Garden.

TRANSPORTATION: Westport, 5 miles away, is 162 miles from Dublin; express trains between Dublin and Westport.

HOTELS: *Jury's* and *Westport* are the principal ones. The traditional hotel is *Cavanaugh's,* centrally located on The Mall.

POINTS OF INTEREST: Along the sea, between Lecanvey and Murrisk, a large stone cross stands on a low green hill. It is an Emancipation Cross and is one of the few left—perhaps it is the only one. Such crosses were raised in 1829 as a happy memorial for the passage of the British Emancipation Act, by which the British Parliament guaranteed to the people of Ireland basic civil liberties in regard to job opportunities, public education and open practice of religion.

LOUGH DERG

The town of Pettigo in the low hills of southern Donegal is known by the Irish for two distinctive reasons.

Pettigo is what the Irish call a "quirky" border town. It is the only border town in Ireland which actually straddles the border. It is divided in two by the Termon river, a narrow stream crossed by a bridge that looks so woebegone and aged it might have been built by the Romans—but couldn't have been, because the legions of Rome never set foot in Ireland. There is a duplication of public services in Pettigo: two post offices, two police stations, two town halls, all administered by two different governments, the Irish Republic's and the one for the British-controlled six-county area of Northern Ireland. The North Ireland customs inspectors operate from a trailer at the side of the road. There had been a customs building, but it was bombed to smithereens. Pettigo was a storm center in 1922 when a speedily suppressed civil war broke out because of the British partition of Ireland, and it has been caught up in the disturbances involving Protestant-oriented and Catholic-oriented militants of Northern Ireland a half century later. The border town is a no-man's land at night.

The other reason for Pettigo's fame is that it is the gateway town to Lough Derg, Ireland's national point of pilgrimage. Lough Derg is described by the Irish as "the toughest pilgrimage in Ireland." It probably is the toughest in the world, for that matter. It is a 3-day pilgrimage of much fasting and prayer. From the day of his arrival until departure on the third day (2 days later) the pilgrim is allowed to eat only 2 "meals" (dry toast and unsugared tea) and to sleep during only one of the 2 nights of the pilgrimage. Throughout the entire time the pilgrim goes barefoot, accepting the sting of the cold church floors and the pain of the stony ground as part of the penance he wants to do.

The pilgrimage site is Station Island, a mass of land 125 yards long and 65 yards wide, one of several dozen small offshore islands in the lake known as Lough Derg. The boat-landing to reach it is 4 miles from Pettigo.

At one time the pilgrimage centered around a cave on the island. An all-night vigil was maintained in the cave, and this was preceded by 15 days of fasting. The length of the fast was reduced to 9 days in the 17th century; then to 6 days. Even as recently as the first half of the past century pilgrims had a choice of a penitential fast of 3, 6 or 9 days. The cave phase of the pilgrimage began fading in the 17th century when, during the suppression of the pilgrimage at the orders of the British government, the mystifying, mystic hole in the ground of Station Island was filled in. After a renaissance of the pilgrimage, the original cave (or a similar one) was excavated and used. But once and for all the cave was sealed in 1789 by the director of the pilgrimage, and ever since the all-night vigil has been restricted to the church.

Patrick's association with the island is accepted, but there is disagreement about the origin of the name of the lake which encircles it. One legend explains the name in a summons Patrick received from the people of the area to come to their aid and slay a terrifying sea serpent. Patrick performed the mission, and the serpent's blood tinged the lake's waters. Thus, it was natural to call it Lough Derg, or Red Lake. Others suggest that the name originally was Lough Deirge, Lake of the Cave.

The main tradition is that Patrick was drawn to the island not to cope with a sea serpent but because the local people were terrified by the heathen gods and demons of the Druids. Patrick had scattered the pagan spirits from their haunts in the south of Ireland, and now they reportedly had found a haven in the cave. The apostle bravely rowed alone across the few hundred yards to the island because no local boatman would go near the place. Patrick entered the cave and, after 40 days and nights, emerged wearied but victorious. He was able to assure the people that the heathen spirits had not only been driven from the cave but out of Ireland as well. During his long combative vigil in the cave Patrick was given a glimpse of the after-world of temporary suffering for the expiation of sins. That gave it the name of Patrick's Purgatory.

While Patrick continued on his travels through Ireland his disciples settled in the area. Some established a monastic settlement on a nearby island (called Saints Island today), and others lived in a series of small cells near the entrance to the cave he had sanctified.

By the middle of the 12th century the renown of Lough Derg had traveled across Europe. An experience related by a knight generally identified as Owen touched off the start of visits by great numbers of continental pilgrims. Owen related that he had followed an extraordinary life of sin and, to do penance, undertook the vigil in the cave. As he prayed, the sight of purgatory, and then hell, and then heaven came to him, and literally so struck him with awe that he had to be carried from the cave. Pilgrims rushed to Lough Derg to have a similar experience, and some hoped for the chance to talk with their dead.

When the rebellion of the Irish chieftains under Hugh O'Neill of Tyrone was put down in 1603, the English stepped up their colonization of Ireland. The London government ordered all the structures and religious dwellings on St. Patrick's holy island razed in 1632, and the cave filled in. Access to the island was forbidden. Pilgrims therefore would gather on the mainland and carry out the traditional program of prayer and fasting. Early in the following century Queen Anne in a statute prescribing fines (and public whippings for those who would not pay the fine) sought to halt the resurging pilgrimage, but within 10 years thousands of pilgrims were back on the island, walking barefoot, fasting, and praying. One summer, not long after the Emancipation Act of 1829, more than 30,000 persons crossed over to the island to make the ancient pilgrimage of penitence.

What may well be the largest rowboat in the world is in the fleet of vessels that transport today's pilgrims to the island. The boat is certified to be capable of carrying 150 persons and is rowed by 6 men using oars 25 feet long. It was built a half century ago and christened *St. Patrick*. All the vessels in the pilgrim fleet are named after Irish saints. Nowadays the *St. Patrick* is rarely rowed. Instead, it is tied to one of three motorboats and towed across. It is a voyage of only 5 or 10 minutes from shore to shore but the lake's waters can be tricky. There is still talk of the Sunday morning in July 1795 when a brief, violent windstorm got the best of a heavily loaded boat and 93 pilgrims drowned.

James Monaghan, who can "chat up" with strangers easily, says that the weather on Lough Derg is so freakish that one day in 1947 he rode across to the island on a bicycle. Monaghan is the caretaker, and lives with his wife and mother in a house built by his father, Patrick, near the boat landing on the mainland. Patrick Monaghan died in 1967.

"My father was eighty-four then," Monaghan says. "He came here as a lad of thirteen, delivering mail from Pettigo. He went to America for a couple of years, as a young man, but came back to Pettigo when the prior of Lough Derg told him he needed some help. Then he helped build the house which became his as caretaker. He used to tell me about the island's history and point out where the original buildings stood. He also talked a lot about Sir John Leslie, who owned the lake, and much of the land around here. He was a big man, my father said, and was a great swimmer. He could swim around the entire island."

Monaghan keeps a cow and chickens. ("It's too far to go into Pettigo for milk.") He is married to a sister of James Snow, a carpenter. He and Snow operate the boats and keep them repaired. During the long nonpilgrimage period (mid-August till the end of May), the two men are the only ones on the island. They travel over to it daily to work on the boats, to fix windows in the hospices—"to do whatever has to be done," Monaghan says.

The pilgrimage fee is 2 pounds. That covers the boat fare, a bunk in the hospice and the 2 bread-and-tea meals. No advance reservations are necessary because there is plenty of room—500 beds in the men's hospice; 700 beds in the women's hospice.

Fasting for the pilgrimage is to start at the midnight preceding the pilgrim's arrival. Pilgrims unaware that they should have been fasting before getting to Lough Derg are turned away, and asked to return the following day.

Pilgrims are expected to arrive for the start of the pilgrimage between 10 A.M. and 3 P.M. At the boat landing they are given a leaflet detailing the program of fast and prayer. As soon as they reach the island they are assigned to a cubicle in one of the hospices. Each cubicle is fitted with two sets of upper and lower bunks, and two washbasins. The new arrivals leave their shoes and their socks or stockings at their cubicle, and are ready to begin the first of the 9 "stations" (rounds) of prayer.

A station consists of 45 minutes of outdoor praying, kneeling and walking (barefoot, always). The number of Paters, Aves and Credos to be said at the various points on the island are listed in the leaflet given on arrival. With his back to St. Brigid's Cross and, stretching out his arms, the pilgrim 3 times announces his renunciation of "the world, the flesh and the devil."

The first day's program calls for the pilgrim to complete 3 stations before 9:30 P.M.

Anytime after the pilgrim has finished his first station, he is allowed his first (and only) meal of the day. This consists of black tea, dry toast and/or oatmeal biscuits. The pilgrim can have all the tea, toast and biscuits he wants, and take as much time as he likes for finishing the meal. But once he gets up from the table, he cannot eat anything or drink anything (except plain water) until the following afternoon.

The all-night vigil begins with religious services in the basilica at 10 P.M. During the night the pilgrims recite together the prayers for the fourth, fifth, sixth and seventh stations, a total of some 1,200 individual prayers.

Pilgrims agree that the second day is the hardest part of the pilgrimage. They are supposed to remain awake throughout the day, after their all-night vigil. Mass and Confession start the second day. Some time during the morning the pilgrim makes the eighth station, a routine of kneeling, walking and praying similar to that of the first day. There is another Mass at noon and a set of evening services. He can pick his own time during the afternoon for the second meal allowed him while he is on the island. At last, at 10 P.M., he can go to bed for his first sleep in more than 36 hours.

The next day—the third and last of the pilgrimage—he is awakened at 6 A.M. for Mass. Before leaving the island the pilgrim completes the last of the 9 stations.

No meal is allowed on the island on the third and final day of the pilgrimage. The pilgrim is required to continue his fast until midnight. Once he has left the island he can have a tea-and-toast meal similar to what he ate on the first two days of the pilgrimage, and drink what the Irish refer to as "minerals." These include soft drinks but not fruit juices or anything alcoholic. "If it has food value, it's out," says Monsignor Thomas Flood, prior of the Lough Derg pilgrimage. "That's the test."

Some pilgrims forget to bring their medicines with them to Lough Derg—diabetics, for example—and become ill. It is always a question whether they really forgot the medicines or whether they were hoping for a miraculous cure.

"Lough Derg is not a place of miracles, except for the miracle of grace," Monsignor Flood says. "No one has ever seen any visions here. There is no emotionalism. It is very low-key, a personal and anonymous pilgrimage, and one that is very rewarding. People go away feeling refreshed, spiritually and physically."

Monsignor Flood is the parish priest (P.P., or pastor) at Dromore, on the other side of the border in Northern Ireland. For 3 months each year he turns over his parish to a curate, and administers the Lough Derg pilgrimage. He has been at Lough Derg for 30 years—the first 16 as assistant prior, and subsequently as prior. He is aided by a staff of 10 boatmen, about 30 young women who serve the meals and make the beds, and a half dozen Our Lady of the Sacred Heart nuns from Ballybay in County Monaghan who are nurses, cooks and secretaries.

"Cardinal William Conway, the Catholic primate of all-Ireland, has made the pilgrimage," Monsignor Flood says. "He did it as a student priest. But it was an American who was the first to make the pilgrimage as a cardinal. Cardinal Timothy Manning has been a pilgrim at Lough Derg seventeen times during the past thirty years. He came first as a young priest, then as auxiliary bishop of Los Angeles, later as bishop of Fresno, and in 1973 as cardinal-archbishop of Los Angeles. He comes incognito. He merely tells the girl at the registration desk that his name is 'Tim Manning.' The last time he had on some kind of a golf jacket and a high-necked sweater. I recognized him of course because I've known him for thirty years. But no one else did. He did not even say Mass while he was here."

For centuries a legal cloud hovered over the Catholic Church's clear title to the ownership of Lough Derg's Station Island. The dispute originated in the welter of land concessions, royal re-grant and confiscation actions of the 16th and 17th centuries. The Leslie family, Protestants from County Monaghan, had acquired the lake and much of the mainland adjoining it. In lawsuits in 1881 and 1917, the family challenged the Catholic claim to the ownership of the island on which the pilgrimage takes place. The question of the island's ownership was finally resolved. The last possible cause for conflict was eliminated in 1960 when the Catholic Church bought the lake itself from the Leslie family. But years before that, the late Sir John Leslie made clear that there were no hard feelings between the Catholic and Protestant neighbors on Lough Derg. On behalf of the Leslie family, Sir John Leslie presented a Madonna painting by Murillo to the prior of the Lough Derg pilgrimage at the time of the consecration of the present St. Patrick's Basilica in 1929. His son, Sir Shane Leslie, while an undergraduate at Cambridge, became a convert to Catholicism, and has written a great deal about Lough Derg and its pilgrimage.

TRANSPORTATION: Pettigo is 144 miles from Dublin; 32 miles, Ballyshannon; 100 miles, Belfast. Buses connect Ballyshannon with Pettigo. There are trains between Dublin and Sligo, which is connected to

Ballyshannon by bus. The Ulster Bus Company travels to Pettigo from Belfast and Enniskillen.

HOTELS: *Great Southern* in Sligo is luxurious. In Ballyshannon, *Dorrians Imperial* and *Royal Millstone* are comfortable, medium-priced.

POINTS OF INTEREST: Near Ballyshannon is the grave of Yeats.

KNOCK

Fifty-two inches of rain, measured out almost precisely at 1 inch a week, sweep each year across the limestone plain of southeast County Mayo and the village of Knock, Ireland's Marian shrine. The nagging wet weather has prompted the construction of an immense new church to provide shelter for the pilgrims who, attracted by the story of an Apparition a century ago, journey by the thousands to Knock year after year. The size and the shape of the church will make it extraordinary for Ireland. It will shelter 5,000 persons inside, and will be round in form. The exterior will be circled by a 20-foot-wide ambulatory, which will be covered by the roof of the church. The overall effect will be that of a tremendous cement umbrella. Father James Horn, administrator of the shrine, says that the umbrella shape of the new church and the village's heavy rainfall are only a coincidence.

"It is cheaper to house people in a round building. Also the altar is in the center, and everybody can see it. I got the idea from the Jesuit church at Auriesville in the Catskills, the shrine of the Jesuit Martyrs. I came across a picture of it while planning our church, and have since visited it."

Even when the new church is built, Father Horn plans to retain on the parish grounds the glass-paneled octagonal structure which is large enough—35 feet in diameter—for an altar. Rain or shine, Mass is now said at the enclosed altar for large pilgrimages, but it will be used only on nice days when the new church is built.

Knock has been a busy point of pilgrimage from the very day townspeople reported sighting an Apparition on the gable of the village church.

The pilgrimage began a little past 7 o'clock on the evening of Aug. 21, 1879, six days after villagers had celebrated the Marian feast of the Assumption. The sacristan's sister, hurrying to lock the church door for the day, noticed that the gable at the rear seemed to be cloaked in a strange brightness, but she did not concern herself with it. From his home a half mile away the aging Patrick Walsh noticed a light around the gable, and wondered why anyone would be foolish enough to build a fire so close to the church. Mary McLoughlin, the parish priest's housekeeper, was on her way to a friend's house when she saw what looked like statues at the church, and figured they were part of some delivery that Father Bartholomew Cavanagh had forgotten to mention to her. On her way home a half hour later the "statues" were still there. A young girl with her was curious and, stepping closer for an inspection, exclaimed that they were not statues, that the figures were moving. Mary McLoughlin told the pastor what she had seen at the church. He assumed the strange sight was nothing but a reflection from the church's stained-glass windows, and let it go at that. A heavy rain did not prevent a score of villagers from hastening to the church to see what was going on. Fifteen of them testified to an episcopal commission 6 weeks later that they saw 3 figures just under the gable, and perhaps 2 feet above the ground. They identified the figure in the center as the Madonna. One of the other figures was recognized as St. Joseph. As for the other figure, a witness said it resembled a statue of St. John the Evangelist she had seen in the church at Lecanvey on her recent vacation. There was also an altar. A lamb was on the altar. Behind the lamb was a cross. For

Brigid Trench, the Apparition was so real that she reached over to kiss the Madonna's feet, but found she was touching the bare wall. The Apparition remained for 2 hours. During that time, the 15 witnesses later testified, they knelt on the wet ground and recited the Rosary. The witnesses were men and women of various ages. Mary Byrne, who had seen the statue of St. John on her vacation, described how the Madonna looked in the Apparition.

"The Blessed Virgin stood erect with eyes raised to heaven, her hands elevated to the shoulders or a little higher. She wore a large cloak of a white color, hanging in full folds and somewhat loosely around her shoulders, and fastened to the neck. She wore a crown on the head, rather a large crown."

Doubters advanced all kinds of arguments against the validity of the Apparition. There were allegations that the Apparition-seers were drunk at the time. It was also suggested that someone had been playing tricks on the villagers by projecting scenes from a magic lantern on the church wall. Critics questioned its spiritual value and meaning, because there was no message.

Church authorities reacted cautiously. The episcopal commission which interviewed the 15 witnesses reported to the archbishop that the "testimony of all, taken as a whole, was trustworthy and satisfactory." But the archbishop made no formal finding of his own, neither stating approval or disapproval. In 1936 the 3 survivors of the original 15 witnesses were interviewed by a new commission. Among them was Mary Byrne. Their sworn stories, more than a half century afterward, differed in some details from the original ones but stuck to the main lines. Four years later the archbishop of the diocese (Tuam) obtained from the Vatican facilities for the acquiring of indulgences by pilgrims to Knock, and arranged for the canonical affiliation of Rome's St. Mary Major Basilica with the shrine. When Monsignor Joseph Cunnane, a native of Knock, became archbishop of

Tuam in 1969 he opened the pilgrimage season that year by heading the diocesan group of pilgrims.

Contemporary Popes have recognized the growing devotion associated with the Knock shrine. On All Saints' Day in the Marian Year of 1954 Pius XII in a solemn ceremony at St. Peter's crowned the Madonna picture entitled "Salus Populi Romani" in the presence of representatives of 400 of the world's Marian shrines. The banner of the Knock shrine was included among the 20 banners formally offered to the Pope on the occasion. On Feb. 2, 1960 John XXIII presented a candle to the Knock shrine, calling it "one of the outstanding places of public devotion to Our Lady." On Nov. 21, 1964 Paul VI closed the third session of the Second Vatican Council by con-celebrating Mass with 24 bishops who were chosen because they represented the main Marian shrines of the world. The Bishop of Tuam was among them.

There are no crutches, braces or other orthopedic devices clustered at the shrine. But there have been cures, Father Horn, the parish priest, says. The crutches and other devices that had accumulated in the early history of the shrine were buried in the foundation of the chapel which was built in 1939 at the church corner, under the gable, where the Apparition was reported.

"Scores of people are cured here," Father Horn says. "We have no medical bureau, however, to attest to the cures. I know of three men who came here on stretchers, as pilgrims, and they have come back each year to help out as stewards. We emphasize the spiritual miracles. Whether physically cured or not, the sick go away with strength and consolation. Our Lady did not ask Her Son to give up His cross, and She may not take the cross from them [the sick pilgrims].

"Two people last year were cured. One was a man from Ballina. He had lost the power of his hands and legs. Then, when he was here on a pilgrimage he saw

big blisters appear on his hands and feet. It was on a
Friday. The blisters suddenly burst, and the man regained his powers.

"People are slow to talk about cures. For one thing
they do not want to face a barrage of questions.
Second, they are superstitious. They are afraid of talking too soon, and that a relapse will come. They do not
want to boast, fearful that God might return them to
their former state. Actually, they are probably wrong.
They probably should make known the cure, and thank
God. God can work in two ways: either in the natural
healing powers of man's body or outside—completely
supernatural—and then you are in the province of
miracles. We don't go into this very much. But a lot of
cures have taken place here which can't be explained
by doctors."

Immediately after the Apparition, pilgrims commenced scraping the cement from the wall on which
the tableau of the Madonna and the saints had been
reported. An archbishop of Tasmania, among the first
pilgrims, said his sight had been restored after applying
some of the powdered cement. About the same time the
archbishop of Perth, Australia, presented a painting to
the shrine, saying he had received a cure through the
intercession of Our Lady of Knock.

Mrs. Delia Gordon told of the first cure on record. On
a pilgrimage 10 days after the Apparition she said that
she had been cured of total deafness. This red-letter
day is remembered by a historic green sash which Mrs.
Gordon had made for her husband, Michael. Michael
Gordon wore the sash on Apr. 29, 1879—4 months
before the Apparition—at the first meeting of the Land
League in Irishtown, County Mayo. The meeting, an
open demand from Irish farm workers that the British
government break up the immense estates, was addressed by Michael Devitt, founder of the Land
League, and Charles Stewart Parnell. The sash is now
in the museum at the shrine. Father Horn created the

museum in the summer of 1973 to show pilgrims the social and educational conditions of the West Country at the time of the Apparition—how the people lived, what they ate, and so on. Among the items on exhibit are a losset (a wooden box for making bread) a *crios* (pronounced "criss") scarf which is made in the pattern of colors used in the bright belts of West Country fishermen, and a wicker basket which belonged to Long Anne of Tuam who, Father Horn says, was a particularly tall tinker woman who used to stand outside Tuam College selling oranges, apples and bananas. There are also photostats of newspapers of the time reporting the Apparition. Father Horn had the newspaper accounts researched at the National Library in Dublin.

"The newspaper clippings are very interesting," he says, "because besides the article on Knock there would be something on the back like Parnell appearing in New York."

Father Horn has known the shrine for a half century.

"I came here as a boy in 1926 when I was a student at St. Jarlath's School in Tuam. I was fifteen, and had just gotten my first bicycle. I came here with a pal. We set off on the eve of August 15, about nine or ten in the evening, and spent the vigil of the feast of the Assumption here, doing the station [round of prayer]. We attended Mass at six A.M. and then cycled home again, exhausted. I was here often after my first visit. I came several times with my parents. In 1963 I was assigned here."

TRANSPORTATION: Claremorris is 3 miles from Knock; 133 miles, Dublin. Claremorris is on main rail line from Dublin.

HOTELS: The one hotel in Knock, *Churchfield House*, has about 20 rooms. In Claremorris, the *Central Hotel* is moderate in price.

POINTS OF INTEREST: A half dozen miles along the highway from Claremorris to Castlebar is a turnoff to the

village of Mayo where, legend says, Alfred the Great
studied and where one of his sons is buried.

THE BURIAL PLACE OF PATRICK

With the precision of a longtime ritual, each evening
as the sky and the Irish sea darken, housewives in Saul
move around the boxlike rooms in their brick houses,
touching a match to the small meshwork hoods in ceiling fixtures. Many houses in Saul still do not have electricity, but the mantles in the gas lamps glow with a
white-hot light that pierces most of the dark corners.
Along the County Down coast near Saul is where
Patrick, according to tradition, first set foot in Ireland
on his return to the land as a missionary. Saul is in
Northern Ireland, about 21 miles south of Belfast.
"Saul" is from the Irish word *sabhal* (barn). The local
chieftain, Dichu, made his barn available to Patrick for
his first Mass on Irish soil, and subsequently became his
first convert to Christianity.

In 1932 for the 1,500th anniversary of the apostle's
coming to Ireland, St. Patrick's Memorial Church was
built by the Church of Ireland (Protestant) on the
traditional site of Dichu's barn at the entrance to the
village. Within the village itself is a Catholic chapel
dedicated to St. Patrick, and across from it on a hill
called the Summit of Saul an 18-foot statue of the
apostle of Ireland has been erected. A woman down the
road from the Summit of Saul says that villagers had
hoped Mass could be said on the hill on St. Patrick's
Day. "They tried it a couple of times, but the weather
just wouldn't cooperate. Too much wind and cold sea
rain, you know? Now the Mass is on the nearest Sunday
to June 18. It is a big celebration, and the bishop usually comes down from Belfast to preside."

The Book of Armagh relates the tradition that Patrick
also died and was buried in Saul, but an early biog-

rapher puts the burial place in Downpatrick, a mile inland. There is a graveyard alongside St. Patrick's Cathedral (Church of Ireland) on a hill overlooking the main street of Downpatrick. Two huge slabs of stone, one atop the other, catch the eye of anyone entering the cathedral graveyard. The upper slab carries the letters remaining from an inscription: PATR. The remainder of the stone, with the inscription, has broken away.

It is believed that the original foundation of the cathedral was laid by Patrick. Many times, starting in the 9th century and continuing for 250 years, Danes and other northerners pillaged the flourishing monastic settlement which had grown up on the site. When the Anglo-Normans moved northward from Dublin in the 12th century, their leader, a Cheshire knight named John de Courcey, built a new abbey. Possibly in a conciliatory gesture to the Irish people he added the name "Patrick" to "Down," renaming the town "Downpatrick," and grouped together the graves of Ireland's three famous early-day saints, Patrick, Brigid and Columcille (Columba). The cathedral had been dedicated to the Holy Trinity, and de Courcey renamed it in St. Patrick's honor. Superstitious local people attributed future misfortunes to this name change, saying de Courcey had replaced the Master with the servant. Misfortune came. Edward Bruce, the brother of Scotland's Sir Robert, ransacked the cathedral in 1316, and in 1538 it was suppressed in the dissolution of Henry VIII. For almost 250 years after the Reformation the cathedral lay in ruins. In 1790 the newly appointed dean pledged 300 pounds of his own salary to finance rebuilding. The cathedral was again opened for services in 1818. Today it is beautifully maintained. A sign near the entrance says:

The dean and chapter bids you welcome;
This cathedral open stands for thee,
that thou mayest enter, rest, think, kneel and pray.

Remember whence thou art, and what must be thine end.
Remember us, then go thy way.

An old legend in Ulster is that when Patrick died,
"for 12 days after, night did not come down."

TRANSPORTATION: Downpatrick is 22 miles from Belfast; 96 miles from Dublin. Buses connect with
Belfast.

HOTELS: In Belfast, *Europa* is alongside the air termi-
nal. *Kilmorey Arms* at Kilkeel is medium-priced.

POINTS OF INTEREST: 1 mile from Saul, on the way to
Strangford, is a chapel dedicated to St. Tassach, a
disciple of Patrick, who is said to have anointed the
apostle when he was dying. St. Patrick's Wells, believed to have been a site of pagan worship until
sanctified by Patrick, are at Struell, 2 miles east of
Downpatrick.

BLESSED OLIVER PLUNKETT

After Oliver Plunkett, the archbishop of Armagh, was
hanged, drawn and quartered for high treason in London on July 1, 1681, parts of his body were carried to
different places in Europe. The main section of his body
is now in the Benedictine abbey at Downside, England,
but the head has been in Drogheda, the historic town of
the Boyne River, since early in the 18th century.
Drogheda is at the southern end of the diocese of
Armagh. For 200 years the head remained in the Siena
Convent of the Dominican Nuns at Drogheda. After
Oliver Plunkett was declared Blessed by Pope Benedict
IV in 1920, the head was transferred to St. Peter's
Church on West Street. But the convent of Dominican
nuns still has a relic of the Armagh archbishop. The
convent is not an actual cloister. Visitors can talk with
the nuns, face to face, in the parlor. But visits take

place over a 2-foot brown fence which divides the room in half. Nuns enter the parlor from a stairway at the far end of the room.

"When the head was taken away," Sister Thomas relates, "Rome said we could have another relic." She is short, bent and probably one of the oldest nuns in the convent, but her eyes brighten like a young girl's when she smiles. "After he was martyred, his body was taken first to Germany. The bishop of Hildesheim gave a relic to the Sisters of our convent. It is nine centimeters long—a rib. It came to us in a glass case, and the Sisters made a reliquary for it. Before the rib was placed in the reliquary, pieces of linen cloth were touched to it. We distribute to visitors a small card with a swatch of the cloth.

"Cardinal Cushing [the late archbishop of Boston] wanted a section of the relic, and there was much correspondence with Rome for a long time before permission was given. Then the procedure was arranged in the presence of a bishop—a bishop has to be present—and the cutting was done by a surgeon. The Sisters took advantage of its exposure to touch additional pieces of linen to it to provide more swatches."

On the Sunday nearest July 12 each year there is a procession through the streets of Drogheda, honoring Blessed Oliver Plunkett, and the relic of the rib is borrowed from the nuns.

In addition to the archbishop's head, St. Peter's Church has the thick wooden door, complete with heavy bolts and hinges, which was on the cell in Newgate Prison where Plunkett spent the 8 months before his execution.

The high-treason indictment against the archbishop of Armagh carried many charges, such as that he had sought financial and other aid abroad to assist the Catholic religion in Ireland, that he had invited the king of France to take over Ireland with an army, and

that he had 70,000 men ready to support foreign troops
in a conquest of the country.

Lord Chief Justice Sir Francis Pemberton, before
pronouncing sentence, declared:

"Look you, Mr. Plunkett, the bottom of your treason
was the setting up false religion than which there is not
anything more displeasing to God or more pernicious to
mankind."

The execution of Ireland's archbishop of Armagh
aroused great interest. It had been over a century since
a Catholic bishop had been executed in England.

TRANSPORTATION: Drogheda is 30 miles north of Dublin; 9 miles east of Slane; train and bus service from
Dublin.

HOTELS: *Boyne Valley* and *White Horse* are medium-
priced, and comfortable.

POINTS OF INTEREST: The Medical Missionaries of Mary
headquarters are here. Six miles west are the ruins of
Mellifont, the first Cistercian monastery in Ireland.
Four miles from the ruins a new Mellifont was
started in 1939.

DUBLIN

The most visited grave in St. Patrick's Cathedral in
Dublin is Jonathan Swift's. He is buried under the
cathedral floor, beside Esther Johnson, the woman he
called Stella. When Stella died, he described her as the
"truest, most virtuous and most valuable friend that I or
any other person was ever blessed with." Shining brass
stars mark their graves.

For 32 years in the first half of the 18th century,
Jonathan Swift was the dean of St. Patrick's Cathedral
which, in the Reformation, became the national cathedral of the Church of Ireland. The Dublin cathedral of
the Church of Ireland is Christ Church, down the hill

from St. Patrick's. Since the Reformation, Dublin has had no Catholic cathedral.

From the days of the apostle of Ireland a church has been on the site of St. Patrick's Cathedral. But after the Norsemen established Dublin in the 9th century, and placed a wall around it, St. Patrick's was beyond the pale. In 1038 Sitric the Dane, king of the Dublin Norsemen, erected a cathedral on the site of the present Christ Church. The church within the walls served in the 12th century as the cathedral for Laurence O'Toole, the first Irishman to be archbishop of Dublin (and the last Irish archbishop for centuries).

The area between the Liffey and the cathedrals is considered the oldest part of Dublin, and is traditionally known as "The Liberties." Archbishop O'Toole is said to have started the Liberty around Christ Church. A Liberty assured sanctuary, and within its boundaries was an independent court and jail.

Jonathan Swift, the 45th dean of St. Patrick's, was born on Nov. 30, 1667 in Hoey's Court (probably at No. 7), practically within the shadow of the cathedral. He was a precocious child, learning to read at 3 and ready to enter Trinity College, Dublin, at 14. When he was 22 he took a post as secretary in Surrey. The housekeeper's child was a vivacious 7-year-old girl. Swift met her. This was Stella. Swift became her teacher. She never had another. At 27 he was ordained, and assigned to the parish of Kilroot, near Larne. He was appointed dean of St. Patrick's in 1713, and at once invigorated the services, the clergy, and the devotion of the people.

Swift knew little about music but he sought to add the finest singers available to the cathedral choir that had been founded in 1432. One story is that Lady Carteret, the wife of the British viceroy, interceded with him for a friend who had wanted to join the choir. Dean Swift politely demurred, explaining that if it was a matter of a bishopric he might consider the request but a singer had to be able to sing. St. Patrick's has the only private choir school in Ireland.

After becoming dean, Jonathan Swift concerned himself increasingly with the political, economic and social conditions of his fellow Irishmen. He gave a third of his salary to charity. He established Ireland's first hospital for the mentally ill, naming it after St. Patrick, although Dubliners took to calling it Swift's Hospital. With enormous indignation, he began writing the freedom tracts that could have brought him jail or hanging. But by this time he was the most prominent and most revered writer of prose in Ireland. "Burn everything that comes from England except the coal," he said to the Irish in proposing a boycott. When Lady Carteret remarked to him about the "beautiful air" in Dublin, it is said that he fell to his knees and implored: "Madam, for God's sake, do not tell that in England, for if you do they will put a tax on it." In the Drapier letters he went to the root of civil liberties for the Irish, saying, "by the law of God, of nature and of nations, and of their own dear country, they are and they ought to be as free as their brethren in England." The letters were written anonymously. British government wall posters offered a reward of 300 pounds to anyone identifying the author. The identity of the author was an open secret, from the "pubs" along the Liffey to Dublin Castle itself. Yet no one stepped forward to seek the reward. The people's response to the reward offer was contained in a verse from the Bible that was pasted on a poster: "And the people said to Saul, 'Shall Jonathan die who hath done this great thing? No, by the living God there shall not a hair of his head be touched!"

Stella died on Jan. 28, 1728. She and Swift had known each other for nearly 40 years. He died 17 years later, on Oct. 19, 1745. He was 78. Near a bust of Dean Swift, in St. Patrick's Cathedral, is his epitaph in Latin: "Here lies the body of Jonathan Swift, D.D., dean of this cathedral, where fierce indignation can no longer tear the heart. Go traveler and imitate, if you can, one who did a man's job in the cause of liberty."

Robert Emmett, another non-Catholic Irish patriot, is believed to be buried in St. Michan's churchyard. The scaffold for his execution was set up in the road in front of St. Catherine's Church. He was hanged on Sept. 20, 1803. A tablet on the church fence says he died "in the cause of Irish freedom."

St. Michan's, now a parish church of the Church of Ireland, was founded in 1096. It is 200 yards south of "Father Mathew Bridge," named after the Capuchin friar, Mathew Talbot, who in 1838 founded the temperance apostolate. Handel played *Messiah* at St. Michan's; Edmond Burke was baptized there, and Parnell (a non-Catholic) presented the church with a movable altar. The night before his burial his body lay in state there. In the burial vaults are the Sheares brothers, leaders of the 1798 insurgency. A strange feature of the vaults is that bodies darken in color but show no signs of decomposing. An unidentified body, a woman next door to the church says, might have been a member of the Third Crusade. "First Crusaders were buried with their ankles crossed; the Second, with their shins. That one's thighs are crossed."

The most popular Catholic church in Dublin is formally dedicated to the Immaculate Conception, but has been known to Dubliners as "Adam and Eve." The unusual name derives from the Adam and Eve "pub" of penal times, a brown-robed friar explains. "Catholics were permitted to drink, but not to worship publicly. The church was hidden behind the pub, and people would say they were going to Adam and Eve's when in fact they were going to Mass."

In the Easter Rising of 1916 the Irish Republic was proclaimed at the General Post office in O'Connell Street. This is a holy place for all Irish.

TRANSPORTATION: Planes connect Dublin with Cork and Shannon and with principal British and continental cities.

HOTELS: *Gresham* is a favorite with Americans. *New Jury's* is extremely modern. *Four Courts* and *Wynn's* are medium-priced and comfortable.

9

Italy

✤

LESS THAN A CENTURY after Christ's death Bishop Ignatius of Antioch used a term to describe the various communities of believers that had formed in Jerusalem, Alexandria, Rome and his own see at the eastern corner of the Mediterranean. He described them as belonging to the universal church, the Catholic Church. The term still endures. Of the various churches created in the time of the apostles, the one of Rome from the very beginning exercised a regulatory role over the others, calling itself the Roman Catholic Church. At the same time its members were being persecuted for their beliefs by the state. Ignatius himself, after a confrontation in Antioch with the emperor Trajan, was hustled to Rome by a picket of legionaries and cast onto the floor of the Colosseum where he was torn to shreds by lions.

The pagans, and their religious beliefs, posed no problem for the pagan emperors and their beliefs. If different, they yet remained consonant. The Christian, on the other hand, professed a belief that was different per se, and which was at odds with every pagan deity, whether venerated by emperor or foot soldier. The series of persecutions by the emperors was almost inevitable. Trajan declared Christianity a crime in itself, punishable by death after trial and conviction. Diocletian masterminded the last and most terrible of the persecutions in the latter part of the 3rd century A.D.

Constantine, with the Edict of Milan, ended the persecutions and ushered in religious freedom. The Christian clergymen now had the same rights as the priests of the pagans. Constantine himself eventually permitted a priest of the new religion to baptize him, becoming known thereupon as the first Christian emperor.

But now the question arose of the relation of the Christian emperor of the Roman empire to the bishop of Rome, the Pope. The answer to the question of the relationship between church and state has occupied clergymen and statesmen over the centuries, not only in Rome itself but wherever its teachings of Christianity have reached—which means everywhere.

With Constantine, the seat of the empire was moved to Byzantium, and although the Pope remained in Rome the city declined in importance. In A.D. 410, Alaric, chief of a northern Barbarian tribe, the Visigoths, crossed the Alps into Italy, and sacked Rome. By the 8th century, the Roman emperor in Constantinople had little control over the remnants of the empire on the Italian peninsula. When the Lombards moved down the peninsula in the middle of the 8th century and made a new attack on Rome, Pope Stephen III appealed to Pepin, the king of the Franks. Pepin routed the Lombards, making the Pope the legal and actual sovereign of Italy. Now the bishop of Rome not only was a spiritual ruler, he was a temporal one, too. Then, a half century later, Charlemagne, Pepin's successor as king of the Franks, was crowned emperor of the West by the Pope in Rome.

While Danish pirates were rampaging in the British Isles, the Dark Ages were visiting the Italian peninsula as well. From the 9th to the first half of the 11th century many Popes reigned just a year—some even less.

Later, there were a number of anti-Popes, false claimants to the see of Peter. Political events in Italy were so alarming in the 14th century that the Popes moved to Avignon in southern France, remaining there almost 100 years.

At the time of the French Revolution, Italy was a political patchwork of independent states—Tuscany, Parma, Naples, Lombardy, the Veneto, the kingdom of the House of Savoy and Rome. Rome was the Papal State, reaching across the peninsula to Ancona on the Adriatic. The other states had various rulers. Lombardy and Venice, in the north, were part of the dominion of the Austro-Hungarian empire. The Papal State had been part of the Napoleonic empire, and it had been permeated with much of the French anticlerical thinking. The presence of the clergy in all public jobs—even clerks—fed the anticlerical spirit directly.

In 1831 the seething rebellion, fusing liberals, anticlerics and patriots, burst forth in Bologna. Austria responded to the appeal of the Pope and sent in forces to quell the political turmoil. As in the tradition of liberation armies, the Austrians lingered on the scene. France, the source of the liberalism wave, moved land and naval forces into the eastern frontier of the Papal State at Ancona. Obviously, the Papacy's temporal rule was ending, and its spiritual rule was jeopardized. Pius IX, coming to the throne in 1846 for a reign that was to last 32 years, introduced temporal reforms which cheered the liberals and irritated the old guard.

When the kingdom ruled by the House of Savoy sought to oust the Austrians in 1848, the Pope remained on the sidelines rather than installing the papal banner in the vanguard. This riled the patriotism of the liberals. A revolution broke out in Rome itself, and Pius IX was forced to flee. The revolutionaries declared Rome independent in November 1848. The life of the new republic of Rome was extinguished the following July when French forces, fighting at the Porta Pia—a few hundred yards from the Quirinale papal palace—captured Rome, and brought it back under the Pope. The French troops remained in the city to guarantee Papal sovereignty.

The patriots from the kingdom of the House of Savoy lost their war with the Austrians, but they waged a vigorous one against the church with more success, suppressing monasteries, expelling religious Orders, and imprisoning priests. After a decade of military regrouping, they made a new attack on Austria in 1859. This time the French joined with them. The Risorgimento was underway. When Austria was defeated, Napoleon III gave Camillo Cavour a free rein. With the aid of forces gathered by Giuseppe Garibaldi, Cavour brought about the unification of the Italian states, except that the Austrians clung to the Veneto and the Pope retained Rome. The Franco-Prussian War siphoned the French forces from Rome, and the Italian troops entered the city, ending the temporal power of the Pope on Sept. 20, 1870.

Now, in a modern context, the 4th-century question of the relationship between church and state, between the spiritual sovereign and the temporal one, had a spectacular immediacy. For the next 59 years, until the signing of a Concordat between representatives of the Papacy and the Italian kingdom, each succeeding Pope took an attitude of isolation, showing his opposition to the turn of events by remaining what has been called "prisoner of the Vatican." The Lateran Pact of 1929 established the Vatican City State around St. Peter's, guaranteeing it complete independence (extra-territoriality) with the right to its own courts, communications and administration. At the end of the Second World War, after the fall of Mussolini, Italians in a referendum terminated the monarchy and established a republic.

Just before the unification of Italy, a General Council of the Church was called for Dec. 8, 1869. The bishops from the world of Catholicism promulgated the doctrine of papal infallibility in the matter of faith and morals. The Franco-Prussian War, which forced the departure of the French troops, ended the Council before its work was finished. The unfinished business—and a general aggiornamento (up-dating) of the church—was taken up in the Second Vatican Council that John XXIII convened in 1962.

The past century and a half has been a turbulent one for the Church of Rome and its Pope. But the period also produced great saints and great Popes.

Paul VI proclaimed a Holy Year for 1975—a quarter of a century since the previous one—basing it on the themes of reconciliation, repentance and renewal.

TURIN

There is a French accent to Turin, because of geographical and historical reasons. Francis I annexed it to France for a quarter of a century and later, in the 17th and 18th centuries, it was attacked by French troops. For 9 centuries, until the end of the Italian monarchy in 1945, it was the main city of the House of Savoy. Today it is Italy's automobile and *espresso* coffee-making-machine capital.

THE HOLY SHROUD

Three different chests—iron, silver and glass—above the Royal Chapel altar in the cathedral at Turin contain what is believed by many to be the "clean linen cloth" which enveloped the body of Christ in His tomb at Jerusalem. The Holy Shroud is a strip of handwoven cloth, 14¼ feet long and 3 feet 7 inches wide. From sepia-colored stains at the upper and lower end of the cloth emerge the blurred impressions of the front and back parts of a human body.

Those who assert its authenticity describe the set of

images as a self-photograph of Christ. Questioners believe the images are some type of artistic reproduction, but no one has yet proved the kind of process that could have produced them.

"Oh, yes, there have been tests," says Giuseppe Viola, a thin, tall man who has been sacristan for 19 years. "In 1969, some tests were made in a room of the royal palace, not far from here. Then, in November of 1973 they made some more tests when it was shown on television. That was the first time it was presented on television. It is not shown to the public often—only on great occasions. The last time it was placed on exhibit was in 1933 for the 19th centenary of Christ's crucifixion."

Paul VI spoke at the time of the television exhibit of the Holy Shroud.

"Whatever historical and scientific judgment scholars may choose to express on this surprising and mysterious relic, we can only pray that it may lead visitors, not only to thoughtful observation of the outward and mortal features of the Saviour's wonderful figure, but also to a deeper insight into His hidden and fascinating mystery," Paul VI said.

The Holy Shroud was acquired by the House of Savoy in 1452 after having been brought to France from Constantinople. It had been carried to Constantinople by Crusaders. The House of Savoy kept it for more than a century in the French alpine town of Chambéry. When a plague struck Milan in 1578, Cardinal Charles Borromeo made a vow to venerate the Holy Shroud in thanksgiving for the swift ending of the epidemic. To spare the cardinal a difficult journey across the Alps to see it, Duke Emmanuel Filiberto had the Holy Shroud brought to Turin. Except for the Second World War when it was safeguarded in the Apennines at the Mount Vergine Abbey at Avellino, it has been in Turin ever since.

"In 1955," the sacristan says, "the cases were opened

privately so a little English girl could touch it. She was a polio victim. She had been brought here by the American pilot who bombarded Hiroshima with the atom bomb. The pilot had dedicated his life to children and the poor. A year or so later, the parents of the child brought some photos of her showing her on her feet, and she seemed to have recovered. I was just starting to work here then."

There are Masses in the Royal Chapel each morning.

"One night in October 1972—the first of October, it was—someone broke in through a cathedral window, and set fire to the altar, but there was no damage. Twenty days later there was a second attempt. When a third try was made—this time it was during the day—the man was caught. He was mentally unbalanced. This was two months later. But since then a good alarm system has been installed. As soon as the machine sees a person entering the chapel it makes the alarm. It does not wait for the person to touch anything. The alarm signal rings in the porter's lodge of the royal palace where there is always someone on guard. Since the alarm was installed, all is quiet, except now and then it goes off at night for some reason. Something moves, probably, and the police come and look around, but all is calm."

THE CONSOLATA

The Madonna, as Comforter, is the patron of Turin. An inscription on the wall of the Basilica of the Consolata carries the notice of the formal dedication: "Amedeo Peyron, mayor of Turin, interpreter of the popular mood, solemnly consecrates the city to the Consolata, June 20, 1954."

Devotion to the Consolata began in the 5th century, according to tradition, but it grew enormously after reports of a miracle that took place on June 20, 1104 when a blind man named Giovanni Ravacchio found a

Madonna statue that had vanished, and at the same time regained his sight. The man was from the other side of the Alps at Briançon.

Don Bosco

In front of the international headquarters of the Salesians is a statue of their founder, St. John Bosco, surrounded by young people. Like the statue of Don Bosco, Salesians are always surrounded by young people. Don Bosco is the patron of youth, and spent his life helping and training the poorest boys, founding vocational schools where they could learn trades.

He was born on Aug. 16, 1815 at Becchi, a tiny community near Castelnuovo, 18 miles east of Turin, the son of a poor farmer who died two years later.

When he was 16 he moved closer to Turin, to the town of Chieri (10 miles east on Highway 10). He had been given a job in the house of a tailor. Along with going to school, he tutored the tailor's son and learned how to sew, bake bread, and repair shoes. The house where he lived at Chieri can be visited. But Turin is the center of Salesian life, and his living and work quarters there are enshrined in a huge complex of buildings that is a small Salesian city.

Why the name *Salesian?*

"He followed the spirit of St. Francis de Sales," says Arnaldo Montecchio, the administrator of the *Salesian Bulletin.* "The spirit of St. Francis de Sales (who is buried in Annecy, on the French side of the Alps) guides me in everything, the saint used to say. Thus, the name *Salesian.*"

The *Salesian Bulletin* administrator is a short, stocky man with a mustache. His offices are on the floor below the 4-room apartment in which Don Bosco lived. Arnaldo says he is from Padua originally, from a family of a dozen children—7 boys, 5 girls. All are alive yet, but the mother has died.

"We were a poor family, and an American friend paid my way to come to the boardingschool of the Salesians here when I was thirteen. That was forty-nine years ago. I have never left the place. I am a lay member of the community, and follow the Salesian way of life."

The remains of St. Don Bosco are presented in a glass container in the Basilica of Maria Ausiliatrice. They are dressed in priestly vestments. The hands and the face are wax masks which have been painted.

COTTOLENGO

The sign above the main door of a building down the street from the Salesian headquarters still carries the name *La Piccola Casa* (The Small House). That was the name used by a priest, Father Joseph Benedict Cottolengo, when he rented two rooms in 1828 and turned them into a reception center for the sick poor who could not be cared for elsewhere. The idea for the center occurred to him when he heard of a pregnant French woman who was traveling through Turin with her husband and 3 children. The Maternity Hospital refused to accept her because she had a contagious disease. Finally she was sent to a municipal shelter which was a catch-all for vagabonds and derelicts.

More than 6,000 persons now live at the Piccola Casa, which is often called "The Cottolengo." It is unique. It is a combination hospital, asylum, convent and school, and the residents represent every known medical affliction. There are tiny orphans, paraplegics, mentally deficient boys and girls, deaf mutes and epileptics. In starting the Piccola Casa, the priest made it the rule that the sicker and the poorer the person, the greater the welcome. This is still the basic guideline. The Piccola Casa never makes any fund drives. Father Cottolengo used to assure his colleagues that Providence would take care of the Piccola Casa.

The work has spread throughout Italy, with 80 branches. The founder has been canonized, and the chapel containing his body is around the corner from the main entrance to the Piccola Casa.

St. Joseph Benedict Cottolengo was born on May 3, 1786 in Bra, a small town 26 miles south of Turin via Highway 393. He died on Apr. 30, 1842 at Chieri, the same town where Don Bosco studied as a youth. Cottolengo had gone to Chieri to be with his brother, a priest.

TRANSPORTATION: Turin (Torino) is 430 miles north-west of Rome. It is linked to Lyons and Paris by rail.

HOTELS: Main hotels are *Palace, Ambassciatori,* and *City. Ligure* and *Suisse Terminus* are less expensive.

PLACES OF INTEREST: The Basilica of Superga, a burial place of kings of the House of Savoy, just east of Turin. It was built to fulfill a vow made by Victor Amadeus II when French troops were attacking Turin in 1706.

MILAN

When Milan's muggy summer weather makes the humidity rise, an attendant increases the central heating in the refectory of the former Dominican Convent of Holy Mary of the Graces. The humidity is kept at a prescribed level to protect the masterpiece, "The Last Supper," which Leonardo da Vinci painted on the dining-room wall nearly 5 centuries ago. A hygrometer constantly measures the humidity, and the attendant adjusts the output of the oil furnace accordingly.

The masterpiece has been prey to the dangers of man and nature a number of times. Gabriele d'Annunzio exclaimed: "Weep, O Poets, O Heroes! for the wonder which will not live again." Troops of the Austro-Hungarian empire bivouacked in the refectory for 3 years in the 19th century. On the feast of the Assumption in 1943, a 2-ton bomb shattered the cloister but, surprisingly, the wall holding the painting did not buckle.

Leonardo came to Milan in 1482 from his birthplace, the village of Vinci in Tuscany. He was 30. The ducal court at Milan was interested in his many talents: military engineering, airplane design, and the creation of musical instruments, such as a new lyre, as well as his painting. A dozen years after his arrival in Milan the Sforzas asked him to paint "The Last Supper" in the Dominican refectory.

Leonardo wanted his painting to reflect the drama and shock of the moment when Christ said: "But behold, the hand of him who betrays me is with me on the table."

The painting is spread across a surface 29 feet wide and 15 feet high. The work took him 2 years, 1495 to 1497. A friar related that some days the artist would work straight through, from dawn to darkness, taking not even the time to eat or drink. Other days, he would sit before the painting contemplatively, not once moving his brush.

TRANSPORTATION: Milan (Milano) is on direct rail line to Rome, 360 miles south.

HOTELS: The main hotels include *Principe-Savoia* and *Sonesta*. The *Commercio* is medium-priced.

POINTS OF INTEREST: The cover of a large burial urn in the Church of Sant' Eustorgio is marked *Sepulcrum Trium Magorum* (Tomb of the Three Magi). The tradition is that Emperor Constantine gave the relics of the Three Magi to Bishop Eustorgius, of Milan, in the 4th century and they were transported from Constantinople by a cart drawn by a young bull. The relics were moved to the cathedral in Cologne, Germany, by Frederic Barbarossa in A.D. 1164. (See Index.)

SOTTO IL MONTE

Until the reign of John XXIII, Sotto il Monte (Under the Mountain), was no better or less known than any other farm village in the Po valley between Milan and Bergamo. Its status as the birthplace of "Good Pope John"—Papa Giovanni, as he is known in Italy—has made it a point of pilgrimage for people from all countries, and religions, too.

It is a typical farm village. Back doors are framed with tomato vines. Mattresses and bed clothing regardless of winter or summer are draped over window sills each morning for a daily airing. Some houses still do not have running water. The men shave on the front porch, setting a wash basin on a chair. On weekends the women of a family—grandmothers to teenagers—do one another's hair. Men go hunting after Mass on Sunday, not so much for the sport as for the chance of bringing home a rabbit or some birds for dinner. *Polenta* is as popular a dish as it was when Pope John was a boy. The Indian corn is ground up, seasoned with herbs, and served with homemade sausages or birds.

Farmers live in the village in two-story houses. Like Pope John's family, many are sharecroppers. The house where he was born on Nov. 25, 1881 is on one corner of the main square. The Church of Santa Maria, where he was baptized, made his first Holy Communion, and celebrated his first Mass is diagonally across the way from the house. While Pope John was still alive, the house was acquired by a congregation of missionaries. It has built a seminary on land next to Pope John's birthplace.

Several pieces of original furniture, a picture of his parents, and a painting of St. Anne and her child Mary are in the simple 10-by-10-foot room on the second floor, where Pope John was born. The old farmhouse is under the official protection of the *belli arti* authorities.

People of Sotto il Monte talk about Pope John like a friend of the family. He had a dozen brothers and sisters. The most colorful of the survivors—because he resembles Pope John so much—is Zaverio. He wears ordinary farm clothes, holding up his trousers with suspenders. Zaverio smiles like his brother, who was a year and a half older. He speaks only Italian but, like his brother, it is easy to communicate with him.

A main pilgrimage date is June 2, a legal holiday in Italy, because the republic was proclaimed on that date. Proclamation Day is the eve of Pope John's death in 1963.

Pope John's friend, the late Cardinal Richard Cushing of Boston, raised funds among Americans to renew the façade of the Church of the Holy Ghost in Bergamo, where Pope John as a young military chaplain used to celebrate Mass.

TRANSPORTATION: Sotto il Monte is 20 miles east of Milan; buses serve the village.

PADUA

The last section of the main street that extends through the city from the railroad station is called the Via del Santo, the Street of the Saint. The square to which it leads is the Piazza del Santo. The immense church on the piazza is the Basilica del Santo. For all of Padua, the *santo* could be no other than the Franciscan friar St. Anthony, who was born in Lisbon (see Index) but who worked and died in northern Italy, and is buried in Padua.

"He was a canon regular of St. Augustine in Portugal, and wanted to be a missionary in Africa," says Fra Luciano, the sacristan at the Basilica of the Saint. Fra Luciano has been at the basilica for 40 years. He is a sturdy, balding, amiable friar. "Twice Anthony headed for Africa. The second time a storm off Sicily stopped the boat, and he decided it was the will of God that he serve in Italy.

"During a chapter of the Order at Assisi in 1221, he met Francis, and was sent to north Italy as the provincial minister. But he was sickly. He was suffering from dropsy, and a friend invited him to Campo San Piero. It is now a small village north of Padua, but then it was only the site of a castle of a rich man who hoped it would help Anthony recover his health. But his health got worse.

"He wanted to die in the house [Franciscan] at Padua, but he never made it. He became worse on the way back here, and was suffering much. The friars accompanying him stopped at a little monastery at Arcella. The monastery was the first convent of the Franciscan Sisters in Padua. He died on a Friday, June 13, 1231.

"After five days his body was brought here. At that time it was the Chapel of Santa Maria Mater Dei, the first house of the friars in Padua."

Why was he kept 5 days in Arcella?

"Because each wanted his body—the Sisters and the friars. When he was finally brought into Padua, children along the route shouted continuously *"Morto il Santo, morto il Santo"* (The Saint is dead, the Saint is dead). He was transported on a Tuesday, so there is a special devotion to him on that day."

Arcella has since been annexed to Padua, and is now part of the main railroad station district. The cell used by St. Anthony is enshrined in the church. At Campo San Piero is the small room where he spent the last days of his life, and where he is said to have been visited by the Child Jesus in a vision.

"The Chapel of Mater Dei was on the site of what is now the basilica chapel holding his tomb," Fra Luciano says. "In 1263, his tomb was opened in the presence of

St. Bonaventure, who was general of the Order. They saw that the body had decomposed, and only the tongue—by a miracle!—was intact. The basilica at this time was three quarters finished. They had started it in 1232, the year after his death. They buried him before the main altar, and his tomb remained there till 1310. At that time they solemnly brought him, in the presence of the cardinal, to the chapel where he now is—more or less where he had been originally. The date of the translation was February 15, 1310, and each year this feast is remembered with a Pontifical Mass. His tongue is in a reliquary in the Chapel of the Treasury."

Hundreds of small hearts of silver and other shiny metals are hung on the walls near the tomb. One wall is filled with photos of automobile accidents. A university student's long tricorne hat, trimmed with dangling trinkets, is among the ex-votos.

The saint's tomb is 5 feet above the ground. Pilgrims walk behind the altar and touch the tomb with their hands. When the basilica is being closed, and the pilgrims are leaving, the friars can be alone with their saint. It is not unusual to glimpse a friar leaning his head against the tomb and remaining there, meditatively, for several minutes.

Part of the original cloister in which St. Anthony lived, the Chiostro del Paradiso, still exists. Near it is a nut tree which does not bloom until about June 1, the period of the saint's feast (June 13). This is a cause of wonder for the friars who recall how the saint was associated in his life with a nut tree. At Campo San Piero, for example, he used to preach under one.

In the tradition of St. Anthony, food and money are distributed daily to the poor. Across from the Basilica of the Saint are a Pilgrims' House and a boardinghouse for students.

"It's mostly for foreign students who don't have much money—Orientals and Africans, for example," Fra Luciano says.

Padua's university, after Bologna, is Italy's oldest. It was founded in 1222. In the Great Hall is conserved the pulpit from which Galileo lectured.

Donatello worked in Padua from 1443 to 1452. Some of his statues and bas reliefs are on the main altar of the basilica.

TRANSPORTATION: Padua is 315 miles northeast of Rome. There is direct train service to and from Rome, Venice and Milan.

HOTELS: *Storione* and *Plaza* are main hotels. *Corso* and *Monaco* are medium-priced.

VENICE

Venice, of course, is a wonder of the world, and of the sea. The doge from his palace on the square named after the Evangelist St. Mark ruled the sea, bringing wealth and culture to this cosmopolis. There is a historical argument as to whether coffee was first introduced into Western Europe through Venice or through Vienna. It is a city of ceremonies, of galas, of spectacles, many with a religious base or history. One old religious ceremonial, one that died with the last doge in Napoleonic times was the marriage of Venice and the Sea. Pope Alexander III, in return for the support of the Venetian republic in his struggles with Emperor Frederick Barbarossa, presented the doge with a ring, symbolizing Venice's link to the sea. On Ascension Day each year the doge would sail ceremonially out to sea where he slipped a ring into the waters, declaring: "O Sea, we wed thee." Voltaire asserted the marriage was not valid because the bride had not given her consent.

The Byzantine style of St. Mark's Cathedral bespeaks the maritime past of the Venetian republic, and its long-range interests in the eastern Mediterranean, the Mare Nostrum of the Romans. Forty-four thousand square feet of mosaics have given St. Mark's Cathedral the title of "the Golden Basilica." The shining mosaics picture scenes from the Bible, and Christ's birth and death. They tell, too, of how the body of St. Mark, after he was martyred in Egypt, was brought to Venice by two sailors who risked their lives by going ashore at Alexandria in search of it. Four life-sized bronze horses embellish its façade. They were a tribute from Constantinople for the part soldiers of the Venetian republic played in the Fourth Crusade. Enemies of Venice used to boast that they would one day "bridle" the horses, but they never did.

Delivery from a plague in 1576, prompted the Venetian senate to order construction of the Redentore, the Church of the Redeemer, and to require the signoria on the third Sunday of July each year to visit it. The church was built by Andrea Palladio. The eve of the feast is saluted with fireworks, music and dancing. For the feast the army's engineering corps strings a pontoon-type bridge across the canal, using boats as the pontoons. On the day of the feast, there is a religious procession across the bridge to the church, with the patriarch of Venice leading and accompanied by the mayor.

Black and yellow directional signs, with inscriptions in Hebrew and other languages, point the way to the old synagogue. It is in a small square, Campiello de la Scuola. A message on the façade says:

"From 1939 to 1945, 200 Hebrews of Venice, 8,000 Hebrews of Italy, 6 million Hebrews of Europe by blind, barbaric hate were hunted, martyred, suppressed in foreign lands. The memory of the most atrocious offense to human civility recalls all men to the holy law of God, to the sentiment of fraternity and love which Israel first affirmed among the people."

TRANSPORTATION: Venice (Venezia) is 330 miles northeast of Rome. It is a main rail center.

HOTELS: Tops are *Bauer Grünwald, Danieli,* and *Gritti Palace. Casanova* and *Flora* are less expensive.

POINTS OF INTEREST: St. Francis of the Desert Monastery, connected to Murano by ship, is where St. Francis arrived on his return from the Holy Land.

RAVENNA

The early Christian history of the Adriatic city of Ravenna, once the capital of the Western branch of the Roman empire, is told in the mosaics which line the interiors of its churches and civic buildings in brilliant colors. The cathedral mosaics are known as Neonian because it was Bishop Neon who ordered the extraordinary decoration. There is also an Arian Baptistry with much the same mosaic design. Emperor Honorius moved the capital from Rome to Ravenna in A.D. 402 after a brief trial of Milan. The Barbarian Ostrogoths took possession of Ravenna at the end of the 5th century, and their king, Theodoric, ruled Italy from Ravenna between A.D. 493 and 526. Theodoric became a Christian. Forces loyal to Justinian I, emperor of the Eastern branch of the Roman empire in Constantinople, seized Ravenna from the Ostrogoths in 540 and brought it under Byzantine rule.

It is one of Christianity's oldest settlements. Its first bishop was St. Apollinaris, a disciple of St. Peter. He is buried in the basilica named after him at Classe, once a seaport but now silted-in, 3 miles south of Ravenna. King Theodoric's tomb is in Ravenna. So is Dante's. There is a large mosaic-covered mausoleum for Galla Placidia, the beautiful, intelligent sister of Roman emperor Honorius. She ruled the Western branch of the empire in place of her son. Palmiro Togliatti, postwar leader of Italy's Communists, was born in Ravenna.

TRANSPORTATION: Ravenna is 230 miles northeast of Rome. There are direct rail connections to and from Bologna, Florence and Ancona.

HOTELS: The largest selection of hotels is at the seaside resort of Rimini, 31 miles south of Ravenna. *Grand* and *Villa Bianca* are luxurious.

PLACES OF INTEREST: The independent republic of San Marino is literally next door to Rimini. At Bologna, in the Dominican church, is the tomb of St. Dominic. (See Index.)

FLORENCE

Florence has been often compared to a palace, a vast palace with hundreds of rooms, each room containing a treasure. The Dominican friar Fra Angelico lived in the San Marco Convent, and painted the walls of the cells, the cloister, and the corridors. Savonarola was its prior at one period. An ascetic, dedicated friar, he sharply attacked the importance given to pleasure and self-comfort. In the lovely Piazza della Signoria, the political forum of Florence in all ages, Savonarola arranged a huge bonfire in 1497 so that penitents won over by his words could do away with their wigs, perfumes, lotions, powders and other accouterments of an easy way of life. He himself was burned to death in the same piazza a year later as a heretic. The spot where he died is marked with a plaque. It is not far from the copy of Michelangelo's statue of "David."

The inside of a Florentine church means frescoes. Giotto's frescoes of the early 14th century are in two chapels of the Santa Croce (Holy Cross) Church of the Franciscans. Giotto began the slender bell tower near the cathedral. The bronze doors of the 11th-century Baptistry depict religious scenes and personages. Michelangelo referred to them as "The Gates of Paradise."

Throughout Florence are souvenirs and signs of the Medicis, of Michelangelo, and of Dante whose *Divine Comedy*, written nearly 7 centuries ago, was the poetic vehicle for him to take a spiritual pilgrimage through the Inferno, Purgatory and Paradise. The house where Dante was born is now a museum. His great inspiration was Beatrice whom he met when she was only a child. Monna Tessa, the nurse in Beatrice's family, suggested to the child's father, Folco Portinari, that something should be done to help the sick among the pilgrims visiting Florence in the 13th century. At her suggestion he set aside some of his property for a small hospital. Monna Tessa was its first nurse, and the Santa Maria Nuova Hospital has grown into an institution with 3,000 beds. Monna Tessa and her companions founded a community of hospital Sisters, adopting a unique veil that is more than 12 feet long and 2 feet wide. The veil, modeled after the head-covering worn by noble ladies of Florence in the Middle Ages, is wrapped into a series of folds atop the head and then falls in the shape of a fan across the shoulders. The congregation of nuns adopted the identifying name "Monna Tessa." The word *Monna* is an abbreviation of "Madonna," a title that used to be applied to domestic servants in the sense of "my woman." *Tessa* is a short form of *Contessa*, Countess. *Contessa* was a popular baptismal name for girls in Florence in the Middle Ages, after Countess Mathilda.

TRANSPORTATION: Florence (Firenze) is 175 miles north of Rome; direct rail connections to principal Italian cities.

HOTELS: *Grand* and *Excelsior* are principal hotels. Other fine hotels are *Baglioni-Palace* and *Minerva*.

POINTS OF INTEREST: The original "David" of Michelangelo in the Gallery of the Accadèmia.

SIENA

Nine popes have come from the Tuscan town of Siena, and two famous saints: St. Catherine of Siena, the patroness of Italy, and St. Bernardine, whom Pope

John XXIII designated as the patron of advertising. Their homes are now sanctuaries.

St. Catherine was born here in 1347 and became a Dominican nun. A most singular act was her success in bringing Pope Gregory XI back from Avignon. She earnestly chided the disloyal cardinals who had taken part in electing an anti-Pope. In the basilica of San Domenico she had the mystical visions which guided her in her pilgrimages across Italy. An authentic painting of her is above the altar of a chapel. A reliquary contains her head. She died in Rome at the age of 33. (Her body is in the Church of Santa Maria sopra Minerva in Rome. Fra Angelico's tomb is in the same church.)

St. Bernardine was a young nobleman, born in 1380, who became a great preacher. He was accustomed to conclude his sermons by holding aloft a tablet with the letters IHS which form the Greek monogram of Jesus' name. He launched the devotion to the Holy Name of Jesus in this fashion.

Long white-stone strips divide the shell-shaped main square into 9 sections, symbolizing "The Nine" (citizens) who administered Siena early in the 14th century after the end of rule by bishops. An opening at the meeting point of the 9 strips catches the rainwater draining off the square. Traditionalists insist it is more than a sewer. Etruscans used to maintain a hole in the ground to communicate with the dead, and since Siena has Etruscan origins the opening is considered to be a link with the past.

Mystical Siena includes famous non-Catholic thinkers, too. Siena is the home of Lelio and Fausto Socino, the two brothers who in the 16th century developed Socinianism, the system of religious thinking associated with the Unitarian sect and the Polish Brethren.

The main square, Piazza del Campo, is the setting each year on Aug. 16, the day after the feast of the Assumption, for Siena's unique horse race, the Palio. It was introduced in the 1500s to honor the Madonna, the city's patron. The festival includes a procession through the streets, followed by the horse race. The prize is a silk cloth (*pallium* in Latin, and thus the Italian word *palio*) which has a representation of the Madonna. The jockeys for the race represent the city's districts (*contrade*). Each *contrada* has its own museum, picture gallery, social club and chapel, and also a baptismal font where children of the district are baptized on the annual feast of its particular patron.

It can be interesting for a visitor to be in Siena at the time a *contrada* honors its patron saint. Men from the *contrada* put on medieval costumes and, accompanied by flag-bearers and drummers, march through the streets to offer the district's respects to the municipal authorities. During the two days of feasting, the *contrada* chapel, picture gallery and museum are open to the public. The feast days of the 17 *contrade* are pretty much bunched in the spring-to-fall period.

At the back of each *contrada* chapel is the *sacra stalla* (holy stable) where the district's entry in the horse race is sheltered for the 3 nights before the race. On the afternoon of the race, the horse is led into the chapel for the official blessing. There is a Palio race also on July 2.

TRANSPORTATION: Siena is 145 miles north of Rome on State Highway SS-2, the ancient Via Cassia.

HOTELS: *Park* and *Scacciapensieri* are leading ones. *Continental* and *Minerva* are medium-priced.

ASSISI

Sister Rosita, S.A., an American nun from Boston, points out that many of the million and a half people who come to this Umbrian hilltown each year are youths. She is in a position to know because she is the superior of the Convent of Franciscan Sisters of the Atonement at Assisi.

St. Francis will have been dead 750 years in 1976. He was born here, near the main square, in 1182, the son of a prosperous cloth merchant and a French mother. Francis, a soldier in his young days in a defensive war against the traditional valley enemy, Perugia, was captured and imprisoned for a year. Later, on his way to join Papal forces on the Adriatic coast, he was confronted by an inner voice challenging him about the direction of his life, till then the life of a well-to-do young man interested in amusements and comforts. He decided that the only princess he would marry would be someone he called Lady Poverty.

San Damiano Chapel, tucked in the side of the Assisi hill, is where Francis was praying one day in 1206 when he heard himself called by name and was asked to restore the house of Christ. Francis thought Christ was asking him to restore the San Damiano Chapel, when actually the request concerned the church itself, confused at the time in heresy and misguided reform. Francis took some bolts of top-quality cloth from his father's shop to raise money for the San Damiano restoration work. The father, angered, brought charges against him and the bishop was called upon to adjudicate the family quarrel. Francis had meant well, the bishop determined, but he had proceeded wrong. The money was returned to the father but Francis, after taking off the clothes his parent had bought for him, publicly renounced him. "Hitherto I have called you father on earth," he said. "Now I say 'Our Father Who art in heaven.' Francis, in his mid-20s at the time, began a life of poverty and public begging.

When a dozen companions had gathered around him, Francis traveled to Rome, seeking approval from Innocent III. The pope, dismayed at the raggedness of the clothes Francis was wearing and the general aspect of penury, turned him away. Francis returned to the pope once more, and this time received papal approbation.

For a time Francis and his companions lived in huts. Then Benedictine monks transferred to him a small chapel at the base of the Assisi hill for the price of a hamper of fish a year. The chapel, known as the Portiuncula (Small Portion), is sacred to the Franciscans as the cradle of their movement. It became a major point of pilgrimage, too, when Pope Honorius granted the indulgence, known as the Pardon of Assisi, to all who come to pray there.

Francis emphasized the humility of his followers by calling them friars *minor*, not *superior*. He founded a second Order, for women wishing to take up the Franciscan way of life. They were called the "Poor Clares," after Clare, daughter of a well-to-do family who was the first recruit. She is buried in the Basilica of Santa Chiara (St. Clare). Nine years later, in 1221, Francis founded a third Order, for lay people who, as Tertiaries, would remain at their regular jobs in the world.

While other friars worked on the phraseology of a canonical rule to govern the Order, Francis wrote a salute to God, "The Canticle of Brother Sun." The hymn of glorification begins:

Most High Almighty Good Lord,
Yours are praise, glory, honor and all blessing.
To You alone, Most High, do they belong,
And no man is worthy to mention You.
Be praised, my Lord, with all Your creatures,
Especially Sir Brother Sun,
Who is daylight, and by him you shed light on us.
And he is beautiful and radiant with great splendor.
Of you, Most High, he is a symbol.

The paean of praise continued with tributes from other creatures of the universe: Sister Moon, Brother Wind, Sister Water, Brother Fire, Sister Mother Earth.

Francis respected all creatures. The birds were his sisters. He called wolves his brothers. He did not fear wolves because he had done them no harm, and thus they had no reason to harm him. Just before he died on Oct. 4, 1226 he cried out: "Welcome, Sister Death."

The title that is used most for him is Il Poverello (the Little Poor Man). The robe he died in belonged to a friar from the Portiuncula. He is buried in the immense basilica in Assisi itself. At the bottom of the hill of Assisi, the Basilica of St. Mary of the Angels has been built around the Portiuncula Chapel. Friars from Assisi have taken the name "the Angels" across the world, using it to describe the geographical center of Spain and to identify what has become California's major city, Los Angeles.

TRANSPORTATION: Assisi is 100 miles north of Rome. The railroad station is at Santa Maria degli Angeli, 2½ miles from the hillside town of Assisi.

ORVIETO

The Etruscans, the ancient inhabitants of Etruria in central Italy, had in Orvieto their main holy place, Fanum Voltumnae, the temple of their goddess. The temple was the meeting place for the representatives of the Etruscan states.

Orvieto is a walled hilltown of Umbria, 95 miles north of Rome. Its cathedral is one of the most sumptuous in Italy.

A tall, husky man near the sacristy door interrupts his conversation with a middle-aged woman to say he is not the sacristan. "I am the *custode*, the guard," he says. He is guarding Orvieto's celebrated Holy Corporal, a small linen cloth on which the host and chalice rest during Mass. The guard says there have been paintings and other articles stolen from churches in Italy in recent years.

"In 1263," the guard says, resuming his conversation with the woman, "a priest was saying Mass in the church at Bolsena, 20 kilometers from Orvieto. When he was proceeding to break the Host, blood appeared on the corporal. The wondrous occurrence astounded the townspeople and it was decided to bring the cloth to the papal court of Urban IV who was residing in Orvieto at the time. About thirty-three popes have lived here, you know. Anyway—to provide a fitting sanctuary for the cloth, priests and people determined to construct a cathedral, and it was started in 1290."

The interior of the cathedral is austere, almost bare. But the façade is a rich, striking object of art. Stories of the Bible are sculpted in the marble across the front, and tiny stones of red, blue and gold stand out like exclamation points in the biblical account. The sides of the cathedral are a horizontal pattern of black and white marble.

A stone tabernacle holds the Holy Corporal. The tabernacle is 5 feet wide, and about the same in height. The gold of the doors glisten against the whiteness of the stone.

"The feast of Corpus Christi was instituted by the Miracle of Bolsena," the guard says. "Each year on the feast the Holy Corporal is removed from its casket, and there is a procession through town with medieval costumes. Later, the Holy Cloth is exposed on the main altar."

St. Thomas Aquinas lived at Orvieto in the Convent of San Domenico, and his biretta and breviary are conserved there.

After Rome was sacked in 1527, Pope Clement VII ordered a well dug to assure a supply of drinking water. The well, more than 200 feet deep, can be visited via an intricate pair of spiral staircases.

There is also an Etruscan necropolis at Orvieto.

TRANSPORTATION: Orvieto is 95 miles north of Rome. It is on main rail lines to Milan, Bologna, Florence and Rome.

THE HOLY HOUSE

Saints, popes and ordinary pilgrims have visited the Holy House at Loreto in the past 7 centuries, but the visitor remembered the most is John XXIII who came on Oct. 4, 1962. His statue is in the square named after him that looks from the hill of the basilica to the Adriatic and the Marches countryside south of Ancona.

According to tradition angels brought from Palestine the house in which Christ was raised at Nazareth, carrying it first to Tersatto, near Fiume, in what is now Yugoslavia, in A.D. 1291. Then on Dec. 9–10, 1294 the Holy House arrived in Loreto in the same miraculous way. It is said that St. Francis on his way to the Holy Land nearly a century earlier paused on the Lauretano Hill here, 190 feet above sea level, and exclaimed: "Blessed hill. O blessed land. What a gift awaits you."

A marble tablet in the sacristy corridor lists holy men who have visited Loreto. The list includes many familiar names: Teresa of the Child Jesus, 1887; Don Bosco, 1877; Peter Canisius, 1558. Another tablet lists popes—11 of them—starting with Nicholas V in 1449. Pope John XXIII was the first pope to visit the Holy House since Pius IX in 1857. But Paul VI came as a cardinal on Sept. 1, 1962, a month before John XXIII's visit. Pius XII was here as a priest in 1900. Pius XI also made a pilgrimage as a priest, but the date is not recorded. Pius X was a bishop when he came here in 1884. Leo XIII, on his visit in 1877, was a cardinal.

Another link to Pope John is that his former secretary, Monsignor Loris Capovilla, is the prelate of the sanctuary of Loreto with the rank of bishop. On the first Saturday of each month he confirms children of the Marches region in a chapel near the Holy House.

The Holy House, its sides encased in sculpted marble, is in the center of the basilica. It is 31 feet long and 13 feet wide. Its present ceiling was added in 1530, and its once-reddish stone walls were covered with paint centuries ago. Under the present altar is another one which, according to tradition, was used by the Apostles. A distinctive element is that the Holy House has no foundations. It rests partly on the ground of what was an open field, and partly on an old country road.

Capuchin friars care for the shrine.

The basilica was started about 1468 at the request of Pope Paul II who reported himself cured of the plague while visiting the Holy House.

Father Luciano, O.F.M. (Cap.), director at the shrine of the world-wide Congregation of Loreto which was founded in 1883, tells about the latest "first."

"In October 1974, a pilgrimage of sick and crippled Americans was scheduled here for the first time," he says. "They were from the New Jersey–Washington area. One of the organizers was the Blue Army."

TRANSPORTATION: Loreto is 170 miles northeast of Rome, and 15 miles south of Ancona; direct trains from Ancona, Brindisi, Bologna and Foggia.

HOTELS: The main hotels are *Giardinetto* and *Marchigiano-Bellevue*. *San Gabriele* and *Santuario* are medium-priced.

PADRE PIO

More than 100,000 persons swarmed into the remote town of San Giovanni Rotondo, 1,827 feet above the sea near the southeastern coast of Italy, for the funeral of the Capuchin friar Padre Pio, who died in 1968. He had been a priest at the Capuchin Convent of Our Lady of Grace for a half century. It is unusual for a friar to remain at the same house so long. Usually he is given another assignment after a few years. But when a transfer of Padre Pio was ordered in 1923 popular demonstrations took place, and it had to be canceled. He was actually restricted to the convent because the cult to him was already developing, and church authorities wanted to be prudent. In 1931 Padre Pio was completely cut off from the public, but the Holy Office two years later lifted the interdiction.

His tomb is in the crypt of the Capuchin church. Flowers are at the corners of the tomb. A plaque on the wall carries the words of Paul VI of Feb. 20, 1971 when he talked of Padre Pio's fame. "Because he was a philosopher?" the Pope asked. "A scholar? Wealthy? No. Because he said Mass humbly, confessed morning to night, and was representative, stamped, of the Stigma of Our Lord. He was a man of prayer and suffering."

The convent is on a spur of the southern Apennines, and is reached across the plains from Foggia. It is a barren hard area of sheep, and of almond trees which burst with pink or white flowers as early as the end of February. The convent is 335 feet higher than the town of San Giovanni. There are 20,000 people living in the town.

"He was known as a saint in his lifetime," says John Howley, who comes from Lakewood in Los Angeles county. John looks singularly tall and slim in his brown Capuchin robes. He is 25. "I had a devotion to Padre Pio, and the Franciscan life, and through a friend of a friend I arranged to be accepted by the Capuchins here. No one brings up the question of money, or payment. Capuchins have a vow of poverty, you know. I guess through Mass contributions and offerings they support me. I help with the correspondence in English, and am studying Italian as a postulant so that I can enter the novitiate."

John knows the story of Padre Pio in detail.

"He was born on May 25, 1887 at Pietrelcina, just a

little west of here, and he was baptized there with the name of Francesco. He entered the Order at the age of sixteen in 1903, taking the name Pio. In the convent of Venafro, in Benevento, before his ordination in 1910, he began his mystical life. Once he fasted two weeks without eating anything but the Host, and he had diabolical apparitions. All these years he was afflicted with a pulmonary sickness. He was always a sickly friar. Some days he was sick; some days well.

"In 1918 he received the Stigmata. At least it was visible continuously then. He first received it in 1910 in his home town of Pietrelcina, but it was only visible for a day or two, and he asked God to remove it so he would not be so embarrassed by people coming to him. In Pietrelcina is a little chapel now at the site where he received the Stigmata for the first time. From then, for the next eight years, he bore this pain until September 20, 1918 when the wounds became visible. He had gone up to the choir loft after Mass to make his thanksgiving, and he received the wounds in his hands, and they stayed there till his death."

Padre Pio had just been assigned to San Giovanni. The friary was old, a place of recollection.

"He had many gifts," John says. "Bi-location, for instance. That made it possible for him to be in two places at the same time. A woman tells of being in St. Peter's in Rome one evening when the basilica was being closed. She wanted to go to Confession but the sacristan said no priests were around, she'd have to wait till the morning. She couldn't wait because she had to go back home to her *paese*. Suddenly, a friar appeared. He invited her to a confessional box, and heard her Confession. The sacristan saw her leaving the confessional a little later, and said: 'I told you there were no priests.' She said that the one in there—and she pointed to the box—had just heard her Confession. The sacristan walked over to the confessional, opened the door. No one was inside.

"Padre Pio also had the gift of emanating an odor of sanctity in perfume, perhaps from the blood of his Stigmata. When he was wanting to help someone who had asked for his prayers, such people often noticed this perfume for a moment, and then it would disappear."

Did he travel much?

"No, rarely. One of the few times he left the convent was to say Mass at the Chapel of Monte Sant' Angelo, the shrine of St. Michael the Archangel, fifteen miles east of here. St. Michael had appeared to the local bishop in the Middle Ages, and asked him to celebrate Mass there. It had been a pagan place of worship, just like San Giovanni (St. John) itself. A temple to Janus had been on the site of the town's Church of St. John the Baptist. It's a round church, and the town's name comes from it, San Giovanni Rotondo."

And the hospital by the convent?

"That was built with offerings from pilgrims. Padre Pio always had the idea of a hospital for pilgrims. So many of them came here with sufferings. It has 900 beds. There are also spastic centers for children here in San Giovanni, at Manfredonia, a town along the coast here, and at Naples."

The entrance to the original church is fitted snugly between the 16th-century cloister and the new larger church. A floor above the sacristy is the Franciscan room, a kind of bridge between the church and the cloister. In the last years of his life, Padre Pio would meet pilgrims in the Franciscan room. Only men were allowed to come up to the Franciscan room because it was in the cloistered area. Women saw Padre Pio in the sacristy. A wooden chair he used is shrouded in plastic.

His cell is just off the Franciscan room. The bed is long enough to fit between the walls. The room is 12 by 6 feet which, John says, is twice the size of the average friar's cell. There are various personal items: a desk, his breviary, an armchair, the black gloves he wore to cover his Stigmata, a washbasin, some books. His half-shoes are in a glass case on the floor. "He couldn't wear shoes too tight," John says, "and slippers were not strong enough for support." There are also some of the candies he used to carry in his pocket to give to children.

The friars have had to protect places and things, such as the chair in the Franciscan room used by Padre Pio, because pilgrims want to take with them any kind of souvenir, whether it is a sliver of wood from the confessional box he used or part of the wall plaster in his cell. The doorway of his cell and the walls of the corridor are covered with plastic. The area in the choir loft where he used to say the Rosary in the evening, when he was too sick to go downstairs, is roped off.

Was his death unexpected?

"The fiftieth anniversary of his Stigmata was to be celebrated on September 20, 1968. That was a Friday. But the observance was held over till Sunday for the pilgrims. Padre Pio celebrated a High Mass. He did not want to, because he was so weak. But the superiors asked him to. He collapsed at the end of the Mass. They carried him into the sacristy, and divested him. He died at two-thirty the next morning."

TRANSPORTATION: San Giovanni is 25 miles northeast of Foggia. By train to Foggia; then, bus.

HOTELS: The *Palace* (luxurious) and *Victor* (moderately priced) are at Bari, burial place of St. Nicholas.

NAPLES

The Miracle of St. Gennarus, the patron of Naples, is the kind that repeats itself year after year, century after century. Gennarus was martyred in A.D. 305. Samples of his blood were placed in glass ampuls, and guarded as relics. In 386, when the martyr's body was being moved to the catacombs of Naples, the blood liquefied for the first time. This phenomenon repeats itself at least twice a year: the Saturday preceding the first Sunday of May (feast of the translation of his body) and Sept. 19 (the feast of his martyrdom). Some years the dry blood also turns to liquid on Dec. 16, the feast of his being made patron of Naples. The liquefaction is manifested by tiny red bubbles. Three people have keys to the elaborate case in which the saint's blood is guarded in the cathedral: the archbishop, the mayor, and a member of Parliament. An intense mood of expectation awaits the start of the liquefying process. Women known as "The Relatives of St. Gennarus" have the right to sit in the first pews in the cathedral and they plaintively invoke the saint's memory and chant salutations to him during the ceremonies.

POMPEII

The ancient city of Pompeii, 14 miles south of Naples, was destroyed in A.D. 79 when Vesuvius erupted in one of history's greatest volcanic disasters. Most of the old city has now been uncovered and one of its splendid monuments is the Temple of Apollo. A Temple of Jove, with triumphal arches at its sides, is near the Forum. The Temple of Isis, the goddess of fertility, is close to the theaters. Frescoes in the Villa of the Mysteries depict the rituals of the cult of Dionysos who was a popular god in southern Italy.

A few hundred yards from the ruins of the ancient, pagan city of Pompeii a new Christian one has risen, dedicated to the Madonna of the Rosary. The builder of the new Pompeii was a lawyer, Bartolo Longo, who was born at Latiano on Feb. 10, 1841. Longo had been baptized a Catholic but drifted to a cult of spiritualism. The example of some friends brought him back to Catholicism, and he eventually decided to devote all his time to works of charity. He married Countess Marianna de Fusco and she became his collaborator. The couple lived in a manorial residence in the valley of Pompeii. It distressed Bartolo that the parish church was almost as much of a ruin as the nearby pagan sanctuary. The Rosary had especial appeal to him because he was a Dominican Tertiary, a member of the Third Order of laymen of St. Dominic. He exposed a statue of the Madonna of the Rosary in the parish church. Soon there were reports of miraculous happenings. Bartolo Longo began to surmise that the Madonna wanted a shrine for herself in this pagan area of international renown. He asked people to contribute the equivalent of a penny a month for its construction. A church was begun on May 8, 1876, and alongside it were built various charitable institutions: schools, workshops, social centers for orphans and for children of prisoners.

The Basilica of the Madonna of the Rosary—enlarged in 1933—is in the main square of the new Pompeii.

Along the porch of the basilica are life-sized statues of 4 holy people who made pilgrimages to the shrine. One statue represents St. Frances Xavier Cabrini (Mother Cabrini), who devoted her life to the building of schools, kindergartens, free dispensaries, and hospitals for the children of Italian emigrants in the United States after she landed in New York on Mar. 31, 1889. She visited the shrine on Mar. 11, 1893 to fulfill a vow she had made during a rough sea voyage. "At Pompeii, I found the Madonna so very good," she is quoted as saying. Another statue is of Ludovico da Casoria, a Franciscan friar and mentor of Bartolo Longo. He made a pilgrimage on Mar. 17, 1884 to "thank the Madonna for the tremendous cure from a fatal illness." The two other statues are Blessed Luigi Guanella who came as a pilgrim in 1913 to "ask the blessing of the Madonna of Pompeii and her apostle Bartolo Longo" for the success of his apostolate in America, and St. Leonardo

Murialdo, founder of a religious congregation which helps young boys, the *Giuseppini* (Josephites). He visited the shrine often.

The main feasts are the first Sunday in October, and May 8. The shrine is administered by the Redemptorists.

TRANSPORTATION: Pompeii is on direct rail line from Rome, Naples and Reggio Calabria.

HOTELS: *Grand Hotel Rosario* is situated between the basilica and the entrance to the ruins of Pompeii. At Naples, *Continental* and *Excelsior* are comfortable; *Domitiana* and *Commodore*, medium-priced.

MONTE CASSINO

The Monastery at Monte Cassino is usually referred to as the most important Benedictine abbey in Europe. If that is so, then it could simply be described as the most important abbey in Europe because St. Benedict founded it in A.D. 529 and he was the father of monastic life in the West. The monastery sits on a hill overlooking the town of Cassino, nearly 1,200 feet below. To the Allied military leaders in Italy in 1944, it was Hill 516, suspected by the New Zealand forces as a redoubt of the Germans. The Americans, under General Mark Clark, did not believe the Germans were in the monastery, and balked at the suggestion of bombing it. But the British Commonwealth military leaders outranked the American Fifth Army commander. The British Commonwealth command decided that the only way to get past the defense line of the Germans blocking the road to Rome was to bomb the monastery. They did on Feb. 15, 1944, shattering it with bombs from more than 200 bombers. The air attack did not crush the Germans. Their line was still at Cassino a month later. The Allies then smashed the town of Cassino, literally wiping it off the map. No one still knows the exact number of casualties because some of the 25,000 inhabitants had managed to flee beforehand, and never did come back. The Italian government after the war financed the rebuilding of the monastery, but no one could replace the manuscripts and art objects that had been destroyed. As it has been for 14 centuries. Monte Cassino is a sacred place of pilgrimage. In the area are 5 war cemeteries with 50,000 graves of British Commonwealth, French, Italian, German and Polish soldiers.

TRANSPORTATION: Monte Cassino is 75 miles south of Rome. Trains to Cassino.

SUBIACO

The emperor Nero founded the city of Subiaco, east of Rome, and for himself had a lavish villa built that was adorned with three artificial lakes. It is a beautiful area of the Aniene River valley, with a narrow gorge, high mountains and rushing water. This was the spot chosen by a young man named Benedict, who was born in Nurcia in A.D. 480, to withdraw from the world. For three years he lived the life of a hermit. Then his twin sister, Scholastica, urged him from his hermitage and with some companions he drafted the monastic rule which ever since has guided the Benedictine Order and the monastic life of the West. The companions were divided into 12 groups, each with a hermitage. All but one of these hermitages were destroyed by the Lombards in their invasion a few centuries later. The hermitage named for Sts. Cosmas and Damian survived, and was later named after Benedict's sister, St. Scholastica. It is a massive structure. High walls surround 3 buildings which in turn encircle 3 cloisters built at different periods. Italy's first printing plant was established in this monastery in 1464.

Less than 1 mile away is the Sacro Speco, the Holy Cave in which Benedict lived for 3 years. It was in the cave that Benedict meditated upon his Rule for the monks, which is highlighted by the motto *Ora et Labora* (Pray and Work). The cave is below 2 churches. Over the door to the Upper Church is the Latin inscription *Sit pax entranti* (Peace be to those who enter). The Upper Church is carved from the red rock of the mountain, and its walls are filled with frescoes by artists from Umbria. Francis of Assisi visited the grotto about 1210, and in a chapel is a painting of Il Poverello, which is said to be the first portrait done from life in the history of Italian art.

TRANSPORTATION: Subiaco is 37 miles east of Rome.

POINTS OF INTEREST: Hadrian's Villa, the Temple of Vesta (Sybil), and the fountains at Tivoli, the vacation area of the Roman emperors.

OUR LADY OF GOOD COUNSEL

Each year at a quarter past four in the afternoon of Apr. 25, just as Vespers is about to begin, villagers and pilgrims, jammed into the Church of Our Lady of Good Counsel in the hilltop town of Genazzano, shout *"Viva Maria!"* For the following 60 minutes the church bells in Genazzano and the surrounding villages ring out, echoing a tradition now 5 centuries old. An Augustinian priest was about to start Vespers on Apr. 25, 1467 when an Apparition of the Madonna was seen on the church wall. The Apparition launched the worldwide devotion to Our Lady of Good Counsel.

Genazzano is a shrine of the Popes. Martin V was born here. Prior to the pivotal Battle of Lepanto, which halted the Saracens in the Mediterranean in the 16th century, Pope St. Pius V offered prayers at the shrine. The entire papal court accompanied Urban VIII to

Genazzano in the 17th century. Benedict XIV initiated the international Union of Our Lady of Good Counsel, and registered as its first member. While held a captive of Napoleon, Pius VII prayed before a small replica of the image of Our Lady of Good Counsel. The Madonna's statue was on the altar when Pius IX celebrated his first Mass. Leo XIII visited the shrine often, starting as a young child. Pius XII, when a priest, said Mass in the church at Genazzano frequently. John XXIII kept a small statue of Our Lady of Good Counsel on his desk and visited the shrine on Aug. 25, 1959, less than a year after he had been elected Pope. Pope John knelt before the altar, and led the pilgrims in saying an *Ave Maria* 3 times: for children of the world, for the sick and suffering everywhere, and for the universal church.

TRANSPORTATION: Genazzano is 30 miles east of Rome.

ROME

Some foreigners leave Rome after a visit of 5 or 6 days convinced that they have seen "everything." Others are not so sure. There are those, too, who have the opportunity of seeing Rome continuously, year after year, and discover something new or intriguing about it every day. Rome is that kind of a city. The religious ceremonies in its basilicas on principal occasions and feastdays proceed with more pageantry and precision than the most rehearsed spectacular on color television. Yet at the church steps chaos seems to reign—in the swirl of the traffic, the noise, the carefree exuberance of everything from the weather to the people.

There are more churches in Rome than in any other city in the world. The Romans say that one could go to a different church every day in the year, and still not see all the churches. Few Romans visit a different church daily. But many do go to *a* church on Sunday— although, perhaps inevitably, they are given an image abroad as being indifferent to the church which is universally identified with their city, and to the Pope who is by definition their bishop.

On the 21st of April each year the policemen of Rome, the *vigili*, wear a cordon of gold braid on their shoulders, and buses make their rounds with the city's colors streaming above the windshield. That is the birthday of Rome. Its exact age is uncertain, but it is generally believed that Rome was founded on the left bank of the Tiber in 753 B.C. From a settlement of shepherds on the Palatine Hill, Rome swiftly grew to be the *caput mundi* (head of the world) in a literal sense, being the chief city and conqueror of every place then known, from the Iberian peninsula across the Mediterranean to Palestine and as far north as England and the banks of the Rhine and the Danube. With the advent of Christianity Rome became the center of the Catholic Church.

Rome communicated with its empire through the roads it stretched across Europe, along the coast of Africa, and into the Middle East. The most glorious of the imperial roads was the Via Appia (the Appian Way), named after Censor Appius Claudius who inaugurated it in a ceremony full of pomp in 312 B.C. The Via Appia, the Queen of the Roads, streamed southeast across the peninsula in a long diagonal aimed at the port of Brindisi, then and now the maritime gateway to Greece and the eastern Mediterranean. Much of the Via Appia Antica has been absorbed or replaced by a new one, Via Appia Nuova. But a 10-mile stretch of the ancient Appian Way still exists at the very door of Rome.

The Via Appia was used by ancient Romans on their way to the temples of the gods in the nearby Alban hills. On his way to Rome the apostle Paul traveled along it. The people not permitted to bury their dead within the city walls—Hebrews and Christians—"deposited" them in underground galleries along the Via Appia. Those who could afford it raised monumental memorials to their dead. Jupiter's temple, as the god of rain, was visible on Mount Cavo from the Via Appia. A crown of clouds on Mount Cavo today tells Romans that the weather is about to turn bad.

Porta San Sebastiano, a gateway in the old Roman wall, is the starting point of the Via Appia Antica. Mars, as god of war, once had a temple on a little hill near the Porta San Sebastiano.

A historic crossroads is just ½ mile from St. Sebastian's Gate. A small church is at the site where Christ and the apostle Peter met, with the latter exclaiming in surprise: *"Domine, quo vadis?"* ("O Lord, whither goest Thou?") St. Peter was fleeing Rome because of the persecutions of Nero. Christ responded: "I go to Rome to be crucified again." Peter turned back. His martyrdom in Rome established the city as the center of the Catholic Church. In the Quo Vadis Church is a copy of Michelangelo's "Christ." (The original is in the Dominican Church of Santa Maria sopra Minerva). A rolling pastureland leads to the St. Calixtus Catacombs where tens of thousands of early Romans, including a dozen popes of the 3rd century, were buried. During the religious persecutions, Romans used the catacombs as underground places of worship.

The Ardeatine Caves are just behind the St. Calixtus Catacombs. A memorial at the caves remembers the atrocities of Mar. 24, 1944 when the Germans, in reprisal for an attack on a column of their troops marching along the Via Rasella in downtown Rome, rounded up 10 Romans, willy-nilly, for each German soldier killed, savagely murdered them, stuffed their bodies into the caves, and then sealed off the opening with dynamite. The victims had nothing to do with the attack. Most were taken from prison where they had been put by the Germans because of their politics or religion. One 14-year-old boy was among those rounded up. Later, when the people of Rome could bury their dead, they recovered the bodies and placed them in graves, side by side, regardless of religion. There were 338 bodies.

It is believed that the bodies of the apostles Peter and Paul, for a time, were kept at the St. Sebastian Catacombs nearby. Between the St. Calixtus and St. Sebastian catacombs are the Hebraic Catacombs. The Hebraic Catacombs are usually closed, but it is possible to visit them. (Requests should be made to the Pontifical Institute of Sacred Archaeology, 1 Via Napoleon III.)

Rome has four basilicas, four *major* ones, that is. There are more than a dozen *minor* ones. *Basilica* was originally used to designate a place of justice or a civic hall. Early Christians adopted the word for churches built over the tomb of a martyr. In more recent times basilica serves as a title of honor. The four major basilicas are St. Mary Major, St. John Lateran, St. Paul Outside the Walls, and St. Peter's. A particular Order of priests is assigned to each: Dominicans at St. Mary Major's; Franciscans (friars minor) at St. John's; Benedictines, at St. Paul's; and Conventual Franciscans at St. Peter's. The priests at the basilicas are special confessors known as Penitenziaries, a term first officially mentioned in church annals in the 5th century. They were designated by early Popes who recognized the burdens placed on the local priests of Rome by the growing number of pilgrims. The Penitenziaries have absolution powers not available to ordinary confessors. The Penitenziaries are also multilingual. In each basilica at least one is always present who speaks English. At St. Mary Major's a Dominican friar speaks Esperanto.

St. Mary Major (Santa Maria Maggiore) is the main church in Rome dedicated to the Madonna. It is sometimes called St. Mary of the Snows because of a legend that Pope Liberius and a wealthy patrician of Rome, in separate visions in the 4th century, were asked by the Madonna to erect a sanctuary to her where they found snow on the following August morning. It snowed on the site where St. Mary Major's now stands.

St. John Lateran (San Giovanni in Laterano) is the Cathedral of Rome and is the Pope's church as the bishop of the city. The name comes from Plautus Lateranus, a wealthy Roman executed in Nero's reign. His property was turned into an imperial palace. In A.D. 312 Constantine the Great presented the property to Pope St. Sylvester I, who made of it the first public place of Christian worship in Rome. Across the street from it is the Scala Santa, the Holy Stairs, a stairway of 28 marble steps encased for protection in wood. According to tradition they were part of the house of Pilate in Jerusalem, and are the steps on which Christ dropped blood as He was descending them. The Scala Santa was brought from Palestine by Constantine's mother, Helena. Some pilgrims ascend the stairs on their knees.

St. Paul's Outside-the-Walls (San Paolo fuori le mura) is built on the burial place of the apostle. He was executed outside Rome, at Tre Fontane (Three Fountains) and buried in the vineyard of a wealthy Christian woman of Rome, Lucina. Constantine built a church over the burial place.

St. Peter's (San Pietro) enshrines the grave of the apostle and first Pope. A small oratory, or *memoria*, was built on the site about A.D. 80, and eventually was expanded to the basilica that is now visually recognized as the center of the Roman Catholic Church. It is an international meeting point. On Easter Sunday when the Pope appears in the loggia above the front door as many as a half million people throng St. Peter's Square and the adjacent area. There are Old Roman Hands who have seen all 7 sacraments performed in St. Peter's on a Sunday, and it is not unusual to see 5 or 6. Some visitors are startled to discover that there is a small coffee-bar near the sacristy. The bar was established to serve foreign priests saying Mass in the basilica who wished to have breakfast right afterward.

The Michelangelo-painted ceiling of the Sistine Chapel and the marvels of the Vatican Museum are some of the many treasures of Rome. Pilgrims like the simple treasures, too. On Sunday at noon they crowd into St. Peter's Square, ringed in semicircles of colonnades created by Bernini, to recite the Angelus with the Pope when he appears at his window.

St. Peter's itself used to be the setting for the weekly general audiences of the Pope. But the number of pilgrims at the audiences increased so much that a special audience hall was built by the architect Nervi, and put into use during the reign of Paul VI. The general audience is Wednesday at 11 A.M.

There is no special procedure for attending an audience. Seats are on a first-come, first-served basis. To be sure of having a seat, a person should write a letter requesting a ticket. The letter should specify the date of the audience one wishes to attend, and where the ticket can be delivered in Rome—the hotel, that is. The letter can be in English. It should be accompanied by a general letter of introduction by someone writing on a letterhead. The letter of introduction can come from a non-Catholic. Religion has nothing to do with it. The letter of introduction helps to screen out cranks.

The audience-request letter should be sent directly to the Prefect of the Apostolic Palace, Vatican City. Some people use intermediaries. The Jesuit Guest Bureau at Borgo Santo Spirito and the Paulist Fathers at the American National Church of Santa Susanna take care of many requests. Most Americans place their requests through the Office for Papal Audiences of North American College, Via dell' Umiltà 30, Rome. A ticket guarantees a seat, except during the springtime audiences.

Even the standing-room tickets are phrased so elegantly one does not seem to mind. They carry the words *Reparto Speciale* (Special Section).

Periodically, as in 1975, a Holy Year is proclaimed by the Pope. In recent times, the Holy Years have been every quarter of a century. They are years of Jubilee, and have their origin in the periodic celebrations of the ancient Israelites. The word "jubilee" comes from the Hebrew *jobel* (ram's horn). The ram's horn when sounded every 50 years transformed the life of the people. The biblical celebration was a time of forgiveness of debts, of restoration of property, of a general renewal of life.

It is not clear when the first Holy Year was held but it took place well before 1300. In that year, some pilgrims pleaded with Pope Boniface VIII to call a Holy Year so that they could have the same indulgences given to pilgrims in Rome a century earlier.

Rome went all out to prepare for that Holy Year. The Pope was a patron of the arts, and the artists of the time were his friends. Giotto and others helped beautify the churches of Rome and of the peninsula. Dante Alighieri was among the pilgrims. In his *Inferno* he contrasted the pilgrims crossing the Tiber to the sinners making their way along a bridge in hell.

Pope Boniface intended that a Holy Year be once a century. But this did not seem often enough to many people. Few had a lifespan potential of anywhere near 100 years, it was pointed out, and thus many would miss out on a Holy Year and its spiritual graces. A delegation from Rome journeyed to Avignon in the middle of the 14th century to petition Clement VI to shorten the interval between Holy Years. In the delegation were the poet Petrarch and St. Bridget of Sweden. The Pope agreed, and reduced the interval to 50 years, proclaiming 1350 as a Holy Year.

This still did not satisfy everyone. The next Holy

Year, therefore, was 40 years later. Pope Urban VI suggested the interval be every 33 years, the length of time Christ spent on earth and the average lifespan of an individual in those days. Pope Nicholas V, in 1450, returned to the twice-a-century schedule, but the once-every-25-year tradition was started by Paul II in 1475. Political conditions in 1800, 1850 and 1875 made a Holy Year impracticable. Otherwise, there has been one each quarter of a century since 1450.

For the Jubilee of 1300, residents of Rome were called upon to visit St. Peter's Basilica and St. Paul's every day for 30 days to acquire the spiritual graces; the daily visits for non-Roman pilgrims were limited to a 15-day period. In the Holy Year of 1350, a visit to St. John Lateran's was added. St. Mary Major's joined the list in 1390. Since then, visits to the four basilicas have been required in each Holy Year.

In addition to the four basilicas, pilgrims of course visit other churches, such as the Gesú, where St. Ignatius of Loyola is buried. Santa Susanna's, the American National Church, is on the list of many. Susanna refused to marry the adopted son of the emperor Diocletian, and was martyred during the persecutions. On the opposite corner from Santa Susanna's is the Carmelite Church of Santa Maria in Vittoria where Bernini's statue of St. Teresa in Ecstasy is on view. Diagonally across from Santa Susanna's a heroic-sized statue of "Moses" dominates the corner fountain. Michelangelo's statue of "Moses" is in the Church of St. Peter in Chains (San Pietro in Vincoli). The church is on the site of the court where St. Peter was condemned. Empress Eudoxia had a church built in A.D. 440 to enshrine the chains that bound St. Peter when he was in the Roman prison. Her mother arranged for the transfer from Jerusalem of the chains that had been used on the apostle there. Both sets of chains are in a bronze case under the main altar.

TRANSPORTATION: Rome is an international air center. Transatlantic ships of the Italian Line call at Genoa and Naples.

HOTELS: *Grand, Hilton* and *Excelsior* are among the finest. *Boston* and *Forum* are also comfortable.

POINTS OF INTEREST: Near Rome are three towns with which St. Thomas Aquinas is associated—Roccasecca, where he was born in 1226; Aquino, where he lived and which has given him his name; and Fossanova, where he died in 1274.

10

Luxembourg

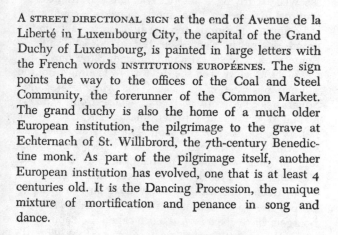

A STREET DIRECTIONAL SIGN at the end of Avenue de la
Liberté in Luxembourg City, the capital of the Grand
Duchy of Luxembourg, is painted in large letters with
the French words INSTITUTIONS EUROPÉENES. The sign
points the way to the offices of the Coal and Steel
Community, the forerunner of the Common Market.
The grand duchy is also the home of a much older
European institution, the pilgrimage to the grave at
Echternach of St. Willibrord, the 7th-century Benedic-
tine monk. As part of the pilgrimage itself, another
European institution has evolved, one that is at least 4
centuries old. It is the Dancing Procession, the unique
mixture of mortification and penance in song and
dance.

ECHTERNACH

After Pope Sergius I consecrated Willibrord bishop,
he became the first archbishop of Utrecht, establishing
his mission among the Frisians and his subsequent title
as patron of the Netherlands. From Utrecht he jour-

neyed to Echternach, building a monastery and a missionary center that further extended the spread of Christianity among the Germanic tribes. A disciple at Echternach was St. Boniface, whom he sent forth to evangelize the land which is now Germany. Willibrord was born in Northumberland in A.D. 657. (See Index.) He died at his monastery in Echternach in 739.

The crypt in which St. Willibrord is buried, in the basilica named after him at Echternach, is the oldest Christian sanctuary in the grand duchy.

Echternach is on the west bank of the Süre River, a tributary of the Moselle. On the other side of the bridge is Western Germany. Along the highway from Luxembourg City robust, smiling women in rubber boots pause in muddy farmyards to stare at the local bus to see who is driving it today. The lanky transmitter of Radio Luxembourg, the most powerful commercial radio station in Europe and the biggest taxpayer in the grand duchy, is planted in the green land outside Echternach, a technical anomaly among the barns, the cows, the tractors. The rue de la Gare leading from the railroad/bus station to Place du Marché (Market Square) is filled with *patisseries* whose front windows exhibit a variety of pastries, made that day in the bakery at the back of the shop. The tarts and pies puff out with whipped cream. Many *patisseries* serve coffee and in their windows are handpainted *Kaffee und Küchen* signs. French is the official language of the grand duchy but with Germany next door the townspeople also speak German. Among themselves Luxembourgers have their own dialect called Letzebürgesch.

The Place du Marché is across from St. Willibrord's Basilica. The small square is rimmed with the town's governmental apparatus. The Hôtel de Ville, a small brick building, houses the offices of the mayor, the *justice de paix* and the police. The town's police car, a red-painted station wagon, is at the Town Hall door.

The driver looks comfortable behind the wheel even though he is quite stocky. He is happy to talk about his hometown. He points to the bell tower of the parish Church of Sts. Peter and Paul at the left of the basilica.

"That's the oldest bell in the country, fourteen hundred and something. It's the alarm bell for the town. In the old days they used to ring it when enemy forces were approaching. Now when you hear it you know there's a fire someplace in town."

In the French Revolution an army from France occupied Echternach, forcing the monks to flee with whatever they could carry. The church and buildings were confiscated and put up for sale. The buyer set up ovens in the basilica to make bricks, and clay pots and dishes. The monks never returned to Echternach.

Meanwhile, the relics of St. Willibrord were gathered together and moved to Sts. Peter and Paul. They remained there until 1906 when they were ceremonially returned to the basilica, which had been restored. The monk's sarcophagus remained on the main floor of the basilica until the celebration of the 1,200th year of his death when it was moved into a chapel in the 8th-century crypt.

"That celebration was in 1939, the year the Second World War started. Luxembourg was invaded by the Germans. When the Allies began pushing the Germans back where they came from, Echternach was in the line of fire—what you call the Battle of the Bulge, and we called the Ardennes offensive. There was much bombing and shelling. Just the other side of the river was the Siegfried Line."

The policeman gazes at the towers of the basilica.

"Those are new. The old ones were destroyed during the Battle of the Bulge—not by the battle itself, though. The Germans blew them up. They said they had to do it for strategic reasons. Part of the nave of the basilica was badly damaged, too. It was good Willibrord's anniversary came when it did, and they had moved him into the crypt. Otherwise his tomb might have been damaged when the nave was."

The restored basilica was consecrated in 1953.

A button-sized red light glows in the dark atrium. It is a push-button light, one of the small economies used by thrifty Europeans. When the button is pushed the vestibule's ceiling light comes on for a fixed time, long enough for the churchgoer to glance at the bulletin board.

The crypt is at the front, with stairways at each side of the nave leading down into it. It is obviously old. The walls are thick, and the vaults form the ceiling into a succession of canopies over the heads of pilgrims. The crypt is just below the main altar of the basilica. At its center is a chapel, 15 by 20 feet, completely closed off by a glass door and a high screen of wrought iron. Through the grille and the glass a notice in German and Dutch is visible. It reads:

"Dutch people—You stand here before the grave of St. Willibrord. Thanks to his effort for the faith, you have received the Christian religion and culture. He is the primary protector-saint of your Dutch nation." (See Index.)

Pilgrim priests say Mass in a small chapel in an alcove on the other side of the corridor. Only once a year, on the pilgrimage day of the Dancing Procession, is Mass said at the shrine.

The starting time for the Dancing Procession is 9 A.M. on the Tuesday of Pentecost (Whit Tuesday), but pilgrims gather long before that for the series of early Masses at the tomb of St. Willibrord. The archbishop of Luxembourg addresses the pilgrims in the courtyard of the basilica, and then the unusual procession of singing and dancing pilgrims moves through the streets of Echternach.

No one knows the origin of the Dancing Procession.

When first written about in 1542 it was described as an ancient tradition. The procession is a great physical effort—singing and dancing for 3 hours. It is also a public act of faith. Some observers consider it "quaint." The physical effort, the public act and the jibes add up to an exceptional type of penance and mortification. This is the general rationale of the Dancing Procession.

People of all ages participate. A few dozen bands are spaced in the line of singers and dancers. There are also individual musicians: pipers, violinists, accordionists. In the old days, church authorities did not deign to participate but for the past half century they have been at the head of the procession.

The participants line up in rows, "holding hands" by clutching the end of a handkerchief held by the singer-dancer alongside. Children are up front, then teenagers, and finally the grownups. The boys wear white shirts and dark trousers. The girls dress in white blouses and skirts with solid colors. There is a special music which is played over and over. The dancers spring forward to the music, hopping from one foot to the other. They used to move 3 steps forward and 2 steps back. But now, because of the immense crowds, the line keeps moving forward, intoning the special litany to the apostle of the Frisians: "St. Willibrord, a true voice of God, pray for us; St. Willibrord, an overthrower of idols, pray for us." The litany is repeated again and again. The goal of the pilgrims is the basilica where the Dancing Procession ends with a Mass. Pilgrims wait patiently for a chance to descend into the crypt, and to end their pilgrimage by making a final leap past the tomb of St. Willibrord.

TRANSPORTATION: Echternach is 23 miles from Luxembourg City. Bus service from Luxembourg City, Ettelbrück and Wasserbillig.

HOTELS: *Bel-Air* is the leading hotel. *Universel* and *Parc* are less expensive.

POINTS OF INTEREST: At Berdorf is an *ara Romana*, a pagan altar of Roman times, raised to honor 4 deities: Apollo, Hercules, Juno and Minerva.

CLERVAUX

In 1910 Benedictine monks built a monastery at Clervaux, a small village 40 miles directly north of Luxembourg City. In the area are a number of medieval churches which have been classified as national monuments. At the monastery there is a permanent exhibit of monastic life. One of the medieval holy places at Clervaux is the Chapel of Notre Dame of Loreto. From olden times the chapel has been a pilgrimage site. On summer evenings the exteriors of the Benedictine monastery and of the Chapel of Notre Dame of Loreto are artistically illuminated.

TRANSPORTATION: Train from Luxembourg City.

HOTELS: *Abbaye, Central* and *Koener* are the leading ones; *Claravallis* and *Parc*, less expensive.

LUXEMBOURG CITY

The capital of the Grand Duchy of Luxembourg is a city of bridges. There are close to 100. It also is a city of historic religious buildings. The Grand Ducal Mausoleum is in the crypt of the Cathedral of Notre Dame. Among those buried in the mausoleum was John the Blind, a king of Bohemia and count of Luxembourg. In the cathedral is the original of the Our Lady, Comforter of the Afflicted statue which is venerated at Kevelaer, Germany. (See Index.) St. Michael's Church was built in the 10th century. The Chapel of St. Quirin is 6 centuries old. Luxembourg City has a Protestant church of the 18th century.

TRANSPORTATION: Bastogne is 36 miles from Luxembourg City; Brussels, 125 miles. It is on main rail line. Luxembourg City is a main air center.

HOTELS: *Holiday Inn* is near Coal-Steel Community offices. *Cravat,* traditional, is downtown.

POINTS OF INTEREST: A double-nave church, built in 1248, is at Vianden, east of Luxembourg City.

11

The Netherlands

THE FIRST OF A SERIES of religio-political confrontations in the Low Countries took place in Roman times along the banks of the Rhine. Christian missionaries following the Roman legions northward early in the 4th century extended the new religion among the Germanic tribes which had filtered south of the river. By the 5th century the Romans were pushed back by the Franks coming from the north, and for several centuries the political climate slowed the growth of Christianity. But Catholic monks had planted the seeds, and ever since towns in different corners of the Netherlands have been associated with them, if not always with the religion they introduced: Servatius in Maastricht; Adalbertus, Egmond; Boniface. Dokkum; Willibrord, Heiloo and Utrecht.

By the middle of the 15th century the various duchies, counties and marquisates of the Low Countries had come under another dominion of the south, the Dukes of Burgundy, and subsequently through them became linked to the Hapsburgs when Mary of Burgundy married the emperor-to-be, Maximilian I. The Hapsburg empire, as Emperor Charles V and his son

Philip II made clear, included the kingdom and the religion of Spain. The independent Dutch, beguiled by the religious reforms engendered by Luther in nearby Germany, chafed at their foreign ruler who simultaneously was imposing a form of government and of religion. For 80 years, 1568 to 1648, they fought for political and religious independence, with William the Silent, Prince of Orange, leading them in revolt.

The political rebellion took some bitter turns, unforgotten today 4 centuries later, making at least one site of battle a point of pilgrimage for Catholics ever since. This is at Brielle, or Den Briel. The Spanish forces, which had been occupying Den Briel, lost it to the revolutionaries under William the Silent on Apr. 1, 1572. At Gorinchem the rebels took the occasion to seize priests and friars, transporting them by the waterways near Dordrecht to Den Briel where they hanged them in a turf barn. There were 19 hangings—most of the victims, Franciscan friars. The hangings took place on July 9, 1572. Since the friars had been in a Spanish-held city and since the Spanish were Catholics, it was assumed they were pro-Spanish. It was a sad misreading of politics and religion. There is a pilgrimage each year, on July 9, to the site of the hangings. On the 400th anniversary in 1972 Catholic Cardinal Bernard Jan Alfrink of Utrecht and ministers of non-Catholic denominations attended services there together.

Amsterdam embraced the new religion of the Reformation in 1578, but some diehard Catholics remained. They attended Mass in living-rooms of private houses and in other secret places. In 1656 the mayor of Amsterdam was given a list of 62 places in the city where, it was charged, Catholic services were being held secretly. Generally, municipal authorities ignored such anti-Catholic protestations. It was in the 17th century, too, that the Dutch gave asylum to Jews who had been driven from the Iberian peninsula and to Protestant Huguenots fleeing from Catholic France.

After the defeat of Napoleon in 1814 the individualistic instincts of the Dutch moved their thinking toward a democratic form of government. In 1815 they founded a constitutional monarchy with William I of Orange as king and chief of state. The Southern Provinces (now Belgium) were included in the rule of King William I, but in 1830 they rebelled, forming their own kingdom.

About the same time as the formation of the new kingdom of the Netherlands, Catholics began reacquiring political and social equality. They were allowed, for instance, to hold public office once again. To speed their political and social evolution, Catholics formed their own institutions, ranging from newspapers to a political party. The Catholic party eventually became the biggest.

But restrictions hung on. Catholics, for example, were not permitted to have processions in the streets without permission of municipal authorities, unless such processions had been a tradition prior to the establishment of the kingdom. When the time came to enforce the law it was discovered that, the Reformation and anti-Catholic feeling notwithstanding, there were places where the Catholics had been holding processions without interruption for centuries. For the most part these procession strongholds were in the southern part of the kingdom. But a procession enclave also was discovered in the north, at Laren, a small town near Hilversum. Laren remained Catholic during the Reformation, and continued the annual procession on the feast of St. John the Baptist. A church constructed in A.D. 1306 was destroyed by Protestants in 1586, but the procession was maintained.

The ban on processions is still in effect. In Amsterdam, it prevents a 14th-century procession that was prohibited during the Reformation, but a way was found to keep alive the memory of the old-time public observance. The tradition of the outlawed Amsterdam procession is that a sick man, after receiving Communion at his home, unwittingly expelled it in a fit of coughing. A woman of the household, fearing contagious germs from the man's disease, placed the Host in the kitchen fire and at once saw an image of the Holy Spirit in the flames. She rushed to the Old Church (Oude Kerk) and told the priest what had happened. He retrieved the Host and put it aside, advising the woman to burn it the next day. When she put it in the fire the following day, the likeness of the Holy Spirit appeared again. This time the priest decided it should be brought back to the church publicly, and the tradition of the procession was born. This was in 1346. When the new kingdom was being established, a Dutch writer retraced the route of the old procession and the custom was revived in a modified form. The procession took place quietly, without singing or praying that could be heard. It was like a quiet walk or, as the Amsterdam Catholics still call it today, a *stille omgang*. The "silent walk" takes place on the Sunday nearest Mar. 15. Until 1973 only men participated in the "silent walk." Now women do, too.

Germany invaded the Netherlands on May 10, 1940 and broke the final resistance of the small country by bombing the port of Rotterdam 4 days later. Many Dutchmen were executed or died in prisons and concentration camps. Tens of thousands of others were carried away to slave labor in German factories and arms plants. Before the German invasion there were 100,000 Jews in Amsterdam, and 40,000 more in the rest of the country. Today the Jewish population of Amsterdam is only 13,000; of all Netherlands, only 25,000.

Today 40 percent of the 12.3 million people in the Netherlands are Catholics. The Dutch Reformed Church has 3.2 million members; other Reformed

Churches, 1 million. Other denominations have ½ million, and a little over 2 million people have no religious affiliation.

ROTTERDAM

Rotterdam is the biggest seaport in Europe. It also prides itself on being "the city of Erasmus." For Americans, Rotterdam has a particular meaning because this was the original departure point for more than a third of the Pilgrim Fathers who arrived off Cape Cod on the *Mayflower* in 1620.

ERASMUS

Rotterdam claims Erasmus as a native son, but some scholars think he might have been born in Gouda, 12 miles northeast of the big seaport. There is dispute, as well, about the date of his birth. It is thought to have been in the latter 1460s. His mother, the daughter of a physician from Sevenbergen, was named Margaret; his father, Gerard, was from Gouda. The parents were not married, and died while he was in his early teens. A guardian persuaded him to enter the Augustinian Order. Not long after ordination, the bishop of Cambrai (France) asked him to be his secretary. This post did not satisfy him long, and he began his travels and studies which took him all over Europe. He was an advocate of reform in the church long before the word became a cause of action. Yet, when the thunder of Luther's Reformation was heard across Europe, Erasmus was assailed by both sides. The Reformers accused him of backing down on what he had been preaching at the critical moment. Fellow Catholics declared that he had laid the Reformation egg which Luther hatched. He stayed within the church, a critic of many of its temporal habits but a foe of religious schism till the end. In 1514 he had moved to Basel, and he died there on July 12, 1536, with the fires of Reformation enflaming hearts across the Continent.

An immense mosaic, near the City Hall Square in Rotterdam, honors Erasmus. The mosaic, several stories high, is along the side of an office building. It shows him as a slender young man on a white horse, traveling along the Rhine which connects Rotterdam and Basel. The rear side of the City Hall and the Post Office next to it were hit during the Second World War. Now the area is booming, crammed with new buildings and wide pedestrian-only shopping plazas.

Another tribute to Erasmus, this time a statue, is in Sint Laurensplaats, an open brick-paved yard alongside St. Lawrence's Church. The statue presents Erasmus in clerical robes and a large hat.

THE PILGRIM FATHERS' CHURCH

The window above the doorway of the sexton's house alongside the Pilgrim Fathers' Church in Delfshaven is filled with stained-glass replicas of two ancient vessels, and the date "1620." One is the 180-ton 3-mast *Mayflower;* the other, the much smaller *Speedwell.* The *Speedwell* was the vessel earmarked to carry to America 3 dozen members of the English Separatist Church who had been living in the ancient university city of Leyden for more than 10 years.

Delfshaven is the oldest area in Rotterdam, dating to the 14th century when it was the port for the city of Delft, famed for its tiles. The Pilgrim Fathers' Church is at 20 Voorhaven, facing a canal and the kind of Dutch bridge that Van Gogh made famous. A few doors from the church is a mid-17th-century building which had been the headquarters of the grain-sack carriers guild, men who specialized in unloading bags of grain from vessels and lugging them to the local distilleries which kept Delfshaven busy as a port and accounted for a large share of the Dutch gin production. The guildhouse has been redone, and is now a museum with a Pilgrim Fathers' exhibit and a display of pewter utensils of the era of the famous emigrants. The museum really comes alive because craftsmen are on hand, fashioning bowls, plates and other articles in molds 3 centuries old.

The church was started in the 15th century, and two centuries later was enlarged. Since the Reformation it has belonged to the Dutch Reformed Church. A bronze tablet remembers the kindnesses of the Dutch to the Pilgrim Fathers. It was presented in 1906 as a thank-you by the Rev. William Elliot Griffin for the Congregational Club of Boston. The New England Society of Chicago gave another commemorative piece, an inscribed stone, on Feb. 7, 1857. It is inscribed with the Greek words *Eis Kyrios* (One Lord).

The church minister, the Rev. S. Kodistra, says the Pilgrim Fathers gathered there to pray the night before they sailed. Some believe they spent the night inside the church, he says. The minister lives several blocks from the church. The inside stairway to the minister's apartment is steep, and consists of 2 narrow flights of steps, one flight after the other. When the outside bell is rung the minister comes to the top of the second flight of stairs, and opens the downstairs door by pulling a cord which, along a series of pulleys, follows the handrail from top to bottom. The cord, when tugged, released the door latch. The minister is of medium height, and solemn. He speaks very little English but like most Dutchmen knows German well. The main room of his apartment is long. It is furnished with a table and some chairs for visitors, a few good-looking prints—a Rubens woman, a churchly looking man (Erasmus?)—and a cosy fireplace. He does not present his wife but she remains seated in a big chair a few yards away at the other end of the room, sewing and listening. The minister wears gold-rimmed glasses, and he clasps his hands as he talks.

"There is a special service on Thanksgiving Day each year in the church," he says. "Last year there was a professor from Leyden University in North America."

The minister carefully explains directions for reaching the actual departure point of the Pilgrim Fathers.

It is on the other side of the canal from the church. Along the quay the same kind of barges are lined up that artists love to sketch or paint when they are moored near Notre Dame in Paris. As the minister said, a tablet with the inscription in English marks the spot where the Pilgrim Fathers from Leyden set out in the *Speedwell* on Aug. 1, 1620 to rendezvous with the *Mayflower* for the voyage to "the New World."

The *Speedwell*, it turned out, was not seaworthy. Twice she and the *Mayflower* set sail from England, and twice both ships had to return to port. The second time they put in at Plymouth, and the *Speedwell* was abandoned. The 35 passengers from the *Speedwell* were transferred to the *Mayflower*, and she cast off on Sept. 16 with 102 persons on board. The *Mayflower* rounded Cape Cod on Nov. 21, and dropped anchor. On board the Separatist Church leaders had drawn up a compact providing for a "civil body politic." All aboard had to sign it before being allowed to land. It was the first of several such governments established in New England by religious groups on the principle of government with the consent of the people and majority rule. The Mayflower Compact began:

In the name of God Amen! We whose names are underwritten, the loyal subjects of our dread sovereign Lord, King James, by the grace of God, of Great Britain, France and Ireland, King, Defender of the Faith, etc., have undertaken for the glory of God and the advancement of the Christian Faith, and honor of our King and Country, a voyage to plant the first colony in the northern parts of Virginia. . . .

TRANSPORTATION: Rotterdam is on main rail line. Ferries connect with Britain.

HOTELS: *Hilton* is tops. *Rijn* and *Skyway Euromotel* are less expensive.

POINTS OF INTEREST: Lovely stained-glass windows in St. John's Church, Gouda. At Oudewater, Arminius established a church for the Calvinist Reformed.

THE HAGUE

Traditionally the Princes of Orange resided in The Hague or, as it is officially known, 's-Gravenhage. Since 1948 the royal family spends most of its time at a residence in the wooded area of Soestdijk, near Utrecht, and the official capital of the nation is Amsterdam. Yet The Hague remains the official royal residence and the seat of government.

The cosmopolitan character of the government center has not changed traditions in Scheveningen, a suburb on the North Sea. On Sunday older residents still wear national costumes to go to the Vissers Kerk, the Fishermen's Church. On Thursdays there is a general market—mostly fish, but also cheese and vegetables. The harbor has increased in importance because a ferry service has been started to Great Yarmouth in England.

There are a number of Huguenot churches in the Netherlands. One is in The Hague on the Vooreinde, a pedestrians-only shopping street in the central area, the Groenmarkt.

SPINOZA

A 15-minute stroll from the Groenmarkt is the house where Baruch Spinoza, the philosopher's philosopher, wrote some of his most important work, and where he died on Feb. 21, 1677. Spinoza was a descendant of Spanish and Portuguese refugees who had to flee the Iberian peninsula because they were Jews. They were welcomed in the Netherlands. He was born in Amsterdam, but not much is known about his early life except that he supported himself as a craftsman, grinding and polishing optical lenses. He left Amsterdam, and for a while lived with friends who belonged to the Collegiate religious sect at Rijnsburg, near Leyden. In 1663 he came to The Hague and in 1671 moved into the house at 72 Pavil Joensgracht which was his final home. It is a 2-story structure of russet bricks. The neighborhood is within sight of the City Hall tower of The Hague, but it looks like another part of the world. There are antique shops which themselves look ancient, and run-down dwellings. In the center of the street is a statue of Spinoza on a massive marble base. He is seated, reflectively. It is still a neighborhood of Portuguese and Spaniards. A badly lighted but well-stocked grocery store of Iberian specialties (sardines, fruits, olives) faces the Spinoza house from the other side of the street. The men lounging in the store are in their 30s and speak Portuguese. It is hard to tell whether they are residents or Portuguese workers who have temporary jobs in The Hague. Four years before he died Spinoza was offered a post at the University of Heidelberg, promised that his philosophy would have complete range of movement. He did not accept the offer. He died humbly in the house with the russet brick front. He had no material wealth. All he left were his writings.

TRANSPORTATION: Frequent train service from Amsterdam.

HOTELS: *Promenade* is outstanding. *Grand Hotel Terminus* is moderately priced.

POINTS OF INTEREST: The Japanese Garden at Clingendael; the Zeiss Planetarium; the miniature city, Madurodam.

MAASTRICHT

The waiter at the sidewalk café overlooking the Vrijthof, the main square of Maastricht, is vague as to why the tables are covered with Persian rugs. "It's traditional," he says. But the waiter is more specific about the history of his city which is in the southeast corner of the Netherlands, touching the Belgian and German borders.

"Maastricht's name comes from the Latin *Trajectum ad Mosam*—'crossing the Meuse,'" he says. "You still cross the Meuse to get from one side of Maastricht to the other. It's an old Roman city. Our first bishop, St. Servatius, or Servace, came here in the 4th century. Because it's been Catholic so long, religious names are used a lot—for streets, for cafés, for buildings. The street named Sint Bernardusstraat, for instance, is a reminder that St. Bernard of Clairvaux preached the Second Crusade here in 1145."

The Dominicain Café, which looks diagonally across the Vrijthof at the Church of St. Servace, obviously gets its name from the old Dominican church nearby. In the suppression of religious orders in Napoleonic times, the church was closed, but the structure still stands. From the outside it still looks like a church except there is a door-button. Churches do not have bells or buttons at the front door. Inside, it looks like a set from a Fellini movie. The church is now used by the City Archives Department and the center aisle is bordered by row after row of head-high bookcases where pews obviously had once been. At the front a lateral stairway leads up to a large glass-fronted enclosure which is directly above the place where the main altar had once been. Two men in shirtsleeves are inside the booth. They are apparently clerks. When the outside bell is rung they can open the door, without moving from the cubicle, by pushing a button. Then they watch intently through the glass as the visitor makes his way down the center aisle.

St. Servace

The basilica built over the grave of Maastricht's patron is a massive structure of huge blocks of stone, and has a fortress look. Servace, an Armenian missionary, came to Maastricht about A.D. 350. He died in Maastricht in 384.

Mass is said in St. Servace Church every day, but it is closed on winter afternoons as a security measure to protect its valuable paintings and treasury. The treasury includes a crucifix that might have been used by Servace. It is plated in gold and speckled with jewels. There is also the crozier he used as the city's first bishop. Part of his head is encased in a glistening shiny bust of copper that is kept in the treasury room. His bones are preserved in a gilded chest in the crypt. The people of Maastricht call it the *noodkist* (emergency chest) because in time of need, such as plague, war, natural disaster, it is borne through the streets in a procession of prayer and piety. The chest is a 12th-century work, also of gleaming copper, a little over 3 feet long and somewhat less than 2 feet in height and width. On the feast of St. Servace, May 13, his bust is carried in procession. Once every 7 years (1976, 1983, and so on) there is a special procession in which all the churches of Maastricht participate by having sacred and ancient articles from their treasuries carried through the streets by parishioners.

Stella Maris

The 15th-century statue that is venerated in a side chapel of Our Lady's Church was found on a ship moored along the Meuse (in Dutch, Maas). The captain of the ship did not pay much attention to the statue, and went about preparations for getting his vessel underway. But he could not move the vessel from the pier. In the hustle and bustle, he thought about the supernumerary cargo, the statue, and took it ashore to the first church he saw. When he returned to his ship, he again made preparations to depart. This time the vessel left the port normally. Because of its association with the river boat, the statue is known to the people of Maastricht as *Stella Maris* (Star of the Sea).

On the Sunday nearest Aug. 15, the feast of the Assumption, there is a procession in the streets of Maastricht with the Stella Maris statue. The members of the escort group dress formally in dark suits and white ties, and carry articles from the Stella Maris treasury. The statue is dressed in a long blue robe. A smaller procession is held on the Monday after Easter. This time a red robe is worn.

THE AMERICAN PRESENCE

Maastricht, the oldest city in the Netherlands, and once considered the strongest fortress on the Continent, has some American connections. America's 30th Division freed Maastricht on Sept. 13, 1944, making it the first Dutch town to be liberated in the Second World War. An American military cemetery with 8,700 graves is 8 miles away. Each grave has been adopted by a Dutch family.

TRANSPORTATION: Maastricht is 135 miles southeast of Amsterdam on the main rail line.

HOTELS: *Casque* and *Derlon* are quite comfortable, and not overly expensive. The modern *Euromotel* is at the airport.

POINTS OF INTEREST: The Mount St. Peter Caves, a labyrinthine network of underground limestone galleries was used as an air-raid shelter by 9,000 persons in the Second World War. The caves, with a nearly constant 50-degree temperature, are a favorite winter home for a dozen of the 15 varieties of bats found in the Netherlands. Only New Mexico's Carlsbad Caverns is more popular with the cold-shunning mammals.

ROERMOND

In every Redemptorist church in the world there is a statue of Our Lady of Perpetual Help, except here in Roermond, a city in the province of Limburg that is about 90 percent Catholic. Instead, the parish church of the Redemptorists in Roermond enshrines a statue known as "Our Lady in the Sand."

"To have two different statues for one person might cause confusion among the people," the rector explains.

Devotion to Our Lady in the Sand is centuries old. Already in 1417 a chapel stood on the sandy banks of the Roer River as a shrine for a wooden statue of a Madonna and Child that was found by a Polish nobleman named Wendelin. The nobleman had wanted to get away from a life in Poland which seemed to him to be too materialistic. On arriving in the area of the Roer River he obtained a job as a shepherd. It was not long before the sheep, searching for water, led him to a spring shaded by a large oak tree. The spring became a regular watering-place for Wendelin's flock, and for him a place of prayer and meditation. One day he found the wooden statue. Soon pilgrims began visiting the site. The chronicles of the city of Roermond for 1578 state that "the Chapel in the Sand, built in honor of Our Lady, is very well known through miracles." That was the year when the chapel was pulled down during the war raging across the Low Countries. But a new chapel was built in 1613. The present brick church, which encloses the shrine, is from 1895.

The church is a few dozen yards from the Roer. Ducks increase the impression the Roer gives of being a pond rather than a river. The spring used by Wendelin's band of sheep is at the altar steps of the shrine.

There is an opening in the floor, covered over now by an iron grating and a sheet of glass 2 feet square. The spring water, 6 feet below, is visible through the opening. The statue of Our Lady in the Sand is in a niche above the altar. In the corridor outside the chapel are faucets where pilgrims can drink water piped from the spring, or collect some to take home. Among the postcards and religious articles on sale in the corridor are half-liter plastic bottles for the spring water. The wall behind the sanctuary altar is crammed with gold and silver pieces, necklaces, and other jewelry. They are behind a protective glass.

"About 10 years ago," the rector says, "ex-votos valued at fifteen hundred to two thousand guilders, and pectoral crosses of two bishops who had died and left their crosses here, were stolen during the night. Watches, necklaces, rings, rosaries, bracelets—things like that—were taken. Now there's a system against burglary. A few pieces were two hundred years old.

"Some people still bring ex-votos every year. It's a way of expressing gratitude with something material and of value, a means of letting Our Lady think of a person. Like a candle. 'She will think of me as long as this candle burns,' a person will say. And with a ring, the same thing. 'As long as it is here, she will think of me.' "

The rector, Father Cornelius van Roermond, is a native of Breda. His name is Roermond, he believes, because his ancestors apparently came from this area. He is heavy-set and middle-aged. He wears a small silver cross in the lapel of a medium-gray suit jacket. "That's how you can tell I am a priest."

The big feast is the Assumption, Aug. 15. On that day, the mayor of Roermond and the bishop lead a procession through town.

Many gilt-inscribed marble thanksgiving tablets are in the corridor leading to the shrine. There is a tablet from the Schaefer family which says: "Our Lady defended us at the moment of the bombing Oct. 28, 1944." A man named J. H. Ververs, from Linne, a village nearby, gives thanks in another tablet for his return from a POW camp.

TRANSPORTATION: Roermond is on the main Amsterdam-Maastricht rail line. It is 51 miles south of 's-Hertogenbosch; 29 miles north of Maastricht.

HOTELS: *Hotel de la Station* is comfortable.

's-HERTOGENBOSCH

For years the Dutch used to refer to St. John's Cathedral at 's-Hertogenbosch, the largest in the Netherlands, as the unfinished cathedral. When the present church dedicated to St. John the Evangelist was being built in the 15th century the plan was to make it bigger than one of 1280. The builders misjudged their finances, and to complete the new structure part of the old one had to be used.

Today the restoration work on the "unfinished cathedral" is described as a never-ending job by Father Jos DeVries, a priest for 16 years. He is tall and slender, and wears glasses. He has on a light brown tweed jacket with a herringbone design, a green shirt, striped tie, and dark brown trousers.

"The restoration work started one hundred years ago, and has been going on nonstop ever since. But the destruction goes faster than the restoration. The stones are powdering away from the gas fumes of the cars and from the chemicals in the air. If the government increases its subsidy, it is possible the restoration will go faster than the destruction. Now we get a half million guilders, but we need more.

"But we're not touching the tower," Father DeVries adds. "During the Reformation the church was given to the Protestants and when it was returned in 1810 with the arrival of Napoleon, the municipal authorities kept title to the tower."

Why?

"Many churches were returned without their towers. Church towers often possessed the only clock in town, and this made them something of general value. It also was expensive to restore them. Since they were a fine sight for the people, the expense seemed logically to be a community matter. Furthermore, bells in the church towers would warn of disaster. I think perhaps that that is the main reason the authorities retained the towers, to have control over the warning bells."

The clock in the tower of the Town Hall presents a show for the people. When the hour strikes cavalry figures appear and march across the face of the clock, simulating a battle of horsemen. At mid-morning on Wednesday and Saturday, shoppers in the open-air market are serenaded with an hour of light music on the carillon. The carillon player then goes to the tower of St. John's where, starting at noon, he plays religious music on the 49 bells.

's-Hertogenbosch is the capital of the province of Brabant which, like Limburg to the south, is mostly Catholic. There used to be an old saying among the Dutch that the Catholics were "below the rivers" (Meuse and Wall), while non-Catholics were in the northern part of the country. The below-the-rivers area is still predominantly Catholic, but Catholics are also in the north, too. A famous son of 's-Hertogenbosch is Hieromymus Bosch, who is known for the demons and monsters that peopled his paintings. Many of his paintings are in the Prado at Madrid—he was a favorite painter of Philip II. The Netherlands has only 3: 1 in the Boymans Museum at Rotterdam and 2 in St. John's Cathedral in 's-Hertogenbosch.

The city gets its name from the woods which filled the Duchy of Brabant. The name is Dutch for "Woods of the Duke." The unusual prefix is not a variation of "saint" but is merely the possessive case. This happens with many Dutch town names, such as 's-Gravenhage, meaning "Forests of the Earl." The Dutch usually shorten that name to Den Haag and, in English, The Hague. Similarly, for 's-Hertogenbosch the abbreviated form is Den Bosch.

At one time St. John's Cathedral was filled with altars. There were about 50. The various guilds of the town, the butchers, the bakers and so on, had their own altar. Small niches in the cathedral pillars are a sign of the old altars. Now empty, the niches used to hold the wine and water cruets for Mass.

The most visited altar in the cathedral for centuries has been the shrine of the Madonna known to the people of 's-Hertogenbosch as the *Zoete Moeder* (Sweet Mother), represented in a small wooden statue. The statue was found by a workingman early one morning in a shop near St. John's. It was a cold morning and the man thought of using it to make a fire. The master of the shop ordered him not to do this, and the statue was given to a cleric named Brother Wouter who intended to install it in his room. On the way, however, the statue became so heavy that Brother Wouter no longer could carry it, and he placed it on the altar of the Sodality of Our Lady in St. John's.

In September 1629 Prince Frederick Henry of Orange-Nassau, son of William the Silent, seized 's-Hertogenbosch from the Spanish. Catholics took the statue into the Southern Provinces (now Belgium), first to Antwerp; then, Brussels. It remained there until 1853 when the first of the new Catholic bishops of 's-Hertogenbosch was appointed. On its return the statue was carried through the streets of 's-Hertogenbosch triumphantly. The route followed the path of a medieval procession when, during the time of a plague, people prayed for help. The procession was repeated annually on the Sunday nearest July 7, the feast of the "Sweet Mother."

The Chapel of Our Lady is about 35 feet square. The statue of the Sweet Mother is on a circular pedestal above a cream-colored altar. It is 3½ feet tall, dressed in a brocaded mantle of maroon and gold. The Madonna holds the Child in her left arm. For the street procession each year the statue is clothed in ermine.

During the first two weeks of July a special altar is set up near the main altar of the cathedral, and the statue is placed upon it. For the festal season jeweled crowns are placed on the heads of the Madonna and Child, and the *Zoete Moeder* holds a scepter in her right hand.

The statue originally was of plain oak, but Emperor Maximilian I suggested that it be painted green and gold when he visited the shrine in 1481. While there his 3-year-old son Philip the Handsome (whose own sons were Charles V and Ferdinand I) was inducted into the Order of the Golden Fleece in a ceremony in the Chapel of Our Lady.

TRANSPORTATION: Express trains from Amsterdam serve 's-Hertogenbosch every half hour. Den Bosch is 50 miles from Amsterdam.

HOTELS: *Euro* leads; *Royal* is medium-priced.

NORTH HOLLAND

From the air Naarden looks like an asymetrical star, or even a bullfrog, surrounded, except for bridges and causeways, by water. Its unusual design was chosen because it had to be heavily fortified, being on the main road to Amsterdam for hostile armies. Four and 5 centuries ago, when its defenses were put in place, the Zuider Zee was at the east of town and water was on the other side, too. In a giant land-reclamation program a large part of the water area has been filled in with *polders* and new towns have sprung up. People who work in Amsterdam are moving to the new towns, living a suburban life-style. Amsterdam is 15 miles northwest of Naarden.

Naarden was founded about 1350. In 1572 it was destroyed by Spanish forces. Only two buildings were left standing: the cloister of 1440 and the St. Vitus Cathedral of 1480 (now the Grote Kerk, the Big Church of the Protestants). They were spared by the Spaniards because they were Catholic institutions. The abbot eventually turned the monastery over to civic authorities for use as an orphanage. Catholics had to live elsewhere because all their homes had been destroyed. When Naarden was rebuilt, the Reformation spirit barred the town to Catholics.

KOMENSKY

A couple hundred yards outside the beautiful fortress town of Naarden is a statue of Jan Amos Komensky—the name Latinized as Comenius—the Czech bishop and pedagogue of the 17th century. The bronze statue, made in Czechoslovakia, is set among trees near a duck pond.

Komensky, as a religious refugee from his homeland, found asylum in the Netherlands and lived in Amsterdam. He is buried in Naarden.

"The same statue we have here in town," says Herman H. J. Heule, "is before the Komensky College in Bethlehem, Pennsylvania, and in Uhersky Brod in Slovakia where some thought for a while he had been born."

Mr. Heule is a husky man with a gray fringe of hair at the side of his head. He has been director of the Komensky Museum in Naarden since 1968. He says it is a "wonderful thing to be director of this museum."

How did he become director?

"I was an Amsterdam insurance broker, educated at Lloyds in London. In 1967 I sold my business and was looking for some feeling of life. I knew Naarden. I had lived here from 1940. I was interested in two men in my life. Booth of the Salvation Army told us about the practice of life, how to help the people around you. Komensky was the man who wrote books about changing the world into a better place. I read his book *De Rerum Humanarum Emendatione Consulatio Catholica*. This was only published completely in 1966. His manuscript had disappeared, and this was found in Halle Germany in 1934.

"My family were Huguenots. My grandfather lived in the Jordaan area of Amsterdam which at that time was outside of town. Refugees in the 17th century came to the Jordaan area, and got tents, and then later small houses. Holland is a mixture of refugees from all countries."

Komensky was born in Nivnice, Moravia on Mar. 28, 1592. He left his homeland (what is now Czechoslovakia) in 1628 at the age of 36, traveling in many parts of Europe. This was the time of the Eighty Years' War (1568–1648) in the Netherlands. In the East, it was the Thirty Years' War (1618–48). Komensky was a minister in the church of Jan Hus which separated from Catholicism in the Reformation, and its members banded together in family groups under the name Moravian Brothers.

"After the Battle of White Mountain," Mr. Heule says, "it was very dangerous to be a member of this church because power was in the hands of the Catholics. Komensky had to leave his country because of the danger to his life."

What brought him to Amsterdam?

"He was a bishop of the Moravian Brothers at Leszno in Poland. There was a big fire in Leszno in 1656. His library was destroyed completely, except for two manuscripts. He was invited by a wealthy businessman in Amsterdam named Laurens De Geer who lived in a fine house on the Keizergracht. The De Geer family had munitions factories in Sweden. The family were Protestant, and did not like this money, and they gave it to

religious refugees around Europe. They were a bene-
factor of Komensky while he was in Leszno.

"The same happened with other groups of refugees,
such as the Walloon Church [Waalse Kerk] who were
Huguenots. The Huguenots were refugees, and came to
Naarden in 1651. And they asked the mayor for some
buildings so they could work weaving cloth, calico.

"Until the arrival of the Huguenots in 1651, the
former Catholic monastery which had survived the
1572 destruction of Naarden had remained an orphanage. Municipal authorities turned it over to them. They
made a chapel out of one end for services, and set up a
weaving plant in the other."

How did Komensky become acquainted with
Naarden?

"Probably through Minister Grouwels, who was the
first minister of the Walloon group in Naarden. We
have an old book in which Minister Grouwels wrote
that he had been paid 15 guilders for the care of a
grave of honor for seventy years for Komensky. The
money had been paid him by the De Geer family. This
was grave No. Eight. Komensky died November 15,
1670 in Amsterdam. We don't know exactly where he
died, but where he lived we know some places, like
Keizergracht 123.

"Komensky was buried [in Naarden] seven days
after his death in Amsterdam. He wanted to be buried
among the refugees, we believe. People were buried
with their feet toward the altar so that on the day of
Resurrection they could stand up and face God.

"In 1870 the Czech people started a search for
Komensky's grave. They knew Komensky had been
buried in a Walloon church, but did not know exactly
where. They wrote to the mayor of Amsterdam. In
1918, after the First World War, Czechoslovakia got its
freedom. One of the first things Thomas Masaryk did
was to try to find the grave of Komensky. He was the

president. The mayor of Naarden at the time was a Reformed Protestant [Calvinist] who said a grave should not be opened. This went on for several years. Finally permission was given, but only for five days, and no other graves were to be opened."

The former Catholic monastery, which successively had become an orphanage and then a chapel and weaving plant for the Huguenot refugees, had been turned into a military casern in 1845. But there were burial records. The Komensky grave of 1670 was known. In 1742 a historian from Amsterdam, Brauwerius van Nidek, member of a refugee family from Austria, was buried in the same grave. Eight years later, the records showed, a French captain living in the Netherlands, Louis Guerre, was also buried there.

"When we opened the grave, we saw the epaulets. We knew this was the right grave. Then Czech and Dutch anthropologists—one of them was Professor Matejka of Prague—examined the skeletons and they determined the racial characteristics of one body were Slavic.

"Now there was another problem. The Czechs asked for the return of Komensky's remains to Czechoslovakia. The mayor again made difficulties. He said this time that it is not possible to move a body from the place where one wanted to be buried. You cannot disturb the body, he said. There were then four years of correspondence between the two countries over what to do with the remains. The solution was found by officially declaring the gravesite to be on Czechoslovak soil so that there was no need to move him. On his birthday, March 28, 1933, the area was formally made part of the territory of Czechoslovakia. This gave the Czechs a chance to build a mausoleum *in their own country*. It took four years to build. Everything in the chapel is from Czechoslovakia.

"The mausoleum was completed in 1937, and the

mayor of Naarden was given the key as the official custodian. It is alongside the former Catholic monastery which since the nineteenth century has been a military casern. The casern is now a NATO base and its entrance is only a few yards from the Czechoslovak territory holding the mausoleum."

Words from a book written by Komensky when he still was bishop in Leszno in 1648 are inscribed on a monument to Thomas Masaryk placed in the chapel in the interval between the two world wars when Czechoslovakia was free: "Some day, I trust, the leadership of your country will return into your own hands."

"Each November 15, the date of Komensky's death, I light three candles held by three hands, the right hands—the Lord's, my neighbor's and my own," Mr. Heule says, referring to a Komensky book, *The Three Right Hands.*

"When Khrushchev was banging on the table in the United Nations with his shoe we were receiving capitalist and Communist visitors here. Each day we receive these groups together in harmony. We have days when Americans and Communists are here together. They sing together, and put down their flowers together. It is very wonderful. Each year the ambassador of Czechoslovakia comes on March 28 (Komensky's birth date). 'Jsem doma,' the Czech people say when they come. *I am at home.*"

At the center of Naarden is the Komensky Museum. A sculpture above the doorway shows the Town Hall, which had been on the site, being attacked by Spanish soldiers in 1572.

"The Socialist government of Czechoslovakia provided a new interior for the museum in 1967, and many of our books are from there. We have a Hussite Bible from 1601. I don't think any other museum has such a Bible—and I got it from the Czechoslovak Socialist government!

"In 1623 Komensky wrote a book, *How Do We Find the Way through the Labyrinth of Life and Find the Paradise in Our Heart?* which tells of how he found life without meaning and that when he discovered Christ he saw paradise in his heart. We had a special exhibit last year on the three hundred and fiftieth anniversary of the book, and the Czech government re-republished the book."

One book exhibited at the museum is *Didactica Opera Omnia,* a huge volume on teaching, which was published in 1657 with money from the De Geer family a year after Komensky arrived in Amsterdam. A notation in the book *Collegij Societatis Jesu Monachij 1667* shows it had been acquired by a Jesuit school within 10 years of its publication.

Individuals from various parts of the world contribute small sums—3 or 4 dollars—to help support the museum.

"We do not want large sums. In order to keep our freedom we do not want any money at all from the Czech government or from groups of emigrants."

A white plaster statue of Komensky, presented by the Communist government of Czechoslovakia, is in the museum. The inscription describes him as "Czech philosopher and teacher; creator of a system of philosophy attempting to improve mankind by education; buried in Naarden; surnamed Teacher of the Nations." There is no mention of religion, or of his having been a bishop.

TRANSPORTATION: By Bus 36 from Amsterdam.

HOTELS: *Euromotel.*

POINTS OF INTEREST: The annual St. John the Baptist procession at Laren, 3 miles from Naarden, is on the Sunday nearest his feastday of June 24. Another northern point where a procession takes place is Dokkum. St. Boniface was killed at Dokkum with his companions in A.D. 755. The procession is on Sunday nearest June 5, feast of St. Boniface.

ADALBERT

Pieter Richardson, the brawny, thirtyish son of a Royal Air Force father and a Dutch mother, can point out where the English Benedictine monk Adalbert, a companion of Willibrord, landed at Egmond, about 25 miles northwest of Amsterdam, after a journey across the North Sea in the 8th century.

"Adalbert landed between Pillar forty-one and forty-two," Pieter says, referring to the pillars installed at 1-kilometer intervals along the coast by the Dutch government as points of reference so that storm-damaged areas—places where raging water has ripped away the land—can be identified easily and precisely.

Heaping sand dunes are only 200 yards from the site where Adalbert built his first chapel and where he was buried. Only persons on foot or on bikes are allowed in the dune area. Pieter's mother was born here.

"My mother tells of how the road leading up from the sea over the dunes—the road Adalbert took—was once paved with seashells, and is still known as the Old Seashell Road. The Nazis replaced the shells with stones in order to move military equipment easier."

The Old Seashell Road, now paved, is still narrow and there is little traffic. Pieter's farmhouse is literally across the road from the site of Adalbert's original monastic cell.

In A.D. 950, when St. Adalbert's Abbey was established—the oldest monastery in the Netherlands—Count Dirk II (Theoderik) of Holland had the monk's remains exhumed. They were moved to a new grave at the monastery, ½ mile inland from the monk's original church. When Adalbert's remains were dug up, a spring burst forth. This is covered over now, and there is a hand-actuated pump above it, as on a country well.

"It's curious about the spring for Adalbert here and the one for Willibrord in Heiloo," says Father Jan van

Dyk, the porter at the abbey. (Heiloo is a town 3 miles away). "People still come to pump the water, old people mostly. They use it like holy water."

The porter's lodge at the monastery is a cramped, smallish room just inside the doorway. Father van Dyk chats as he makes tea on a hotplate for some women guests who are in the church. "They are Père Foucauld Sisters," he says, after a few moments. "They are the ones who work with Eskimos in the North Pole, the natives in the Sahara, with the poor everywhere. They came here today on their bikes from Heiloo with a Sister who lives on a canal boat in Amsterdam."

As he pours the tea, Father van Dyk jokes about his name. It is spelled without the "c," he emphasizes.

There are really three Egmonds, all within a mile or two of one another: Egmond-by-the-Sea, inland Egmond (the town), and Egmond-on-the-Heights, which is capped by the ruins of a castle.

"The castle belonged to the Count of Egmond, a descendant of the oldtime administrator of the monastery lands. Through time and many generations the administrator became increasingly important and eventually came into concurrence with the abbey—in conflict. He also made Philip II angry. Philip II accused him of disloyalty to Spain, and had him beheaded. The people of the town remember the story of the Count of Egmond, and as you know he is immortalized in music."

There are 30 monks at the abbey.

"In the Reformation the monks were dispersed. They took their books and other articles to the Bishop of Haarlem who was the last pre-Reformation abbot. In the time of Philip II it was customary to make the local bishop head of an abbey because then he could support himself and his see with income from the taxes on lands owned by the monastery.

"The monks also took the body of Adalbert to the bishop's residence in Haarlem. Then, in the nineteenth

century, after Napoleonic times, the relics were given to
the parish church of Egmond town—the monks had not
returned yet. All the relics were brought to the parish
church, except the skull. Then, when the monastery
was reactivated in 1935, the bishop of Haarlem brought
the skull to the monks. St. Adalbert's feast is on June
15."

The present abbot of St. Adalbert's happens to have
the same name as the patron of the abbey.

Is he young?

"He was forty this year," Father van Dyk says. The
monk has a small pocket notebook and he looks in it to
check the age of the abbot. He keeps a record of the
birth dates of all the monks so that a birthday does not
slip by unnoticed.

What do monks do on a monk's birthday?

He laughs, and says: "We smoke a cigar."

He laughs again, and adds: "At Easter and Christmas, and on major feasts of the Order, we also smoke a
cigar."

TRANSPORTATION: By local bus from main-line railroad
station at Heiloo.

HOTELS: *Bellevue* at Egmond-on-the-Sea is comfortable.
Altenburg and *Frisia* are medium-priced.

HEILOO

Many churches in the Netherlands are named after
Willibrord, the 8th-century English monk who was the
first archbishop of Utrecht and who is buried in Luxembourg. (See Index.) Near the Utrecht Cathedral (now
Dutch Reformed) the monk is shown on horseback as a
missionary. A spring is named after him in Heiloo, a
neighboring town of Egmond, site of a spring named
after another English Benedictine, St. Adalbert. St.
Willibrord's spring is near the Town Hall. A half mile
away, a private psychiatric center, with 500 in-patients,

also bears St. Willibrord's name. The center was started by the Brothers of Our Lady of Lourdes, of Ghent, in 1930. Each year on Nov. 7, the day of Willibrord's death, Mass is said in the chapel and a reliquary is exposed. A statue at a side altar is inscribed: "St. Willibrord, patron of our center, pray for us."

A spring was also discovered on the site of the shrine of Our Lady of Need which is near the Amsterdam-Alkmaar railroad tracks. The shrine is set in woods in a remote, isolated area of town. Along one side of the road are a few houses, a café and a 2-story brick house with the biblical name Ain Karim (Vineyard Spring) where the priest lives.

"No one is sure about the origin of the shrine," a man in the café sipping coffee from a glass says. "They have documents from the early fifteenth century which mention it. During the Reformation the shrine was destroyed, and the people secretly kept the devotion at the site, and had prayers. It was existing again in 1830 when the reign of the first Orange king of Holland, William the First, a Protestant, started. Apparently because a concordat was being negotiated at the time with the new king, the Holy See ordered the public devotion to cease. Then, early in the twentieth century, it began again publicly. Land had been bought around the site of the old chapel and a new sanctuary was built. Since the land was private, a procession could take place and the law couldn't stop them."

TRANSPORTATION: Heiloo, 17 miles north of Amsterdam by train.

HOTELS: *Oude Herberg* is a typical, pleasant village inn.

AMSTERDAM

To religious refugees of yesterday Amsterdam was a welcome haven, a place where they could practice their religion without harassment. In recent days Amsterdam has become a home for "The Children of God," who have opened a reception room and shelter across from the Central Station. They are a Bible-oriented group which evolved from the religious revolution at Huntington Park, Calif., in 1968. Their mentor, or guru, is an American man in his early 50s named David Moses who writes out his thoughts in general letters which, after being translated, are distributed on street corners by members of the Children of God community. The Children of God believe in God and socialism. They say the U.S.A. is materialistic. They do not like the atheism of the U.S.S.R. The community accepts all young people arriving in Amsterdam who need food and lodging, and maintain a dormitory for those without money. No questions are asked about a person's religious beliefs. "Some speak so many languages we don't know that it would be hard to even discuss religion with them," a youth from Houston says.

THE OLD JEWISH QUARTER

The most famous religious refugees who found a home in Amsterdam were the Jews of the Iberian peninsula. They had been expelled from Spain in 1492 and, after fleeing into Portugal, were driven from there, too. From the Old Jewish Quarter of Amsterdam have come men who have helped make the world a better place by their intellect, artistic skill, moral values and, of course, courage. At 61 Waterlooplein the philosopher Baruch Spinoza was born. In a nearby park is the bronze heroic-sized statue of a husky figure in cap, and with sleeves rolled up. This is "The Docker," a reminder of the spontaneous outrage shown by the city's longshoremen at the inhuman actions of the Nazi occupying forces in the Second World War. The Nazis rounded up 400 young Jews, beat them brutally, and then hauled them from the country. The people of Amsterdam were shocked, and the dockers showed the city's feelings by defiantly leading a general strike of protest on Feb. 25, 1941.

One of Europe's most beautiful houses of God, the Portuguese Synagogue, is essentially the same as it was when built by refugees 3 centuries ago. Brass chandeliers hold candles which supply the only light. Long benches are the only seats. Wood from the Cedars of Lebanon was used for the ceiling.

REMBRANDT'S HOUSE

Rembrandt was in his teens when he moved to Amsterdam from Leyden 3 centuries ago. The son of a miller, he wanted to study painting. There are traces of him everywhere, but especially in the Old Jewish Quarter. On his arrival in Amsterdam he resided first in the corner building at 2 Jodenbreestraat (Jews Broad Street). This was his residence and his atelier, and he and Saskia lived there after their marriage in 1634. It was one of their residences until he bought the house next door at No. 4 Jodenbreestraat. This house is now a museum. All the places they lived were in the same neighborhood and local landmarks figured in his drawings and paintings. The 15th-century Waag (Weighing House), for instance, was where he did his famous "Anatomy Lesson of Dr. Tulp." At the time Amsterdam's guild of surgeons used rooms in the fortresslike building for its meetings.

THE JEWISH MUSEUM

Amsterdam has never got out of its old habit of welcoming homeless Jews. Baruch Cyklik came to Amsterdam in 1946. He had been in the Russian army from 1939 to 1945. The way he capsulizes his family history is as low-key as the vital statistics on a tombstone: "I had four sisters in Amsterdam before the war.

One came back from Bergen-Belsen. A brother-in-law was in Auschwitz. He came back. He has a number on his hand yet." Baruch Cyklik is an attendant at the Jewish Museum in the Waag, the Weighing-House.

The Jewish Museum exhibits many articles, some of great art, which were associated with the religious life of the newly arrived Jews of Amsterdam. There are also documents, papers and passes which are sorrowful testimony to recent sufferings. Part of the story of occupied Holland, for instance, is told in the listing of "Anti-Jewish Regulations" imposed by Arthur von Seyss-Inquart, the German commissioner in the Second World War.

"They tell me almost every day there was a new *Kennisgeving* posted on the walls of the quarter—another regulation for the Jews," Baruch Cyklik says. There are dozens and dozens of regulations in the listing, and each is dated:

Nov. 7, 1941—a pass must be obtained for inter-city travel; moving from one house to another is forbidden; membership in non-Jewish tennis, bridge, dance and other clubs is prohibited.

Nov. 21, 1941—use of non-Jewish hotels, theaters and swimming pools is forbidden.

Jan. 1, 1942—the hiring of non-Jewish domestic personnel is forbidden.

Jan. 9, 1942—enrollment in public schools is forbidden.

Jan. 23, 1942—in passports Jews must be identified with the letter "J."

Mar. 25, 1942—marriage to non-Jews is forbidden.

Mar. 26, 1942—sale of household furnishings is forbidden.

Apr. 24, 1942—all Jewish butcher shops are closed.

May 29, 1942—all (*volledig, alles*) travel is forbidden: train, tram, automobile.

June 12, 1942—shopping for vegetables in non-Jewish shops is forbidden.

All bicycles and automobiles must be turned over to the commandatura.

July 8, 1942—telephoning is forbidden.

A Jew is not permitted to visit a non-Jew.

July 17, 1942—Jews may shop only between 3 and 5 P.M.

July 31, 1942—barbershops are out of bounds for Jews.

Sept. 8, 1942—In The Hague, Jews are not permitted to sit on benches in city parks.

Sept. 15, 1942—university education is prohibited.

THE CHURCH-IN-THE-ATTIC

In the early days of the Reformation, Dutch Catholics used code names for the secret hideaways where they attended Mass. A Catholic would whisper to a Catholic neighbor that he was on the way to some such place as "The Parrot," "The Tree," "The Mail Bugle," or "Chalk Mountain." Gradually the need for secret places of worship declined, and they either disappeared or grew into large churches. But oldtime code names often stuck to the new public churches built on sites of secret ones, even though given formal religious designations. A life-sized model of a parrot on a perch in the middle aisle of Sts. Peter and Paul Church in downtown Amsterdam reminds Catholics of its past.

One of the oldtime secret places of worship has survived as a museum, and as a "parish church" for Amsterdam's artists. Its code name was "The Deer" or "The Hart," because the name of the businessman who built it in the attic of his 5-story home in 1661 was Jan Hartman. Hartman made clear in his will that his heirs could not sell the building because he wanted to make sure there was a church for his neighbors. But the family needed money and a few years after his death sold the building to a non-Catholic. Catholics feared that they would have no place for Mass. But the new owner of the building rented the attic to them.

Catholics got into the habit of saying they were going to "Our Dear Lord in the Attic." The attic church is still called that today. The building was bought by a nonprofit foundation, the Amstelkring, when St. Nicholas parish church was built in 1887.

It is just down the street from the Oude Kerk (Old Church). Everything is on a small or special scale. The pulpit, for instance, takes up half of the altar area. After it is used, it can be rolled behind the altar.

About 200 persons crowd into the attic for the Artists Mass at 11 A.M. on the first Sunday of each month. Marika Schnitker estimates that 20 to 25 weddings and christenings take place each year. Marika is tall, long-haired, blonde and young. She is the caretaker of the attic church and its museum on Saturdays. During the week she attends art classes in design and crafts. The name? She laughs.

"One grandmother was Marie; another, Rika."

THE OLD CHURCH

Carillon concerts are played in the towers of the Old Church, the West Church and a few other churches—now, all Dutch Reformed—in the summer. Schedules are posted at the church door. The rest of the year brief recitals are also given by carillonneurs, usually at noon and early in the evening.

The Old Church was consecrated in 1306, and Rembrandt's wife is buried under a whitened stone in its floor. The stone says simply: "Saskia 19 June 1642." Rembrandt himself is buried in the West Church.

An observation platform is in the 220-foot-tower of the Old Church. The view of Amsterdam is worth the climb.

THE BEGUINAGE

The Beguinage (in Dutch, *begijnhof*) is in the very center of Amsterdam, but because it is, in effect, a large inner court with 50 three-story buildings it looks like an attractive Dutch village. The Benguinage is operated by a Catholic foundation. The houses are red brick, and the windows are trimmed in white. Father Bert Overgaag says each house has a sleeping room, a living room and a kitchen. He is a priest at the Open Door, a Catholic-sponsored storefront at 37 Heiligeweg in the middle of Amsterdam's shopping district. Father Overgaag or a colleague keeps the Open Door open quite late in the evening to respond to anyone's question about anything to do with religion.

"About one hundred to one hundred and fifty women live in the *Begijnhof* now," Father Overgaag says, "but they are not beguines. They are widows or single women. Some work. The older ones are retired. They pay a small rent to the foundation—seventy or eighty guilders a month. The last beguine died five years ago."

Two churches practically face each other. One, originally Catholic, became Protestant in the Reformation. In the 17th century Catholics received permission to build a new church, and made one from two houses.

On the façade of the English Reformed Church a tablet was erected "to the Glory of God in Christ Jesus" by a company of the clergy of the Reformed Church in America in 1927. The inscription on the tablet says it was placed there as a tribute to the Pilgrim Fathers "who settled first in the city of Amsterdam in Holland, the country of their asylum, a shining exemplar of civil and religious liberty, many of whose institutions, transmitted to America through the English Pilgrims and the Dutch who settled in New York, have given to the New World a distinctive character."

THE REBUILDER OF THE JESUITS

A museum with various personal articles of Dutch Jesuit Father Jan Philip Roothaan is alongside St. Francis Xavier Church where he made his First Communion and served as an altar boy. Father Roothaan was born at 62 Laurierstraat on Nov. 23, 1785. Because of the suppression of the Jesuits in many countries of Europe during Napoleonic times, he went to Russia when he was 19 to join the Society of Jesus, and became a priest there in 1812. After the lifting of the anti-Jesuit ban, he was elected General of the Society of Jesus in 1829. He is called the "second founder" of the Jesuits. The cause for his canonization has been started and Father P. C. J. Ligthart, S.J., organizer of the museum and a biographer, is its vice postulator. "I had a brother in California whom the people called 'Lightheart'," the Jesuit says pleasantly.

The desk Father Roothaan used as general of the Jesuits is in the 1-room museum. It is a simple piece of furniture, 5 feet long and 18 inches wide, with a bank of 4 drawers on each side. His Russian passport is on exhibit, too. It is a folded piece of paper, a little larger than legal size. One side is written in Russian; the other side, in German, identifies the czar as Alexander der Ersten.

A wig of dark brown hair about 4 inches long is among the exhibits.

"He began wearing a wig when he was old. During a visit in Holland in 1849 he forgot one of his wigs. He had several. We found the one he left behind here."

Many books are exhibited. One biography, *The General Who Rebuilt the Jesuits,* published by Bruce in Milwaukee, Wis., was written by American Jesuit Father Robert G. North, the noted archaeologist and biblical scholar. It is dedicated to "the Mother of a Jesuit."

Father Ligthart tells of having talked to Father North, and mentioning the biography. He had written it before ordination, while still a scholastic. "That was a sin of my youth," he quotes Father North as saying, and laughs.

TRANSPORTATION: Frequently scheduled planes and trains link Amsterdam with other cities in the Netherlands and Europe.

HOTELS: *Hilton, Europe,* and *Amstel* are main hotels. *Doelen, Krasnapolsky* and *Esso Motor* are not too expensive.

12
Portugal

THE CONCORDAT signed by the government of Portugal and the Holy See on May 7, 1940 notes that Catholicism is the traditional religion of the Portuguese people.

But the tradition has been broken a number of times during the nearly 9 centuries of Portugal's existence. In the succession of revolutions and governments a little over a half century ago, only one Catholic church in all Lisbon was open, and that one escaped closing because it belonged to foreigners, the Irish Dominicans. The three little shepherds who reported seeing the Madonna at Fatima were kidnaped by a local official and threatened with death if they did not change their story about having witnessed the Apparitions. Three times the Jesuits have been expelled from Portugal.

The bishop of Oporto, Portugal's second city, was able to return to his diocese from an enforced exile abroad of more than 10 years after the bloodless overthrow of the government of Marcello Caetano (successor of Salazar) in April 1974. The bishop's "sin" was that he had written a letter to Salazar proposing the removal of press censorship, the formation of a Christian political opposition party, and a bigger share for the north in government spending. Coincidentally, in the 1910 revolution the bishop of Oporto was sent out of the country.

Portugal's monarchy collapsed in the 1910 revolution and the present republic was established. There were cries of "No God! No Religion!" by the anticlerical republicans. Afonso Costa, the new minister of justice, predicted that in two generations the Catholic religion would be extinct in Portugal.

The constitution provides for religious freedom, and 95 percent of the people are Catholic in name at least. The percentage of Massgoers drops as one moves southward, varying from almost 100 percent in Braga and the north to 5 percent deep in the Algarve.

Catholic Portugal has less priests per capita than any other nation in Western Europe. Some 5,000 priests serve a nation of 9 million people in 3,800 parishes, barely more than one priest to a parish. Large parishes need several priests, and this is balanced by assigning 3 or 4 small parishes to one priest. Our Lady of Help parish in the Boa Hora (Good Hour) workers parish of Lisbon has 50,000 parishioners, and is served by 4 priests. In the Beja district, 60 miles from Lisbon, one pastor has as many as 6 or 7 parishes.

Yet, as the concordat observes, there is a long Catholic tradition in Portugal.

One of the great saints of all time, the Franciscan friar known as Anthony of Padua was born in Lisbon in 1195. John XXI, who ruled the church from Rome in the 12th century, was a Portuguese. Portuguese explorers carried the cross around the world. Millions of pilgrims have journeyed to the obscure hinterland area called Fatima, because of the Apparitions there in 1917.

Portugal was Catholic from its very beginning as an independent nation over 8 centuries ago. The man who brought about Portugal's independence from the kingdom of Leon and Castile was a French Crusader from

Burgundy, Count Henry, who had come to the Iberian peninsula to help turn back the Moors. His son, Afonso Henriques, led the Christian army which routed the Moors in a key battle at Ourique in 1139, and was acclaimed king of the new nation. Afonso and his father laid out the ecclesiastical organization for the church in the territory regained from the Moors, establishing the seats of dioceses at Braga and Coimbra, and bringing two monks from France to fill them.

Before the establishment of the kingdom of Portugal the religion of the inhabitants varied with the occupants. About the 6th century B.C. pagan Celts coming from the north entered what is now northern Portugal. Phoenicians and Greeks settled along the south, having made their way through the straits of Gibraltar. About 185 B.C. came an invasion by the Romans. They subjugated the Lusitanians who were descendants of the Celts, and by 38 B.C. controlled the Iberian peninsula. Germanic barbarian tribes crossing Europe reached the Iberian peninsula in the 5th century A.D. Of the four main tribes the Swabians were the ones who entered Galicia (northwest Spain) and northern Portugal. Then, in A.D. 711, the Saracens crossed from North Africa into Spain and in a half dozen years took possession of almost every part of the Iberian peninsula. After the establishment of the kingdom in the north, the entire country was reconquered from the Moors by the start of the 13th century. (In Spain, it was 1492.)

With the establishment of the kingdom of Portugal Catholicism, like the new nation itself, prospered for centuries.

The church's difficulties began in 1755 when an earthquake devastated Lisbon. The city was rebuilt by the prime minister, the Marques de Pombal. But this talented gentleman still felt insecure and, specifically, feared that the Jesuits might weaken his influence with the king. Through a series of maneuvers he effected the expulsion of the Jesuits from Portugal in 1759, the first victory in a Europe-wide attack on the Society of Jesus. The Jesuits were not allowed to return until 1831. It was a very brief stay—three years. They returned from their second expulsion in 1860, and remained in Portugal till 1910 when they and all religious orders were banished once more.

Fatima gave Catholics hope.

After the end of the monarchy in 1910, there were 16 revolutions, 8 presidents and 43 changes of government. The armed forces seized power in 1926. Two years later they invited Antonio de Oliveira Salazar, an economics professor at the University of Coimbra, to straighten out the economy as finance minister. In 1932 he became prime minister and from then until 1968 when he was incapacitated by a stroke that eventually brought death, Salazar ruled Portugal like a dictator.

The new constitution of 1933 by permitting the existence of associations tacitly indicated that religious orders (including the Jesuits) could be reestablished. But the relationship between church and state in the long period of dictatorship was never an easy one. Some described the church as being in a golden straitjacket: she looked fine, but actually could not move.

BRAGA

No city in Portugal is older in religious history than Braga, the capital of Minho province in the north. Count Henry, the French Crusader and father of Portugal's first king, Afonso, is buried in Braga Cathedral. Afonso was born in Guimarães, southeast of the city, and was crowned by Braga's archbishop. The archbishop bears the title of "Primate of All the Spains," outranking in a sense even the archbishop of Toledo because Braga, in the reconquest from the Saracens, reverted to Christianity earlier. The cathedral is on the site of a pagan temple which the Romans dedicated to Isis, the goddess of fertility. A plaque from the old temple hangs at the entrance to St. Gerald's Chapel. A 14th-century image of Mary is exhibited in the Chapel of the Madonna.

It is a poor area. But many little girls have rings of gold in their pierced ears. At the railroad station, a woman serves as baggage porter. Under the arcades at the Café Vianna side of the main square men of all ages stand. They wear caps and are huddled together, yet are apart, just standing. In winter Braga is umbrella country. It is an area of religious devotion. In the hills outside the city are two shrines: one for Jesus; the other for the Madonna. On Sunday many pilgrims make a day of it, walking up one side of the hill to the Madonna shrine and returning by the "Good Jesus" shrine on the other. Bus drivers have rosary beads draped over their rearview mirrors.

NOSSA SENHORA DO SAMEIRO

After Fatima, Nossa Senhora do Sameiro (Our Lady of Sameiro) is the largest Marian shrine in Portugal. It is atop a hill, 5½ miles from Braga and is reached by a road that twists and turns through vineyards and woods. The taxi driver takes off his cap as he passes the roadside shrines along the way. Women food vendors have set up shop at the roadside. They are dressed completely in black—skirts, blouses, sweaters, stockings. From wooden tables covered with white cloths they sell homemade bread rings from high stacks.

Four statues stand on tall pedestals at the entrance to the shrine. The saints represented are associated in their devotion to Mary. An inscription describes the first as "St. Cyril of Alexandria, great doctor and Marianist, an intrepid defender against Nestor of the divine maternity of Our Lady." The second is St. Bernard of Clairvaux, "mellifluous doctor, inspired singer of the excellencies of Mary and tireless promoter of her cult." The third, St. Anthony of *Lisbon,* is identified as "teacher, doctor and Marianist. His golden tongue exalted with unequaled brilliance the greatness of the Most Holy Virgin." The fourth statue is St. Alphonsus Liguori, "the doctor of the glories of Mary, Paladin of the Immaculate Conception and of the universal mediation of Mary."

Wall plaques inside the church list sums of money offered for further development of the shrine. A tablet dated Aug. 9, 1953, for example, tells of a *grandiosa* pilgrimage of the textile workers of Concelho de Braga, and notes that "in appreciation and thanks for so many benefits received" 27,000 escudos were offered.

A statue of the Madonna is on the main altar.

"It was made in Rome and blessed by Pius IX before being brought to Braga in 1878," says Father L. S. Mascarenhas. He is a delightful person. He is 74 years old now and says until 3 years ago he could touch the floor without bending his knees. He is tall and husky. He was born in the onetime Portuguese colony of Goa and for 45 years was a missionary in Burma.

"Once in a while the statue is taken from the shrine and brought elsewhere for something special, like for this year's national Eucharistic Congress in Braga.

"There is a golden crown for the statue which weighs three kilos. It is solid gold. It was made in 1904 with gold offered by the women of Portugal to commemorate the fiftieth anniversary of the definition of the dogma of the Immaculate Conception. There was no Fatima then. A priest from Braga wanted to encourage devotion to the Immaculate Conception. He put a statue on top of Sameiro Hill in 1870 and three years later built a chapel. That's how the shrine started.

"Even poor people are generous here. In building this place much of the money has come from the people. A woman for example makes a promise and vows that if her son becomes well, she will give her earrings. Poor people do that. Poor people are more generous than the rich. I always found it that way."

Four years ago a 3-story house of retreat, the Mater Ecclesiae Apostolic Center, was built. Its dining-room is popular for wedding receptions because it looks across treetops to the roofs of Braga.

BOM JESUS

Bom Jesus do Monte (Good Jesus of the Mountain) is a half hour's walk through the woods from the Marian shrine. Chapels and monumental stairways are along the hill which is crowned by a large statue of Christ.

"The sanctuary has existed since the eighteenth century," the missionary from Goa says.

He points to the Calvary scene reproduced above the main altar, with Christ, the two thieves, the Madonna, Mary Magdalene, Roman soldiers.

"Last week someone said it was worth coming from the States just to see it."

TRANSPORTATION: Braga is 35 miles northeast of Oporto. Transfer to train for Braga at Nine.

HOTELS: At Braga, *João XXI Hotel* is convenient; *Francfort* is medium-priced. At Bom Jesus do Monte, *Elevador* is luxurious; *Parque,* moderate.

FATIMA

A statue at the entrance to the paved esplanade at Fatima shows Paul VI kneeling, bareheaded, and praying as a pilgrim during his visit of pilgrimage on May 13, 1967, the 50th anniversary of the Apparitions. One million people crowded into the sanctuary area on the occasion of the Pope's visit. The esplanade is almost 8 football fields in length, and half that in width. Even so, sometimes it is not big enough to accommodate all the pilgrims.

The other end of the esplanade from Pope Paul's

statue is closed by a lacy white basilica which resembles a wedding-cake decoration. This impression is strengthened by its popularity with couples being married.

At the left side of the esplanade, a small, open-sided chapel marks the spot where 3 farm youngsters said they saw the Madonna at noon on May 13, 1917 while they were watching a flock of sheep. The young shepherds were Jacinta Marto, 7; her brother, Francisco, 9; and her cousin, Lucia dos Santos, 10.

Lucia, the only survivor of the 3 children, for years has been a nun, Sister Lucia of the Immaculate Heart, at the Carmelite Convent of St. Teresa in Coimbra. She described the experience this way:

"It was a Lady clothed in white and brighter than the sun, radiating a light more intense and clear than a crystal cup would be, were it filled with sparkling water and illuminated with burning sunlight."

The children told their parents that the Lady promised she would appear on the same day, the 13th, for each of the following 5 months.

On June 13, a month after the first Apparition, the annual parish fair was being held and the parents of the children wanted them to attend it. The youngsters protested that they had an appointment which they could not break even though the fair honored the patron of the parish, St. Anthony. About 30 persons were present when the children reported they had again seen the Lady. For the third Apparition on July 13, 1917, almost 5,000 persons packed the fields.

This was too much for the young subprefect, the administrative head of the district. He was ambitious and, like the government in Lisbon, anti-Catholic. The day before the fourth appearance of the Lady was expected, the subprefect kidnaped the 3 children. He kept them imprisoned for 2 days, threatening to dump them into a cauldron of boiling oil unless they changed their story about the Apparitions. When the children refused to alter a word, he at last let them free. Although missing their appointment with the Lady on Aug. 13, they saw her 6 days later, a Sunday, while they were with their sheep in the Valinhos Hills behind their home.

A throng of 70,000 persons was on hand on Oct. 13 for the sixth and last of the Apparitions. As usual only the 3 children reported seeing the Lady, but many in the crowd reported that something strange happened in the sky. The most typical description of the phenomenon was that "the sun started dancing."

Still there remained many unfriendly to the story of the Apparitions. After the sixth one, pilgrims erected on the site a wooden marker shaped like an inverted U. A few nights later it was destroyed, and the pieces carted away. To block pilgrims streaming to the site the government posted troops along the roads. This did not stop the pilgrims. They left the roads, and trudged through the fields.

If church authorities did not discourage the devotion, they did nothing to encourage it. Caution is always the church rule under such circumstances, but in this case the ecclesiastical officials were particularly prudent. They feared that the anti-Catholic government of Lisbon might use the Fatima events as an excuse for outlawing all forms of public religious worship. Immediately after the first Apparition was made known, the cardinal-primate of Portugal ordered the clergy of the diocese to maintain a hands-off policy. It was not until the fourth anniversary in October 1921 that the bishop of the diocese, Monsignor José Alves Correia da Silva, authorized the saying of a *low* Mass at the site on days of major pilgrimages. He waited another year before beginning the usually routine "canonical process" of naming a commission of 7 members to investigate and report on the events at Fatima.

The commission took 7 years for its inquiries, and the completion of a report. Bishop da Silva did not rush the report into print. He spent another year in going over it.

At last, 13 years after the sixth and final Apparition, Bishop da Silva made known the official view of the church. In a pastoral letter made public on Oct. 13, 1930 the bishop formally declared that the Apparitions which the 3 children had reported were "worthy of belief," and he gave official approval to the devotion to Our Lady of Fatima. There were more than 100,000 pilgrims at the shrine for the announcement.

Bishop da Silva headed the diocese until 1956, a total of 36 years, and in that long period never viewed his role as that of someone who was to carry out an intensive promotion campaign to develop the shrine. He told the priests of his diocese that if the Madonna wanted the world to know about Fatima, she would take care of the publicity program herself. He had the same view about money. If the Madonna wanted money for her shrine, she would provide him with it, and he would spend it. But he himself would not make any appeal for funds. That is still the policy at Fatima.

Although one of the most visited places in the world, Fatima is virtually as isolated as it was in 1917. The nearest railroad station is identified as *Fatima* but it is more than 15 miles from the sanctuary. Passengers arriving by train must wait until it pulls out so that they can literally walk across the tracks to the station exit. There is no underpass or overpass.

Farmers say that the oil produced from the olive trees around Fatima is the purest in all Portugal. Like wine, olive oil has its good years and its bad years. In good years, the people manage. In bad years, life is hard.

Twenty-five small hamlets depend on the parish church of Fatima. The shrine is 2 miles away. Ajustrel, where the 3 children were born and where their families still live, is 1 mile. Wheat and corn are ground at the windmill behind the parish church. The families of

Fatima make their own bread. For feasts they usually bake cornbread because it goes well with pork and sardines. The houses in Ajustrel are small stone buildings. The cisterns, which collect and hold rainwater, are topped by a cross so that God will protect the water and keep it drinkable.

Lucia's two sisters and the sister-in-law of the dead youngsters, Jacinta and Francisco, like the women of Fatima generally, cover their heads with large black scarves knotted gracefully at the back. Men still wear caps. A photograph of a half century ago shows Francisco wearing a *carapuço* cap, similar to a large black stocking, that flows from the back of the head. Youngsters can be seen today in the streets of Fatima with such caps.

The bodies of Jacinta and Francisco are buried in the basilica. Francisco died on Apr. 4, 1919 after becoming ill with the "flu." His sister Jacinta took sick the following year, and died on July 20. Her body, when it was exhumed on Sept. 13, 1935, was intact, while Francisco's had disintegrated.

An English-speaking community of cloistered Dominican nuns of the Perpetual Rosary was established at Fatima in the Marion Year of 1954 by a Philadelphian, Mother M. Louis Bertrand, O.P. She had been prioress of the congregation's convent at Camden, N.J.

Rafael Palacios, manager of the Blue Army's 250-bed hospice and international center, says that 43 religious congregations have already established houses around the shrine. He is in his 30s. He was born in the Holy Land during British Mandate times. His father, who died in 1947, was a Palestinian; his mother, Spanish. She died in Madrid recently. His wife was born in the Holy Land, too, and they have 2 children. His brother, Father Alfonse Salah Palacios, is at the Latin parish in the Zababdeh quarter of Jenin, south of Nazareth.

The Blue Army is a laymen's organization that was

founded in 1947 by Father Harold Colgan, a pastor in
Plainfield, N.J. When he became critically ill after the
Second World War he made a promise that if he recovered his health he would do everything he could to
"make known the conditions of Our Lady of Fatima for
the conversion of Russia." He was cured and a few
weeks later in a sermon to parishioners said.

"Atheists have developed a Red Army. . . . In this
parish let us be a Blue Army of Our Lady to fulfill her
conditions for their conversion."

Monsignor Colgan and his principal layman associate, John Haffert, gathered a million signed pledges by
1950. The international headquarters were opened at
Fatima 6 years later. Haffert is now international lay
delegate. Monsignor Colgan died in 1973.

"Today," Rafael says, "the Blue Army has twenty-
seven million members in fifty-two countries, and the
number keeps growing each year. There are one hundred thousand in South Vietnam alone.

"Every year the Blue Army takes what we call a
'pilgrim version' of the statue of Our Lady of Fatima
from place to place to propagate the message of
Fatima. I was on the trip last year to the Eucharistic
Congress in Melbourne. There were two hundred of us,
mostly Americans. They are the only ones who can
afford it. We did a round-the-world trip. Twenty-one
days. We took with us small statues, and rosaries, and
scapulars which we gave out.

"The Blue Army's statue always travels open, and it
has its own seat on the plane. In 1972 the statue wept
in New Orleans. That statue is in the American center
of the Blue Army at Washington, New Jersey. It has
been examined by scientists. The sculptor who made it
is still alive."

The Message of Fatima is not a single statement but
a number of declarations made to Jacinta, Francisco
and Lucia. Prayer and repentance are the basic themes.

For example, in the fourth Apparition, the Lady of Fatima asked that the Rosary be recited every day.

It fell upon Lucia to write down the details of the Apparitions, and she did this, amplifying on her account through the years. The children had spoken of a "secret." After becoming a nun Lucia disclosed part of the secret. Sister Lucia said the message had revealed the imminent deaths of Francisco and Jacinta and the part she would play, as survivor, in helping to spread the devotion to the Immaculate Heart. From the general public Sister Lucia (who is still alive) held back one part of the secret, and asked that it should not be disclosed before 1960 or her death—whichever came first. But Pope John, when 1960 arrived, said nothing and neither did his successor, Paul VI, on his visit to Fatima for the golden jubilee of the Apparitions. There is speculation that the undisclosed secret contains something sensational. Those close to the events of Fatima do not seem to think so, feeling that what has already been disclosed is sensational enough. For example, at the third Apparition the Lady of Fatima said:

"If my wishes are fulfilled, Russia will be converted, and there will be peace; if not, then Russia will spread her errors throughout the world, bringing new wars and persecutions of the church; the good will be martyred, and the Holy Father will have much to suffer; certain nations will be annihilated. But in the end my Immaculate Heart will triumph. The Holy Father will consecrate Russia to me, and she will be converted, and the world will enjoy a period of peace."

There is an intriguing association between Russia and Fatima. The October Revolution of the Bolshevists took place in 1917, the year of the Apparitions.

TRANSPORTATION: By train to Fatima; then, bus or taxi.
HOTELS: *Santa Maria* and *Tres Pastorinhos* are new.

Among the first-class religious institutions are the

Blue Army hospice, and *Beato Nuno,* named for Count Nuno Alvares Pereira, a general in the 14th-century battle of Aljubarrota, who gave all his property to the poor and became a Carmelite friar. It is operated by Carmelite Fathers.

PLACES OF INTEREST: The Santo Antonio grottoes, 3 miles from Fatima, are beautifully illuminated, although no wiring is in sight.

COIMBRA

The University of Coimbra, Portugal's intellectual center, was founded in 1290, and students follow ancient customs. Most customs apply to the male students because it is only in relatively recent times that women have been admitted. A black cape for men is traditional, and it is usually frayed and tattered. Some say each dangling strip represents a romance. Others ascribe the custom to the old days when all the property in a family went to the oldest son who, because of his wealth, did not have to go to the university. His younger brothers, on the other hand, were poor and needed an education. But they lacked the money to buy a new cape when the first one wore out. Colored ribbons hanging from bookbags of students tell what they are studying: red, law; violet, pharmacy; yellow, medicine; dark blue, philosophy and literature; brown, engineering; green and white, agronomy; and light blue and white, mathematics.

A main beauty spot is the Penedo da Saudade, a pine-filled bluff overlooking the Mondego River. Behind the Penedo da Saudade is the Carmelite Convent of St. Teresa where Sister Lucia (the survivor of the 3 children of Fatima) lives a cloistered life. In 1921, after the deaths of her 2 cousins, Lucia left Fatima and went into an orphanage. She was 14 then. Four years later she entered the Convent of the Sisters of St. Dorothy, and in 1928 made her vows as Sister Maria Lucia of Sorrows. She joined the Carmelites in 1948.

TRANSPORTATION: Coimbra is on the main Lisbon-Oporto rail line, and is 60 miles from Fatima.

HOTELS: *Bragança* and *Astoria* are quite comfortable.

SAGRES

Ships heading for, and leaving, the Mediterranean watch for the lighthouse at Cape St. Vincent on the southwest corner of Portugal. The adjoining finger of land, the Cape of Sagres, is known as "Portugal's Jerusalem." Prince Henry the Navigator assembled mapmakers and mathematicians at this barren point of land early in the 15th century and trained the sailors who explored the world for Portugal. Still clearly visible on the sunbaked ground is the elementary compass, the Rosa dos Ventos, which he traced out with stones.

TRANSPORTATION: Sagres is 175 miles south of Lisbon. There is air service to Lagos.

HOTELS: *Posada de Infante* and *Baleeira* are excellent.

LISBON

The capital of Portugal is known as the "Princess of the Tagus," after the river which flows past it into the Atlantic. Lisbon is as lovely as the loveliest princess. Its famous river is spanned by a 3,323-foot bridge, the longest in Europe.

Towering above the bridge itself from a nearby hill is a 350-foot statue of Christ the King, erected in 1959 after a nationwide subscription. Portugal's cardinal-primate had promised to raise a statue to honor Christ if the country was saved from involvement in the Second World War.

Along the shore, between the bridge and the Atlantic, is an extraordinary monument to the Discoverers, shaped like the prow of one of the caravels which carried Portugal's explorers around the world. Vasco da Gama is buried in the long, elaborately decorated Jerónimos Monastery which is just inland from the monument. Anchors, compasses, flowers from the tropics, and other articles linked to the explorations of Portuguese navigators have been laced into the ornamentation of the monastery in the exuberant Manueline architectural style which gets its name from Manuel I, the Discovery King. It was during his reign that the explorations, prepared and launched by Prince Henry the Navigator a century earlier, reached their zenith. There was a saddening nadir, too. Manuel I introduced the Inquisition and, in order to marry the daughter of Ferdinand and Isabella of Spain, he yielded to their demands that Portugal cease offering a haven to Jews.

The Corpo Santo Church was founded in 1659 by Irish Dominican friars who had to flee Ireland because of the religious persecutions. During the long "troubles" in Ireland, Corpo Santo served as the seminary for the Irish province of the Dominicans. In the religious persecutions of 1910 in Portugal, British diplomatic authorities intervened and protected the Irish church. It remained open while other churches were closed.

Opposite the Lisbon Cathedral is St. Anthony's Church, enshrining the house in which the Franciscan friar known as Anthony of Padua was born. At Mafra, outside Lisbon, King John V having received an answer to his prayers for an heir built a monastery to honor St. Anthony. It is the largest monument in the world dedicated to the Lisbon-born friar.

The Estrela Basilica was the first church in Europe dedicated to the Sacred Heart. It was built in 1780 by Queen Maria I as a thanksgiving offering for an heir.

In return for an answer to his prayers the average Portuguese makes a promise, *promessa,* to do something that in line with the means at his disposal is equivalent to the basilicas raised by kings and queens. The more difficult the *promessa,* he feels, the greater the chance his prayers will be answered. It will be more effective to walk to Fatima than to go there by bus, for instance. Saying the Rosary is fine, but even better is to say it kneeling. Lighting a candle helps, but if the candle is as tall as the petitioner the chances of receiving the favor are improved. Saints are often reminded of a sick child, or the afflicted leg of a family member, by the placing of a waxed replica of a child or a leg near the statue of the saint to whom one is praying. The saints whose aid is beseeched with wax images of arms, legs and other parts of the human body are known as *santos de cera* (wax saints). The shrine of Our Lady of Grace is filled with wax images.

TRANSPORTATION: Lisbon is an international air hub. There are overnight train connections to Paris and Madrid. First-class *Fuguete* express trains operate during the day between Lisbon and Oporto.

HOTELS: *Ritz* and *Sheraton* are among the finest. *Capitol* and *Presidente* are moderately priced.

POINTS OF INTEREST: Feasts of the popular saints on Avenida da Liberdade, outdoor celebrations—St. Anthony, June 12–13; St. John, June 24; St. Peter, June 29.

13
Scandinavia

THROUGH THE DARK MONTHS of winter, Scandinavians long for the coming of spring and of the Midnight Sun that never sets. The first of May ignites a merry, carefree outdoor season brightened by a sun which casts a wide swatch of daylight across much of Scandinavia, night after night, until it falls out of sight at the end of summer.

Many centuries ago the ancestors of contemporary Scandinavians waited for the sun, too, but for them its arrival touched off a great religious ceremony. The sun was at the center of the religion of ancient Scandinavia, and the places of worship can be identified today. At Östfold, near the Swedish border in the southeastern corner of Norway, rock carvings point to a farming community which existed there 3,000 years ago and focused its religious life on the sun.

On the eve of each first of May Swedes continue to celebrate Walpurgis Night, the sabbath of pagan times when witches gathered and reveled. Today the Swedes mark the feast by lighting fires on the mountains and along the lakes. The bonfires symbolically signal the coming of the sun. In olden times they were lighted to ward off evil spirits.

For most of the 4 centuries before the Reformation, Catholicism reached across Scandinavia, from the cathedral in Norway's Trondheim to a Dominican priory in Finland's Turku. In the 4 centuries since the Reformation Scandinavia has been almost solidly Lutheran. It was only in the past century that any other religion was tolerated. (One small exception was in Finland which, at one time politically linked to Russia and also physically close, has had an Orthodox community for several hundred years.)

Sweden allowed foreign diplomats to practice Catholicism openly, starting in 1783, but it was almost a century before the Swedish people themselves could do so. Even then they could not drop out of the state church without joining another Christian denomination. This restriction stayed on the books until 1951.

It was much the same all over Scandinavia. Permission was given for a Catholic church in Helsinki in 1860 for Polish soldiers in the Russian czar's army. But the Catholic Church itself did not resume its activity completely until after the independence of Finland in 1917, and the subsequent voting of religious-liberty laws 5 years later.

In the north birth rather than baptism makes one a Lutheran. Non-Lutheran parents of a newborn baby must make a formal report that the child is not a Lutheran.

The state church is supported by taxes assessed against the people in the same way and with the same obligation as state taxes. In general, Scandinavians can be freed from the church taxes by formally declaring that they no longer belong to the Lutheran Church.

In Stockholm it is estimated that as few as 1 percent of the Lutherans attend church—and, at that, generally at Christmas only. Elsewhere in Sweden and Scandinavia, regular church attendance is rarely higher than 2 or 3 percent. Christianity is more intact in Norway and Finland, which have had similar destinies, than in other countries of the North. They are ancient, farm-based civilizations which were urbanized and industrialized much later than in Denmark and Sweden, great powers in their time.

Catholicism shows few signs of making a comeback. The number of Catholics in some cities of the four Nordic countries can be counted on one's fingers. There are people who have never met a Catholic layman, much less a priest.

The role of Catholicism in Scandinavia's future was raised a half century ago with Sigrid Undset, Norway's Nobel Prize-winning writer, and a Catholic convert. When asked if her country would ever become Catholic again, she replied cautiously:

"I don't know about that. But what I do know is that the only Christians who will remain in Norway in a not too distant future will be Catholics."

DENMARK

Denmark's transition to Christianity is carved in runic stones at Jelling, near Vejle, on the island of Jutland. This is where Danish kings assembled their court 10 centuries ago. One stone in the group is carved with the oldest representation of Christ in all Scandinavia.

KING CANUTE

At the middle of Denmark on the island of Fyn, the capital city, Odense, is noted for two famous sons. Hans Christian Andersen, Denmark's favorite writer of fairy tales, was born in Odense in 1805. In 1186 King Canute, the patron saint of Denmark, was murdered there. King Canute, who was subsequently canonized as a saint, is buried in the crypt of St. Alban's Cathedral where he was slain by angry farmers who had chased him all the way from Jutland. He had called for a raid on England, and warriors responded from the farms of the kingdom. Ships were assembled in the fjords. But there was no agreement on who should command the raiding force. Time passed, and harvest time approached. Such raids by the Norsemen on the British Isles had been a tradition for centuries, but they were always carried out between planting and harvest time. King Canute was not popular with farmers, in the first place, because he was strict and his taxes took most of their money. The dragging-out of the raid was the last straw. The farmers jumped ship, sought out King Canute, and kept after him in his desperate flight to the south. Reaching Odense he took refuge in St. Alban's. The attacking farmers did not follow him into the sanctuary, but from outside the church they fired stones and arrows, killing him.

TRANSPORTATION: Odense is on main rail line from Copenhagen.

HOTELS: *Grand* is fine. *Ansgar* and *Odense* are mission hotels, and moderately priced.

Jutland remembered King Canute with a church built for him, and given his name, at Fredericia in the 17th century. It is the oldest of the post-Reformation (1537–1849) Catholic churches, and was allowed in Fredericia, "the town of Frederick, a free town established by King Frederick." To stimulate growth in areas which were dull and stagnant, or to spur cultural life and development it was customary for European rulers to create "free towns" which would welcome refugees— if they were gifted and had initiative—who might be barred in other parts of their kingdom because of political or religious beliefs. The post-Reformation ban on other faiths did not apply. Jesuits, Jews and monks were subject to the death penalty if they set foot in Denmark, but this did not affect new settlers of Fredericia. (Actually, the penalty was rarely enforced.) The Jesuits were allowed in Fredericia (and Copenhagen, too) because they had been invited by the king to serve as chaplains for the Danish professional army of Spanish, German and other mercenaries who were Catholics. King Canute's feast as a Catholic saint is observed on Jan. 19. When Father Knud Nielsen, a Jesuit in Denmark, is asked about King Canute's qualifications for sainthood, he says thoughtfully: "By today's standards he may not have been holy. He had several wives, for example. But he was just and good to his people."

TRANSPORTATION: Fredericia, is on main rail lines.
HOTELS: *Landsoldaten*, good. The mission hotel is *Ny Missionshotel*.

HOLY SPRINGS

In the post-Reformation period a holy woman named Kirsten who lived in the forest a half dozen miles north of Copenhagen one day happened upon a spring she had never seen before while she was out walking. She followed the path of water which flowed from the spring past centuries-old oak trees, and it led her back to her home in the forest. Word of the spring spread, and people began coming to see it for themselves. Its water was considered to have healing powers. As the number of pilgrims grew, vendors tagged along to sell sausages and biscuits. Bakken, the area in which the spring is located, developed into a center not only of pilgrimage but of family fun in the outdoors. Bakken is Denmark's oldest amusement park. (*Transportation:* S-train—the suburban railroad—from any station in Copenhagen to Klampenborg).

Even before Kirsten discovered the spring at Bakken, springs were associated with Catholic pilgrimages. Until the Reformation there were more than 100 holy springs in the kingdom of Denmark, all identified by religious names. Most were dedicated to the Madonna, but St. Michael and St. Anne were also popular as patrons. Karup, in the heart of Jutland, is now known mostly as the site of a NATO base but centuries ago its spring was a major point of pilgrimage.

AARHUS

A spring named after St. Nicholas is near the harbor in Aarhus, Denmark's second city, a cheery seaport on the east coast of Jutland. In all Danish ports there is invariably a chapel or church dedicated to St. Nicholas of Bari (originally of Myra, Turkey), the patron of seamen. A St. Nicholas church had been in Aarhus but after it was assigned to the Dominicans, the friars rededicated it to the Madonna as *Vor Frue Kirke* (The Church of Our Lady). It was built around A.D. 1300. In its crypt is the oldest vaulted chapel in Scandinavia. St. Clement's Cathedral (now Lutheran) dates from the 13th century. It has a 300-foot nave, the longest in Denmark, and its baptismal font is 5 centuries old.

TRANSPORTATION: There is air and ferry service to Aarhus from Copenhagen. Rail travel is not practicable.

HOTELS: *Atlantic, Marselis* and *Mercur* are tops. The mission hotels are *Ansgars* and *Merci*.

NEW PILGRIMAGES

Once a year, during May, Jutlanders journey to the ruins of the Cistercian monastery at Øm, 20 miles southwest of Aarhus. In the Middle Ages Øm was the high place of Cistercian life, and the monastery surrounded by lakes was known to the monks as Cara Insula (Beloved Island). King Christian III demolished Cara Insula during the Reformation and used its bricks for his nearby residence at Skanderborg and for roads in the area.

Another new pilgrimage route is to the Benedictine Monastery of Our Lady (*Vor Frue Kloster*) at Aasebakken, between Elsinore and Copenhagen.

COPENHAGEN

The university student in Copenhagen's Vartov Church, where Denmark's great preacher and hymnwriter N. F. S. Grundtvig was minister for 33 years in the 19th century, agrees that it is unusual for a pulpit to be installed directly above the main altar.

"In Sweden I visited one thousand five hundred churches, and saw six with pulpits located that way," he says. "And maybe of the eight hundred to nine hundred churches I visited in Denmark, I saw five with such pulpits. I visit churches when I'm traveling on my own, either by bike or car. Parish churches are handsome, and they're good places to make an interlude in your journey. You get fresh air as you sit in your car, and you see some beautiful things. Most Danish churches go back to medieval times and that means beautiful buildings. In any part of the country—all over Scandinavia, for that matter—you have fine parish churches. If you are on a long journey, you should make a few stops along the way."

He is one of a dozen university students living in the Vartor Church complex. The church and related buildings face one another across a large courtyard. The voices of small children playing in the courtyard mingle with the sounds from the church where someone is practicing the organ for the coming Sunday's services. At the center of the yard is an immense statue of N. F.

S. Grundtvig, dressed in his ministerial robes and kneeling as he draws water from the Spring of Baptism.

The youth identifies himself as Andreas Hens—"the name is like female grown-up chickens," he says in good English. He is tall and wears black-rimmed glasses. He smokes a cigar that is stuffed in the thick bowl of a meerschaum pipe. "It's the only way to smoke cigars. The pipe is no good for smoking tobacco." He lives in a ground-floor room, next door to the church, and apologizes that it is so cluttered. Books, sketches, and enlarged photos are all over the place, including the desk. The window is completely bare but a black cloth, heaped on a chair, obviously serves for a drape at night and a darkroom curtain whenever he is developing or printing his photos. The photo-enlarger rests on a chair near the desk. The room is 9 by 15 feet. A bathroom is at one end. He goes into the space at the other end of the room and returns with two Carlsbergs. The wall photo of a log, he says, he took in a parish church in Sweden. "You can tell from the texture of the wood, and the gnarled lines, that it is seventeenth century." He looks over at another wall photo which has caught a white swan in a generally agitated manner as its wings reach for flight. "I had to wait a half hour to catch her in that mood of motion and emotion."

Pages for the master's thesis he is working on are stacked on the desk. "I will probably teach history, but that depends on whether my professors say I am able." His thesis deals with the way parish priests several centuries ago were used by the government to gather data about their area, historical as well as current information concerning the farmers—what they were planting, how many animals they owned, and so on.

"This information-gathering system started with a rescript of the Danish government of August 11, 1622. It asked bishops to have their parish priests report on what ancient documents they had, if there were any stones in the parish with runic lettering, what is said locally about ancient places such as fountains. It also asked for a general description of the parish, and the number of farmers and other inhabitants. A writer in Copenhagen would then put all this information together. In 1781 the government issued the first general description of the country, the *Pontoppidan*, the Danish Atlas, based on the reports from the parishes."

About 200 persons attend Sunday morning services at the Vartov Church. The simplicity of the interior is accented by the wooden pews. The only relief to the drab green decor is the replica of a 3-masted wooden schooner which hangs over the center aisle. Wooden boats are in most Danish churches, Andreas says.

The Vartov Church complex has evolved from the Holy Ghost Hospital which Catholic Bishop Jens Krag of Roskilde established along with a monastery in A.D. 1296. The Holy Ghost Church, now Lutheran, still exists at Amagertorv 22, a section of Copenhagen's "walking street," the Strøget. Following the Reformation, in 1536, the hospital was independently supported and early in the 17th century was moved ½ mile away to the Vartov estate (across from the present Town Hall) which had belonged to the astronomer Tycho Brahe. The name remained Holy Ghost Hospital, but people began calling it and its new church by the name "Vartov." By the time Grundtvig was assigned as minister to the Vartov Church in 1839, the hospital had been made into an asylum for 450 old and feeble people.

"Grundtvig was progressive and therefore unwanted in the public churches," Andreas says. "The king thought by sending him here to preach to old women, he would not be so dangerous. But instead of dying away, Grundtvig became more popular than ever. People came from all over town to hear him, and the hymns that he wrote here were sung all over the country."

Grundtvig was born at Udby in southern Sealand,

and died in Copenhagen in 1872. He is buried at Køge, an old market town with a beautiful church, 23 miles south of Copenhagen. The burial site is atop a hill in a wooded area 1½ miles from town. The only others buried on the same hill are his 3 wives and 2 children. It is not a cemetery. His second wife owned a country home at Køge. (*Transportation:* Køge is a 1-hour train or bus ride from Copenhagen.)

On another hill, this one in the northern part of Copenhagen, a memorial church honors Grundtvig. It is in the Bispegjerg (Bishop's Mountain) district. (*Transportation:* Buses 16 and 19 from Town Hall Square. Ask to be let off at the Grundtvig *kirke*.)

Relics of St. Ansgars, the patron of Copenhagen, are in the pro-cathedral named after him at 64 Bredgade, a few blocks from the royal palace. On the first floor of the rectory (behind the church, at the right) exhibits in a museum depict the life of the Catholic community in Copenhagen since 1754.

TRANSPORTATION: Copenhagen is on the main air route between the rest of Scandinavia and of Europe.

HOTELS: Various organizations associated with the Lutheran Church operate in Denmark, Norway and Sweden dozens of moderately priced, comfortable and well-furnished "mission hotels." They are fine places to stay. Religious services are held in most a few times a week, but no one is required, or even asked, to attend them. A number have cafeterias or restaurants that serve low-priced family-style meals of high quality. The biggest mission hotel in Copenhagen is *Missionhotellet*. Names of other mission hotels can be obtained from the Sekretariat, Danmarks Missionshoteller, 2 Nørrebro, Sønderborg, Denmark. Other hotels are the *Angleterre*, aristocratic, excellent, across from the royal theater; *Sheraton*, beautifully furnished; *Palace*, conveniently located in Town Hall Square.

POINTS OF INTEREST: Roskilde, a traditional burial place of Danish rulers and one of the country's oldest towns. The *Domkirke* (cathedral church) at Roskilde is 8 centuries old. (By train, 19 miles from Copenhagen.)

SWEDEN

The people of modern-day Sweden are extraordinary for many reasons. One is their religious attitude. The Gallup Poll surveyed a number of nations some years ago in regard to belief in the existence of God. Of the countries surveyed Sweden placed lowest in the poll. Noting this, the Swedish Institute in a publication of July 1972 made the following additional points:

It should be noted, however, that the population has a broad range of generally benign attitudes toward Christianity. At one end of this spectrum there are those with a vague feeling for Christianity as related to human values which one would wish to see preserved. At the other end there are those with a deeper personal commitment. Thus, in a poll in 1969, no fewer than 73 percent of the parents would like to see their children receive a "Christian upbringing," but only 13 per cent declared that they would want their children to become believing Christians.

Sweden was one of the last among the countries of Europe to accept Christianity. Missionaries arriving in Sweden from England and Germany discovered that a heathen temple was still standing at Uppsala. It was at Uppsala, too, that one of Sweden's first Christian martyrs died. That was not until well into the 12th century when King Erik was killed in a battle at Uppsala. Architects and sculptors were brought from France around the end of the 13th century to build an appropriate cathedral in Stockholm as a shrine for this Swedish king-saint who is said to have brought Christianity to Finland. A 14th century Swedish saint, Birgitta (or Bridget), founded a religious congregation of women who, known as Birgittines or Bridgettines. St. Bridget and her nuns made Vadstena a lakeside town in south-central Sweden, the spiritual center of the country in the Middle Ages. All things considered, it probably still is today.

VADSTENA

St. Bridget was born in 1304. She belonged to a noble family and married a Swedish prince. After some years of marriage, and 8 children, Bridget and her husband agreed to separate. The prince entered the Cistercian Order of monks and died in 1344 when Bridget was 40 years old. At the time, Sweden was ruled by King Magnus and Queen Blanka. King Magnus moved around his kingdom a great deal, and on the eastern shore of Lake Vättern he possessed a large estate known as Vadstena. It was while serving in the court of King Magnus at the Vadstena Palace that Bridget received the first of a series of visionary revelations. From these visions, which she reported to her confessor, Bridget filled out details of the congregation of nuns she was to found, the Order of St. Saviour, and the design of their abbey. She related her vision to King Magnus and in 1346 he and the queen made a gift of the Vadstena domain to the future abbey. The first followers of Bridget took up residence in the manor vacated by the Swedish rulers.

"We in the Protestant Church of Sweden do not pray to saints," Mrs. Göran Grefbäck says. "We admire them. We take them as models. We believe Birgitta was a modern woman."

Mrs. Grefbäck is the wife of the Lutheran pastor of the Kloster Kyrkan (The Big Church) which is the original abbey of the Bridgettines, and St. Bridget's remains are preserved in a chest there. When Catholic nunneries were suppressed by the Reformation in the 16th century the Bridgettines left Vadstena. When they returned in 1930, the ancient palace which had been their first convent was a hospital and their abbey church, Kloster Kyrkan, was still in the hands of the Lutherans. The Bridgettines bought an old house and some land near St. Bridget's medieval abbey, and on July 23, 1973, celebrating the 600th anniversary of her death, they opened a new church, convent and guesthouse. A dozen Bridgettines are in the newly established community at Vadstena.

"There are many religious groups here," the wife of the Lutheran pastor says. "The Greek Orthodox were here till lately. There's a Protestant group of nuns dressed in blue called the Daughters of Mary. Their convent is near the Big Church. The Baptists, the Salvation Army, the Philadelphia Congregation (Swedish Pentecostalists) are here, too."

The name of the minister's wife is Birgit. "Birgitta is a popular name in Sweden," she says, "and many variations of it are used."

She is tall, strong in appearance, active, handsome, blonde. She and her husband Göran met as university students at Uppsala. He was studying theology; she, to be a teacher. For 5 years (1957–62), they lived in Philadelphia where he had been assigned as a minister for Scandinavian seamen. They have 3 children. The oldest is a young woman of 20. The two boys are Pieter, 8, and Michael, 13. She agrees that Pieter will be tall. "He was a tall baby," she recalls.

They live in a large 2-story frame-and-brick house. Without, apparently, even giving it a second thought they maintain an Open Door.

"Come in," she calls out hurriedly, when a total stranger rings the doorbell. "I'm on the phone to Stockholm."

The entrance room, next to the kitchen, looks like a

busy office, rather than a formal parlor for receiving callers. A wooden chest, with dozens of compartments, is at the end of the room near the kitchen. It is a ready archive for church bulletins. Two desks are back to back, with chairs on each side of them. One imagines the minister and his wife working together across the desks. As she talks on the phone Pieter sketches fences, animals and stairways on a pad.

Mrs. Grefbäck happily shows off her house. The kitchen is large and high-ceilinged. It is American-style —or is it Swedish-style? One side of the room is solid with built-in cupboards and tables. Refrigerator, electric stove and dishwasher are on the other side. The dining-living section is L-shaped, and immense. The long dining-room table, she says, serves both for family meals and for parish conferences. The living area is furnished with two bulky white sofas that are casually set at a right-angle. There is still plenty of space to spare for a Colonial-style chest brought back from America. She points out that the double-set of handles seem to indicate that there are two drawers at the top. When she tugs on the handles she shows that it is only a single drawer without even a middle divider. "That's how they make things now," she says. An antique Swedish inlaid chest of drawers was a gift from her mother-in-law. She looks around the living-dining area, and says: "There's plenty of room." Upstairs are all the bedrooms.

A 2-story building, known as the Bishop's House, is in the yard. It was built by Bishop Henrik Tidemansson in 1470 and used by him when he made his visits to the Abbey of the Bridgettines, and to the monastery of monks that had also been established in Vadstena.

"The bishop must have been a modern man, a real commuter," she says. "His house is almost the way it was. No one has restored it. King Johan III gave the house to whoever is rector of the Big Church, so right now we own a bishop's house, but don't know what to do with it. You can see the feet of animals on the floor, who walked in the brick before it dried. There is a heating system, a medieval type of thing. You can see holes where hot air was led into the room, and it came from a fire they had some place else. They led the hot air through pipes into the room, and then covered the holes when it was warm enough. It's great fun to see how they did things like this so long ago."

Two rooms are on each floor. The house is fitted with some pieces of furniture, and is not locked.

"Guides are always taking people in here in the summer," she says. "We have used it for one or two parties, as it is ours for the time being. But we have nothing against people walking in and out."

About 200,000 persons visit Vadstena each year. Big crowds come between July 19 and July 25, Bridget's Week, when the saint's feast is celebrated.

Pastor Grefbäck appears briefly. He has been at one parish meeting, and is headed for another. He is tall, lighthaired, not too heavy. He gives his wife a peck on the cheek and pats 8-year-old Pieter before rushing away. Mrs. Grefbäck thinks of her other son, Michael. She smiles.

"Mike is an American. He was born in Philadelphia. He is the only one in the family who can be president of the United States."

TRANSPORTATION: Vadstena is about halfway between Stockholm and Hälsingborg. There is no rail service to Vadstena. The nearest train station is Motala. Excursion boats on the Göta Canal stop at Vadstena.

HOTELS: A guesthouse for 40 persons has been installed in the ancient palace of King Magnus. The Bridgettine Sisters also operate a guesthouse. The *Hotel Solgården* is small, moderately priced.

POINTS OF INTEREST: The courthouse, the oldest in

Sweden—a judge comes from Motala a few times a year to hold court in it; Omberg, a mountain considered sacred from pagan times; Dagsmosse Bog, an excavated site of a Stone Age settlement; the Rök Stone, in church at Rök, the most celebrated runestone in Scandinavia; ruins of the 12th-century Cistercian abbey at Alvastra.

ISLAND OF CHURCHES

Gotland probably had more churches per capita than any other inhabited island of the Old World. In the Middle Ages, 98 churches were constructed. Gotland lies in the Baltic, off the southern coast of Sweden, and is the home of 60,000 people. Its 300-mile shoreline is a frame for dozens of species of wild-growing orchids, for the strange marine stacks formed by the sea over thousands of years, and for the natural refuges used by its famous narrow-billed diving guillemots. Gotland's geographical position, on a direct line between Russia and the European continent, made it a prosperous, cultured crossroads in Hanseatic times, and thus it could not only build churches but fill them with stained glass, paintings, sculptures of wood and marble, and other art works. Its cultural history literally vanished from sight during Reformation times when murals in the churches were covered over with whitewash. But this did not prove to be the calamity that it seemed at the time. When the religious climate in Sweden turned milder, the whitewash was removed from the walls, revealing a superb collection of religious paintings of the Middle Ages. The capital city of Visby is a favorite with visitors, and describes itself as a "holiday town with medieval atmosphere and modern comfort."

St. Maria is the only one of the medieval churches of Visby which still has a roof. *St. Nicholas* was the church of the Dominican friary established about A.D.

1230, the first one in Scandinavia. Although in ruins, St. Nicholas comes to life each summer when it is used as the setting for a mystic pageant opera presented in the Visby Festival. The opera is named after Petrus de Dacia, its protagonist, who was a prior at the Dominican friary in the 13th century and is considered to be Sweden's first author. *Helige Ande* (Holy Spirit) has an unusual 2-story form, with a towerlike nave. It was started at the end of the 12th century.

TRANSPORTATION: Öland is now linked to the mainland by the longest bridge in Europe: 3½ miles. In summer passenger vessels traveling between Helsinki and Travemuende (West Germany) call at Gotland. Air service to Visby is available from more than 100 points in Sweden.

HOTELS: *Snäckgärdsbaden* is the leading hotel at Visby; *Donnersplatz* is moderately priced.

LAKE SILJAN

Each village along this beautiful lake of the Dalarna region, 200 miles northwest of Stockholm, has a Maypole wreathed in flowers. Around the village Maypoles merrymakers dance in a rite going back to pagan times on the first of May. Maypoles are not unusual in Sweden, which celebrates the first of May with great verve and enthusiasm. What makes the Lake Siljan Maypoles different is that they remain standing, and decorated, all year around. In olden times villagers rowed across the lake to church. Today many villagers still row to church on Sunday. In July there is a spirited rowing competition among the villagers, who are mostly farmers and artisans, and the contestants represent the various village churches. The Lake Siljan villagers dance around their Maypoles again at Midsummer, the feast of pagan origin which marks the longest day of the year and is the time when nature looks its best. At

Leksand, at the southern end of Lake Siljan, a Bible-based allegorical play is presented each July in the open air. Note: In 1896 the townspeople of Nås seemingly had the same idea at once of emigrating to the Holy Land. Most of them followed through on their idea, journeying there together. Some remained. Each June/July an open-air outdoor religious play recalls this mass pilgrimage of the past century.

ANCIENT CHURCHES

Churches with deep historic and cultural roots are to be found in all parts of Sweden. Among the oldest and most noteworthy are:

Dalby (*Skåne*): Built A.D. 1060; oldest stone church in Sweden.

Hemmesjö (*Småland*): 12th-century church; murals.

Husaby (*Västergötland*): According to tradition Erik, Sweden's first Christian king (and saint) was baptized here. The first episcopal see was established here. Ancient tombs.

Kiruna (*Lappland*): Built early in this century in the northern region occupied by the Lapps. Sweden has 10,000 Lapps. Till well into the 19th century they had remained pagan, using drums and magical signs in their religious rites. Now all have been Christianized. The Church of Sweden conducts religious services for the Lapps in summer at Saltuluokta and Staloluokta.

Lund (*Skåne*): The 12th-century cathedral is the finest example of Romanesque style in Scandinavia.

Roslagsbro (*Uppland*): A celebrated 13th-century image of Erik, the Swedish saint-king, is in the church.

St. Olof (*Skåne*): A 12th-century chapel honoring Olav, the Norwegian king-saint.

Sjösås (*Småland*): A 13th-century Calvary group.

Skånela (*Uppland*): A 16th-century Madonna statue in a Romanesque-style 12th-century church.

Södra Råda (*Värmland*): A 13th-century wooden church.

Uppsala: The cathedral is the outstanding example in Scandinavia of French Gothic architecture. Has shrine of Erik, Sweden's king-saint.

STOCKHOLM

The network of islands is reminiscent of Venice; the cosmopolitan quality, of Paris; the contemporary, ball-bearing-smooth life-style, of San Francisco; the cultural interest and history, of Rome; the memories of great empire, of Vienna. Stockholm has many sides. Winter or summer, whether its waters reflect the sun or are frozen solid, Stockholm is the loveliest city of the north.

Its cathedral (*Storkyrkan*) was built in the 13th century, and later enlarged. Among its art works is a sculpted wood group of life-sized figures representing St. George and the Dragon. The Riddarholm Church, built originally as a Franciscan friary in the 13th century, has been the burial church for Swedish kings for the past 300 years.

TRANSPORTATION: Stockholm is 350 miles from Helsingborg. There is an extensive rail and air network within the country. Rail service is very good. Passenger-car ferries connect Sweden with Denmark at Helsingborg and Malmö. There are ship connections with Helsinki and northern ports of Western Germany.

HOTELS: Moderate-priced, comfortable mission hotels are throughout Sweden. Mission hotels in Stockholm are *Excelsior, City, Gamla Stan, Tegnérlunden, Ansgars,* and *EFS*. In various regions there are mission *pensionat* (pensions). For information on Sweden's mission hotels, write Kristliga Hotellföreningen i Sverige, Bäckgat. 7, 582 45 Linköping, Sweden. The Hjelmseryd Stiftelsen (foundation) has a guesthouse, a church and rooms for retreat at Gamla Hjelmseryd, a small village in Småland, north of Växjö. (The Swedish-American of the Year is honored on Minnesota Day each August in Växjö. A House of Immigrants, where genealogical research can be made, and a Glass Museum are at Växjö.) Other hotels in Stockholm are *Sheraton, Park, Apollonia* and *Grand* —all excellent. *Castle, Domus, Foresta, Oden* and *Wellington* are somewhat less expensive.

POINTS OF INTEREST: The royal palace (the state, Bernadotte and guest apartments can be visited); Tower of the City Hall; Skansen, the open-air museum with original houses and artifacts of Sweden of another day; the 17th-century *Wasa,* a man-of-war that sank in harbor on commissioning and was later salvaged; the seaside resort of Saltsjöbaden, offering a pleasant viewpoint of the archipelago (less than ½ hour by train; 12 miles by highway); Gripsholm Castle, a historic landmark, with important portrait collection (open June to August only; boat from quayside at City Hall; by highway, 45 miles); Vaxholm, a particularly attractive village of the archipelago (1 hour by boat; 25 miles by highway); Skokloster Castle, built by Field Marshal Wrangel, a military figure of the Thirty Years' War (45 miles by highway). NOTE: In the Swedish language, the letters Å, Ä and Ö come at the end of the alphabet.

NORWAY

An argument as old as the mountains ringing the Norwegian fjords continuously engages Norway and Austria. Each country claims to be the birthplace of skiing. There is no argument, however, that Norwegians are outdoors, sports-oriented people who like to ski when there is snow—and some can be found somewhere in Norway most of the year—or at least be out in the air. This is the explanation usually given for the low church attendance. Only 3 percent of the members of the State Church of Norway (Lutheran) participate in Sunday religious services regularly. An old aphorism says that Norwegians prefer to sit on a mountain and think of God, to sitting in a church and thinking of a mountain. The proliferation of transistor radios has blunted the mountain-church confrontation. Religious services are broadcast on the radio on Sunday mornings. Norwegians heading for the mountains take their transistors with them.

TRONDHEIM

Trondheim is one of the 3 largest cities in Norway, with a population of 130,000, and it has the third largest fjord, stretching 77 miles from mouth to head. Trondheim also has the oldest point of pilgrimage in Norway. This city on the west coast of northern Norway was founded a few years before A.D. 1,000 by the Viking king Olav Tryggvason, who because of his successful efforts to replace the pagan religion with Christianity became honored as a saint. From Karlstad, the capital of the present Swedish province of Värmland, which is at the mouth of the estuary where the Klarälven (the biggest river in Sweden) empties into the Vänern (the biggest lake in Sweden), pilgrims in the Middle Ages traced a route to the grave of the holy Olav. The route of the medieval pilgrims—in Swedish, *Pilgrimsleden*—is still identifiable and, what's more, followed. From Karlstad it follows the Klarälven, along Highway 62, to Stöllet (Sweden) and then along Highway 235 north to Långflom, at the Swedish-Norwegian border. In Norway, the Pilgrim's Route continues north along Highway 26 through Nybergsund and Sølen to Trondheim, passing through moors and lowlands, valleys and peaks.

Trondheim's Nidaros Cathedral was built around the original shrine of the saint-king early in the Middle Ages. The cathedral replaced a smaller church started by Olav's son, Magnus the Good, and completed in the middle of the 11th century. The cathedral is the largest medieval building in Scandinavia. It was begun in 1150, and is a combination of Norman and late English Gothic style. Olav the Holy is Norway's patron saint (and also patron of the Swedish island of Gotland), and Trondheim's annual festival is fixed at the cathedral named after him. Trondheim was the chief episcopal see during the Middle Ages. There are still memories of pagan times. Munkholmen, one of the islands in the Trondheim fjord, was used by the pagans as a site of executions. Sometime after King Olav's arrival, a monastery was built on it. The monastery on the pagan island was probably the first in Norway. In Reformation times the monastery was made into a fortress and its basement was used as a prison. The island is now a popular bathing beach. (Hourly boat service.)

TRANSPORTATION: Trondheim is served by air, rail and sea from Oslo and Bergen.

HOTELS: There are two mission hotels in Trondheim, *Trøndelag* and, somewhat smaller, *Norrøna*. The chief hotels of Trondheim are *Ambassadeur Sjømann-shjemmet*.

POINTS OF INTEREST: The remains of an early 13th-century Cistercian monastery are on the island of Tautra, called the "kitchen garden" of the Trondheim fjord. A 12th-century church identifies the battlefield at Stiklestad where King Olav defeated an army of farmers in 1030. Each summer a pageant recalls the historic event. The Stiftsgarden, a royal residence in Trondheim, is northern Europe's largest wooden building.

BERGEN

Another Olav, King Olav Kyrre, founded Bergen, the second city of Norway. It has a population of 215,000. Bergen was founded A.D. 1070, and about 70 years later St. Mary's Church (*Mariakirken*) was consecrated. It still exists, and on Thursday evenings during the summer (roughly, mid-June to the end of August) there are services of the Norwegian State Church in English. Bergen was the home of composer Edvard Grieg for more than 20 years.

Two churches, St. Jørgen and Fantoft, present special aspects of Norway's religious life. St. Jørgen was the church for the old St. George's Hospital which was founded in the Middle Ages for lepers, although present buidings are only a few centuries old. Norwegian doctors traditionally have devoted their lives to aid lepers and to provide something to comfort those afflicted with leprosy while they hunt for the eventual cure.

STAVE CHURCHES

Fantoft, the other notable church of Bergen, represents a style of construction that is almost exclusively Norwegian, and in any case is not found outside of Scandinavia. Fantoft, built in the middle of the 12th century (and restored a number of times) is a wooden church made of staves, or struts. The staves served as pillars which rested on a wood or stone base. In the Middle Ages nearly 1,200 stave churches were built. By the early part of the past century only 100 or so survived. Today there are less than 3 dozen. Stave churches also were built in Sweden and Denmark, but not to the same extent as in Norway.

None of the original stave churches of Bergen exists any longer. The Fantoft stave church was actually

moved to Bergen from the Sogne Fjord area. The Sogne
Fjord is north of Bergen, and its banks were the
foundation for a number of stave churches, including
one at Urnes which was built in the 12th century. The
Urnes church is small, actually tiny. Scholars believe
that the pagans worshiped the gods Tor and Odin in
the stave churches. Christian bishops, on their arrival,
decided it would be more effective to retain the old and
familiar places of worship while changing the religion of
the people. The stave churches of the pagans, therefore,
were brought into the Christian sphere.

TRANSPORTATION: Bergen is a main air center. It is on
the main rail line to Oslo. Steamers sail to Newcastle
and Cuxhaven in England, and to Amsterdam. There
is hydrofoil service to Stavanger and Haugesund. By
highway it is about 300 miles from Oslo.

HOTELS: The mission hotels are *Terminus*, *Bibelskolens*
and *Skandia*. Other comfortable Bergen hotels are
Hatleberg and *Fantoft*.

POINTS OF INTEREST: Norwegian composer Edvard
Grieg lived in Bergen for 22 years on Nordås Lake.
He and his wife Nina are buried at the villa called
Troldhaugen. One of Europe's finest aquariums is on
Nordness peninsula. (Bus No. 6.)

OSLO

Sometime after the death in 1047 of Magnus the
Good, the son of Olav the Holy, a market town was laid
out at what is now Oslo. This was a strategic seaport in
the power struggle between the men of Norway and the
Danes and it primarily provided the chief inland link to
Trondheim, the ruling point. King Harald Sigurdson
made Oslo the eastern seat of his kingdom, and built a
royal residence at the mouth of the Alna River. During
the reign of his successor, King Olav Kyrre, Oslo be-

came a cathedral city in the latter part of the 11th century. The present cathedral (*Domkirken*) is from the 1690s. Oslo of the Middle Ages was built mostly of wood. Each succeeding fire destroyed old landmarks, and produced a new architectural style. The original St. Hallvard Cathedral was erected on a hill at the edge of town. On Aug. 17, 1624 it was caught up in the big fire which burned for 3 days and wiped out the town. The cathedral's ruins can be seen in the Old Town. Gamle (Old) Aker Church, built of stone about 1100, has survived fire and time, and is still in use as a parish church. It is the oldest stone church in Scandinavia. Today's *Bispegata* (Bishop's Street) is the successor of the episcopal roadway of 8 centuries ago. The newest church project in the Oslo area has been the construction of a Catholic chapel and laymen's center, *Maria-holm* (Mary's Farm), on Lake Øyeren, 30 miles east of Oslo. The center is used for conferences, seminars and retreats, and has 36 two-bed rooms for guests.

TRANSPORTATION: There are overnight ferries to Danish ports. Oslo is 9 hours from Stockholm by train; about the same from Copenhagen; 4½ hours from Gothenburg.

HOTELS: The mission hotels in Oslo include *Ansgars* and *Det Nye*. Other Oslo hotels are *Scandinavia*, near the royal palace, and the newest; *Continental* and *Viking*, traditional and excellent.

POINTS OF INTEREST: Ruins of a 12th-century Cistercian monastery (plundered and burned in 1532) at Hove-døya; the Viking Ships House, with 3 ancient vessels raised from the Oslo Fjord.

FINLAND

Christianity is a relative newcomer in Finland, not reaching here till the middle of the 12th century. The

Finns themselves are newcomers in the area. They can be grouped with the Scandinavians of Norway, Sweden and Denmark in a geographic sense—all are neighbors along the Arctic Circle—and possibly in a political sense, since Finland for centuries was integrated into the Swedish kingdom. The origin of the Finns is as obscure as a winter evening in Lappland. Everything about them, starting with their language, is different from the counterpart in Norway, Denmark and Sweden. Across the Gulf of Finland in the Soviet republic of Estonia young women keep up on the latest news and styles of fashion by watching Finland's television and listening to its radio. The people of Estonia understand Finnish. There is also a similarity between Finnish and Hungarian. It is thought that the people of Finland migrated to their present home from western Asia about A.D. 1,000, or a bit earlier. They brought with them a pantheistic religion which was well developed. It concentrated on nature. There were gods for the countless lakes and endless forests, for the sea at their doorstep which freeezs over solid in the bitterly cold winters. There was a superior god, as well. The religion of the early-day Finns was abruptly changed in 1155 by a Crusade-type incursion from Sweden. St. Henrik, archbishop of Uppsala, led with the king of Sweden the first of three crusades. Sweden extended Christianity's borders, and its own, to encompass Finland. Until early in the 19th century, Finland was part of Sweden. Freed of Sweden on the west, it was annexed by czarist Russia on the east. Finally in 1917 Finland arrived at independence.

About 93 percent of the Finns today are Evangelical Lutherans; 1.3 percent, Orthodox. The Lutheran and Orthodox cathedrals are on the waterfront at Helsinki.

Finland's Catholics have more priests per capita than any other country in Europe: 1 for every 135 laymen, or 8 times the European average. The impressive ratio is due to the small number of Catholics, about 2,700. St. Bridget's is the only Catholic church in Turku (capital in Swedish times), a city of 150,000 inhabitants. Only 140 of the 250 members of St. Bridget's parish live in Turku. The others live as far off as 100 miles. The number of native-born Catholic priests in all Finland since the Reformation can be counted on one hand—3. Dominican friars established a friary in Helsinki early in the 13th century. The Dominicans are active once more. One of the native-born priests is a Dominican.

TRANSPORTATION: Helsinki, the capital, is connected by air with New York, and with the Scandinavian and other European capitals. Daily ferry service between Helsinki/Turku and Stockholm; somewhat less frequent service to Copenhagen and Travemuende (West Germany).

HOTELS: *Inter-Continental* is tops; *Helsinki,* moderate priced.

POINTS OF INTEREST: Hameenlinna, birthplace of Sibelius.

RUSSIA

Day-long excursions are made from Helsinki to Tallinn, capital of Estonia, in summer. Chance to visit Russian Orthodox churches. No visa is necessary.

ICELAND

The sagas of Gunnar and other early-day Icelandic heroes are read, and remembered, all over this island country in the North Atlantic between Norway and Greenland. It is possible to make a saga tour of Iceland following the steps of legendary heroes. Such a tour would include the Saga of Bishops, and lead to Skálholt where Christianity first took root in Iceland. One of the churchmen told about in the old sagas is Bishop Pall Jónsson, who was considered the most cultured of all early bishops. His stone tomb was unearthed not long ago, and it is in the crypt of the modern memorial church that has been built at Skálholt.

TRANSPORTATION: Air service from, to, and within Iceland is good.

14

Spain

꙳

THE USE OF THE TERM "Catholic Spain" can be logical. The Rosary is recited on the national radio of Spain each day. On Good Friday, offices, shops and factories are shut tight. This is particularly impressive when one realizes that well into the afternoon on Good Friday even the Vatican post offices in St. Peter's Square are open, and in Rome itself there is business as usual all day.

Like most thumbnail descriptions, the term "Catholic Spain" needs some footnotes. The Spanish Civil War of 1936–39, neatly presented as a struggle between the reds and the blacks, Communism and the church, buttressed in many minds the image of "Catholic Spain," some happily; others, not. Spain's identification with the Inquisition, the unique tribunal set in motion by the Lateran Council of 1215 to search out, try and punish heretics, seemed to confirm the orthodoxy of Spain's Catholicism, if not its depth and extensiveness. For Ferdinand and Isabella, known to Spaniards and history as *los reyes Católicos,* the Catholic monarchs, the year 1492 was totally extraordinary: their protégé,

Columbus, discovered America; colonial empire was founded for Spain; and the Moorish centuries-long hold on the Iberian peninsula ended with the fall of the Alhambra. Sadly, such positive happenings were stained that very same year by their order for the Jews to become Christians or leave Spain.

Nonetheless, it is not difficult to make a solid case for the term "Catholic Spain."

St. James the Greater and the apostle Paul brought Christianity to Spain in the years 61 to 67. The burial place of St. James at Compostela in Galicia became with Rome and Jerusalem one of the major places of pilgrimage in the Middle Ages, and still is.

Catholicism was used as a spiritual support and a rallying-cry in the long struggle to reconquer Spain from the Moors.

Spain has given the church some of its greatest saints: It was Dominic who established the first religious Order, properly called, setting a pattern of organization for the nearly 8 centuries since. Before his Order of friars-preachers there had been monks and canons-regular. He himself was superior of the canons regular of Osma. But such monks and canons were bound to a particular monastery or religious house. Dominic had in mind a vast mobile army of spiritual warriors, ready and able to move anywhere they were needed. In 1205 he accompanied his bishop across the Pyrenees to France. There he encountered the results of the Albigensian heresy, and saw the need for a group of ascetic, intelligent and theologically informed preachers. Before his death in 1221, the Dominican Order had been canonically established and recognized by the Pope. Three centuries later Ignatius of Loyola established another Order of spiritual warriors, the Jesuits, with a mission of readiness to serve the Pope wherever he needed them. Teresa, the Castilian from Ávila, after joining the Order of cloistered Carmelite nuns, spent the rest of her life in reforming its convents across Spain, reviving contemplative life. John of the Cross helped reform and revive the Carmelite friars.

Spanish sailors explored the world in the 15th and 16th centuries, and wherever they went the missionaries with them planted the cross. Hernan Cortés put flag and cross in Mexico in 1522, and Christianity soon traveled along a Spanish trail into the southwest United States. From St. Augustine and Santa Fe to Lima and Buenos Aires, Spaniards brought Christianity, reaching also to the western fringe of the Pacific among the islands of the Philippines.

The earliest settlers, the Iberians, get their name from the river which rises in the northern part of Castile (near the Basque Country) and flows eastward into the Mediterranean. Now it is called in Spanish *Ebro*, but the Latin name for it was *Iberus*. They were a people of mystery who gathered in mountainous areas for protection. About the 6th century B.C. Celts settled in the northwestern part of the Iberian peninsula (what is now Galicia and northern Portugal). The southern part of the peninsula, meanwhile, was being settled by Phoenicians from the eastern Mediterranean, and by Greeks. But Carthaginians from North Africa soon moved into southern Spain and, immediately after completing their occupation in 218 B.C., had to contend with new arrivals, the Romans. There were three Punic Wars before supremacy was determined. After the second one, an agreement was made giving the Romans hegemony over everything north of the Ebro; the Carthaginians, everything south. Hannibal sought to outwit and outflank the Romans, crossing the Pyrenees beyond Barcelona and heading for the Alps. The Romans turned to North Africa, destroying Carthage itself in the Third Punic War in 146 B.C.

By the early part of the 5th century A.D. the Romans were in decline and Germanic Barbarian tribes were crossing the Pyrenees. The Visigoths were the most cultured of the four main tribes. They conquered Spain, and made Toledo their capital. The Visigoths believed in Arianism, the heresy of the Eastern Mediterranean. This religious problem was solved at the Council of Toledo, A.D. 589, in a far-reaching reconciliation during which king, nobles and those bishops espousing Arianism made formal submission to Catholicism.

The traditional interrelationship of the Spanish church and state, with its benefits and drawbacks, began in Toledo. The church was extremely nationalistic. The king appointed its bishops, and everything revolved around the primatial see, Toledo.

In A.D. 711 Arabic-speaking followers of the Islamic prophet Mohammed, who had died 79 years earlier, swarmed across the 10 miles of open sea at the Straits of Gibraltar and almost overnight captured the entire Iberian peninsula, except for a few enclaves of resistance along the north. The reconquest of Spain from the Moors started at once, but it took nearly 8 centuries to complete.

Spain's grandeur waxed after the fall of the last Moorish king in Andalusia in 1492. For a century she remained a great world power. Then things started going the other way. The Spanish Armada was defeated by England in 1588. European possessions—Flanders, Milan, Sardinia, Sicily—were lost in 1713. Napoleon put his brother Joseph on the Spanish throne. Church property was seized. In the Spanish-American War, Spain lost Cuba, Puerto Rico and the Philippines, setting off decades of unrest, plots and anarchy. The heavy vote of antimonarchy republicans in the municipal elections of 1931 encouraged King Alfonso XIII to abdicate. In the chaos of the following years, churches were burned and monasteries ransacked. Three years of civil war started in 1936 with a revolt by some army units led by General Franco.

Spain is now emerging from the isolation induced by the Civil War. So is the Spanish church. Tourist revenues have fortified the Spanish economy. Church-state relations are not as cosy as they were at the time of the Visigoths. Often, Catholic priests are on the barricades with the workers and students. Thoughtfully, the Vatican's Concordat with Spain makes provision for the conditions of the arrest and imprisonment of priests.

ASTURIAS

The land of the Astures, along Spain's north coast between Galicia and Castile, grows apples, iron ore and descendants of Celt-Iberians who refuse to be dominated. Asturias has also grown the seeds for two major events in Spain's history. Asturian miners in 1934 revolted at economic-political conditions. They marched into the main city, Oviedo, putting fire to the university and other buildings, and setting loose shock waves of revolt across Spain. It turned out to be the opening shot in the Civil War that started, formally, two years later. Back in A.D. 718 King Pelayo of the Astures defeated the Saracens in a battle at Covadonga. Only 7 years earlier the Saracens had entered Spain. Pelayo's victory was the first step in the reconquest of Spain from the Moslem invaders. The Madonna appeared to Pelayo during the battle, Asturians say, and encouraged him. The spot where she appeared, near a waterfall along the side of a cliff, is sacred to the Spaniards. The Madonna of Covadonga is venerated as the patroness of Asturias, and the Mother of the Spanish people. The valley town of Cangas de Onis, 6 miles from Covadonga, was made the first capital of Asturias by King Pelayo, and thus the first capital of the reconquered Spain.

COVADONGA

Pelayo had been a prince at the court of the Visigoths in Toledo. When Toledo fell to the Moors many of the

Spaniards and their Visigothic leaders, fleeing north-ward, crossed the Pyrenees. Some, like Pelayo, took refuge in the mountains along the coast of Asturias. At the approach of the Saracens, Pelayo led the resistance. The tradition is that there were hermits in the mountains around Covadonga, and one invited Pelayo to pray to the Madonna in a grotto of Mount Auseva. Pelayo and his followers placed an image of the Madonna in the cave. Most historians think the statue was installed after the victory as a sign of thanksgiving. Pelayo died in the 19th year of his reign.

Devotion to the Madonna was expanded by Pelayo's daughter, Queen Hermesinda, and her husband, King Alfonso I. They built a chapel near the site of the grotto. They established also a monastery of Benedictine monks, with the mission of singing the praises of Mary day and night.

The site of the victory of Pelayo became a point of pilgrimage for the Asturians, and was given the name "Covadonga." *Cova* apparently came from *cueva*, the word for "grotto"; *donga*, possibly from Doña, meaning "Lady."

In 1383 the Benedictine monks were replaced by canons regular of St. Augustine. The monks had acquired from the kings various privileges and rights over nearby towns—such as the power of the abbot to name mayors and act as judge. The canons regular were followed in 1635 by canons secular whose way of religious life did not follow a fixed rule (*regula*, and thus "regular"). The canons secular were poor, and did not live at the monastery, working instead in parishes of the zone.

The statue of Our Lady of Covadonga was crowned on Sept. 8, 1918 in the presence of King Alfonso XIII and Queen Victoria Eugenia, the 12th centenary of the Battle of Covadonga.

Covadonga was caught up in the calamitous Civil War which lasted from July 17, 1936 to Apr. 1, 1939. During this time all Asturias, except Oviedo, was under the full control of the Loyalist (anti-Franco) forces. Covadonga was occupied. The bejeweled crowns for the Madonna and Child statue, given by Asturians on the 1,200th anniversary of the Battle of Covadonga, had been prudently taken to Oviedo beforehand. But the statue itself had disappeared. All sorts of rumors circulated about its fate, but no one knew for sure.

Toward the end of the Civil War a young Asturian at Spain's embassy in Paris—which had remained under Loyalist control—informed a priest at the city's Spanish Mission Church that the statue of Our Lady of Covadonga was among the treasures which had been secreted out of the country, and hidden there. It was feared that the treasures in Paris would be sold by the Loyalists, or removed to Russia, and the youth was told to try to hide the statue until the new ambassador arrived. The bishop of Oviedo, when told about the discovery of the statue, assembled a committee to make plans for its triumphant return. On Sunday, June 11, 1939 the statue entered Spain at Irun, after spending the night in the parish church at the French border town of Hendaye. From then on there was a succession of festive days in northern Spain, as the statue moved from town to town, accompanied by prominent notables, farm families, and fishermen. It was exposed on the fifth of July in Cangas, the site of Pelayo's ancient kingdom, and the following day was returned to the chapel in the grotto at Covadonga.

Covadonga sits in a cup formed by mountains whose walls are more than 3,000 feet high. The road into the area is lost among the trees. The basilica with its twin rose-shaded towers rests on a clump of land reaching out from the circle of mountains. There is not much in the way of physical structures—houses for the canons; the school and residence of the Escolania, the choir of 60 boys; a long, single-story arcade with a few souvenir shops; a hotel named *Pelayo* which is popular for wedding receptions (200 to 250 a year); and the grotto chapel across from the basilica.

The gray-haired, thin woman in the black dress behind the wooden counter of the grocery store estimates about 30 people live in Covadonga, "not counting the canons—there are eight of them—and the Guardia Civil [the national police]."

The woman's small granddaughter appears behind the counter from the living quarters in the back of the store. The child's black hair is piled in soft curls atop her head. She busies herself closing a foot-square plastic schoolbag after cramming into it her illustrated reading book, *TA, TE, TU*.

"About a dozen or so children go to the school," she says. "They range in age from Maria Covadonga, who is a little over four, to fourteen. After fourteen they either go to work or to high school in Cangas."

Maria Covadonga?

"That's her name, all right. It's not unusual. Many Spanish girls have that name. There's a woman reporter on Radio Nacional in Madrid named Maria Covadonga. I've heard her several times. She's quite pretty, too, I hear."

The Battle of Covadonga is celebrated on Aug. 1, the woman says, but September is the big pilgrimage month.

"September 8 is the feast of the Nativity of Mary in the diocese, and the archbishop of Oviedo leads a procession here. The statue then wears the crown of gold and platinum and diamonds and pearls which was made by a priest from Asturias, a real craftsman. The people of Asturias donated their jewelry, and he made the crowns—one for the Madonna, and the other for the Child. During the Civil War the crowns were kept in a bank in Oviedo. The silver crowns were lost, though—the ones which used to be on the statue on ordinary days of the year."

The Chapel of the Holy Grotto is on the face of a mountain. On the underside of the grotto water collects from 3 main sources and falls along the mountain wall into a stream. The chapel consists of an altar and 6 wooden benches. The continuous roar of the waterfall blocks out all other sounds, but the area is so isolated that except for a bus or an automobile of pilgrims few outside noises intrude. Pelayo's body, buried originally at Cangas, was later transferred to the Holy Grotto.

The statue of Our Lady of Covadonga shows the Madonna standing. She holds in her left arm the Child. The statue had been in the cathedral at Oviedo as a replica of one exhibited in the Holy Grotto in the Middle Ages. When fire destroyed the Holy Grotto and its statue in 1777, the bishop of Oviedo presented the replica to the shrine at Covadonga.

TRANSPORTATION: Covadonga is 55 miles east of Oviedo. A private railway serves Arriondas from Oviedo; at Arriondas, connecting buses.

HOTELS: At Covadonga *Pelayo Hotel* is comfortable. At Oviedo, *Jirafa; Principado,* less expensive.

GALICIA

This is a land of the Celts. Men wear close-fitting dark blue berets, and drink red wine from white bowls while they play dominoes. It is a land of beauty, with sharply bright green hills and long slender waterways called *rias*. Materially, Galicia is poor. The farms are small and except for shipbuilding there is not too much industry. For the average Galician youth, Switzerland does not mean ski resorts and alpine meadows, but the workshop of his father or his brother—or of himself some day. The people of Galicia speak a special language, *Gallego*. Language in Galicia, as in the Basque Country and in Catalonia (Barcelona), is a nationalistic instrument, and the central government in Madrid seeks to discourage the use of Gallego. "The government spreads the word to people like my mother that only the lower classes speak Gallego," a young naval officer says. "So she corrects me when I try to speak it with her at home. But I speak it with my friends." Galicia is also a land of superstition. Fire is important, a thing of wonder. It can be used to scatter demons and evil spirits from the fields. On the feast of St. John, at midsummer, fields are sown magically. In the 6th century St. Martin, a holy man from Dumio, wrote about the superstitions of the Galicians. Some people don't think times have changed much.

COMPOSTELA

On New Year's Eve, about a dozen times a century, the archbishop of Santiago de Compostela taps with a silver hammer on the Holy Door of the cathedral in this university town of Galicia. The ceremony marks the start of a Holy Year for the shrine where the apostle St. James the Greater is buried. The Holy Year takes place each year that his feast, July 25, falls on a Sunday. The last Holy Year was in 1971. The next will be in 1976. The Holy Year was established in 1122 by Pope Calixtus II.

A reliquary in the crypt below the main altar of the cathedral holds the remains of St. James. It is customary for Spanish churches to have a statue of their patron above the altar. A 12th-century statue of St. James is above the main altar in Compostela's cathedral. The statue can be reached by stairways behind the altar and many pilgrims, after making the climb, embrace the statue while they pray.

Santiago is a contraction of *Sanct' Yago* (St. James, in Latin). Compostela, it is thought, comes from the phrase *campus stellae* (field of the star).

St. James had preached Christianity in Galicia, and on returning to Palestine was sentenced to death by

Herod. His body was then brought to Galicia. Pilgrimages began, but they were intermittent because of the succession of persecutions—first, by the Romans; then, by the pagan Barbarian tribes; and finally by the invading Saracens. The saint's sepulchre had to be hidden. When the land of Galicia ceased being a battleground temporarily in the 9th century, a bright star shone over a field and pointed to the place where the saint's remains had been hidden in a tomb of stone. This happened about A.D. 813. King Alfonso II hurried to the site, and had a chapel built. The local bishop moved his diocesan headquarters to the *campus stellae*.

But the wonder of the "field of the star" reached the ears of the Moors as well as those of Christians. The Emir Almanzor was impressed. He saw that the rediscovery of St. James's body had given the people hope, and had encouraged them in their determination to reconquer their land. If the shrine was destroyed, Almanzor reasoned, so too would the people's will to fight. He attacked the community in A.D. 997, setting its buildings afire. The flames stopped short of the crypt holding the saint's body. The Moors were incredulous. They fled. Their booty included the bells of the church which they took to the main mosque at Cordoba.

The present cathedral was started at the end of the 11th century.

Medieval pilgrims were distinctive. A wide-brimmed hat protected against the sun. A strong stick was a walking aid. Their food was in a backpack. A gourd held a supply of fresh water at their side. But they were identifiable primarily by the scallop shell fastened to their cloak. The shell came to be an emblem. Immense shells of silver, some as big as a deep-sea turtle rather than an offshore scallop, are used in ceremonies at the cathedral on major feastdays.

Origin of the scallop shell as a pilgrim's badge is not clear. Some think the scallop shell was used to scoop up water from springs along the pilgrim's route. Or pilgrims asked for alms with it at a church or monastery door. Traditionalist Galicians have their own theory. They tell a story of an armored knight who was dragged from a boat by a sea monster. St. James saved the knight, plucking him from among a bed of scallop shells. The knight, in relating the rescue later, remembered that there were scallop shells clinging to the saint's cape. Pilgrims hearing the story took the scallop shell as a sign of the saint's protection.

The shrine itself needed protection late in the 16th century. Compostela is only 20 miles from the Atlantic shore, and English pirates made forays along the coast. When Sir Francis Drake entered the port of nearby La Coruña with a squadron of English ships, Archbishop San Clemente removed the saint's body to a secret place.

For 3 centuries the relics of St. James remained hidden. Canons of the cathedral, from one generation to another, remembered the location of the relics by praying to the apostle each day at the point behind the altar where they had been buried by the archbishop. Excavations were started in 1878 to locate the relics. They were found and dug up. The archbishop of Compostela, proceeding under rules set down by the Council of Trent, consulted experts and appointed a commission. Chemical analyses and anatomical studies were made. Rome reviewed the findings but, before acting, waited for the results of an on-the-spot inquiry made by a papal emissary. Whereupon Leo XIII—"all doubts and discussions ended"—authenticated the relics, issuing the *Deus Omnipotens* Bull. The bull related the history of the shrine, and concluded: "Let all the faithful start again on pilgrimages to that holy sepulchre, according to the custom of our forefathers."

Santiago de Compostela unmistakably is a university town. The university was established in the 16th century by Archbishop Fonseca to make an education possible for all poor youths of Galicia. Now it is operated by the state. On school days at 1 P.M. and 7:30 P.M. students pack the narrow, sidewalkless main street, the Calle del Franco. The street is named not for General Franco but for the Frankish pilgrim of the Middle Ages who typified all foreigners for the local people. In scores of small coffee-bars students sip wine that costs a few pesetas and eat the food of the area: fresh mussels, soup made from potatoes and greens, potato or spinach omelets, roast merluza (a kind of codfish) with tomatoes, thin slices of meat fried with potatoes. As typical of Santiago de Compostela as the student bars are the *soportales*, arcadelike street passageways which protect against the drizzly rain that often blows in from the sea.

José-Maria Ballesteros, a local official, was born in the town but his spirit becomes animated when he talks about the way the feast of St. James is celebrated. He is tall and about 40.

"The big feast is July 25," he says, "but all the last half of July is a time of celebration. There is a religious celebration and a folkloristic Galician one, with both overlapping. The folklore festival lasts four days, starting around July 21 in the square behind the cathedral.

"On July 24, the eve of the saint's feast, the center of activity becomes the square in front of the cathedral, the Plaza del Obradoiro. That's a Galician word meaning, roughly, 'Square of the Artisans,' because the stonemasons and the other craftsmen who built the cathedral used to have their workshops and homes across the way, where the Town Hall is now located. At noon on July 24 the 'Square of the Artisans' is packed with people for the procession of the *Gigantes y Cabezudos*, the Giants and the Big Heads. They leave the cathedral exactly at noon. There are about eight giants, and many other figures with large heads. The tradition is that the giants represent the different people who have come here on pilgrimage. There are blacks and whites, and browns and yellows—all colors. There are American Indians with their feathers, and Orientals in turbans. There is an admiral of the navy and his wife representing Europe. They're called El Coco and La Coca, but it is hard to say exactly what the words mean. They're traditional. That's all. The children love this, although the tiniest ones get frightened at the big heads. The giants dance in front of the cathedral until the hidden men, who carry them on their shoulders, get tired.

"Anyway—after dancing in front of the cathedral, the Giants wander through town, greeting the people in the street in a friendly way. It's all quite pleasant, and charming. At midnight there are fireworks in the square in front of the cathedral.

"The next morning is the religious celebration. There is the High Mass in the cathedral, a Pontifical Mass. During the Mass there is the *ofrenda nacional* to St. James, the national offering of a sum of money to him as patron of Spain. In the holy years Franco himself has been present to make the offering. In other years he sends a representative.

"During the Mass the giant censer, the *botafumeiro*, is used. It is about five feet high, and it takes eight men to move it.

"In the evening at seven o'clock a procession leaves the cathedral, and goes through the whole city."

The Portico of Glory, the main entrance of the cathedral, is considered one of the finest pieces of medieval sculpture. The artist, Mateo, left a small self-portrait in stone just inside the doorway. Centuries ago students adopted the statue, nicknaming it Saint Tap-on-the-Head. It is their tribute to a great master. On entering the cathedral students bow to the statue or tap their head against it. The gesture calls to mind the genius of the past and indicates their hope that they themselves will be endowed with artistic and intellectual ability.

TRANSPORTATION: Santiago de Compostela is 390 miles from Madrid; 70 from Tuy, at the Portuguese border. It is on a direct rail line to Madrid.

HOTELS: *Hotel de los Reyes Católicos,* converted from a 15th-century royal hospital, is easily one of the most magnificent hotels in Europe. A similar establishment is *San Marcos* at León, a medieval halt on the Pilgrim's Route. *Peregrino, Gelmirez* and *Compostela* are less expensive.

THE BASQUES

The Basque people help to make Spain such a magnificent country. They also contribute to its pleasant touch of mystery. The Basques are open, friendly, happy-go-lucky people. They are mysterious nonetheless. No one knows where they come from. No one knows the origin of their language. They live along the northern coast of Spain near the corner of southwest France. They are short, but ruggedly built, and have all the old-fashioned virtues: honesty, thriftiness, industriousness, and so on. Some think the Basques migrated from the Caucasus. There is a theory that they are the descendants of the original Iberians. The origin of their language is just as baffling. No one but Basques understand it, although some of its words crop up in other languages. The Basque word for "water," for instance, is *ur*. It is intriguing to note how *ur* becomes part of names and places associated with water—Lake *Ur*mia in Iran, for example; the ancient city of *Ur*uk, near the Euphrates; the *Ur*al river which flows into the Caspian; *Ur*uguay, a South American river as well as nation; and so on. An autonomous movement has been simmering in the Basque Country for generations. When the monarchy fell in 1931, the Basques had a fling at autonomy under the provisional government. Autonomy ended with the victory of the Franco forces in the Civil War. Since then the central government in Madrid has viewed autonomous movements as separatist and therefore harmful to the unity of the nation.

Although they were the last on the peninsula to receive Christianity, the Basques are a religious people. They kept to their naturalist religion until the 9th century, making deities out of such natural forces as thunder and lightning, and honoring the sun with awesome titles like "The Eye of Light" and "The Eye of God." It is still possible to see the sun used in the décor of old buildings in the Basque Country. One of Christianity's greatest saints, Ignatius, founder of the Jesuits, was a Basque. So was his associate, Francis Xavier, the apostle of the East.

LOYOLA

When Inigo de Loyola was born here in 1491, the son of a noble family, only about 20 families were in the area. The population has not increased very much. Several oldish men in big berets sit in the sun on the wooden bench of the railroad station each morning. They are there because the station is a congenial meeting place. They are certainly not there to watch the trains. Only a few trains a day pass by. Ox carts rumble through the little community that is centered around the railroad station. The main changes in 5 centuries are the railroad station and the basilica.

The basilica is immense. It has been built alongside the manorial house in which Ignatius (Inigo) of Loyola was born. One can walk through the rooms used by Ignatius, and see the room in which he convalesced after having been seriously wounded in his defense of the Castle of Pamplona on May 20, 1521. He was a captain in the army of Castile, and Pamplona with the support of France was opposing Spain. The battle wounds at Pamplona gave Ignatius time to reflect upon his past life, and his future. He determined to devote himself to a life of poverty and spirituality. The new path was not always smooth. At one point he was imprisoned, at Salamanca, suspected of being a heretic.

In the basement of the house in which Ignatius was born, contemporary Jesuits have established a radio station. It is one of a number of privately operated stations permitted by the government throughout the country to broadcast locally, under the general name *Radio Popular*. The Jesuit station is ideally located. Loyola is almost equidistant from each of the 4 Basque provincial capitals. Bilbao and Pamplona are 30 miles away; San Sebastian and Vitoria, 25.

The Jesuit Order continues to reflect its Spanish heritage. There are 600 Jesuits in the Basque Country, and 4,500 in all Spain. But the Jesuit link to Spain through Loyola has not dispensed the Society of Jesus, on its home grounds, from the type of troubles which have visited the Order elsewhere. In the 19th century alone, the Jesuits were expelled from Spain 5 times; in this century—so far—once.

TRANSPORTATION: A private railway serves Loyola from San Sebastian.

HOTELS: At San Sebastian, *Orly* and *San Sebastian* are major hotels; *Avenida* and *Gudamendi*, less expensive.

PAMPLONA

Navarre, one of the early kingdoms in Spain, is usually considered as a Basque province because its valleys between the Pyrenees and the Ebro are inhabited by Basques. Its capital, Pamplona, is the city of the "running of the bulls" which Hemingway wrote about in *The Sun Also Rises*.

In the sidewalk of the Avenida San Ignacio a brass plate marks the spot where Ignatius fell wounded in the battle of May 20, 1521 over control of Pamplona Castle. The brass plate is in front of a church dedicated to St.

Ignatius. Curiously, the church is administered not by the Jesuits, but by the Redemptorist Fathers. Thirty-five miles southeast of Pamplona is Javier, birthplace of Francisco de Javier. Francis Xavier was in Paris teaching philosophy at the Sorbonne when Ignatius was injured at Pamplona, but his brothers fought on the side of Navarre against the Castilian forces of Ignatius. Later, the two met and Ignatius won Francis over to the new Order, sending him in 1541 at the request of the king of Portugal to the fledgling Catholic mission in India. He is buried in Goa.

Pamplona houses the University of Navarre, the only private university in Spain and, some say, the best. It was established in 1952 by Opus Dei, a unique organization of Catholic men and women, founded in Spain in 1928 and spreading afterward to 30 or more other countries, including the United States.

It is an old city. Some believe Pamplona's original name was Pompeiopolis, the city of Pompey. The running-of-the-bulls through the streets on July 6 honors the city's first bishop, St. Fermin, whose feast is the following day. Fermin had been a heathen but became a disciple of St. Sernin, bishop of Toulouse, which is on the French side of the Pyrenees. This was in the 3rd century. The saint's feast used to be celebrated in October, but city authorities formally requested the diocesan synod to change the date to July 7, saying this would be more convenient. The request was granted. That was in 1591.

TRANSPORTATION: Pamplona is connected to San Sebastian by train and bus.

HOTELS: The outstanding hotel is *Los Tres Reyes*. *Maison-nave* and *Orbi* are quite comfortable.

RONCESVALLES

At the northern edge of Navarre, 30 miles north of Pamplona, is the historic settlement of Roncesvalles, among the brambled valleys which give it the French name. Charlemagne's forces were defeated here on Aug. 15, A.D. 778. The memorable tragedy of that defeat was the death of the medieval hero, Roland. Roncesvalles was a main route across the Pyrenees for the pilgrims on the way to Santiago de Compostela, and an important *Hospital*—the word having the Latin meaning of "hospitality"—was established in the latter part of the 12th century. Roncesvalles itself had become a point of pilgrimage in the 9th century when an abbot of the monastery founded by Charlemagne reported seeing a vision of the Madonna, accompanied by a deer and a choir of angels. The vision appeared to the monk at a time when he feared that he would fall into the hands of the Saracens.

A 13th-century image of the Madonna is at the collegiate church. Many of the medieval kings and bishops of Navarre are buried at Roncesvalles.

Roncesvalles is near the French border. (*Casa Sabina* is an unassuming inn.)

BARCELONA

Barcelona is one of the brightest cities of the Mediterranean. It is the capital of the northeastern region of Spain known as Catalonia, the land of the Catalans, a special people whose counts once extended the kingdom across the Mediterranean. The Costa Brava, the ragged, rugged line of shore between Barcelona and the French border, has become synonymous with tourism. The language of Catalonia, Catalan, is somewhat like the Provençal that used to be spoken and sung in southern France. As in the Basque Country, language in Catalonia has nationalist undertones.

The people of Catalonia like to sing and dance, and the favorite setting is the square of the village church on Sunday. The square in front of the Gothic cathedral in Barcelona itself on Wednesday evening and at noon

Sunday becomes the stage for the spontaneous dancing of Catalonia's national dance, the *sardana*. It is a dance in which the dancers hold hands as they form a circle. Scores of couples regularly meet at the cathedral to dance, and everyone is welcome to join the circle.

The cathedral crowns the city's lacey Gothic quarter which is built on the ruins of the original Roman settlement. On the return of Columbus from America, Ferdinand and Isabella welcomed him in the Tinell throne room of the palace. A replica of the discoverer's flagship, the *Santa Maria*, is moored at the waterfront. The former royal chapel in the palace is a favorite wedding site for young Barcelonese.

Barcelona is a leisurely place. Bird and flower markets along the string of pedestrian malls on its main street encourage easy going.

The 575-foot Mont Juich (Mountain of the Jews) gets its name from a Jewish cemetery of the Middle Ages. Many of the old stones, with Hebrew inscriptions, have survived.

Gaudi, the contemporary architect and artist, used all of Barcelona as a workshop. His creations are everywhere. The most renowned is the Church of the Holy Family.

TRANSPORTATION: Barcelona is 400 miles from Madrid. There are fast day trains to Madrid and Paris.

HOTELS: *Arycasa* and *Colón* are among the leading hotels. *Covadonga* and *Gaudi* are medium-priced.

MONTSERRAT

The Benedictine Monastery of Montserrat is the shrine of the Madonna patroness of Catalonia. The monastery's official symbol is a saw, which symbolizes the huddled teethlike peaks northwest of Barcelona that shelter the old monastic settlement. The word *Montserrat* itself means "serrated mountain." To some the mountain tips are more like fingers reaching outward than like teeth of a saw. The dual symbolism of saw and fingers at times can be applied by different persons to the same situation on Montserrat.

When Abbot Aurelio Escarré, O.S.B., made a statement in *Le Monde,* a decade or so ago, about the situation of church and state in Spain, his words must have cut like a saw across the political nerves of government leaders. Perhaps with even more teeth, a similar declaration by his successor, Abbot Casia Just, O.S.B., a half dozen years later, could have had only the same effect. So, too, would the sit-in protest of several hundred intellectuals at the monastery at the time of the Burgos court martial of 15 Basques (including two priests) who were brought to trial under a new banditry-terrorism decree. The protesters included the great Catalan artist, Joan Miró, then well past his 75th birthday, and young people like Ramon, the singer. Spain's minister of justice telephoned the abbot, asking why he had permitted the protesters at the monastery. The abbot replied that he was merely receiving people who wished to manifest themselves in favor of justice. He was not taking part in any political act, the abbot said, but rather, something fundamental in the life of man. The minister then asked if the abbot would request the protesters to leave. The abbot agreed to do so once the minister assured him there would be no reprisals.

About 1 million people visit Monserrat a year. The monastery is a center of liturgical development and of ecumenism. Its choir school is Europe's oldest and the Catalan name for it, Escolania, has been accepted by the National Academy as a regular part of the Spanish language.

The statue of the Virgin of Montserrat is a polychrome wood-carving of the 12th or 13th century. The Madonna is seated with the Child in her lap, facing forward and with her right hand raised. The face is dark. She is known as the "Black Madonna" and, familiarly, as *La Moreneta* (The Little Dark One).

Hermits had settled in the Montserrat area, 4,000 feet above sea level, in the early centuries of Christianity. In the 11th century, Abbot Oliba of Ripoli Abbey in the Catalan province of Gerona established the monastery on Montserrat.

In Napoleonic times the monastery was burned to the ground. It was rebuilt in the latter part of the 19th century.

Montserrat is particularly popular with newlyweds. An old saying in Catalonia is that a man is not "properly married" until he and his wife have made a pilgrimage to the shrine.

The choir sings in the abbey church each day at noon and at 7 P.M., and on Sunday at the High Mass at 11 A.M. Monastery records indicate that the choir school existed in the 13th century, beginning as a training center for altar boys in the liturgical chant. There are 50 boys, ranging in age from 10 to 14, in the choir. They live at the monastery, attending a regularly accredited school, and studying voice and a musical instrument. The monks are the teachers.

"There are a hundred applicants each year for a dozen vacancies," says Father Alejandro Olivar. "The sad thing is when the child has a good voice and intellect, and his voice changes—and he has to leave. That's sad."

Father Alejandro is in his 50s, and is of medium height and build. His hair is thinning out. He wears glasses, and has a sense of humor. He is a patrologist, a specialist in the Fathers of the church.

Does the choir travel?

"Yes, all over Europe. They have been invited to America, but have not accepted as yet. There are different opinions in the monastery. There is a grand pluralism in the monastery, happily. We can't be closed. We must be open in our views. Some think it's too far to go. But it will happen. It is too great a temptation, a chance to make Montserrat more known."

Father Alejandro is one of 90 monks at the monastery.

"I myself have seen two hundred."

Part of the decline in numbers is due to dropouts, but most to the slowing of the vocation rate.

"There are two or three vocations a year. That's enough for now. We could admit more, but it is better to be demanding, to accept only those who are certain the monastic life is for them. Accepting those who are not certain would mean departures that would disturb the community life, and be discouraging."

Some of the fall-off in the monastery's population has been caused by its foundations.

"In the past twenty years we have established two foundations—one in Colombia; the other in Bethlehem. The one in Colombia is a normal foundation.

And in the Holy Land?

"In the Holy Land, there is a project, with six of our monks and laymen—professors and students of different religions—who have an Ecumenical Institute of Theological Advanced Studies at Deir et-Tantur. The young students there are preparing doctoral theses, and doing research. They eat with the monks, although their living quarters and way of life is independent of the monks. The monks give the Institute a place of prayer. An institute cannot be only an academy.

"Within the monastery there was a question of who should be sent to Jerusalem. It was definitely decided to send the best monks of the community. If we were going to undertake such an important work, we should do it seriously, we decided, even though it might be a sacrifice to lose good men. We feel that by sending our best, God will take care of us, and fill our ranks with very good men again. It is always a temptation in a religious community to answer the request for assistance by sending the restless ones, and those who are having some difficulty. But that does not do anyone any good, generally, and if we did that in this case the project would be doomed to failure."

What do they do at the Ecumenical Institute?

"They study problems of theology, not ecumenical ones. They study Bible questions. If a Protestant and Catholic study together the problems which separate them, there is a likelihood they would become more separated. It is better for them to study the theological questions arising from what unites them—the Bible. A good Catholic, a good Protestant will listen to what the other says, and will reflect on it. That is important, that is the one essential. I don't tell a Protestant to be a Catholic. I tell him to be a good Protestant."

Any ecumenical activity at Montserrat itself?

"Yes, indeed. Even before the Council, Montserrat was ecumenically oriented. Americans are in the ecumenical group meetings at Montserrat. I myself am a member of a society called Societas Liturgica. It is an international organization founded in Holland, and many theologians of different nations and religions are in it, including American Episcopalians. It meets every two years. In August of 1974 the Societas met at Montserrat."

And progress?

"In Spain there is a general feeling that research is a waste of time. One does not see any quick results. Research is a luxury. So, too, is ecumenical work. Results may take years, lifetimes. But we have to be able to afford these so-called luxuries of research, of ecumenical effort."

Montserrat's research resources are considerable.

"Our library," Father Alejandro says, "has two hundred thousand volumes. We also have a Biblical School, and an Oriental Institute. There are monks in the monastery who have permission to celebrate the Liturgy in the Byzantine and Syriac rites. I don't like that. You

know why? It is folklore. If I am Latin, then I should
follow the Latin rite."

Some of the books in the library were written by
Montserrat's monks, such as an oldtime abbot, Garcia
de Cisneros. He wrote a *Manual of Spiritual Life* that
has influenced present-day asceticism. The monks still
write, and publish what they write in their own printing plant. They publish four reviews.

"All but *Studia* are in Catalan."

So, Catalan is permitted?

"Oh, yes. We are allowed to publish books and
reviews in Catalan, but not newspapers—because
newspapers are more widely read."

The cloister of the monastery is small, a square of
arcades in a yard connected to gardens at a slightly
higher level. The refectory entrance is near the cloister.
Five minutes before mealtime the cloister becomes a
busy meeting place for monks who wish to pass on a
message or exchange information.

"About fifty of the monks are priests," Father Alejandro says. "We do not use the term *Brother* for those
who are not priests, and we don't divide up into priests
and nonpriests. All are treated the same and have the
same rights and the same vote. All eat together, all are
mixed up, in the same refectory. That's democracy."

How does the monastery support itself?

"Besides the printing plant, we have an atelier,
where some of the monks make pottery, and a goldsmith's works. As Benedictine monks, we have the
traditional distillery. A liqueur is made here called
Aromas del Montserrat. The two hotels, the two restaurants and self-service cafeteria, the few shops—all the
buildings on the mountain belong to the monastery. If it
was otherwise, there would be a danger that the commercial aspect would infringe on the site. This way, we
can control the atmosphere. The big problem is finding
enough space on the mountain to accommodate the

automobiles and buses. We are trying to solve it by building garages in the mountain itself. We already have a three-level garage in the side of the mountain that can handle seven hundred cars."

The main days of the pilgrimage at Montserrat are Apr. 27, the feastday of the "Black Madonna," and Sept. 8, the traditional feast of the sanctuary. On feast-days, the "Black Madonna" wears a crown of 2,400 diamonds, 146 emeralds, 30 pearls.

Historic reminders are everywhere.

The lobby of the Hostal Abad Cisneros is a setting of antique Spanish furniture: desks, tables, benches. An enormous tapestry, 30 by 25 feet or more, hangs across one wall. It is the only major furnishing that is obviously not Spanish.

Is it French?

"It's Spanish," the woman desk clerk says. "Spanish in the sense that it is Belgian—from Flanders, in the time of Charles V and Philip II, when Flanders belonged to the Spanish empire."

TRANSPORTATION: The Catalanes private railway serves Montserrat. Montserrat is 38 miles from Barcelona.

HOTELS: *Hostal Abad Cisneros* is quite comfortable. *Monasterio* is inexpensive.

VALENCIA

The delightful seaport cosmopolis of Valencia, producer of oranges, paellas, festas and beauty in general, is Spain's third city. Valencians believe it is the country's first. Victor Hugo counted 300 belfries. They seem numberless when seen from the 200-foot bell tower of Valencia's cathedral, dedicated to the Virgin of the Abandoned (*Los Desamparados*), the patroness of the city.

Each Thursday at noon the cathedral's "Door of the

Apostles" becomes the setting for a unique court. Leather-backed chairs are set in the sculpted enclosure outside the cathedral entrance and the *Tribunal de las Aguas,* the Water Court, begins its weekly session. The judges are 8 working farmers. They are elected by the farmers served by the 8 irrigation canals which channel water from the Turia River across 55,000 acres of highly productive agricultural lands. The judges dress in knee-length black smocks, the traditional clothes of Valencia farmers. The mission of the court is to hear charges of violations of water rights and to assess penalties against those farmers it finds guilty. Its decisions are final, and cannot be appealed to any other court in Spain.

It is Spain's oldest court. The generally accepted date for its founding is A.D. 960, a time when Spain was being ruled by the Moorish caliphs of Cordoba. Its meeting place, until the reconquest, had been inside the Grand Mosque. The reconquerors of Valencia razed the mosque and, in 1262, built the present cathedral where it had stood. Because some Moslems remained in Valencia among the farmers after the defeat of the Moors, the cathedral itself was not automatically acceptable as the courtroom for the Tribunal de las Aguas, either because of the reluctance of Moslems to enter the church of the Christians or because of the refusal of the Christians to permit access to the nonbaptized. The doorway of the cathedral was the solution. The court is called into session by its bailiff, the *alguacil. Alguacil* is one of many Arabic-derived words which have survived in the Spanish language from Moorish times.

The cathedral's treasury contains the chalice which, tradition says, was used by Christ at the Last Supper.

St. Vincent Ferrer, the Dominican missionary, was born in Valencia in 1350, and was baptized in St. Stephen's Church, near the cathedral. The daughters of El Cid were married in St. Stephen's.

Valencia is known for its *festas*. The festivals usually are of religious origin, such as Corpus Christi with its procession, but they invariably involve music, dancing and fireworks. For the feast of Valencia's native son, Vincent Ferrer, on Apr. 5, children act out episodes from his life on open-air stages around the city. The feast of St. James, July 25, is marked with a *corrida* featuring Spain's top bullfighters. Hemingway told about this in *Death in the Afternoon*. The most famous celebrations are the week-long *Las Fallas* which climax spectacularly on Mar. 19, St. Joseph's Day, and the start of Spain's bullfighting season. The word *falla* means "bonfire" in the Valencian dialect, and each neighborhood during the week of celebration erects in the local square carnival-like figures of papier-mâché and wood which satirize contemporary personalities. On the final night of *Las Fallas* each neighborhood makes a bonfire of its exhibit, and it seems as if all Valencia is ablaze.

TRANSPORTATION: Valencia is 220 miles south of Barcelona. Express train and frequent air service to Barcelona and Madrid.

HOTELS: *Astoria Palace* and *Reina Victoria* are the main hotels. *Alhambra* and *Ingles* are less expensive.

ANDALUSIA

The last stronghold of the Moors in Spain was the region of Andalusia along the southern coast. The Moorish domination of Spain ended in 1492 when their last king, Boabdil, went into exile in the Sierra Nevada, but many of their customs and much of their language remained behind with the people.

Spain's best bulls come from Andalusia, and this is important because bullfighting is the nation's main spectator drama, whether sport or spectacle. So, too, is Andalusia the birthplace of the leading bullfighters.

This follows because Andalusia is not a land of wealth, and the bullring has encompassed the hopes of poor youths for generations. In the slum district of Seville, which is the aristocratic city of Andalusia, bullfighters pay homage to a Madonna statue known as the Virgin of La Macarena. La Macarena is the name of the poor district. Traditionally, bullfighters visit the Madonna shrine in the Basilica de la Macarena before leaving to face the bulls in the ring.

All over Andalusia Holy Week is celebrated with spectacular processions and rituals. Perhaps the most impressive are those at Seville.

SEVILLE

Churches with square towers in Andalusia usually were mosques in Moorish times. All the Christians did was make a bell tower out of the Moslem minaret. At Seville, when the Christians built their cathedral they made it the largest in Spain, the third largest in Christendom, and retained its elegant minaret, the towering La Giralda. The courtyard where the Moslems washed their feet before entering their mosque has been retained, too, as the Patio of the Orange Trees.

Throughout the year the cathedral is the point of origin for the spectacular religious celebrations of Seville. One of the oldest is the dance done before the main altar by a group of choir boys dancing with solemnity and dignity to the measured tone of the castanets (*castañuelas*) they hold in their hands. The oldtime name for the group is *Los Seises*, the 6-year-olds, but they usually are 10 or 11 years of age. They do their unusual dance on the feasts of Corpus Christi and of the Immaculate Conception. For Corpus Christi they dress in red; for the Marian feast, it is blue. When news of the dancing before the altar with castanets first reached Rome, the Pope is said to have been astonished, and ordered its halt. But the people of Seville persisted, explaining that it was a liturgical dance of respect, and had always been performed. The Pope relented somewhat, saying that the dance could be continued as long as the robes of the choir boys lasted. The tradition is that the robes worn by the choir boys are from the 16th century, carefully handled so that they can last indefinitely. The choir boys of the cathedral are from the slums of Seville, and are being educated on scholarships.

Corpus Christi is marked, too, with a procession through the streets of Seville. It starts early because, during the night, the streets have been covered with a sheet of fresh ferns by municipal employees. The feet of those in the procession crush the ferns, and a mintlike aroma floats through the air.

During the processions of Holy Week people along the route stand on their balconies, singing a special type of song called a *saeta* which has Moorish undertones in its wailing, throbbing melody. The *saetas* are restful, poetic greetings to a particular image, such as the Virgin of La Macarena, when it comes into view. "Of all the women in the world, you are the most beautiful," is an example of a *saeta* salutation.

Christopher Columbus is buried in the cathedral.

TRANSPORTATION: Seville is 340 miles south of Madrid. Express trains connect Seville and Madrid. There is air service to and from all major cities of Spain.

HOTELS: *Alfonso XIII, Cristina* and *Luz* are among the principal hotels. *Colón* and *Inglaterra* are less expensive.

POINTS OF INTEREST: The ruins of the Roman settlement, outside Seville, where the emperors Hadrian and Trajan were born. Among the ruins are the remains of what was the largest Roman theater in Spain.

CÓRDOBA

Washington Irving made a journey on horseback through Andalusia with a Russian diplomat in 1829, starting from Seville, and ending in Granada. En route they paused at Córdoba, the captivating headquarters of the caliphs and the capital of Moorish Spain from the 8th to the 11th century. In those days it was the most populated city in Europe—1 million inhabitants. It is about a fifth of its former size. Fortunately, the 8th-century Mezquita, the Great Mosque, was not destroyed in the reconquest. It is a gem of Arabic art, with myriad peppermint-stick columns supporting horseshoe-shaped arches curving above a score of naves. The Mezquita was made a cathedral in the 13th century.

Near the Mezquita is the old Jewish quarter of Córdoba, indicated by the word JUDIOS in large, raised letters on a whitewashed wall. The inscription is merely a historic note. There are no Jews in Córdoba today. The ancient Jewish colony of Córdoba was one of the most cultured in the world. The "Street of the Jews" is 100 yards long. In the 15th century gates at either end closed it off from the rest of the city. In the street is a synagogue, built in 1314–15 in Mudejar (Christian-Arab) style by Isaac Mejeb. It is quite small, 25 by 20 feet.

After the expulsion of the Jews from Spain in 1492, the synagogue was used first as a mental hospital and eventually for Christian religious activities. In 1885 it was made a national monument. Inscribed plaques in the patio of the synagogue carry tributes to the medieval philosopher, physician and rabbi, Maimonides (Moisés ben Llaimón), who was born in Córdoba in 1135 and died there in 1204. One plaque says: "Córdoba, his homeland, offers him the veneration of her memory." The second: "Spain, his nation, expresses her homage to the immortal genius of Judaism." The square at one end of the Jewish quarter is named after him, Plazuela Maimonides. In another little square, Plaza de Tiberiades, is a statue of him seated. It carries the dates 5724 and 1964.

Another philosopher, the Roman Seneca, was born in Córdoba about A.D. 2.

In the Plazuela Maimonides is Córdoba's Municipal Bullfighting Museum.

But the shrine for bullfight fans is the 2-story white-front house at No. 6 Calle Torres Cabrera, a narrow street behind San Miguel Church. On July 4, 1917 Manuel Rodriguez Sanchez was born there. He was known by the diminutive of Miguel (Michael), "Manolete," and was one of the greatest bullfighters of all time. His face is on photos in bars and restaurants throughout Córdoba and most of Andalusia. There is no name on the photos. Everyone knows him. He is thin-faced, solemn. His left cheek is scarred from an injury during the 1944–45 *temporada* (season) at Valencia. An Englishwoman once asked Manolete why he always looked so solemn. "Madam," he replied, courteously, "the bull is always solemn." Like American baseball fans who can recite batting averages, bullfight aficionados know that it was a bull named Islero from the Mura ranches in Jaen province of Andalusia that killed him at 5 o'clock in the afternoon of Aug. 28, 1947 in the Plaza de Arenas at Linares in Jaen.

TRANSPORTATION: It is 250 miles south of Madrid. There is direct train service to and from Madrid and Seville.

HOTELS: *Melia, Gran Capitan* and the government *parador* are the main places to stay. *Colón, Niza* and *Marisa* are medium-priced.

GRANADA

Sacro Monte, Holy Mountain, is named for Cecilio and other Christian missionaries who were martyred on it in the days when the Romans occupied Spain. Gypsies have been living in small caves on Sacro Monte since Ferdinand and Isabella conquered the Moors in 1492. Two Ave Maria schools were founded on the mountain in 1888 for the gypsy children. The founder was Don Andres Manjon y Manjon, a law professor at the University of Granada and a canon in the ancient Abbey of St. Cecilio at the far end of Sacro Monte. He is buried in Our Lady of the Assumption parish church. No name, no tribute of any kind is on the sheet of marble covering his grave. He did not wish any. The only inscription are the letters "A" and "M," the initials of his name and of *Ave Maria*. The church's large statue of Christ is carried by the gypsies in the Holy Thursday procession along the Sacro Monte road. They light fires and sing haunting *saetas* as extemporaneous tributes to God.

Spaniards say that God, if He loves someone, makes it possible for that person to live in Granada. Washington Irving, on his horseback tour of Andalusia in 1829, resided for several months within the walls of the Alhambra. The Moors called it al-Hamra (The Red) because of its deep color of orange. Within its walls they raised a citadel, a palace, fountains and gardens.

The Mexican poet Francisco de Icaza resided in Granada early in this century. His words of homage are engraved on the Tower of La Vela which guards the approaches to the Alhambra:

> Give him alms, good woman,
> As in one's life there isn't
> A misfortune so great
> As being blind to Granada.

The banner of Castile was unfurled from the Tower of La Vela by Queen Isabella on Jan. 2, 1492, marking the end of the Moorish empire in Spain after nearly 8 centuries. She and Ferdinand carried out the successful siege from the military fort at Santa Fe, now an attractive Andalusian town of 10,000 residents, 6 miles west of Granada on the Seville highway. After the Alhambra fell, Isabella and Ferdinand met at Santa Fe with Christopher Columbus, agreeing to support the expedition which led to the discovery of America. An ornamental plaque on the parish church wall commemorates the undertaking Columbus received on Apr. 17, 1492.

The tombs of Ferdinand and Isabella are in the royal chapel of Granada Cathedral.

Boabdil, the last king of the Moors, is said to have paused at *Suspiro del Moro* (Sigh of the Moor) to take a farewell look at the kingdom he had just lost before going into exile in the Alpujarra range of the Sierra Nevada. A marker at the side of the Motril highway, 7 miles south of Granada, identifies the spot. Washington Irving says that Boabdil's mother severely rebuked him in his defeat. "You do well," she chided him, "to weep as a woman over what you could not defend as a man." When Emperor Charles V (Charles I of Spain) was told about this, he remarked (according to Washington Irving): "Had I been he or he been I, I would rather have made this Alhambra my sepulchre than have lived without a kingdom in the Alpujarra."

But the New Yorker who wrote *Tales of the Alhambra* as well as *The Legend of Sleepy Hollow* observes: "How easy it is for those in power and prosperity to preach heroism to the vanquished! How little can they understand that life itself may rise in value with the unfortunate, when nought but life remains."

TRANSPORTATION: Granada is 270 miles south of Madrid. Direct trains from Madrid.

HOTELS: *San Francisco Parador, Luz* and *Melia* are out-

standing. *Washington Irving* and *Guadalupe* are less
expensive.

POINTS OF INTEREST: The prehistoric cave paintings at
Nerja.

MADRID

The Hill of the Angels, the geographical center of the
Iberian peninsula, is 6 miles from Madrid. Philip II, the
son of Emperor Charles V, was born in Madrid, and
chose it as the capital in 1561, moving the royal court
from Toledo. Madrid is in *New* Castile, meaning the
southern part which was freed last from the Moors.
Castile is speckled with castles which in turn gave the
region its name—from the Latin *castellum*, "fortress."

The Escorial is an extraordinary castle of Spain. It is
a combination church, palace and royal mausoleum
675 feet wide and 525 feet long. Charles V had it built
4 centuries ago because he wished a fit-for-an-emperor
burial place. It is in the bleached foothills, 30 miles
west of Madrid. A marble sculpture of Christ by Ben-
venuto Cellini is in the basilica. Ten miles away is a
tremendous war memorial for the Civil War dead. A
900-foot-long basilica has been built within a mountain, topped by a 500-foot cross (with an observation
platform).

At Segovia, 55 miles northwest of Madrid, is the
"Lady of Spanish Cathedrals." Segovia Cathedral gets
its title from the elegant way it seems to float in the air.
During the Holy Week and Corpus Christi processions
a gilded carriage, propelled by 4 men hidden inside,
takes the lead. An aqueduct from Roman times and an
alcazar (castle-fortress) from the Moors indicate the
wide span of Segovia's history.

In Madrid, when the city celebrates in May the feast
of its patron, St. Isidore the Farmer, there is a full week
of bullfights. St. Isidore was born outside Madrid, and

was canonized on Mar. 12, 1622, the same time as Ignatius Loyola, Francis Xavier and Teresa of Ávila. It is said that before going out into the fields each morning to do his farm work Isidore would attend Mass. The legend is that he was able to spend a great deal of time in prayer, and still get his work done, because angels helped him.

At St. Anthony's Church in Madrid young girls, especially seamstresses, make a pilgrimage on his feast-day (June 13) to pray for a fiancé who will bring them a happy marriage. The ritual involves dropping a pin into the holy-water font. The girls usually cover their heads with a white mantilla and drape a white shawl, called a *mantón de Manila,* across their shoulders. Manila was a seamstress. One day, rushing to St. Anthony's on his feast, she hurriedly cloaked herself with the silk covering from a piano. The improvised shawl was adopted by the young women of Madrid and given Manila's name.

TOLEDO

Livy, the Roman historian, writing about Toledo 20 centuries ago called it *Toletum* and described it as a "small fortified town." It is one of the oldest cities in Christendom, having had a bishop in the 1st century A.D. When Reccared became king of the Visigoths in A.D. 586 he announced that he was going to be a Catholic. In the Council of Toledo in A.D. 589 Arianism was rejected, and Catholicism became the religion of the kingdom. Toledo had already been made the capital of the Visigothic king; now it was the primatial see of the church in Spain.

Early in the 8th century the Saracens captured Toledo. It was reconquered in 1085. Starting about the 13th century Toledo, with its School of Translators, became a center of art and knowledge as Jew, Christian and Moslem worked together. The demise of Toledo began with the expulsion of the Jews from Spain in 1492. Although the capital was moved to Madrid in the 16th century, Toledo continued to be the religious capital of Spain.

Because El Greco masterpieces are everywhere, Toledo is practically an open-air gallery of his work.

The 10th-century Christ-of-the-Light Mosque is the only structure surviving from the pre-reconquest era. The Christians remaining in Toledo during the Moslem rule—Mozarabs—were allowed to have their own churches, such as San Sebastian and Santa Eulalia. Unfortunately, such churches have little from Moorish times because they were practically rebuilt after the reconquest. The post-reconquest churches were constructed in the combination Christian-Arab style called Mudejar. Fine examples are San Vicente, El Cristo de la Vega, and Santo Tomé. El Greco's "The Burial of Count Orgaz" is in Santo Tomé Church.

There were many synagogues in Toledo because persecutions elsewhere drew Jewish refugees to the city in the second half of the 12th century. Only two synagogues survive, and both were built in Mudejar style. The oldest, now known as the Church of Santa Maria la Blanca, was built as long ago as 1260—perhaps earlier. Santa Maria dominates the Tagus from the "Gate of the Jews" in the western part of Toledo, and had the rank of a major synagogue until 1405 when it was transformed into a Catholic sanctuary—thus the name. In 1550 the archbishop of Toledo, Cardinal Silvio, used it as a "refuge for repentants" and from Napoleonic times until the middle of the last century it was a warehouse.

The synagogue El Transito is not far from Santa Maria. Its building was ordered by Samuel ha-Levi, master of the treasures of King Peter I of Castile in the middle of the 14th century. A singular feature is the series of wall inscriptions of medieval quotations in Hebrew. Its ceiling is sculpted from Cedars of Lebanon.

Construction of Toledo Cathedral was started in 1226, but not completed until 1492. On feastdays a monstrance is used which was made from gold Columbus brought back from America.

El Greco's house is now a museum and in it, besides some of his paintings, are various personal articles, such as a spinning wheel used by his wife.

TRANSPORTATION: Toledo is 44 miles south of Madrid. Direct train service.

HOTELS: *Conde de Orgaz Parador* is excellent; *Maravilla* and *Almazara*, medium-priced.

ÁVILA

Ávila, the birthplace of the mystic and Carmelite reformer of the 16th century, calls itself the closest spot to heaven of all Spain. It is at an altitude of 3,670 feet, 70 miles from Madrid. It is a walled city, perched on a hill, and physically reminiscent of Jerusalem. It was Christianized in the 1st century by Bishop San Segundo. A statue of Teresa dominates the main square.

A monastery named for the saint was built in 1636 on the site of the house where she was born and where she lived for 20 years before going across the valley to the Encarnación Convent of the Carmelite Nuns, 1 mile away. She had fled from home because she sought a religious life and her father had planned a domestic one for her. Teresa entered the convent in 1535, and remained cloistered there for 27 years, leaving then on her mission of reforming the Carmelite convents of Spain. She began with St. Joseph's Convent in Ávila. Both St. Joseph's and Encarnación convents can be visited.

Teresa's mother died shortly after she became a

Carmelite, and then her father died. The house of Teresa's birth was abandoned. Later (1630) the Carmelite friars bought the property and soon built a monastery around it. Nothing remains of Teresa's original house, but the friars have localized the place where she was born. She died on Oct. 4, 1582 in Alba de Tormes near Salamanca. It is a little over 50 miles from Ávila. Her body is in a reliquary in the main altar of the Carmelite convent church there. (Train service both to Ávila and Salamanca from Madrid is frequent and fast. The leading hotel at Ávila is *Valderrabanos*.)

The Encarnación Convent at Ávila, which Teresa joined, is a 2-story building of huge stones. It was built in 1515. It includes a museum, with furniture of the epoch of Teresa. One room contains several musical instruments: a guitar, a harp of beautiful wood, a drum. Another has chalices. One chalice had been used by St. John of the Cross, another native of Ávila. A leather-backed chair which had been used by St. John of the Cross for hearing confessions of the nuns is also exhibited. There is a block of wood, 18 by 6 by 6 inches, which the woman serving as a guide says Teresa used as a pillow. She is one of several women living as Carmelite Tertiaries at the convent. She points also to the *toca*, the now-yellowed white coif of the saint's. Visible through a grille is the large square room in which Teresa lived for 3 years when she was prioress of Encarnación. She had a 2-room suite, with a small room for her oratory. The Tertiary presents a leaflet with Teresa's prayer. It reads:

> Let nothing disturb thee,
> Let nothing affright thee;
> All things are passing,
> God never changeth.
> Patient endurance
> Attaineth to all things.
> Who has God,
> In nothing is wanting.

TRANSPORTATION: Madrid is on international air routes, and on the main rail lines from Paris, Barcelona and Lisbon.

HOTELS: *Castellana, Ritz* and *Palace* are among the chief hotels. *Carlos V* and *Emperatriz* are in medium-price range.

15
Switzerland

CHRISTIANITY is as old in Switzerland as it is in almost any other country of Western Europe. From the earliest days of the Christian religion holy men sought out refuge for prayer and meditation in the alpine heights which give the land of the Swiss almost unequaled beauty and character. In the second half of the 4th century a church was built at St. Maurice in Valais canton to honor an officer in the Roman army who with his men had been martyred by Emperor Maximilian because they had become Christians. The crypt at Chur is the oldest north of the Alps. St. Gall, an Irish monk, came to Switzerland in the 6th century, giving a name to a city, St. Gallen, that has been a cultural and religious center century after century.

In monasteries at Einsiedeln and Engelberg, Benedictine monks have been praying and working for more than 1,000 years.

A Frenchman, John Calvin, brought the Reformation to the French-speaking people of Geneva, but a native son, Ulrich Zwingli, was the apostle of reform in the larger German-speaking area, and literally fought and died for his religious beliefs.

Swiss of all religious views honor a saint, Nicholas von der Flüe, for his remarkable conciliatory efforts which kept together the Swiss confederation at a critical moment in the 15th century.

Celts known as Helvetii occupied most of the territory that is now Switzerland in the centuries before Christ. The Romans seized Helvetia in 58 B.C., and maintained control for 5 centuries. The movement of the Barbarian tribes brought invasions in the 5th century. The Burgundians moved into the western part, adapting themselves to the Latin language that was spoken (and which eventually became French), and the German-speaking Alamanni invaded the eastern and central areas, installing themselves and their language.

In 1291 three of the forest cantons (states) around Lake Lucerne—Uri, Schwyz and Unterwalden—signed a Perpetual Covenant of mutual support and defense. At the time the 3 cantons were part of the Germanic Holy Roman empire and, its rulers, the Hapsburgs were guarantors of their rights as guardians of the alpine passes of central Switzerland. The 3 cantons agreed to defend and protect their rights against everyone, including the emperor. Their covenant, entered into on Aug. 1, 1291, marked the foundation of the Swiss Confederation. By 1353 the Confederation had expanded to include 8 cantons; by 1815, 22.

When Protestant encountered Catholic in the Reformation, religious wars were ignited—4 of them—which tore the land and spirits for almost two centuries. Protagonists in the wars of religion were the "Catholic cantons" (the 3 founding ones and Lucerne) and Zurich, the mission land of the reformer Ulrich Zwingli. Zwingli, a Catholic priest turned reformer, was a *feldprediger*, a battlefield (or combat) chaplain, with the military forces of Protestant reform. He died on the battlefield outside Zurich.

From the outset the cantons have fiercely guarded

their rights, giving to the confederation jurisdiction over only a limited group of matters—foreign affairs and national defense, primarily. The eligible voters of a canton vote on matters which elsewhere in the world are handled routinely by legislative or executive bodies of government. The residents of Zurich, for example, go to the polls on an average of once a month and, frequently, a dozen or more measures are on the ballot.

Most cantons now officially recognize 3 religions: Protestant, Catholic and Old Catholic. There are exceptions. It was only in 1963 that Zurich voted to give official recognition to the Catholic Church. The constitution of the Italian-speaking canton of Lugano declares that the Roman Catholic religion is the religion of the state (canton). On the other hand, Vaud (Lausanne) does not recognize the Catholic Church. The basic effect of recognition is that the canton will collect church taxes for the support of a resident's local parish. In a small number of cantons church taxes are not obligatory. In 1947 Geneva introduced a voluntary church tax system. Next door in heavily Protestant Vaud canton there is no church tax machinery at all. The Protestants are financed directly from the public treasury. (Discussions to finance Catholic parishes in the same manner have been started.)

One view held by all 22 cantons is that a child is born into the religion of the parents. Later, if he wishes to renounce the religion of his birth, change to another religion, or be recognized as a nonbeliever, he must make a formal declaration. Otherwise, when the child reaches tax-paying age, he pays church taxes in accordance with the practice of the canton. There are very few "dropouts" to escape church taxes.

Relations between church and state vary from canton to canton, too. In the Catholic canton of Fribourg, cantonal officials make a formal New Year's Day call on the bishop. In the canton's capital city, also named Fribourg, officials attend Mass in the cathedral on feastdays and participate in the Corpus Christi procession.

Some cantons have a say in the naming of a bishop. In the Basel diocese, cathedral canons submit a list of 6 names for consideration by municipal (Basel) and cantonal (Solothurn) authorities. The officials have the traditional right to strike 2 names from the list. For at least a half century, the officials have never vetoed any of the nominations. Even if they do veto a name, Rome is still free to appoint anyone it wishes, whether on the list or not.

Switzerland is a pluralistic society, with many religions, languages and ethnic groups. About 3.8 million of the 5.5 million Swiss speak German; 1 million, French; and a bit more than ½ million, Italian. (Approximately 50,000 in the St. Moritz area speak the Latin-based Romansch language). A little over half of the Swiss are Protestants.

The Swiss constitution calls for approval by the federal government before a new diocese is created. The constitution, adopted in 1848, restricted the establishment of any new monastery. It also banned Jesuits from "work in church and school." By a popular vote the constitutional interdictions were suppressed in 1973.

At Schoenbrunn, in the Catholic canton of Zug, the Jesuits have a retreat house, and springs on the grounds are the source of part of the city of Zurich's water supply. Ironically, in the 19th-century campaign against the Society of Jesus, the Jesuits were—among other things—called "poisoners of the wells."

ST. NICHOLAS OF FLÜE

For the Swiss, St. Nicholas of Flüe is a national hero in the same category as William Tell. No one is certain as to the date of his birth—sometime in March 1417—but all Swiss know how he saved the growing confederation from a disastrous civil war between city and county cantons. The federal parliament had met a couple dozen times in various parts of the country to work out a peace, and never succeeded. When the legislators convened in Sachseln in 1481 they met the saintly man known as Brother Claus, then in his mid-60s. He spoke with them and a nation-saving peace was agreed upon within an hour. As a result, he is considered as a father of his country. He is buried at Sachseln, 5 miles from his birthplace at Flüeli. He died on Mar. 21, 1487 at the age of 70. His feast, Sept. 25, is a day of pilgrimage.

TRANSPORTATION: Sachseln can be reached by train from Zurich.

HOTELS: At Flüeli-Ranft, *Paxmontana;* at Sachseln, *Mot-Hotel Kreuz.*

PLACES OF INTEREST: Nearby is the Benedictine Monastery of Engelberg.

ALPINE SAINTS

Maurice was an officer who headed the Theban legion of Rome. He became a Christian in the latter part of the 3rd century and with all his men was put to death by imperial decree in what is now the canton of Valais, south of Lake Geneva. In the 4th century St. Theodore, the first bishop of the diocese, who lived at Martigny, erected a church over the graves of Maurice and his men at the site known today as St. Maurice-en-Valais. In A.D. 515 King Sigismund of Burgundy enlarged the church of St. Maurice, and settled a community of monks whose mission was psalmody. Day and night, continuously, the monks sang the praises of God, the first monks in the Western world to practice such a ritual. The monks remained at St. Maurice-en-Valais until the 9th century when they were replaced by canons. In 1127 the canons adopted the Rule of St. Augustine.

Meanwhile, St. Bernard of Mont Joux built a hospice along the pass that still carries his name, the Great St. Bernard, to care for and give shelter to travelers making their way through Europe's highest mountains. The hospice was installed at the 8,020-foot level at Bourg St. Pierre. In the 10th century, the Saracens destroyed St. Bernard's hospice. It was reestablished in the 11th century by canons who, like those at neighboring St. Maurice, adopted the Augustinian Rule.

Construction of the Mount Blanc and Great St. Bernard tunnels notably reduced the traffic through the Great St. Bernard Pass and, at the same time, the need for the traditional assistance of the "monks" of St. Bernard and their handsome, helpful dogs. Nowadays, a chapel remains on the mountaintop for use primarily in summer. The Augustinian canons have reestablished their Great St. Bernard Monastery in the lowlands at Martigny. The St. Maurice and St. Bernard monasteries, the only Augustinian ones in Switzerland, belong to a confederation of Augustinian congregations created by John XXIII in 1959. The first abbot-primate of the world's Augustinian congregations was the abbot of St. Maurice (1959–68). He was succeeded by the abbot of Klosterneuburg, which is outside Vienna (See Index.)

TRANSPORTATION: St. Maurice-en-Valais and Martigny are on rail line from Lausanne.

HOTELS: At St. Maurice, *Interalps Motel* and *L'Écu du Valais* are tops; *La Gare* and *Des Alpes* are less expensive.

PLACES OF INTEREST: The fairyland cave known as *Grotte aux Fées*.

ST. GALLEN

St. Gallen, near the shores of Lake Constance, has been at the center of Christian culture and civilization for more than a dozen centuries. At St. Gallen Monastery the language spoken by the Germanic tribes was put into written form for the first time. The monastic library contains a number of "first editions": the oldest German version of the *Pater Noster;* the oldest manuscript in German (about A.D. 770); the oldest Bible in Greek; the oldest copy of the Rule of St. Benedict.

In the town which developed around the monastery of St. Gallen the residents, 7½ centuries ago, developed a textile industry that remains Europe's finest. The standards were high. Linen-makers who did not meet them risked having what they produced burned publicly and they themselves would be barred from working at the craft for a year.

A city of 80,000 inhabitants has grown on the site where an Irish monk, Gall (in Latin, Gallus), installed his hermit's cell in A.D. 612. While Gallus was exploring the area, his foot became tangled in a briar patch and it was several minutes before he could shake it loose. For Gallus this was a sign from heaven. He decided to make this the place for his hermit's cell. Other Irish monks joined him. After he died (A.D. 646) settlers along Lake Constance as well as people on the other side of the Alps made pilgrimages to his grave. A monastery was built and the monks, after following an austere Irish discipline for nearly a century, adopted the Rule of St. Benedict in A.D. 720. As the settlement grew, the name St. Gall (in German, Gallen) was given to the monastery; to the town which grew up around the monastic settlement; and, a century ago, to the canton.

Today, a little over half the residents of St. Gallen are Catholics. Just before the Reformation everyone in town was a Catholic. During the Reformation the townspeople literally chose the circle in which they wished to live. Catholics lived behind a wall in the inner circle around the monastery; the Protestants, between walls, in an outer circle. Each group was forbidden to cross into the other's circle. Passage through the circles was made by a kind of Berlin corridor.

St. Gallen Monastery survived the Reformation, but not the French Revolution. The monastery was suppressed in 1805, the buildings secularized, and the monks sent away. When the diocese of St. Gallen was established in the middle of the last century, the church of the former abbey became the bishop's cathedral. It is the most magnificent church in Switzerland. St. Gallus is buried under the main altar. His feast on Oct. 16, the anniversary of his death, is a major day of pilgrimage.

Over the library entrance of the former monastery, Greek words say: "Medicine Chest of the Soul."

TRANSPORTATION: St. Gallen is 50 miles east of Zurich on main rail line.

HOTELS: *Valhalla* and *Portner* are excellent. *Metropol* and *Montana* are less expensive.

EINSIEDELN

The name of the town Einsiedeln tells its background. In German, the word *einsiedler* means "hermit." The hermit was a young nobleman named Meinrad who, according to legend, had descended from the Counts of Hohenzollern. Early in the 9th century Meinrad became a monk in the Benedictine monastery at Reichenau on Lake Constance. He was assigned to teach at the monastery school but this work did not please him because it kept him too close to the everyday world. With the permission of the abbot he set out to find a place where he could live in solitude. In A.D. 835 he settled at what is now Einsiedeln in the canton of Schwyz. He lived a solitary life for 26 years, his only companions being two crows. Then one night in the year 861—the traditional date is Jan. 21—two wandering men clubbed him to death, and fled. The crows followed them, hovering above and shrieking in a strange manner until the two murderers, on arriving in Zurich 30 miles away, were captured by suspicious residents. Meinrad's body was brought back to Reichenau, and other monks took up living at the place of his hermit's cell. In A.D. 934, a monk from Strasbourg, named St. Eberhard, established a formal monastic community under the Rule of St. Benedict.

Einsiedeln is always alive. In summer, buses squeeze along the narrow main street. In winter, snow brings skiers. There are always pilgrims. An outdoor food vendor, roasting large fat sausages over a fire, looks expectantly for clients in the crowd.

It is a small, cosy town of 10,000 residents. Townspeople out shopping greet perfect strangers they meet on the street with the friendly Swiss-dialect salutation *Gruezi*. The traditional greeting goes back to the days when the people of Einsiedeln wanted to let pilgrims know they were welcome.

The main street leads to the square in front of the monastery. The monastic complex, with the twin-towered basilica at the center, resembles a stage setting. It is vast. The monastery, with the basilica at the center, is more than 300 feet wide. The two bell towers are nearly 170 feet high. Behind the wide, calm façade the monastery reaches back hundreds of yards, with workshops for the monk-repairmen, barns for the milk cows, stables for the thoroughbred horses that are sold to the Swiss army.

At the very top of the basilica is a statue of the Madonna, flanked by two angels. Just below, in a recessed niche, is a statue of St. Maurice, the Roman officer-martyr of the 3rd century. Still lower on the façade are statues of Meinrad and the monk Eberhard who built the first church.

Ancient documents tell of a remarkable happening at the time of consecration of the church on Sept. 14, 948. A vigil and a fast were observed on the evening before the day of consecration. Two bishops were present, Conrad of Constance and Ulrich (later canonized) of Augsburg. As the two bishops knelt in prayer they all at once observed Christ standing at the altar with angels and saints beside Him. When Bishop Conrad proceeded to consecrate the church at the ceremony the following morning, an angel held him back. The angel announced that Christ had consecrated the church the night before. The anniversary of the consecration has been a main day at Einsiedeln ever since.

When Meinrad arrived from Reichenau in the 9th century he had with him, according to tradition, a wooden statue of the Madonna. At least as far back as the 12th century the monks honored Our Lady of Einsiedeln in a chapel within the church. A statue of the Madonna, possibly the one brought by Meinrad, was above the altar of the chapel and pilgrims came to pray to Our Lady of Einsiedeln. That statue is not the one now in the chapel. A fire in 1465 destroyed the church, the chapel and its statue. A new Madonna statue was acquired by the monks and, except for a hegira caused by the arrival of French Revolution forces, has been in the chapel continuously.

The chapel, a black marble structure, is at the center of the splendid Baroque basilica, not far from the entrance. The chapel is a perfect Baroque square, 20 feet high, wide and deep.

Centuries of candles lighted by millions of pilgrims have darkened the once flesh-colored features of the Virgin, who is standing, and the Child she holds in her left arm. As a result, pilgrims refer to her as the "Black Madonna."

The 4-foot statue is dressed in a robe of red and gold brocade. There are special robes for feastdays and days of major pilgrimage. The custom of robing the statue in ornate garments apparently began under the Spanish influence of Emperor Charles V (who was also Charles I, king of Spain). There is a collection of crowns which change according to the feastday. One silver crown carries a black pearl that had been in the ring worn by Charles V.

Beneath the statue of the Black Madonna is a miniature baldachin in which is exposed, behind a delicate mask of gold and precious stones, the head of St. Meinrad. Other relics of the first hermit of Einsiedeln are in a reliquary at the main altar. The relics were brought from Reichenau in 1039.

Two cannon balls are among the ex-voto offerings in the chapel, among the plaques and paintings recording miraculous cures and protection in time of danger. The cannon balls were presented by townspeople of Lindau, a Lake Constance resort, and Villingen, thankful that their villages had been spared during the cannonading by Swedish soldiers in the Thirty Years' religious war of the 17th century.

The chapel itself was not spared when Napoleon's troops invaded Switzerland. The tremendous size of the monastery and basilica defied the French forces, so they concentrated on the fragile Chapel of Our Lady of Einsiedeln. The chapel's stone, marble and wood were smashed into bits, and hurled into the square in front of the basilica.

The statue of the Black Madonna was not endangered. Before the troops arrived someone from the monastery hastily buried it in the hills near the shrine. From this hiding place, after 3 weeks, it was taken on a long escape journey that continued for 5 years. The first place of refuge was a Benedictine monastery in Voralberg, the westernmost Austrian province which borders Switzerland. The Voralberg Monastery did not remain secure long. Napoleon's men moved into western Austria and the statue for several years had to be transferred from one place to another. At last, when religious institutions no longer were considered safe, an Austrian villager carried the statue over the Alps to Trieste. There, the villager turned the statue over to a friend who promised to keep it safe in his house. The friendly protector happened to be a Protestant.

The political situation eased by 1803, and the Black

Madonna began the long journey home. On Sept. 29, 1803, the statue made a triumphal entry into Einsiedeln. Each year, on the anniversary, a High Mass is celebrated in the chapel and the statue is dressed in the same gold-embroidered white robe it was wearing when it made its safe return.

The shrine was not left empty during the enforced journey of the Black Madonna. Another statue was substituted. When the troops of Napoleon reached the basilica they seized the substitute statue and, thinking it was the miraculous image of Our Lady of Einsiedeln, took it with them. A few years before his defeat at Waterloo, Napoleon sent a message to the monks at Einsiedeln offering to return the miraculous statue. The monks informed him that the Black Madonna was already safely back at the shrine.

Late each afternoon, after reciting Vespers in the basilica, the monks proceed to the Chapel of Our Lady of Einsiedeln. In pairs, in 2 long columns, they proceed through the vast church with their arms folded under their long black scapulars. They are grouped according to seniority, with the novices first and the abbot at the end of the processional columns. At the chapel of the Black Madonna the monks chant the *Salve Regina,* a melodious prayer believed to have been written by a monk named Hermannus Contractus at Reichenau nearly 1,000 years ago.

The custom of the daily *Salve Regina* began at Einsiedeln during the Reformation. Till then the prayer had been chanted only on Sundays and certain feast-days. But in 1547, during the upheaval caused by the Reformation, the Cistercian monks were expelled from their monastery at Maulbronn in Württemberg, Germany, and the last abbot, Johannes von Lenzingen, took refuge in Einsiedeln. He presented a gift to Einsiedeln Monastery on condition that, from then on, the monks would sing the *Salve Regina* each day.

The 120 monks at Einsiedeln still successfully blend

their agricultural and cultural activities, says Father Wolfgang Renz, a tall, 50-year-old monk with black hair which he combs back. Father Wolfgang is named after St. Wolfgang, the first apostle of Hungary and noted bishop of Regensburg, who started his religious career as dean at Einsiedeln. Father Wolfgang has the Latin title of *cellarius* at the monastery, meaning that he is in charge of guests, of the monastery's food, and of all housekeeping arrangements.

"We are in a pre-alpine region, three thousand feet above the valley meadowlands," Father Wolfgang says, "and this is privileged by the state. Small peasants give up farming. They work hard, but the income is not enough. The government wants the area farmed, otherwise it will be ruined. So, when we sell cheese, we get help from the state in the form of a subsidy. This is everywhere the same in the pre-Alps. The government wants to encourage farming in such areas. We sell milk, too. We have ninety cows, and they are machine-milked. We used to have three cow barns. Now, we have only one, but it is new and very fine, and electrically equipped.

"For a thousand years we have been raising our own breed of horse. We have twenty to thirty horses now, but we used to have sixty to seventy. We can't sell them the way we did because the army [Swiss] does not use so many horses anymore."

"The monastic day has been shortened a bit at Einsiedeln. The first Mass used to be at four-thirty A.M., and the monks would rise in time for it. Now the first Mass is at five-thirty A.M. Then at seven-thirty A.M., there is a conventual High Mass—'conventual' meaning 'convent' or 'monastery'—and all the monks are at this except those who are parish priests or who have work to do. This High Mass is in Gregorian plain chant. Then, at twelve o'clock, exactly at noon, we have midday prayer. At four P.M., there is Vespers, followed by the procession to the chapel to sing the *Salve Regina*. At eight P.M. we chant Compline."

On the feasts of Corpus Christi and of the Assumption there is a procession in the square, with the abbot and the monks participating. The procession is at 3 P.M. There is also an outdoor procession on the days of major pilgrimage: Sept. 14, anniversary of the 10th-century consecration of the church; and the feast of the Rosary, the first Sunday in October.

Whenever a monk at Einsiedeln is asked about miracles, he usually refers to the words of Johannes Scherr, a 19th-century historian who, although long an unbeliever, was impressed.

"Is it not also a real miracle," Scherr asked, "that millions of people come, their heart filled with troubles, to deposit their burden before the Black Madonna, and go away consoled?"

TRANSPORTATION: Einsiedeln is 30 miles south of Zurich, with change of trains at Wädenswil.

HOTELS: *Drei Könige* is excellent. *Bären* is less expensive.

POINTS OF INTEREST: Every 5 years (1975, 1980, etc.) the Corpus Christi play of the Spanish poet and Franciscan friar, Don Pedro Calderon de la Barca, is presented in the evening during the summer in the square fronting the basilica. Hundreds of Einsiedeln villagers take part in the religious pageant.

MARIA STEIN

The first impression given by the Benedictine abbey of Mariastein, 14 miles south of Basel, is that it could easily be the most rundown of the active abbeys remaining in Europe. Chunks of plaster have been torn from the walls in the main corridor, many parts of the building are bare of paint, and there is a general ramshackle air. Then one learns of the 2 miracles that first attracted pilgrims to the site centuries ago. A third miracle, one concludes, is that the monastery still exists.

Maria Stein Monastery—Mary of the Stone and, in French, Notre Dame de la Pierre—is built near the edge of a cliff in the foothills of the Juras. The Marian Chapel, although enclosed, has been erected along the side of the cliff, and one descends into it by an inner stairway near the abbey entrance. The shrine is at an altitude of 1,713 feet. A little hamlet at the site calls itself Mariastein but it consists only of a small hotel, a few dwellings and Maria Stein Monastery.

A monk named Augustine tells of the miracles of Maria Stein. Father Augustine is slight in build, his hair is thinning, and he is in his 30s.

"Pilgrimages began here in the fourteenth century after a child, playing, fell from the rock. The child landed safe and sound fifty meters below at the entrance to a grotto. The people at first put an image of the Virgin in the grotto, and then later constructed a chapel in the rocks where the child fell. It was an open grotto, but they built an outer wall to make it into a chapel.

"In 1540 there was another miracle. Another child fell again in the same spot, and escaped injury. Of this event we have a *mirakelbild* (painting of the miracle) which was made three years afterwards.

"The Benedictine monastery was not here at the time of the second miracle. It was at Beinwil, twelve miles to the northeast.

"In the century after the second miracle, the monks were invited by the cantonal government of Solothurn to reestablish their monastery here, and take charge of the pilgrimages."

Why did the invitation come from the canton, and not from the bishop?

"Who knows? It is a historic point."

The abbot of Einsiedeln sent monks to help in the construction. The monastery was completed in 1648.

"For more than two centuries," Father Augustine says, "everything was normal. Then, in 1874, the cantonal government launched a kulturkämpf, a liberalismus, and the monks were expelled. They went at first to Delle, in the French Juras, where they built a monastery and a *collège*, a secondary school. In 1900, in the anticlerical movement in France, they were expelled from there, and went to Austria, to Dürnberg. They had only a house in Dürnberg temporarily. In 1906 they recommenced monastic life at Bregenz [in the Austrian province of Voralberg], and during the same year some of the monks began teaching at Altdorf in Uri [one of the 3 original Swiss cantons].

"In 1941 the monks were expelled from Bregenz by the National Socialists [the Nazis who occupied Austria]. They thereupon asked the cantonal government of Solothurn for permission to return to Maria Stein. The government gave permission but only until the father-abbot had found something else. But the monks did not look any further. They decided this was their homeland, and their home.

"They then hired a lawyer who studied the ancient expulsion decree [of 1874] in light of the federal constitution [of 1848] which prohibited construction of any new monastery. The lawyer discovered that the decree simply said it was no longer desired that the monks be here. But the important word *aufheben* (suppress) was not in the decree. Thus it was not a matter of constructing a new abbey. The old one had never been suppressed. But since a vote of the people sanctioned the 1874 expulsion order, a new vote was needed to revoke it, and this took place on June 6–7, 1971. Since then, the abbey has been recognized by the cantonal government, and we are now beginning to restore it.

"In the monastery yet is a school of the canton which will be there for another year or two. And some families have been living in the monastery till recently."

Then monastic life has resumed at Maria Stein?

"It never really ended. Since the expulsion in 1874, the cantonal government always allowed two or three monks to remain here to care for the pilgrims."

How many monks are now in the community?

"There are forty-nine of us, but only eighteen are here at present, along with the abbot. The other monks are at our school at Altdorf in Uri, which is about one hundred eighty miles from here. With a school so far from the monastery it is difficult to maintain a normal monastic life."

And the abbot?

"In 1971, after we were officially recognized in our home by the cantonal government, the abbot who had been guiding us through all these difficulties since 1937 renounced his lifetime rule. He was seventy-eight then. The new abbot was forty-seven."

How is the restoration paid for?

"The cantonal government has given us some money for the restoration work. We try to earn money, too, by teaching catechism to the students who have been attending the cantonal school in the monastery, and also in some of the neighboring villages. We are now putting central heating in the church."

Fifty-six steps lead down to the main floor of the Chapel of Grace that was built along the side of the cliff from which the two children fell. Ex-voto plaques, in French and German, are on the walls. One in French says: "Mary, protectress of their son during the siege of Neuf-Brisach; the father and mother are grateful; Mariastein, 12 November, 1870." A small plaque in German, with no name, says in gold letters: "Mary has helped."

The "miracle painting" of the second child who fell

from the cliff in 1540 hangs in the monastery's Chapel
of the Seven Sorrows. It carries the date "1543." It is an
unusual painting, also, because it depicts all members
of the Holy Trinity. God the Father is seated; a dove,
for the Holy Spirit, is behind Him; and Christ is shown
on His cross. Mary is also in the painting.

TRANSPORTATION: Basel is on main rail line from Zurich,
France and Western Germany. A narrow-gauge railway connects Basel with Flüh where there is a bus
to Mariastein.

HOTELS: At Mariastein, *Hotel Post* is quite comfortable.
In Basel, leaders are *Trois Rois* and *Schweizerhof*.
International is a bit less expensive.

POINTS OF INTEREST: The shrine of Notre Dame of
Vorbourg is at Delémont. Many of its ex-votos are
little paintings.

GENEVA

Geneva today is an international city but John Calvin
made it a world center for religious refugees and a
religious center for the world in the 16th century. Himself a religious refugee from his native land of France,
Calvin is buried somewhere in the Plainpalais cemetery,
½ mile from St. Peter's Cathedral where the people of
Geneva on May 21, 1536 unanimously adopted the
Reformation. There is no tomb for Calvin, no indication
of where he lies buried. He specifically asked that no
name or sign of any type be placed over his grave. Yet
his name is all over Geneva. The city has been called
"the Protestant Rome." In the Reformation, religious
refugees flocked to Geneva, choosing it as a likely
haven because the people there had voted to "live
according to the Gospel." Six thousand Protestant exiles
crowded into a city that had a population of just
12,000. But they were made welcome. There were

British, and Dutch, and Italian, and Spanish refugees. Geneva became a beehive of Reformed activity, the principal center of the Reformation in the French-speaking world.

While the English refugees remained in Geneva from 1556 to 1559, John Knox of Scotland served as their pastor. The English exiles produced the Geneva Bible which was known also as "The Breeches Bible" because, in describing the leaves which served as coverings for Adam and Eve, they modestly referred to them as "breeches." The liturgy developed at Geneva by Knox became the model for the order of worship of the Church of Scotland. It is, too, the base for the Presbyterian liturgy throughout the world today. From Geneva, scores of trained pastors entered France in this same period.

Geneva, at the time of Calvin, was essentially a seat of knowledge. He believed, in fact he insisted, that the reform of religion and of life had to be rooted in a profound understanding of the Holy Scriptures.

THE JOHN CALVIN AUDITORIUM

There were sufficient churches for the citizens of Geneva in the beginning days of the Reformation. For the refugees from elsewhere, Reformed and Presbyterian, the Auditorium was their parish church.

The Auditorium is a small Gothic vaulted church, somewhat larger than a chapel, across from St. Peter's Cathedral. The World Alliance of Reformed Churches, meeting in General Council at Princeton in 1954, voted to restore the Auditorium. Dr. Harrison Ray Anderson of Chicago was named to head an international fund-raising committee.

The Auditorium is on the site of a 5th-century church. After the acceptance of the Reformation in Geneva, the church was not used and in 1545 became a foundry for the production of military weaponry. In

1557 John Calvin and other ministers of Geneva began using the church for weekly meetings of "The Congregation," a group of Genevese and exiles who met together at 7 o'clock in the morning, before going to work, in order to learn about the Bible and Reformed doctrine. It soon acquired the name "Auditorium," like a university lecture hall. Calvin was a pastor at the Auditorium from 1562 to 1564. (He had arrived in Geneva in 1540).

. The Auditorium is known also as the John Knox Chapel and as the National Protestant Church of Geneva. The Church of Scotland (Presbyterian), the Dutch Reformed Church (Protestant Gemeente) and the Evangelical Waldensian Church of Italy have regular services in the Auditorium. Each Sunday at 11 A.M. is a service in English.

Three tall plain-glass windows are at the front of the Auditorium. The table used for the service is 8 feet long. Its 4 legs are joined together in a frame. The table is from Calvin's time. On the table is a gilded cross inscribed "To the Glory of God and in memory of the members of the Fourth Presbyterian Church of Chicago who gave their lives for freedom."

Alcoves along the side which once housed altars now contain exhibits and memorabilia concerning Calvin and the Reformation. There is a reproduction of a 16th-century portrait of Calvin as a young man—long tapering beard, and strong dark eyes. An engraving of Calvin at the age of 48 makes him into a biblical patriarch.

One item on exhibit indicates the religious sufferings of the past. It is a copy of a large certificate, an *Acte de Liberation,* releasing a French Huguenot, Jacques Pecher, who had been condemned as a slave to row a galley because of his Protestant religion. The certificate, dated Apr. 15, 1699, begins: "We, François Arnoul de Vaucresson and Michel le Vasseur, advisers of the king, commissioners and general controllers of the Galleys of

France. . . ." The *Acte de Liberation* calls upon all governors, lieutenants of the king, mayors, district aldermen, provosts, and captains of ports, bridges and passages to "let Pecher enjoy the liberty granted him by His Majesty."

Among the other exhibits are copies of title pages to the Geneva Psalter of 1565, to the first edition of Calvin's *Christianae Religionis Institutio,* to the English translation of the Geneva Bible in 1560, and to the Geneva Confession of Faith of 1537. (Originals of documents exhibited are at the university library or Historical Museum of the Reformation.)

When the restored John Calvin Auditorium was dedicated on June 1, 1959 in the presence of 100 delegates from the world's Reformed and Presbyterian churches and of the Geneva Company of Pastors, Dr. Anderson said:

"Now the Auditorium is finished. It is as it should be. True to the past, useful for today, and ready for tomorrow."

CALVIN COLLEGE

The main entrance and the long sloping roof of Calvin College, the foundation stone literally of the University of Geneva, are intact after 4 centuries, and its pedagogical principles are as sound as when it was founded by the local government in 1558 at the insistence of Calvin.

There was only one private school in Geneva at the time. Calvin proposed the creation of the college to prepare men who could serve God and the government. It is a 4-year high school. Until 1969 only boys attended the Calvin College. Since then girls have been admitted, as well.

Excavations in the school yard have unearthed several inscriptions left by the Roman legions. One is dedicated to the god Apollo; another to a woman who was priestess at a pagan temple.

In the courtyard now are parked the bicycles, motor scooters and motorbikes of the students. At the center of the façade, above the yard, is the coat of arms of Geneva with a large representation of the sun, representing Light—that is, God.

MONUMENT OF REFORMATION

Among the messages on the 100-yard wall which tell the story of the Reformation are a few words from John Knox: "A man with God is always in the majority."

Knox is one of the churchmen represented in the massive international Monument of the Reformation, a gleaming rampart of quartz. Actually, the monument is amid the remains of Geneva's 16th-century ramparts. It was built in 1909 with funds contributed by Reformed congregations in the United States and Europe.

Across the face of the monument in huge letters is the inscription POST TENEBRAS LUX (After the Darkness, Light).

The 4 churchmen who were in Geneva when Calvin College was dedicated are among the 10 heroic-sized statues. Three of them are French; the fourth is Knox, the Scot. There are Calvin himself who became the leader of the Reformation not only in Geneva but in France; William Farel, of Dauphiné, who traveled through western Switzerland preaching the doctrine of Reform; and Théodore de Bèze, a native of Vézélay, who succeeded Calvin as the head of the Geneva Reformed Church and who was the first rector of the new university.

Political and social leaders who helped spread Reformed principles are depicted in other statues. They are: French Admiral Gaspard de Coligny, leader of France's Huguenot party; William the Silent, who supported the cause of Protestants in the northern Low Countries (now the Netherlands); Stephen Bocskay, fighter for religious freedom for Hungarian Protestants in the 16th century; Oliver Cromwell, English general and statesman of the 17th century; Friederich William, founder of the Prussian State, who gave a haven to French Huguenots when the Edict of Nantes was abrogated by Louis XIV (part of his Edict of Potsdam, welcoming the religious exiles, is inscribed on the wall); and Roger Williams, member of the company of Pilgrims that arrived on the *Mayflower* in 1620 in the Massachusetts Bay Colony. The preamble of the Mayflower Compact is produced on the wall in Old English.

INTERNATIONALISM

Geneva is home of the World Council of Churches, the World Health Organization, the International Committee of the Red Cross and the International Labour Organisation.

TRANSPORTATION: Geneva is 180 miles southwest of Zurich on main rail routes.

HOTELS: *President, Des Bergues,* and *Richemond* are among the fine hotels. *Eden* and *Ambassador* are less expensive.

POINTS OF INTEREST: The Chair of Calvin in St. Peter's Cathedral; at No. 12 rue de l'Hôtel de Ville, the house where Agrippa d'Aubigné, a Huguenot captain, poet and "defender of the Faith," lived from 1552–1630; the statue of Rousseau; and the Russian Orthodox Church. St. Francis de Sales is buried at Annecy, across the border in France. He was bishop of Geneva in 1602. At Castle Thorens in Annecy is a collection of souvenirs of the saint.

ZWINGLI'S BIRTHPLACE

The spiritual teachings of Ulrich (also, Huldrych) Zwingli reached into all parts of German-speaking Switzerland. The Swiss Reformer was born on Jan. 1, 1484 at Wildhaus, in the eastern part of Switzerland. It remains an area of milk cows and beef cattle, of butter and cheese, and of delightful alpine meadows and Gothic alpine peaks. His father, Bartholomew Zwingli, was in public life, as a burgomaster, but a brother of his mother was abbot at the Benedictine monastery of Fischingen, and a brother of his father was the pastor at Wessen. As a young man, Zwingli showed great musical aptitude, and could play nearly a dozen instruments. He taught at St. Martin's Parish School in Basel. His interest in theology was not great until he became aware that religion and humanism were not automatically incompatible. He was consecrated a Catholic priest in Constance (see Index), and said his first Mass in his home town of Wildhaus. His first sermon was preached at Rapperswil. He was made pastor in the town of Glarus, and remained there for 10 years.

He was a man of dynamism, and twice while still a young priest took on assignments as a battlefield chaplain. But he was a man of learning most of all, and he studied Greek in order to be able to read the New Testament in its original language.

In 1516 he was assigned to Einsiedeln to assist the pilgrims. The number of monks had dwindled to a handful. Some of the former noblemen among the monks had gone to live in the manor houses and castles of their families. A parish priest, such as Zwingli, was engaged by the monks as a *leutpriester* (literally, people's priest) to serve the pilgrims. Zwingli was impressed by the number of people who came to the shrine to seek the intercession of the Madonna. But their devotion caused him wonder, too. "Why do we want to go to another rather than to Him?" he asked himself. "Isn't that showing contempt for His open grace and mercy?" He pondered such questions during the several years he remained at Einsiedeln.

The place where Zwingli was born at Wildhaus is a 2-story wooden building, made of heavy beams. The house is much like an oversized wooden box, with practically no windows along the sides or back. At the front are large windows made from handblown glass, similar to those in Calvin's house in Noyon. A few wooden steps are at the front door. The ground floor is divided into several rooms. All are small, except the living-room which takes up half the floor. There are some pieces of furniture of the period and engravings—one of the sword and helmet that belonged to him as a battlefield chaplain; one of the Gross Münster in Zurich. The bed upstairs has a wooden canopy.

TRANSPORTATION: Wildhaus is 10 miles northwest of Buchs. By train to Buchs; then, bus.

HOTELS: *Acker* and *Hirschen* are the principal ones. *Friedegg* is across from the Zwingli house.

POINTS OF INTEREST: The delightful principality of Liechtenstein is just across the Rhine from the eastern border of Switzerland. Liechtenstein's ancient shrine at Schaan is virtually opposite Buchs. Liechtenstein is ruled by Prince Franz Josef II, the 12th prince of Liechtenstein, a member of the oldest dynasty in the German-speaking area with a family tree rooted in the 12th century. No troops existed to safeguard the 60-square-mile principality at the outbreak of the Second World War. On Easter Monday 1940 Prince Franz Josef went to the shrine at Schaan as a pilgrim, and like his ancestors dedicated himself to the Madonna, asking her protection. "Guard my country from all internal and external dangers," the prince prayed. "In spite of my country's smallness let it be a kingdom of your Son where Justice and Peace reign." The 3½-century-old family art collection is probably the most valuable private one in the world. Leonardo da Vinci's *Gianevra de Benci* is in the collection. It is the only Leonardo in private hands.

FRIBOURG

Fribourg is called a small Rome. There are numerous religious houses in the city, and all during the Reformation it remained Catholic.

It was built as a passage to guard the bridge over the Sarine River in 1157 and its founder, a lordly landowner, Berthold de Zaehringen, gave the people certain rights in order to encourage them to live here, and guard the bridge.

"At the Reformation," Father Rosetti says, "it was the government of Fribourg that decided to remain Catholic. The curés had little or nothing to do in the decision. Five or six times in the sixteenth century, the government assembled the people in the town square and had them take an oath to remain in the Catholic faith. Several priests were asked to leave Fribourg because they wanted to introduce 'new ideas.'"

Father Rosetti, a secular priest, is robust, middleaged and affable. He is rector of St. Michael's College which was founded by St. Peter Canisius, the former Jesuit general who was born in the Netherlands.

"Canisius came here in 1580. He was already aged, about sixty then. He was sent by his superiors to found a college [secondary school] because the government and the provost of the collegiate church wanted a place where Catholic children could study. There were Protestants all around Fribourg, you see. Gregory XIII, the Pope of the new calendar, encouraged the government to do this, and to make it possible for the Jesuits to live here he suppressed a decadent monastery of the canons of Pre-Montré near Bulle. Only five or six canons were still there. So the Pope turned this property over to the Jesuits, and the government agreed to build the school.

"First they built the school, then the church, then a house for the priests. The whole thing was built in the shape of a U so that the sun was always in the courtyard—typically Jesuit.

"While waiting for the priests' house to be finished, Canisius lived in town in the rue de Lausanne. There still is an argument about exactly where. He was here seventeen years, and he died on December 21, 1597 in the room next door to mine.

"Canisius named the school after St. Michael. He had a great devotion to the saint. He was born on May 8 which used to be a feast of St. Michael. Now the school is officially a cantonal school. The Jesuits were suppressed in the eighteenth century, and returned at the start of the nineteenth century. Then in 1848 they were expelled again [by the constitution] and for a while the name St. Michael was dropped and it was called the Cantonal School. In 1856 it was once again St. Michael's School, and the priests of the diocese were made directors."

Father Rosetti says Canisius's room was made into a chapel in 1641. On a wall is a painting of St. Michael which used to be above the domestic altar that Canisius used for Mass. The ground-floor room looks across the sunny courtyard. Two sundials are in the yard. They have Latin inscriptions: *Transit umbra, manent opera* (The shadow passes, works remain) and *Dico lucidas, taceo nubilas* (I tell of the bright days, I keep silent about the cloudy ones).

The relics of St. Peter Canisius are in a glass reliquary below the main altar of the church.

"He was certainly well named," Father Rosetti says. "His family name was De Hondt, and in accordance with the custom of those days it was Latinized as Canisius. The name means 'The Dog.' They called him the Watchdog of the Faith."

NOTRE DAME OF BOURGUILLON

Fribourg shows its age when one follows the route, Beau Chemin, which Canisius used to take on his way to the shrine of Notre Dame of Bourguillon. It is on a hill across the valley from St. Nicholas's Cathedral. Scores, perhaps hundreds, of stone steps lead down from the cathedral area through the huddled-together houses of the *basse ville*, the low part of Fribourg. The steps are a playground for children from the small houses crouched along the hillside. The pretty route crosses the Sarine River, passes the Church of St. John, and lazily ascends a wide green hill.

Bourguillon is a commune of Fribourg. It is nearly 1 mile high. Linguistically, it is on one of Switzerland's language borders. Just on the other side of Bourguillon, people speak German rather than French. There are about 300 residents.

The tiny church of the shrine is at a fork in the road in the center of town. A cemetery is at the front door. The church's name is written on the façade. Under the name, in French and German, is the statement: "In this place the Blessed Virgin has often performed miracles." The walls inside are filled with ex-voto plaques. A large one, dated July 18, 1933 at Asseris, and signed by the Charles Barby family, says: "Roger Barby (18) fell under a hay wagon weighing 800 kilos. It passed over his legs. His father invoked Notre Dame of Bourguillon. The child had nothing broken. A scratch and some blue marks attested to the accident and the protection of Mary."

The statue of Notre Dame of Bourguillon is life-sized. It is cloaked in a white neck-to-foot robe decorated in gold. A cape, fitted under a high gilded crown, covers the head and falls across the shoulders. The Child, held in the left arm, is dressed the same way, except for the cape, and wears a crown.

Father Gachet, the rector of the sanctuary, says that the statue was solemnly crowned on Oct. 8, 1923, the 400th anniversary of Fribourg's "maintenance of the Faith." He is a small, aging but lively man who has been rector 8 years. Before that he taught at St. Michael's College.

"Notre Dame of Bourguillon played a role in the maintenance of the Faith in Fribourg," the priest says. "The government of the city would organize pilgrimages of the people to the shrine to pray for strength in guarding their faith. From this moment, the statue acquired the title 'Guardian of the Faith.' This is the popular title, rather than the ecclesiastical one."

Father Gachet says that the statue, and the Gothic choir of the chapel, have existed since the 14th century.

"At first it was a chapel for the lepers. The government of Fribourg had installed a leprosarium here in the 13th century because the site was outside the city. It was a solitary area. All that was here were the lepers in a building, and the chapel. Why it became a place of pilgrimage no one knows. But pilgrims and lepers were here together till the sixteenth century, maybe the seventeenth. At that time the leprosarium was closed."

There are 3 major pilgrimages: one in June (the date varies) for the sick; the feast of the patroness, Notre Dame of Carmel, July 16; and the feast of the Rosary in October.

TRANSPORTATION: Fribourg is 95 miles southwest of Zurich on main rail lines from Bern and Lausanne.

HOTELS: *Duc Bertold* and *Fribourg* are the main ones. *Terminus* and *Central* are medium-priced.

ZURICH

Every official document issued by municipal authorities of Zurich shows 3 holy people carrying their heads. They are Felix, Regula and Exuperantius, the patron saints of this superb city.

Felix was a captain in the Roman legions which occupied the present area of Zurich. He had his sister, Regula, come from Rome to be his housekeeper, and then later sent for the servant Exuperantius. Felix became a convert of Christianity, and since the Roman settlement at Zurich was still pagan he, his sister and Exuperantius were persecuted for their religious beliefs, and then beheaded. Like holy men of ancient Greece, *cephalophors,* they carried their heads from the site of the beheading—an islet on the east bank of the Limmat—and walked across a small wooden bridge. They collapsed a short way up the hill on the other side of the river. Later, people of Zurich said this must be a holy sign, and they erected the Gross Münster (cathedral; literally, Big Monastery) on the spot where they died, and the Wasserkirche (Water Church) at the place where they were beheaded. Meanwhile, the soldiers of the Christianized Roman legion were persecuted, and chased into the Grissons area. They settled there, and introduced the street Latin of Rome, a language that is still spoken in the area as Romansch. Indeed, Romansch is the official language of St. Moritz.

In the 9th century, the daughters of King Ludwig the German, Princess Hildegard and her sister, Princess Bertha, were on their way into Zurich from their father's hilltop palace on the Ütliberg on the edge of town. On the way they were met by a deer with lighted candles on its antlers which escorted them to the west bank of the Limmat, and then disappeared. The two princesses told their father about the occurrence, saying that it was a sign from heaven to build a church. The king agreed with them, and had the Frau Münster (Lady Monastery) built on the site which, according to legend, was where Felix, Regula and Exuperantius were buried.

Frau Münster

King Ludwig the German built the Frau Münster as an abbey in A.D. 853 for his daughters Hildegard and Bertha. For centuries the princess-abbess of the women's monastery was the Lady (*Herrin*) of Zurich. In 1524 Abbess Katharina von Zimmern voluntarily turned over the church to the Zurich city council. This was in the time of Zwingli. Katharina was the last abbess. Since then the Frau Münster has been a Reformed church.

All statues had been removed from the church during the Reformation and, thinking it too bleak, a wealthy Zurich family some years ago engaged Marc Chagall to enliven it. He created a series of five stained-glass windows telling the biblical story. The walls of the cloisterlike area between the church and the City Hall tell the story of the two princesses and the deer in a series of frescoes.

Gross Münster

Zurich summoned Zwingli as a *leutpriester* (people's priest), a vicar, in 1518, and the Gross Münster (Big Monastery) was his cathedral. Zwingli was a dynamic man with a mission.

"The life of Jesus has remained concealed from the people too long," he declared. "I shall draw only from the source of the Holy Script and without any human explanations following will give what I have found by careful comparison and hearty prayer."

A statue of Zwingli is on the quay of the Limmat, alongside Wasserkirche. Its only inscription is the dates "January 1, 1484" for his birth and "October 11, 1531" for his death. At the corner of Kirchgasse and Neustadtgasse is the House-by-the-Column (*Haus-zur-Sul*) where Zwingli lived from 1522 to 1525. In those days houses were not numbered, and were identified by a descriptive word or phrase. Not far from the House-by-the-Column are old dwellings called the Black Eagle, the Ship, the Golden Deer and so on. The House-by-the-Column is now used as a kindergarten for children of working mothers.

A few dozen yards from the House-by-the-Column, at 13 Kirchgasse, was a subsequent residence of Zwingli. From here on Oct. 11, 1531, grabbing his helmet and sword, he rushed to the suburban fields at Kappel where the Protestant forces met in battle with the men of the Catholic cantons. Zwingli never returned from Kappel. The inscription on the house says he "died there for his faith." The building is church property and, in addition to serving as a residence for a clergyman, is used for Sunday school.

Kirchgasse leads into Zwingli Platz, the square surrounding the Gross Münster. At No. 4 is a severe-looking cement-finished building with a balcony window painted in blue and yellow. It is a 3-story building with a gabled roof and is the *antistitium,* in effect the residence of the head of the Swiss Reformed Church. It is also the parish house for the Gross Münster. Before the Reformation the building was the residence of the provost of the Gross Münster canons. In 1536 it became the residence for the *antistes* (an ancient Latin title for high priest) of the Zurich Church, Heinrich Bullinger. He was the head rector of Gross Münster after Zwingli's death, and authored the Second Helvetian Act of Faith. A statue honoring Bullinger (1504–75) is on the wall near the entrance to the Gross Münster. On a column by the entrance is a faded fresco of the Madonna and Child.

Before the Reformation, the Gross Münster had been the Church of the Canons of St. Felix and St. Regula, and was the only parish church on the right bank of the

Limmat (across from the City Hall). Zwingli and his successor Bullinger made it the Mother Church of the Swiss Reformation.

It is a Romanesque church, built between 1100 and 1225 on the site of an older basilica. The interior is extremely severe, solemn, with the only brightness issuing from the stained-glass windows at the front. It is completely unadorned now. There are no altars. They were removed by the Swiss Reformers.

"They were the most puritan, the most progressive of all," the caretaker says. "The Calvinists in Lausanne have an altar. So do the Lutherans. But not here."

The Roman-style crypt contains a statue of Charlemagne, made nearly a century before the Reformation. The statue had been on the tower facing the river and overlooking the city. Gravestones of pre-Reformation canons are also in the crypt.

THE SWISS NATIONAL MUSEUM

Zwingli and the Roman martyrs of Zurich come together in the Swiss National Museum which is behind the city's main railroad station.

In the exhibit room of seals is the original seal of Zurich of 1364 showing 3 headless persons. Klaus Deuchler, the museum's information officer, points out that an earlier seal of 1250 contains only 2 heads, those of Felix and Regula. Exuperantius, the servant, was added to the Zurich seal later.

Klaus is a youngish, slim, well-informed man with glasses. He is extremely helpful, and meticulous about his work.

"That was found in 1938," he says, referring to a painting on wood of the 3 Roman martyrs. "A house in the Old Town called Zum Königsstuhl (At the King's Throne) was being demolished, and a medieval wall with this painting turned up.

"A series of panels telling the whole story of the

beheading," Klaus says, "used to hang in the Gross Münster. How many there were no one knows because in the storming of the Gross Münster by the iconoclasts some were destroyed. We now have the five surviving panels in the museum. Three of the panels are of the martyrs, and the two others show the scene along the river. The latter two panels were overpainted in Reformation times, to hide the saints. A small section of the original painting has been uncovered. But it is more interesting at the present time to show Zurich of the 16th century, in the overpainting, than an artist's representation of the beheading that happened many centuries before he was born. Notice how in one panel you can see the Frau Münster Church and the Ütliberg where the two princesses who saw the deer lived."

The Ütliberg is part of the Albis Range in which is situated the community of Kappel, the site where Zwingli died. Till the Reformation there was a Cistercian abbey at Kappel with beautiful stained-glass windows. It is now an asylum. The stone statue that had stood outside the abbey church is in the museum, but in poor condition. The statue shows Christ and Mary, with their heads back to back. Mary's face was destroyed almost completely by the iconoclasts and Christ's also was disfigured.

Zurich's acceptance of Zwingli's teachings touched off the Battle of Kappel which was fought for political as well as religious reasons. The Catholic cantons to the south of Zurich looked upon the Reformation-oriented city as a traitor to the confederation.

"The Catholics were coming from the south," Klaus says. "The men of Zurich heard the cry, 'They're coming, They're coming,' a the-Russians-are-coming type of thing. Kappel is about twenty kilometers from Zurich, but the oldtime Swiss of Zwingli's time were tough, hardy men and could cover great distances fast. The men of Zurich rushed out of town in a kind of disorder, figuring it would be no problem to stop the southerners. Zwingli accompanied them as *feldprediger*, as battlefield chaplain. Nowadays, chaplains do not carry weapons but in those days they did, and Zwingli had a huge sword."

What are believed to be the helmet that Zwingli wore onto the battlefield and the 4-foot iron sword he carried with him are exhibited in the weapons room. On display also is the large blue, white and red banner of the Zurich forces. A man of Zurich named Adam Näf saved the banner from capture. His sword has a leather scabbard fitted with pockets for 2 short knives, used for cutting.

"They had no forks in those days," Klaus says. "They ate with their hands."

He points to the 16th-century painting of Hans Asper which shows Zwingli in his famous black cap with the long visor.

"Reformed clergymen of Zurich still like to call their sons Ulrich [Huldrych]," Klaus says.

The Confederated Catholic forces were stronger than the men of Zurich, and the Battle of Kappel turned into a rout. Klaus says the people of Zurich were good men but were not well led.

On the day after Zwingli was killed, his body was taken to a spot on the mountain where wood had been heaped high for a pyre. His body was thrown on the mound of wood, a torch was touched to it, and a fire that could be seen in Zurich roared across the range. Later, when the fire had cooled, the cinders were tossed helter-skelter into the wind.

TRANSPORTATION: There is major air service to Zurich directly from New York, Chicago and Boston. The Swiss National Railroads network covers all Switzerland with speed and comfort.

HOTELS: *Baur au Lac*, and *Zurich* are outstanding. *Atlantis* is at the foot of the Ütliberg. *Alexander Garni* is moderately priced and comfortable.

POINTS OF INTEREST: Zurich is one of Europe's loveliest cities. The Old Town, near the Gross Münster, is perfect for exploring on foot. Nearly a dozen old towers remain, including one named after Rudiger von Manesse, a 12th-century troubadour who took the trouble to write down the words of his songs in an illuminated script. In Spiegelgasse, a few blocks from the Gross Münster, Lenin lived from Feb. 21, 1916 to Apr. 2, 1917. St. Peter's Church has the largest clocktower in Europe. It is an easy drive to idyllic settings on the Rhine. The Carolingian church at Müstair has superb frescoes. At Riva is a 6th-century church. At Locarno a funicular railway leads to the Madonna del Sasso (Madonna of the Rock) shrine which has a superb view of Lake Maggiore.

16
Turkey

❦

CHRISTIANITY WAS BORN in Palestine, but it grew up in Turkey.

At Antioch (the present Antakya), the word "Christian" was used for the first time. The name of the first Christian emperor, Constantine, was given to the great city on the Bosphorus. It was called Constantinople until seized by the Turks in 1453 and renamed Istanbul. St. Paul was born in Tarsus. Popes from Peter to Paul VI have prayed on the soil of Turkey. Some think that Mary, after Christ's death, came to Ephesus with John the Evangelist and spent the rest of her life there. It is believed that St. John died at Ephesus and is buried there. The first church in Christendom dedicated to the Madonna was built at Ephesus. Many Christian martyrs of the 1st century died in the Bythnia district which includes the renowned Council city of Nicea (now Iznik).

The early centuries in Turkey were times of propagation of the faith, foundation of chapels and churches, and persecutions. Persecutions ended in the 4th century with the Edict of Milan establishing freedom of religion in the empire as a right of Roman citizenship.

Turkey witnessed, too, the decline of Christianity. Nicea (Iznik), the place of the first General Council, is identified with Arianism. After the Council of Ephesus, Nestorianism developed. The Monophysite heresy is linked to the Council of Chalcedon (on the Asian side of the Bosphorus). The heresies separated the people from the Church of Rome, as well as from the emperor. Increasing power was centered in the Eastern emperor at Constantinople which eventually became the city of schism between the Latins and the Orthodox.

Decline of Christianity in Turkey was speeded by the invasion of the Arabs in the 8th century who brought with them from the Arabian peninsula the Moslem religion. Latin Crusaders on their way to the Holy Land in the 11th century reconquered much of the land that had been "Arabized" either in the sense of race, religion, or language. Seizure of Constantinople in the middle of the 15th century by Moslem Turks who had come from the East meant the almost total extinction of Christianity in Turkey.

During the centuries of rule by the Ottomans, France came to be accepted at the Sublime Porte as the representative of the religious interests of the West. Even today France is remembered as Protector of the Christians in Turkey. Each Easter the Latin bishop of Izmir (Smyrna) celebrates a Mass for the French consul. In Izmir's St. Polycarp's Church is a special reserved seat, fitted in velour, for the French consul and his wife. On the feast of St. Polycarp tradition is for the consul to be solemnly saluted with incense. The incensing ritual was dispensed with a few years ago because the consul was not a Catholic. He voiced a protest on behalf of the French government and word later came from Rome that the consul of France was always to be incensed, as traditional.

Except for a relative handful of the 35 million citizens, the religion of Turkey is Moslem. Priests and ministers are few, and churches are even fewer. The archdiocese of Izmir stretches across most of southern Turkey. But it has only 2,000 Catholics. There had been a relatively large Greek Orthodox community in Izmir during the Ottoman empire. When the new republic of Turkey was formed following the First World War, ancient political feelings were stirred, and many Greeks were expelled. The Orthodox community at Izmir has not had a regular priest. For Easter and Christmas services a priest comes from Istanbul. Services are held in a small chapel which Dutch Protestants make available. During the 19th century Protestants and Catholics operated many schools and hospitals, but these activities have dwindled.

The Great Powers of the First World War called upon Turkey in the peace treaty to preserve the ancient religious communities. Turkey has done this, scrupulously permitting complete religious freedom. But, administratively, there has been a tendency, as traditional, to stick to the status quo. What already exists is permitted. On the other hand, authorization for a new church or for the immigration of additional foreign personnel, whether a hospital nurse or a priest, is a slow process.

ANTIOCH

Geographically, Antioch (Antakya) is at the end of the line. It is in a pocket of south-central Turkey between the Mediterranean and Syria. The western and northern borders of Syria are less than 20 miles away.

Religiously, Antioch ranks as the fifth most sacred city in Christendom, preceded only by Jerusalem, Bethlehem, Nazareth and Rome. Paul made the city his headquarters, and from Antioch began his 3 major journeys. Luke lived here. The followers of Christ, persecuted by the Romans in Jerusalem, fled to Antioch in the first years after the Crucifixion. They referred to Him as the Messiah, which comes from the Hebrew word for "the Anointed One." Kings were ceremonially anointed with oil and for the followers of Jesus, He was the king of kings. In Greek, the word for "the Anointed One" is *Christos*. Greek-speaking Gentiles did not realize the significance of the term *Christos* applied to Jesus. They associated oil with athletes and the sick. Derisively, they used the adjective for *Christos* to describe the refugees from Palestine. The word "Christian" took hold, and now applies to about a billion people in the world.

In Antioch, Christian is used today for about 1,000 of the 70,000 residents. The Orthodox are the most numerous, with nearly 900 members. They had 4 priests at one time but recently were reduced to one. After saying an early Sunday Mass at St. Anthony's Church in Mersin, 150 miles away, an Italian friar once a month journeys to Adana (site of an American NATO base) to say Mass there and then continues on to Antioch for Mass at 5 P.M.

Early in the 19th century French-speaking Europeans settled in the city, and the French government sought authorization for a Catholic church. St. Peter's School and a hospital were built. But, as elsewhere in Turkey, there was a fall-off in the Christian practice once more after the establishment of the modern republic.

The great schism that split Christianity in the imperial city of Constantinople in the 11th century still separates the Christians of Antioch, but not completely. The joy of birthdays and marriages is shared in the Christian community. Orthodox and Latin comfort one another in sickness and at time of death. When the late French Capuchin friar, Father Leonard, celebrated his golden jubilee as a priest, four-fifths of the people in the Latin chapel were Orthodox residents of Antioch.

Antioch today is an administrative center for a vast farming area where fine tobacco, cotton and wheat are grown. Small shops sell everything from olives to pieces of gold jewelry. In the dusty main street the pilgrim can simultaneously encounter a band of sheep, a Mercedes taxi, and men riding donkeys.

February 22 is celebrated as "St. Peter's Chair at Antioch," a reminder that he established the diocese and served as bishop. On St. Peter's feast, June 29, Mass is said in a hillside grotto named for him.

TRANSPORTATION: Nearest airport is at Adana, 100 miles northwest of Antakya. Long-distance buses and trains from Istanbul, Ankara and Izmir.

HOTELS: At Adana, *Ener Motel* is quite good. *Magarsus Motel* and *Ipek Palas Hotel* are medium-priced.

TARSUS

For Christians a main day in Tarsus is June 30, the feast of St. Paul who was born in this city on the Mediterranean in south-central Turkey. For all the 80,000 inhabitants of this predominantly Moslem city, the main day of celebration is Mar. 18. On Mar. 18 in 1923 Ataturk made a ceremonial visit to Tarsus. That visit is remembered each year. School children carrying a large portrait of Ataturk march in solemn procession to the Tarsus railroad station to give a symbolic welcome to the father of modern Turkey. He had arrived by train and the events of that historic day are reconstructed and followed faithfully. Among the school children "welcoming" Ataturk are the 300 youngsters of the Tarsus American College, a secondary boarding-school for boys, which was founded in 1888 by an American Protestant mission group. It was originally called St. Paul's Institute but was given its present name, and a secular image, in 1923 when modern

Turkey was being built under Ataturk. Tuition fees provide most of its budget needs, but 15 percent of its finances comes from the United Church Board for World Ministries in New York City. In keeping with the low religious profile encouraged by Turkish nationalism, the American missionary board is referred to in school literature as UCBWM without any further explanation. The principal, Wallace M. Robeson, of Janesville, Wis., is a minister in the United Church of Christ which, he explains, is a grouping in recent years of Congregational churches, the Christian Church, the Evangelical Church and the Reformed Church. When he is addressed as "Reverend," he says, "My name is Wally."

Principal Wally is tall, somewhat heavy and in his early 40s. He is affable and his face is bright. He operates a taut ship. Students wishing to go home to a nearby town for the weekend must get his personal permission along with that of the instructor on duty.

"Back in 1810," he says, "some Williams College students felt they should make some contribution to society, and they formed the American Board of Commissioners for Foreign Missions, the predecessor of the UCBWM."

During the latter part of the 19th century American Protestant missionaries were working among the Armenians who inhabited the plains around Tarsus. There were churches, but no schools.

"In the spring of 1885 Elliott F. Shepard, of Jamestown, New York, came to Tarsus. He wondered why there was no school here where there had been a great school of philosophy in which people like Nestor had taught and studied. There has to be a Christian school in the town of St. Paul, he decided. Shepard was a lawyer, one of the founders of the New York State Bar. He was a military man, too. The Fifty-first Regiment was named 'Shepard Rifles' in his honor."

The first principal was Thomas Christie, of New York City. Principal Wally corrects himself.

"An Armenian headed the school at first. He asked for help and an American ministry family was sent. After a year they said they couldn't work with this man, and they were moved. A second family had the same experience. Then, in the third year, Christie was sent. After a year the Armenian said he couldn't stand Christie. The Armenian left, and Christie was principal till about 1915."

The United Church Board operates a girls' school in Izmir and one at Uskudar, the Asian side of Istanbul.

"About twenty years ago," Principal Wally says, "Eartha Kitt had a song about Uskudar."

While Principal Wally is talking, students, teachers and visitors wait their turn to speak with him. One visitor is a middle-aged, neatly dressed Turkish man who with 2 brothers graduated from the American school before the Second World War. One brother is an orthopedist; the other is a veterinarian. This man is an agricultural engineer. In order to apply for a job in the Netherlands he needs a certificate regarding his fluency in English. At first Wally suggests that perhaps the English teacher should be the one to give the test, but that would mean delaying it until the next week. The man does not seem to mind. Principal Wally concludes it ought to be done right now.

"I'll tell you what," he says to the man. "Write a couple of pages on some subject—maybe why you want to go to Holland—and I will certify that this was done by you without any assistance. I'll tell you what I'll do. I'll give you a good sheet of paper and also a work sheet. You can write in the office next door."

The man goes into the empty office and for more than a half hour concentrates on his English test. When the man returns, Principal Wally looks at what he has written and, noncommittally, says he will have his secretary prepare a covering letter of certification on

Monday. The man can pick it up at any time on Monday morning.

Tarsus is well supplied with banks, but a restaurant is hard to find. There is only one quite unassuming hotel. Few women wear veils—an Ataturk reform—but almost all of them cover their heads with shawls of different colors. Men sit in austere cafés long after they have finished their small glass of tea.

At the Mersin end of town, a monumental arch stands at the center of the street. It had been part of the old city wall. A sign identifies the arch as Cleopatra's Gate, a reminder that the Egyptian queen in the 1st century before Christ sailed to Tarsus to meet Mark Antony, the Roman general and triumvir.

"They used to call it St. Paul's Gate," Principal Wally says, "but with *Antony and Cleopatra* being such a movie success, authorities thought it would have more tourist recognition if they made it Cleopatra's Gate."

The well associated with the apostle is in a district teeming with dwellings and shops. Municipal authorities have cleared the nearby market area so that St. Paul's Well is set apart like a wayside shrine. The mouth of the well is circled by a 3-foot-high ring of stone and is protected by a heavy metal cover. The stubs of 2 Roman columns flank the well like palace guards. Some local people think the well water is good for one's health, a man in shirtsleeves is telling a group of visitors. Traditionally the well has been linked to St. Paul, but the reason is not known.

"Some Americans are planning to make excavations to determine whether this was the site of the ancient Jewish community. If this was established they could go on and determine many important things related to the well and to St. Paul."

TRANSPORTATION: Tarsus is 18 miles east of Mersin, and 27 miles west of Adana. It is on the Istanbul-

Baghdad rail line, 29 hours by train from Istanbul.

HOTELS: *Toros Hotel* at Mersin is comfortable.

POINTS OF INTEREST: The tomb of the prophet Daniel is
in the Green Mosque. Lekman Hekim, a 9th-century
Arab physician, is buried in the Great Mosque. The
Old Mosque near the Roman Baths used to be an
Armenian basilica.

IZMIR

Izmir, the ancient Smyrna, is a mosaic of 50 centuries
of civilization, sharing with Athens the most varied and
longest history of any Mediterranean city. Homer, it is
said, was born in Izmir. Tradition is that the legendary
king Tantalus founded Izmir. It was rebuilt by Alexander the Great. It is a cosmopolitan city of nearly 1
million inhabitants on the western flank of Asia Minor,
350 miles south of Istanbul.

With the collapse of the Ottoman empire in the First
World War, Greece and Italy sought possession of
Izmir. The Lausanne Treaty of 1923 returned sover-
eignty to Turkey. In the main square of the onetime
European quarter is an equestrian statue of Kemal
Ataturk, founder of modern Turkey and its first presi-
dent (1923–38).

Mount Pagus, the "pagan mountain," 550 feet high,
wraps around part of Izmir like an amphitheater. In a
valley at the left are ancient aqueducts and the headquarters of NATO's 6th Tactical Air Force. The *agora*,
marketplace, of the 2nd century A.D. is visible from the
Pagan Mountain. Residents of Izmir look to the Pagan
Mountain for the latest weather. A lamp with the
power of a beacon signals the weather by the color of its
light—fair, blue; rain, green; snow, red; fog, yellow.

Near a Turkish air-force cemetery on the mountain is
the site of the stadium in which the first bishop of
Izmir, St. Polycarp, met a martyr's death in A.D. 155 at

the age of 92. His feast is celebrated on Feb. 23 in the church named for him. Polycarp was a disciple of St. John the Evangelist.

EPHESUS

"I am Saul of Tarsus," a lanky man in a white shirt says in a loud voice as he stands in the middle of the Roman amphitheater at Ephesus, facing the rows of empty stone benches. The man speaks English. He is a Turk, and identifies himself as "the Old Fisherman." His black hair is speckled with gray, and his face is deeply lined. He is now a guide but, at some time in the past for reasons which he does not specify, he has been a political prisoner. He is fascinated by the history of Ephesus, a religious and commercial center which the Greeks settled about 1400 B.C. They built a temple to Artemis (associated with the Roman deity Diana) which was one of the 7 wonders of the ancient world.

"This is about the fourth or fifth Ephesus," the Old Fisherman says at Selçuk, a town of 10,000 residents. "Ephesus used to be on the coast but the silting-in of the harbor and the marshy area forced the people to keep moving inland."

Oriental music from house radios tuned to the same station emanates through open windows, encompassing the valley with the vigor of a sandstorm. A caravan of camels plods in single file along the road. The houses are round, and have red-tiled roofs. Women at an outdoor well, a few dozen yards from the Basilica of St. John the Evangelist, wear baggy silk ankle-length trousers and matching blouses of bright colors. Long white cloths, fastened to their hair, stream down their backs. The basilica area is enclosed with a barbed-wire fence. The well for the villagers is just beyond the fence. At a booth a blonde, pretty Turkish woman in a

Western-style blue uniform sells admission tickets to the area for a small fee. Her name is Fatma.

A mammoth Byzantine mosque is nearby, and a few hundred yards away are the ruins of the Temple of Artemis.

St. John's Basilica is believed to be on the site of an early Christian chapel erected over the grave of the apostle who wrote the Fourth Gospel in Ephesus. For years the shrine stood in ruins, a gaunt frame. Restoration work was carried out by the American Society of Ephesus, Inc., which was founded by the late George B. Quatman, of Lima, Ohio.

In Latin and Turkish a tablet on a column of Roman stones says: "Pope Paul VI in this holy building raised prayers on July 26, 1967."

Mary's House is at the other end of the splendid mile-long Arcadian Way, a thoroughfare of glistening slabs of marble, named for its restorer, the emperor Arcadius (A.D. 395–408). Hadrian's Temple, the Celsius Library, and other Roman monuments line, or are near, the Arcadian Way. Not far from the marble road is the shell of the Council Church, the site of the General Council of A.D. 431.

"Pilgrims used to leave colored scarves in a corner," the Old Fisherman says, pointing to one of the small rooms which comprise Mary's House. "One of the Little Brothers of Foucauld, a French priest who has been working with the poor in Middle Eastern countries for over thirty-five years, stopped the practice. He did not think it was suitable. With a couple of other Little Brothers he had worked for almost five years at a leprosarium in eastern Turkey. When it looked as if the government would end their residence permits, one of them, Brother François, applied for Turkish citizenship and obtained it, and he now is working in Iskenderun, near Antioch. Brother Joseph later applied for citizenship, too, but it was too late. The lawyer who had handled the application of Brother François had been heavily criticized, and he was not anxious to do the same thing again."

A small chapel is in Mary's House. A tablet in the floor covers an ancient hearth in which ashes were found.

Mary's House is known by the Turkish word *Meyremana,* literally "Holy Lady." It is only a few miles from the coast and usually the Greek island of Samos is visible. The Turkish government recently built a wharf at Kuşadasi, 13 miles from Selçuk, and cruise boats call there.

TRANSPORTATION: Izmir is a main air center with frequent flights to Istanbul. Taxis are available at flat rates for the journey from Izmir to Ephesus.

HOTELS: *Ephesus (Efes) Hotel* in Izmir is luxurious. *Taner* and *Izmir Palas* are less expensive.

POINTS OF INTEREST: The excavated site of ancient Smyrna is in the Bayrakli zone, 5 miles north of Izmir. A temple, a fountain, and a defense wall are among the ruins uncovered. On the mountain behind Bayrakli is the tomb of Tantalus, mythological founder of Izmir. Statues of the gods Demeter, Poseidon and Artemis were discovered in excavations at the *agora* and are exhibited there.

IZNIK

Iznik (Nicea), where the first General Council of the Catholic Church was held in June, A.D. 325, is on the eastern shore of Lake Iznik, south of Istanbul. Emperor Constantine summoned the bishops of the Roman world to discuss the controversy arising over a heretical doctrine preached by Arius, a priest of Alexandria. Three hundred bishops attended, most coming from the Eastern empire: Egypt, Palestine, Syria and the present

Turkey. The Pope sent 3 representatives. The emperor presided, and the language was Greek.

Mountains rise from the southern shore of Lake Iznik. Fruit trees fill the fields along the north. Sheep with red markings on their foreheads graze at the roadside, indifferent to passing trucks. Most men in the villages near Iznik wear white headdresses. Many women are barefoot. Donkeys are the major means of transport, with a pair of wicker baskets straddling their backs. At Çakirca, numerous dwellings and barns are made from adobe brick.

A funeral procession passes through the streets of Iznik, with about 100 men, almost all wearing caps. Some have beards and turbans. No women are in the procession but many, in bright pantaloons, look out from doorways. The casket is green and made of wood, and shaped more or less like a human form. At the front of the casket are metal replicas of a star and crescent. The casket is carried on 2 plain wooden poles that might have been borrowed from a farm for the occasion. The men take turns for the honor of carrying the coffin—a few steps, then someone else comes forward and the one in front moves to the back.

The huge Santa Sophia Church, long unused, is a monument to Iznik's Christian past. At the lakefront blocks of stone poke from the water. They remain from the Palace of Constantine in which the Council Fathers assembled.

Nicea has kept its Eastern character. Some people speak Greek, but Western languages generally are unknown here. A policeman in the street tries to be helpful, and asks: "Do you speak Bulgarian? Russian?"

TRANSPORTATION: By boat from Istanbul across Marmara Sea to Yalova; then, bus to Iznik, 35 miles away.

HOTELS: *Reis Motel* at Yalova is comfortable.

ISTANBUL

About two dozen Christian churches are in the lovely city of Istanbul which the Greeks still refer to as Konstantinoupolis (The City of Constantine), 5 centuries after its capture by the Turks.

It is difficult to see the Christian churches. They seem to be playing hide-and-seek. This is due to an order of the Sublime Porte after the Turks seized Constantinople from its last Greek emperor in 1453. The Sultan directed that in the future façades of churches could not face a public thoroughfare. The Franciscan Church of St. Anthony's, for instance, is in Galatasaray, the busiest district in Istanbul. But it is set back from the street, almost hidden by 2 large apartment buildings which reach across the yard in front of it. The Catholic cathedral of the Holy Spirit is across the street from the Hilton Hotel. But hotel guests could walk or drive by the cathedral all the time they are in Istanbul, and not notice it. The cathedral is screened from the street by a stagelike façade.

Istanbul's splendid mosques, immense, squat and magnificent with their missilelike minarets pointing skyward, line the Bosphorus, producing a vista unique and beautiful. The Blue Mosque is the most celebrated of the mosques in use. Santa Sophia, once a Christian church built in A.D. 450, is no longer used as a mosque but is more of a museum or historic monument. St. Sophia does not honor a saint named "Sophia" but was called after one of the attributes of God, the Greek word for *wisdom*. Similarly, the Basilica of St. Iraneus, which is probably older than St. Sophia, takes its name from the Greek word for *peace*, another attribute of God.

TRANSPORTATION: Istanbul is on the main line of international express trains. There are easy air connections from Istanbul with the rest of Europe and of Turkey. It is 165 miles from the Greek border at Kipi/Ipsala.

HOTELS: *Hilton* is tops. *Park, Cinar* and *Maçka* are less expensive.

PLACES OF INTEREST: Near the main bus depot in the Tokapi district are the old city walls.

17
Eastern Europe

A QUARTER CENTURY after the arrests, imprisonments, show trials and persecutions of the postwar era, things in Eastern Europe have not turned out the way either the leaders of Communism or those of Christianity had expected. Christians had hoped that religion by now would be free. It is not. The Communists looked forward to its complete extinction. It exists.

The deep and long religious faith of Eastern Europeans accounts for the survival of Christianity against incessant attacks of atheists. History was on the side of Christianity. In every Western European country religious belief had been suppressed, vilified or outlawed at one or more times in 20 centuries, but never was it halted. Nor was Communism successful in ending religion in the Eastern Europe of the mid-20th century.

Each country of Eastern Europe has employed different methods to dissuade its citizens from the path of religion. Government control on religious activity varies from one country to the other.

As far as the visitor is concerned, everything would seem to be normal. To a great extent, it is. Churches are open, services are conducted, prayers are said, priests and ministers are being trained, children learn the fundamentals of their religion. The government controls that continue to exist deal with such crucial if remote matters as the number of priests and ministers allowed, official permits for construction of new churches, the location and number of seminaries and training colleges.

In some countries of Eastern Europe religious orders are still banned because they are international and thus, according to the Communist theory, more subject to outside influence than local clergy. Yugoslavia has not banned religious orders. At Opatija and other cities along the Adriatic coast Jesuits preach in the churches. In a city in East Germany, on the other hand, a small group of Jesuits live like civilians in an apartment in a lower-middle-class neighborhood with only their family names on the mailbox. One Jesuit in his 50s spends his time writing books about Palestine, Lourdes and other holy places. He has never been to any of the places he writes about. Although he has consistently requested permission for travel, he has never been given a visa. But the government permits him to write letters abroad requesting research material for his books. "Es geht," he says. It works out.

In these times of fluid travel, Eastern European countries are getting on the bandwagon and allowing larger numbers of their people to go abroad on "organized and guided tours." Still it is surprising how few priests and ministers receive government authorization to go where they want to when they want to—one of those rights that is taken for granted in the West. In August 1974 the Order of Preachers founded in 1216 by St. Dominic met in general chapter at the 16th-century Marian Shrine of the Madonna of the Arch near Naples to elect a new master-general, a friar to head the world's Dominicans. Nearly 200 delegates were present from those countries in which the Order has members. Poland and Yugoslavia were represented, but the delegates from Hungary and Czechoslovakia did not receive permission to travel to Italy.

Lutheran ministers in East and West Germany are able to have meetings twice a year thanks to the East German government's promotion policy for the Leipzig trade fair. The fair is held each year in March and September. During the fair, the government relaxes its visa requirements, and a visit at least to Leipzig by West German clergymen is a simple formality.

As a matter of fact the desire for tourism revenue has induced the Eastern European countries to simplify visa requirements. Yugoslavia and Romania for years have routinely issued visas at the border.

With the way currencies have been fluctuating on the international money market in recent years it is at times possible to obtain a "good rate" on a particular currency in New York or Zurich, for example. But it is foolhardy to dabble in financial transactions involving Eastern European currencies. Fines are stiff, and jail terms are possible.

Another caveat is to avoid discussing politics with clergymen. At the least the subject can be embarrassing. It could be harmful to the Eastern European, too.

The camera fan can take all the pictures he likes within a church or religious institution. Outdoors, it is important to turn the camera lens away from anything that could be considered a military subject. If there is any doubt, it is best not to click the shutter until someone has been consulted—a policeman, a shopkeeper.

There is much to photograph among the shrines of Eastern Europe. The ancient city of Cracow calls itself "the Polish Rome." It has many churches—about 75. The notorious Nazi concentration camp and gas chambers, Auschwitz, is on the outskirts of Cracow. One million Poles were at the shrine of the Black Madonna of Częstochowa on Aug. 26, 1956 for the 300th anniversary of the day when King John Casimir designated Mary queen of Poland. At the time Stefan Cardinal

Wyszyński, primate of Poland, was in prison but he sent a message that was read to the multitude of pilgrims. The cardinal called upon the Polish people to make a series of promises—fidelity to God and to the church, defense of unborn children, faithfulness in marriage, education of the young as Catholics, strengthening of families through spiritual graces, application of love and justice to social life. The 1,000th anniversary of Catholic Poland was 10 years away, and the cardinal proposed a promise for each year leading to 1966.

Someone is always at prayer at the shrine of the Infant of Prague. The celebrated statue of the Holy Infant, which is duplicated in countless churches around the world, is in the Church of Our Lady of Victory in Prague, not far from the lovely Charles Bridge.

In Bucharest, weekly devotions to St. Anthony in St. Joseph's Catholic Cathedral bring Orthodox and Latin together. The Franciscan friar is as popular with one as he is with the other.

There are always candles, always visitors, always flowers in the cathedral at Zagreb before the grave of the former archbishop, Aloysius Cardinal Stepinac. For many he has been a symbol of the struggles, and the hopes, of Christianity in Eastern Europe. Pius XII made him a cardinal in 1952. Archbishop Stepinac at the time was serving his sixth year in prison. The Pope's bold, dramatic support for Archbishop Stepinac so outraged the Yugoslav government that it broke off diplomatic relations with the Holy See. But Yugoslavia mellowed. When Cardinal Stepinac died on Feb. 10, 1960 the Yugoslav government granted formal permission for his burial in Zagreb Cathedral and for visits to his grave.

Crowds outside St. Stephen the Martyr's Church after Mass on Sunday in Budapest are as numerous as those in an American parish. Two old religious orders survive in Hungary, the Benedictines and Franciscans.

The Hungarian saint-king, Stephen, invited the sons of St. Benedict to Hungary in the 11th century to teach his wandering Magyars how to cultivate the land. Two years after the death of St. Francis in 1226, Franciscan friars were settling at Esztergom, the seat of the primate of Hungary. The massive cathedral at Esztergom had been Cardinal Mindszenty's church.

The first home of Pope John when he arrived in Sofia as a young papal diplomat in 1925 is now a convent, and can be visited. It is on Ulitsa Todor Stoianov. Nearby is the St. Francis Chapel where a statue of the Infant of Prague is exposed. A cloister of Carmelite nuns had been established in Monsignor Roncalli's (Pope John's) former residence, but the international community of Sisters was expelled by the government in one of its periodic crackdowns on religion. Later the government permitted a Bulgarian congregation, the Eucharistine Sisters, to move in. When the Carmelites were authorized to live together as a community once more there was no place for them to go. At last they moved into the choir loft of St. Francis Chapel, fashioning a makeshift cloister by partitions of fiberboard and glass.

The Communists have their own shrines, too. In the center of Sofia is a huge mausoleum with the body of Georgi Dimitrov, a patriarch of international Communism. He led an insurrection in 1923, went into exile, and then in 1933 was arrested in Leipzig by the Nazis on the charge of having participated in the burning of the Reichstag. On his return to Bulgaria after the Second World War, he became prime minister and party leader. There is a line on the downtown sidewalk to his tomb every day.

Luther memorials are all over Europe, but there are special shrines for him in East Germany. He was born in Eisleben in the Harz Mountains, 50 miles west of Leipzig. He studied at the University of Wittenberg (35 miles north of Leipzig), was a parish priest there, and on the church door according to tradition nailed his Ninety-Five Theses. He died in Eisleben, too. The Augustinian monastery where Luther lived and worked in Wittenberg was suppressed, ironically, by the Reformation which he brought into being, and it is now a Luther Museum of memorabilia. The *propst* (dean) of Wittenberg lives there. Luther is buried in Wittenberg in the Schlosskirche (Castle Church).

The Catholic cathedral in East Berlin, St. Hedwig's, is a shrine for the Polish people as well as for German Catholics. It was consecrated in 1773 by a Polish bishop of Silesia because Poland had been placed in charge of the mission land of Prussia. St. Hedwig's was the first Catholic church built in Berlin since the Reformation, and it was named to honor the patron of Silesia. The first church in Berlin in pre-Reformation times was St. Nicholas, now in ruins from Second-World-War damage and not high enough on East Germany's priority list for restoration as yet. The second oldest is the Maria Church, now Lutheran, which is near the new, splendid observation tower.

St. Hedwig's was destroyed on Mar. 2, 1943, but rebuilt after the war, and its new high altar was consecrated on Nov. 1, 1963. It is just off Unter den Linden, and a few blocks from The Wall. The barrier built by the Communists in August 1961 is the most visited place in Berlin. From East Berlin, visitors stare at The Wall in silence. On the West Berlin side young people, mostly, place wreaths of flowers at memorial crosses which mark places where men and women died after having been shot by East Berlin "vopos" (*volkspolizei*) in an unsuccessful attempt to get over The Wall to freedom.

Index

Aachen, Germany, 144–145
  hotels, 145
  transportation to, 145
Aarhus, Denmark, 395
Aasebakken, Denmark, 396
Adalbert, St., 361–363
Adana, Turkey, 498
Admont Monastery (Austria), 19
"Adoration of the Mystic Lamb, The," 61–64
Aigues-Mortes, France, 81–82, 85
Airplane travel, 4
Aix-en-Provence, France, 75
Alacoque, Margaret-Mary, St., 96–97
Albi, France, 76
Albigensians, 76–77
Alès, France, 84, 87
  transportation to, 87–88
Alfred the Great, 274
Alps, the, 100
Alsace-Lorraine, 79
Altenburg Monastery (Austria), 23

Altötting, Germany, 148–153
  hotels, 153
  places of interest, 153
  transportation to, 153
Altötting, Our Lady of, 148–153
Amsterdam, the Netherlands, 364–372
  Beguinage, The, 369–370
  Church-in-the-Attic, 368–369
  hotels, 372
  Jewish Museum, 366–368
  Old Church (Oude Kerk), 369
  Old Jewish Quarter, 365–366
  Rembrandt's house, 366
  transportation to, 372
Andalusia (Spain), 445–449
Andersen, Hans Christian, 392
Anne, St., 108, 130
Anthony of Padua, St., 374
Antioch (Antakya), Turkey, 494, 496–498

Antioch (cont'd)
 transportation to, 498
Antwerp, Belgium, hotels in,
 71
Apostoline Sisters, 60
Appolonia, St., 48
Aquino, Italy, 329
Arles, France, 80
Ars, France, 95
 hotels, 96
 transporation to, 95
Assisi, Italy, 304–307
 transportation to, 307
Asturias, Spain, 422
Athens, Greece, 248–249
 hotels, 249
 transporation to, 249
Athos, Mount, 216, 220–243
Augustine, St., 183, 186, 187,
 189
Austria, 7–40
 Burgenland, 36
 Carinthia, 27
 Lower, 19
 religious history of, 7–9
 Styria, 18–19
 Tyrol, 24
 Upper, 28
 Voralberg, 30
 See also names of cities
  and towns
Avignon, France, 80–81
Ávila, Spain, 455

Bakken, Denmark, 394
Ballyshannon, Ireland, 268
Bamburgh, England, 185
Banneux, Belgium, 52–60
 hotels, 60
Baptists (England), 210–211
Barbizon, France, 127
Barcelona, Spain, 436–437
 hotels, 437
 transportation to, 437
Bari, Italy, 314
Bartholomew, St., 78

Barton, Elizabeth (the Nun
 of Kent), 170
Basel, Switzerland, 471–475
 hotels, 475
 points of interest, 475
 transportation to, 475
Basques, 432–433, 434
Bats, 348–349
Bayeux, France, 109
Beauraing, Belgium, 64–69
 hotels, 69
 places of interest, 69
 transportation to, 69
Beauvais, France, 127
Becket, Thomas, 168–169,
 186, 188–189, 192
 relics of, 193
Beco, Mariette, 52–59
Bede, The Venerable, 184–
 185
Bedford, England, 211
Beguines, 47
Belfast, Ireland, hotels in,
 276
Belgium, 41–73
 religious history of, 41–44
 See also names of cities
  and towns
Benedict, St., 100, 318–319
Benedictines, 11, 100, 134–
 136
Berchmans, St. John, 47–48
Berdorf, Luxembourg, 334
Berg Isel (Austria), 24
Bergen, Norway, 412–413
 hotels, 413
 points of interest, 413
 transportation to, 413
Bermont, France, 91
Bernadette of Lourdes, St.,
 113–123
Bernadine of Siena, St., 302–
 303
Bernhardt, Sarah, 126
Bildstein, Austria, 31
Birgittines. *See* Bridgettines

Birmingham, England, 196–197
transportation to, 197
Blieskastel, Germany, 136
Bologna, Italy, 301
Bom Jesus do Monte, Portugal, 379
Boniface, St., 136–137, 360
Bosco, St. John, 290–291
Bourguillon, Notre Dame of, 485–486
Bouschet-de-Pranles, France, 85
Braga, Portugal, 376–379
hotels, 379
Nossa Senhora do Sameiro, 377–379
transportation to, 379
Bregenz, Austria, 30
Breughel, Peter, 72
Brian Boru, 253
Briançon, France, 86
Bridget, St., 401–402
Bridgettines (Birgittines), 401–402
Brigid, St., 253
Bristol, England, 211
Brittany (France), 108–109
Brückner, Anton, 29
Bruges, Belgium, 60–61
hotels, 61
transportation to, 61
Brussels, Belgium, 72–73
hotels, 73
transportation to, 73
Bucharest, Romania, 512
Budapest, Hungary, 512–513
Bunyan, John, 199, 211
Burgenland, Austria, 36
Burns, Robert, 180
Busman, Hendrick, 145–147

Caen, France, 109
Calderon de la Barca, Don Pedro, 471
Calvin, John, 17, 83, 88–89, 458, 475–479
Calvin Museum (Noyon, France), 88–89
Camisards, 86
Canaan (spiritual retreat in Germany), 165–166
Cannes, France, 106
Canterbury, England, 185–195
archbishop of, 190
Boys' Choir, 189
Cathedral, 186–190
Dane John, 194
hotels, 195
memorial to Protestant martyrs, 194–195
St. Augustine's Abbey, 190–191
St. Augustine's College, 191
St. Dunstan's outside West Gate, 192–193
St. Margaret's Church, 191
St. Thomas's Church, 193–194
transportation to, 195
Canute, King, 392–394
Cape Sounion, Greece, 248
Capet, Hugues (Hugh), 83
Cara Insula (Denmark), 386
Carinthia, Austria, 27
Carloman, 76
Catherine Labouré, St., 124–125
Catherine of Siena, St., 302–303
Catholic Young Workers of Austria, 9–10
Cévennes mountains (France), 82, 84–85, 86
Chagall, Marc, 488
Charlemagne, 52, 76, 114, 129, 144–145, 184
Charles I (Spain). *See* Charles V, Emperor
Charles II (France), 83

Charles V, Emperor, 8, 41, 61, 131, 160, 162
Charles VII (France), 77
Chartres, France, 98–99
    hotel, 99
Châteaudun, France, 99
Chevetogne, Benedictine Monastery of (Beauraing, Belgium), 69
"Children of God, The," 365
Chollerford, England, 185
Church of England, 170
Claremorris, Ireland, 273
Clervaux, Luxembourg, 334
    hotels, 334
    transportation to, 334
Clingendael, Netherlands, 345
Clovis, 52, 125
Cocteau, Jean, 106
Coimbra, Portugal, 386–387
    hotels, 387
    transportation to, 387
Coligny, Gaspard de, 83
Cologne, Germany, 139–144, 293
    hotels, 144
    points of interest, 144
    transportation to, 144
Columba, St. 181
Combes, Émile, 79
Comenius. *See* Komensky, Jan Amos
Compiègne, France, 91
Constance, Council of, 157
Constance, Germany, 157–160
    hotels, 160
    transportation to, 160
Constance, Lake, 30
Constantine the Great, 132–133, 168, 217
Copenhagen, Denmark, 396–400
    hotels, 399
    points of interest, 400

transportation to, 399
Córdoba, Spain, 448–449
    hotels, 449
    transportation to, 449
Corps, France, 101–105
    hotels, 105
    transportation to, 105
Cottolengo, The (Turin, Italy), 291–292
Counter-Reformation, 8, 18
Covadonga, Spain, 422–426
    hotels, 426
    transportation to, 426
Cracow, Poland, 511
Cranmer, Thomas, 170, 173, 186
Credit cards, 5
Croagh Patrick (Ireland), 253–259
Cromwell, Thomas, 171
Crusades, 76, 82
Curé of Ars, The (Jean-Baptiste Marie Vianney), 95

Dachau, Germany, 153–156
    transportation to, 156
Damien, Father, 45–47
"David" (Michelangelo), 302
Defoe, Daniel, 200
Delémont, Switzerland, 475
Delfshaven, Netherlands, 341
Delphi, Greece, 245–246
    hotels, 246
    points of interest, 246
    transportation to, 246
Demetrios, St., 226, 243–244
Denis, St., 123
Denmark, 392–400
    See also names of cities and towns
Diest, Belgium, 47–48, 51
    points of interest, 48
    transportation to, 48
Dokkum, Netherlands, 137, 360

Dominic, St., 77, 301
Dominicans, 77, 105, 510
Domrémy, France, 90–94
 hotels, 94
 transportation to, 94
Downpatrick, Ireland, 275–276
 transportation to, 276
Downside, England, 276
Driving in Europe, 5–6
Drogheda, Ireland, 276–278
 hotels, 278
 points of interest, 278
 transportation to, 278
Dublin, Ireland, 278–282
 hotels, 282
 transportation to, 282
Dunfermline, Scotland, 179–180
 transportation to, 180
Dunois, Jean, 99
Duns Scotus, Blessed John, 141–143
Durand, Marie, 85
Durham, England, 184
Dympna, Princess, 70–71

East Berlin, Germany, 514
Eastern Europe, 509–514
Echternach, Luxembourg, 329–334
 hotels, 334
 points of interest, 334
 transportation to, 333
Edict of Nantes, 84
Edict of Tolerance, 84
Edinburgh, Scotland, 173, 175–179
 Greyfriars Kirk, 179
 hotels, 179
 St. Giles's Cathedral, 173, 176–178
 transportation to, 179
Egmond, Netherlands, 361–363
 hotels, 363

 transportation to, 363
Einsiedeln, Switzerland, 465–471
 hotels, 471
 points of interest, 471
 transportation to, 471
Eisenstadt, Austria, 36
Elizabeth I (England), 171–172
Eloy, St., 108
Emancipation Cross, 260
England. *See* Great Britain
Enns, Austria, 29
Ephesus, Turkey, 503
Erasmus, 44, 72, 192, 340–341
Erik, St., 400, 407
Escomb, England, 185
Estonia, 415, 416
Europa Bridge (Innsbruck, Austria), 27
Europe
 driving in, 5–6
 Eastern, 509–514
Eurail Pass, 4–5

Fatima, Portugal, 374, 376, 379–386
 hotels, 385–386
 places of interest, 386
 transportation to, 385
Faughart, Ireland, 252
Fell, Margaret, 212
Fere, Greece, 244
Filippi, Greece, 244
Finances, personal, 5
Finland, 391, 392, 414–416
 See also names of cities and towns
Fisher, Bishop John, 170
Five Children of Beauraing, 65–69
Florence, Italy, 301–302
 hotels, 302
 points of interest, 302
 transportation to, 302

Foggia, Italy, 314
Fontainebleau, France, 127
Fossanova, Italy, 328
Fox, George, 212
France, 74–127
  religious history of, 74–79
  See also names of cities
    and towns
Francis of Assisi, St., 300,
    304–307
Francis I (France), 77
Frankfurt, Germany, 165–
    166
  hotels, 166
  transportation to, 166
French Riviera, 105
Freud, Sigmund, 37
Fribourg, Switzerland, 483–
    486
  hotels, 486
  transportation to, 486
Fulda, Germany, 136–139
  hotels, 139
  transportation to, 139

Galicia, Spain, 426–432
Ganges, France, 86
Genazzano, Italy, 319–320
  transportation to, 320
Geneva, Switzerland, 475–
    480
  Calvin Auditorium, 476–
    478
  Calvin College, 478–479
  Frau Münster, 488
  Gross Münster (Big Mon-
    astery), 488–490
  hotels, 480
  points of interest, 480
  transportation to, 480
Genevieve, St., 125
Germany, 128–166
  religious history of, 128–
    131
  See also names of cities
    and towns
Gheel, Belgium, 70–71
  hotels, 71

transportation to, 71
Ghent, Belgium, 61
  hotels, 64
  places of interest, 64
  transportation to, 64
Giles, St., 82
Glasgow, Scotland, 180–181
  hotels, 181
  transportation to, 181
Goethe, Johann Wolfgang
    von, 165
Gotland, 405–406
  hotels, 406
  transportation to, 406
Göttweig Monastery (Aus-
    tria), 22–23
Gouda, Netherlands, 344
Granada, Spain, 450–452
  hotels, 451–452
  points of interest, 452
  transportation to, 451
Gran-du-Roy, France, 81
Graz, Austria, Cathedral at,
    18
Great Britain, 167–215
  religious history of, 167–
    172
  See also names of cities
    and towns
Grenoble, France, 100–101
Greece, 216–249
  northeastern, 244
  religious history of, 216–
    220
  See also names of cities
    and towns
Grotte aux Fées (Switzer-
    land), 463
Grotto of the Demoiselles
    (France), 86
Grotto Trabuc (France), 86
Gurk, Austria, Cathedral at,
    27
Gutenberg, Johann, 165

Haddington, Scotland, 173–
    174
  transportation to, 174

Hague, The, Netherlands, 344–345
  hotels, 345
  points of interest, 345
  transportation to, 345
Hallein, Austria, 35–36
Hartlepool, England, 185
Haydn, Franz Josef, 16, 36
Hebrides, 168
Heiligenkreuz Monastery (Austria), 23
Heiloo, Netherlands, 361, 362, 363–364
  hotels, 364
  transportation to, 364
Helsinki, Finland, 391, 416
  hotels, 416
  points of interest, 416
  transportation to, 416
Henry IV (France), 78, 84
Henry VIII (England), 167–171, 186, 189
Hitler, Adolf, 9, 37, 134, 149, 154–155
Holland. *See* Netherlands, The
Holy House (Loreto, Italy), 309–310
Holy Island. *See* Lindisfarne
Holy Shroud (Turin, Italy), 287–289
Holy Springs (Denmark), 394–395
Holy Tunic, 132–133
Homer, 216–217, 502
Hovedøya, Norway, 414
Hubert, St., 72
Huguenots, 78, 79, 80, 82, 83–87
Hungary, 512–513
Hus, Jan, 157–160

Iceland, 416–417
  transportation to, 417
Ignatius of Loyola, St., 433, 434
Innsbruck, Austria, 24–27

Hofkirche (Court Church), 26
  hotels, 27
  points of interest, 27
  transportation to, 27
Iona (island), 181–182
  hotels, 182
  transportation to, 182
Ireland, 250–282
  religious history of, 250–253
  See also names of cities and towns
Istanbul, Turkey, 507–508
  hotels, 508
  places of interest, 508
  transportation to, 507–508
Italy, 283–328
  religious history of, 283–287
  See also names of cities and towns
Izmir, Turkey, 502–505
  hotels, 505
  points of interest, 505
  transportation to, 505
Iznik (Nicea), Turkey, 505–506

James, St., 427–430
Jarrow, England, 184–185
Jesuits, 9, 48, 79, 370–371, 375–376, 510
Jews
  in Amsterdam, 365–368
  in London, 203–205
Joan of Arc, 77, 90–93, 99
John the Baptist Procession, St. (Laren, Netherlands), 360
Joseph II, Emperor, 8–9, 18, 21, 37, 61
Jutland, 392, 393, 395

Kalambaka, Greece, 247
Karup, Jutland, 395
Kennedy family, 104

Kevelaer, Germany, 145–147
  hotels, 147
  transportation to, 147
"Key of St. Peter," 52
Kilkeel, Ireland, 276
Klagenfurt, Austria, 27
Klosterneuburg   Monastery
  (Austria), 23
Knock, Ireland, 268–274
  hotels, 273
  points of interest, 273–274
  transportation to, 273
Knox, John, 167, 172–174,
  176–178, 479
  house of, 175
Kolping, Father, 141–143
Kolping Society, 142–143
Komensky, Jan Amos (Co-
  menius), 355–360
Kortembois, Belgium, 48
Korycaean Cave (Greece),
  246
Krems, Austria, 23
Kremsmünster Monastery
  (Austria), 18, 29–30

La Salette, Notre Dame of
  (France), 101–105
Labouré, St. Catherine. See
  Catherine Labouré, St.
Lachaise, Père, 126
Lambach Monastery (Aus-
  tria), 30
Lambert, Bishop, 52
Landerneau, France, 108
Langadas, Greece, 244
Laren, Netherlands, 360
Leksand, Sweden, 407
Leo III, Emperor, 218
León, Spain, 432
Liechtenstein, 482
Liège, Belgium, 51–52
  hotels, 52
  transportation to, 52
Lindisfarne (island), 183–
  184

transportation to, 184
Linz, Austria, 28
  hotels, 29
  points of interest, 29
  transportation to, 29
Lioba, St., 138
Lisbon, Portugal, 375, 387–
  389
  hotels, 389
  points of interest, 389
  transportation to, 389
Lisieux, France, 110–113
  hotels, 113
  transportation to, 113
Livingstone, David, 180
Locronan, France, 108
Loire Valley, 98
London, England, 198–215
  Baptists, 210–211
  Church of the Sacred
    Heart, 172
  hotels, 215
  Jewry, 203–205
  places of interest, 215
  Quakers, 211–212
  St. Paul's Cathedral, 208–
    210
  transportation to, 215
  Wesley's Chapel, 200–203
  Westminster Abbey, 212–
    214
  Westminster Cathedral,
    214–215
  Wren churches, 205–208
Loreto, Italy, 309–310
  hotels, 310
  transportation to, 310
Lot region (France), 107
Lough Derg (Ireland), 260–
  267
Louis IX (France), 81–82
Louis XIII (France), 78
Louis XIV (France), 78, 82,
  86
Louis XVI (France), 79, 84
Lourdes, France, 113–122

hotels, 122
transportation to, 122
Louvain, Belgium, 43, 44
    American College, 45
    Irish College, 45
    transportation to, 47
Louvain, University of, 41–42, 43–44
Loyola, Spain, 433–434
    transportation to, 434
Luther, Martin, 129–131, 160–162, 513–514
Lutheran Church, 8, 391
Luxembourg, 329–335
Luxembourg City, Luxembourg, 329, 334–335
    hotels, 335
    points of interest, 335
    transportation to, 335
Lyons, France, 95
    hotels, 95

Maastricht, Netherlands, 52, 345–349
    hotels, 348
    points of interest, 348–349
    Stella Maris statue, 343–348
    transportation to, 348
Macbeth, 179–180
Madrid, Spain, 452–453
    hotels, 457
    transportation to, 457
Madurodam, 345
Magdeburg, Germany, 162
Maimonides (Moisés ben Llaimón), 448–449
Marbach, Austria, 20–22
    transportation to, 22
Margaret-Mary, St. *See* Alacoque
Maria Laach, Germany, 134, 144
Maria Plain (Austria), 31
Maria Saal (Austria), 27
Maria Stein Monastery (Switzerland), 471–475
Maria Taferl shrine, 20–22
    hotels near, 22
Marian Year, 2, 9
Mariastein, Switzerland, 471–475
Mariazell, Austria
    hotels, 14, 18
    Marian shrine at, 7, 9–18
    restaurants, 14
    transportation to, 10, 18
Marseilles, France, 74, 75, 95
Martel, Charles, 76
Martigny, Switzerland, 463
Martin of Tours, St., 99
Marx, Karl, 132, 136
Mas Soubeyran, France, 86, 87
    transportation to, 87–88
Matthias, relics of, 132, 134–135
Matisse, Henri, 105
Matisse Museum (Nice), 106
Mayo, Ireland, 274
Mazarin, Jules, 78
Médicis, Catherine de, 83
Melk, Austria, 19
    monastery at, 22
Mellifont Monastery (Ireland), 278
Mercator, Gerard, 44
Mersin, Turkey, 501–502
Meteora Rocks (Greece), 247
Methodism, 168, 195–199
Michael, St., 72, 109
Michelangelo, 60
Milan, Italy, 292–293
    hotels, 293
    points of interest, 293
    transportation to, 293
Modestus, St., 27
Mont Aigu, Notre Dame of, 49–51
Mont St. Michel (France), 109

Mont St. Michel (cont'd)
hotels, 110
transportation to, 110
Montcalm, Gen. Louis Joseph de, 81
Monte Cassino, Italy, 317–318
transportation to, 318
Montserrat (Spain), 437–443
hotels, 443
transportation to, 443
More, Thomas, St., 169–171, 192–194
Moses, 1
Mount Athos, 216, 220–243
Mount Nebo, chapel on, 1
Mount of Calvary, 36
Mount St. Peter Caves (Netherlands), 348
Mozart, Wolfgang Amadeus, 31, 33
Mühlheim, Germany, 141
Munich, Germany, 147–148
Museum of the Desert (Cévennes France), 86–87
"Mystic Lamb," mystery of the, 61–64

Naarden, the Netherlands, 354–360
hotels, 360
points of interest, 360
transportation to, 360
Naples, Italy, 314–315
hotels, 317
Napoleon, 79, 100–101, 125, 132–133
Narbonne, France, 75
Nås, Sweden, 407
Nea Fokea, Greece, 245
Neri, St. Philip, 196
Nerja, Spain, 452
Nero, 318
Netherlands, The, 336–372
religious history of, 336–340

See also names of cities and towns
Nevers, France, 122–123
hotels, 123
transportation to, 123
Newcastle, England
hotels, 185
points of interest, 185
transportation to, 185
Newman, John, 195–196
Nice, France
hotels, 106
Matisse Museum, 106
transportation to, 106
Nicea. See Iznik, Turkey
Nicholas of Flüe, St., 459, 461–462
Niederalteich, Germany, 153
Niel-As, Belgium, 48
Nîmes, France, 80–88
hotels, 88
Normandy (France), 109
Northumbria, 182–183, 184
hotels, 185
Norway, 390, 391, 392, 409–414
stave churches in, 412–413
See also names of cities and towns
Nossa Senhora do Samiero (Portugal), 377–379
Notre Dame of Mont Aigu (Belgium), 49–51
Noyon, France, 88–90
hotels, 90
points of interest, 90
transportation to, 90

Oberammergau, Germany, 156
hotels, 156
transportation to, 156
Oberndorf, Austria, 34–36
Odense, Denmark, 392–393
hotels, 393
transportation to, 393

Ogilvie, Blessed John, 181
Olympia, Greece, 246–247
  hotels, 247
  transportation to, 247
Øm, Denmark, 395
Omberg (Sweden), 405
Oratorian Fathers, 51
Orléans, France, 91
Orvieto, Italy, 307–309
  transportation to, 309
Oslo, Norway, 413–414
  hotels, 414
  points of interest, 414
  transportation to, 414
Ostfold, Norway, 390
Otto I, 129
Oudewater, Netherlands, 344
Our Lady under the Four
  Pillars (Austria), 24–25
Oviedo, Spain, 425, 426
Oxford, England, 195–196
  places of interest, 196
  transportation to, 196
Ozanam, Frederic, 125

Padua, Italy, 295–298
  hotels, 298
  transportation to, 298
Pamplona, Spain, 434-435
  hotels, 435
  transportation to, 435
Panteleimon, St., 227
Paray-le-Monial, France, 96–
  97
  hotels, 97
  points of interest, 97
  transportation to, 97
Paris, France, 78, 123–126
  hotels, 126
  Notre Dame Cathedral, 74
  points of interest, 126
  transportation to, 126
Parnassos, Mount, 246
Parpaillots, 87
Passion Play, 156

Passports, 3
Patrick, St., 106, 251–258,
  261–262
  burial place of, 274–276
Pepin the Short, 76
Pépinster, Belgium, 59
  transportation to, 59–60
Peter, St., 52
Pettigo, Ireland, 260–268
  hotels, 268
  points of interest, 268
  transportation to, 267–268
Pio, Padre, 310–314
Plunkett, Blessed Oliver,
  276–278
Poland, 511–512
Polycarp, St., 502–503
Pompeii, Italy, 315–317
  hotels, 317
  transportation to, 317
Pont du Gard (France), 82
Portugal, 373–389
  religious history of, 373–
  376
  See also names of cities
  and towns
Pöstlingberg (Austria), 28
Praemonstratentian Monas-
  tery (Austria), 24
Prague, Czechoslovakia, 512
Presbyterianism, 168
Procession of the Holy Blood
  (Bruges, Belgium), 60
Protestant Reformation, 8,
  41, 77, 78, 82, 89, 129,
  167, 172–173
  monument of, 470–480
Prouille, France, 77
Provence, France, 75, 81

Quakers (London), 211–212

Rabanus Maurus, St., 138
Rankweil, Austria, 31
Ranquine, France, 125

Ravenna, Italy, 300–301
  hotels, 301
  places of interest, 301
  transportation to, 300–301
Reformation. *See* Protestant
  Reformation
Rein Monastery (Austria), 18
Rembrandt
  burial site, 369
  house of, 366
Renoir, Pierre Auguste, 105
Rheims, France, 91, 126
Richelieu, Cardinal, 78
Rimini, Italy, 301
Ripon, England, 185
Riviera, French, 105
Roc Amadour, France, 106–
  107
  hotels, 107
  transportation to, 107
Roccasecca, Italy, 328
Roermond, Netherlands,
  349–351
  hotels, 351
  transportation to, 351
Rök, Sweden, 405
Rome, Italy, 320–328
  hotels, 328
  points of interest, 328
  transportation to, 328
Ronan (Irish hermit), 108
Roncesvalles, Spain, 435–
  436
Roothaan, Father Jan Philip,
  370–371
Rotterdam, Netherlands,
  340–344
  hotels, 344
  Pilgrim Fathers' Church,
  341–344
  points of interest, 344
  transportation to, 343
Rouen, France, 92
Rubens, Peter Paul, 72
Russia, 416

Sachseln, Switzerland, 462
Sacre Coeur Basilica (Liège,
  Belgium), 52
Sagres, Portugal, 387
St. Albans, England, 215
St. Andrews, Scotland, 174
  transportation to, 174
St. Bartholomew's Day Mas-
  sacre, 78, 83, 173
St. Benoit-sur-Loire, France,
  100
Saint-Denis, France, 123
St. Elorian, Austria, 29
St. Gallen, Switzerland, 463–
  465
  hotels, 465
  transportation to, 465
St. Giles, France, 82
St. Helena, Greece, 245
St. Honorat, island of
  (France), 106
St. Jean-du-Doigt, France,
  108
St. Lambert's Monastery
  (Austria), 11
St. Maurice-en-Valais, Swit-
  zerland, 462–463
St. Pölten, Austria, 10–11
St. Veran, France, 86
Ste. Ann-d'Auray, France,
  108
Ste. Anne-la-Palud, France,
  108
Saintes-Maries, France, 81
Saints, Alpine, 462–463
Salesians, 290
Salonika, Greece, 220–244
  hotels, 244
  transportation to, 244
Salzburg, Austria, 31
  churches of, 33
  hotels, 33
  points of interest, 33
  transportation to, 33
Samothraki, Greece, 244

San Giovanni, Italy, 310–314
  transportation to, 314
San Marino (Italy), 301
San Sebastian, Spain, 434
Santiago de Compostela, Spain, 427–432
  hotels, 432
  transportation to, 432
Santo Antonio grottoes (Portugal), 386
Saul, Northern Ireland, 274–276
Scandinavia, 390–417
  religious history of, 390–392
  See also Denmark; Finland; Norway; Sweden; and names of cities and towns
Scherpenheuvel, Belgium, 49–51
Scotland, 167, 172–181
Sea travel, 4
Seckau Abbey (Austria), 19
Servace, St., 52, 346, 347
Seville, Spain, 446–447
  hotels, 447
  points of interest, 447
  transportation to, 447
's-Hertogenbosch, Netherlands, 351–354
  hotels, 354
  transportation to, 354
Siena, Italy, 302–304
  hotels, 304
  transportation to, 304
"Silent Night, Holy Night," première of, 34
Siljan, Lake, 406–407
Skálholt, Iceland, 416, 417
Smyrna, 502–505
Society of Friends. *See* Quakers
Society of Jesus. *See* Jesuits
Sofia, Bulgaria, 513

Sotto il Monte, Italy, 294–295
  transportation to, 295
Spain, 418–457
  religious history of, 418–422
  See also names of cities and towns
Spinoza, Baruch, 344–345
Spurgeon, Charles Haddon, 210
Stadl-Paura, Austria, Trinity Church at, 30
Station Island (Ireland), 261
Stevenson, Robert Louis, 127
Stocker, Franz, 149
Stockholm, Sweden, 391, 400, 408–409
  hotels, 408–409
  points of interest, 409
  transportation to, 408
Stone, St. John, 194
Struell, Ireland, 276
Sturmius, St., 137–138
Styria, Austria, 18–19
Subiaco, Italy, 318–319
  points of interest, 319
  transportation to, 319
Sully-sur-Loire, France, hotel at, 100
Sunderland, England, 185
Superga, Basilica of (Italy), 292
Sweden, 391, 400–409
  ancient churches in, 407–408
  See also names of cities and towns
Swift, Jonathan, 278–280
Switzerland, 458–493
  religious history of, 458–461
  See also names of cities and towns

Tallinn, Estonia, 416

Tarbes, France, 125
Tarsus, Turkey, 398–502
  points of interest, 502
  transportation to, 501–502
Tassach, St., 276
Tautra, island of (Sweden), 411
Teresa of Ávila, St., 455–456
Teresa of Lisieux, St., 110–113
Tertiaries, 77
Tewkesbury, England, 211
Theotokos, 218
Thomas Aquinas, St., 328
Three Magi, 140–141
  relics of, 293
Toledo, Spain, 453–455
  hotels, 455
  transportation to, 455
Tongrès, Belgium, 51
Toulouse, France, 76, 77
Tourist offices, 6
Tours, France, 99
  hotels, 99
Transportation, local, 6
Traveling
  advice concerning, 3–5
  by air, 4
  by sea, 4
  Eurail Pass and, 4–5
  source of information, 6
Tréguier, France, 108
Trier, Germany, 131–136
  hotels, 136
  points of interest, 136
  transportation to, 136
Trondheim, Norway, 391, 410–411
  hotels, 411
  points of interest, 411
  transportation to, 411
Turin, Italy, 287–292
  Consolata, The, 289–290
  Cottolengo, The, 291–292
  Holy Shroud, The, 287–289
  hotels, 292
  places of interest, 292
  transportation to, 292
Turkey, 494–508
  religious history of, 494–496
  See also names of cities and towns
Turku, Finland, 391
Tyrol, Austria, 24

Ulverston, England, 212
  transportation to, 212
Undset, Sigrid, 392
Uppsala, Sweden, 400, 408

Vadstena, Sweden, 401–405
  hotels, 404
  points of interest, 404–405
  transportation to, 404
Valencia, Spain, 443–445
  hotels, 445
  transportation to, 445
Van Eyck brothers, 61
Vaucouleurs, France, 91
Vauvert, France, 81
Vence, France, 105
Venice, Italy, 298–300
  hotels, 300
  points of interest, 300
  transportation to, 299
Veria, Greece, 244
Verviers, Belgium, 60
Via Crucis (Austria), 36
Vianden, Luxembourg, 335
Vianney, Jean-Baptiste Marie. *See* Curé of Ars, The
Vienna, Austria, 36–40
  Boys' Choir, 38–39
  churches, 36, 40
  hotels, 39–40
  points of interest, 40
  St. Stephen's Cathedral, 36
  transportation to, 39
Villefranche, France, 105

Vincent de Paul, St., 124–125

Visby, Gotland, 405–406

Voltaire, 78

Voralberg, Austria, 30

Wagrain, Austria, 35

Waldenses, 86

Walpurgis Night, 390

Walsingham, England, 197–198
  hotels, 198
  transportation to, 198

Wesley, Charles, 200–203

Wesley, John, 168, 195, 199–203

Westminster Abbey, 212–214

Westminster Cathedral, 214–215

Westport, Ireland, 253–260
  hotels, 260
  points of interest, 260
  transportation to, 259

Wiener-Neustadt, Austria, Our Lady's Church at, 24

Wilde, Oscar, 126

Wildhaus, Switzerland, 481–482
  hotels, 482
  points of interest, 482
  transportation to, 482

Wilfrid, St., 186

Wilherinn Monastery (Austria), 30

Willibrord, St., 329–333, 361, 363

Wilton Basilica (Austria), 24

Worms, Germany, 10, 161–165
  hotels, 165
  Jewish cemetery, 162–163
  Liebfrauenkirche (Church of Our Lady), 164
  Luther monument, 161–162
  synagogue, 163–164
  transportation to, 164

Wren, Sir Christopher, 205–208

Wycliffe, John, 195

Yalova, Turkey, 506

Yeats, William Butler, grave of, 268

York, England, 185

Yugoslavia, 510, 511, 512

Yves, St., 108

Zacchaeus, 106

Zagreb, Yugoslavia, 512

Zeppelin, Count Ferdinand von (Graf), 158

Zurich, Switzerland, 486–493
  hotels, 492
  points of interest, 493
  Swiss National Museum, 490–492
  transportation to, 492

Zwingli, Ulrich, 459, 488–492
  birthplace of, 481–482